A History of Political Thought

Once again, and always, for Gary and Georgia

A History of Political Thought

From the Middle Ages to the Renaissance

Janet Coleman

London School of Economics and Political Science

First published 2000

2 4 6 8 10 9 7 5 3 1

Blackwell Publishers Ltd
108 Cowley Road
Oxford OX4 1JF
UK

Blackwell Publishers Inc.
350 Main Street
Malden, Massachusetts 02148
USA

British Library Cataloguing in Publication Data

A CIP catalogue record for this book is available from the British Library.

Library of Congress Cataloging-in-Publication Data has been applied for

ISBN 0–631–18652–2 (hbk)
ISBN 0–631–18653–0 (pbk)

Typeset in 10½ on 12 pt Bembo
by Ace Filmsetting Ltd, Frome, Somerset
Printed in Great Britain by MPG Books Ltd, Bodmin, Cornwall

This book is printed on acid-free paper.

Contents

Preface

I have greatly enjoyed writing *A History of Political Thought*, especially because so many of the issues raised and for which I have tried to provide some explanations, are the result of discussions with generations of remarkable undergraduate and postgraduate students at the London School of Economics and Political Science. Coming from a wide variety of departments in the School, and individually from a range of international backgrounds, they have approached the thinkers of a long-distant past with energetic idealism and critical astuteness. This is all the more remarkable since the new managerialism and vocational functionalism dominating today's universities would lead us to believe that what an ancient Greek or a medieval Christian had to say about living a successful human life in a structured community in which they played active roles in contributing to collective governance, would have no interest for today's students. But in addition to the small number of Government Department students for whom an introduction to the history of western political theorizing is a requirement of their degree, at the LSE the course is also taken as an open option by hundreds of students specializing in a variety of other social science subjects. And both more advanced undergraduates and our post-graduate political theorists choose to follow up the introductory course by focusing in depth on some of the thinkers discussed in these volumes. If we are meant to treat students as consumers who vote with their feet then I am delighted to inform the more sceptical among us that the history of political thought is alive and well, and this because students quickly see that the ideas to be studied here mattered and continue to matter.

At times I have had the impression that students are frankly relieved to be given the opportunity to look at world views that emerged from within historical, intellectual and social settings that are different from their own. And it has given some of them a space in which to reflect on their own, previously unexamined, but cherished views on what politics is for. It has also astonished them to see how much their own cultures are more or less reliant on certain strands of these earlier epistemologies, moral philosophies and theories of the 'state'. They have been both delighted and appalled. And everyone discovers a favourite thinker and (at least) one they most love to hate.

Because my students are asked to read set texts themselves and then to read as much historical background to get a sense of the 'theatrical backdrop' to these differing philosophical and political perspectives, as well as a selection of secondary analytical commentaries on these works, I am aware that I overload them in what is already an overloaded university curriculum. My aim in *A History of Political Thought* has been to provide as much of a historical and cultural setting as would make the texts they are asked to read look full of plausible and important arguments, given the dilemmas and circumstances their authors sought to address. Students cannot help asking themselves whether there are ideas here which just might be applicable to the present, and there is much shouting about whether or not past whole theories can be brought into a different and modern world. They are helped to make up their minds by seeing what specialist commentaries can tell them.

But academic disciplines have become increasingly specialized over the years and it is now virtually impossible to cover the results of international research undertaken by classicists who specialize in philosophy or history, to say nothing of the enormous amount of fascinating research on the early years of Christianity, the early Middle Ages, the political history, philosophy and theology of the high Middle Ages and the explosion of texts, written and printed, during the Renaissance. While I have tried to reflect a variety of current academic preoccupations in all these different fields of expertise – and here I have benefited tremendously from having edited the journal *History of Political Thought* from the beginning, when Iain Hampsher-Monk and I founded it in 1980 – I have also provided, as a consequence of my own years of research, some original and possibly controversial perspectives on some of these thinkers.

Had I been asked to write a textbook on these thinkers, say, twenty years ago, it would have looked more like a reasoned synthesis of other specialists' views and the footnotes would probably have been longer than the already over-long text. But at this stage in the game, I fear I know too much about how current perspectives penetrate the reading and interpretation of past texts that are none the less held to have something to say to us. All these years down the road I have come to realize, as I had not when a student, how there have been interpretative trends, often dominated by contemporary ideological preoccupations, which have closed off alternative readings. If nothing else, I have realized that certain utterances by past political theorists get differentially high-lighted in different generations. I have tried to indicate where I think certain current orthodoxies distort what an old text could have been taken to be saying by a past audi-ence for whom it was originally written. In believing this to be the least I could do, I have undoubtedly put my own imprint on a variety of texts despite the enormously generous guidance given me by Dr Paul Cartledge of Clare College, Cambridge for the Greeks; Dr Andrew Lintott of Worcester College, Oxford for the Romans; Professor Robert Markus, formerly of Nottingham University, for St Augustine; and Professor Nicolai Rubinstein of the Warburg Institute for Machiavelli and Renaissance Florence. I also owe a considerable debt to Professor Antony Black of the University of Dundee and Professor Brian Tierney of Cornell University, who offered their judicious com-ments especially on volume two concerning medieval and Renaissance political thought. I can only hope that where they do not agree with my interpretations or emphases, they will at least allow me to acknowledge with heartfelt thanks that I could not have come even to these views without their help. It is also to the numerous writings and friendship of two distinguished medievalists, Professor Dr Jürgen Miethke of Heidelberg Univer-sity and Professeur Jean-Philippe Genet of the University of Paris, that I owe a continu-ing debt of gratitude because they have kept me actively in touch, through off-prints and their invitations to conferences, with research done in Germany, France and other European centres, where approaches to the texts studied here adopt perspectives that often differ from those current in British and American universities.

It is not clear to me that there is any longer the institutional will to train students, as I was trained, in the languages, histories and philosophies that enable one to approach the texts of classical, medieval and Renaissance intellectual history. Today, a student who is drawn to a study of pre-modern ideas and historical settings will be asked why on earth such an irrelevant subject matter should attract any interest or indeed, funding. The student will probably require independent means and if persuasive, might be able to become enrolled in several university departments at once and for at least five years at postgraduate level in each. In Politics and Government Departments there has been a tendency to keep alive small pockets of normative theorists who have neither interest in nor knowledge of the history of their own discipline or of the languages they use with such confidence. This is to say nothing of what appears to be the sad fact that one department's agenda and methodology is now increasingly seen as incommensurable with that of another, so that specialists no longer seem to have either time or inclination to read each other's work. But the history of political thought is above all an interdisciplinary endeavour and that is by far one of its chief fascinations for staff and students alike. Of all the courses a student is likely to take at university, this is the one students tell me prepares them for being a serious tourist, and I have a stash of postcards going back over twenty-odd years sent from Athens, Rome, Paris, Avignon, Munich, Florence, Padua, Cordoba with statements like: 'it's seeing this landscape daily and the possibility of working in these buildings, and the quality of this strange light everywhere that made me realize why Aristotle or Marsilius or Machiavelli could say what he said the way he said it'. Furthermore, there is a sheer pleasure, physical and intellectual, which comes from a serious confrontation with the plausibility of alternative views on the living of a successful life. It is also a privilege to be able to read the musings of great thinkers, even if one is also aware that it is no longer quite possible to grasp wholly what they meant and why it so mattered to them – especially if one thinks them wrong. To try to listen to plausible, coherent and 'other' perspectives on human nature and its socio-political organization develops patience and tolerance, but more than that, a kind of reverence for the extraordinary creatures humans have shown themselves to be over the centuries. In defending their truths with such eloquence and energy they give us the courage to challenge that mentality which always seems to have been in our midst and which has sought to manage the creativity of individual and collective agency, not least by labelling people with critical ideas 'the chattering classes' and by pretending that a successful life lived in common is reducible to the 'social inclusion' that is supposedly achieved through market economics.

Several years ago I was astonished to read in Blackwell Publishers' current list of new publications that my long-awaited *History of Political Thought* was to appear imminently. I am thoroughly embarrassed at how long I have kept them waiting and I am grateful for their long-standing (and discreet) encouragement. It was meant to appear as the precursor to Iain Hampsher-Monk's excellent *A History of Modern Political Thought* (1992). Through the efforts of Jill Landeryou at Blackwell Publishers my 'long awaited' history of political thought now appears in two volumes: volume 1 *From Ancient Greece to Early Christianity* and volume 2 *From the Middle Ages to the Renaissance*. I am immensely grateful for her enthusiasm, advocacy and patience. But textbooks, no matter how original, are not highly regarded in intellectually ambitious centres like the London School of Economics, not least because national Research Assessment Exercises have financial consequences for departments and universities that seek to retain their high-flyer research-orientated status. Hence, during the years I had hoped to complete this history of political thought I was otherwise engaged in writing and publishing the work that was meant to matter. I have, however, been able to draw on this research material in these books and I hope that more advanced students and colleagues will find it useful, stimulating and contentious. In so far as the scholarly research has shaped the contents of what is meant to be a more introductory text, I can only hope that what I have done here gives students a view of how at least one academic sees the ancient, medieval and Renaissance worlds of political discourse as having sustained certain continuities and fictitiously constructed others. The primary hope is that it will get students to go back to the original texts and argue about them, thereby countering the tabloid scepticism about politics which has come to sound so loudly in all our ears.

Janet Coleman

Introduction

There are many and varied reasons why a student may become interested in studying the political and social thought of what we now call the Middle Ages and the Renaissance. A student may first confront medieval and Renaissance thinkers after having become acquainted with their forebears among the ancient Greeks and Romans in courses dealing either with the history of philosophy or with the history of political thought. He or she may ask: 'Did the ancient Greek and Roman legacies survive and in what form?' A student may also discover an interest in the development of perspectives on politics and social living as expressed among the earliest Christians. He or she may then wish to see how later and different peoples who adhered to Western forms of Christianity sought to use the language and ideas of those early Christians in order to answer the question: what is the appropriate Christian perspective on 'the political'? Or perhaps a student may simply be fortunate enough to spend a summer, maps in hand, wandering around the Western European landscape and coming upon some extraordinary building which has survived, in whole or in part, and which the tourist information dates to the twelfth or some even earlier century. 'What kind of society built this', one asks, 'and are there any voices left from that past which might provide some barely comprehensible explanation?' One might go further and ask: 'How different were such people's conceptions of the social world from our own and is there any way in which some of their ideas are still alive for us?'

One way to find out something more about these remains and relics, and the societies which caused their appearance in the landscape, is to enter into a dialogue with a chronologically arranged set of discourses. These are known as the canonical texts of Western debate on the principles and practices of good government. This canon of great texts was written by men who have been taken to be the key figures in the history of European political thought. In the introduction to volume 1 of *A History of Political Thought* I discussed the ways in which Europeans have constructed their tradition(s) and why this canon is itself contentious, not least because it is selective, retrospective and has often silenced many contemporary voices in favour of others. One could say that the canon of great texts is an extraordinary expression of European prejudices about themselves and others. This is precisely why it is important. Hence, the kind of dialogue we engage in when we read these texts needs to be much more complicated and reflexive, historically and philosophically, than the one in which pre-modern readers of their ancient legacy believed themselves to be participating. In the introduction to volume 1 I have tried to explain at greater length why I believe this to be the case.

In this volume, we look at some of the ways in which thinking about and discussing values and institutions emerged in Western Europe after the decline and fall of the Roman Empire. The voices of the ancient Greeks and, even more so, the Romans are still there. We shall often need to refer to the discussions in volume 1 of their ethical and political theories, not only in order to grasp to what later medieval and Renaissance thinkers were referring but also to understand what they assumed their audiences already knew. But we must also remind ourselves that the voices of ancient Greece and Rome came to be heard and understood through other mediations – most notably, that of the Bible and its commentators, known as the early church Fathers, along with traditions of collective living that were modified in practice across the centuries. For this reason I have treated the political theories or political philosophies of the medieval and Renaissance centuries as embedded within a good deal of socio-political history in order to elucidate why these texts ask and answer certain questions rather than others. Like the Greeks and Romans, the authors of such political theories can be viewed as representatives of groups, parties, all of them positioned in structures not of their own making. These theorists are not, then, to be treated simply as individual linguistic agents in speech situations; rather, they are taken to be representatives of local kinds of arguments set in contexts that were not purely linguistic. The contexts survive for us through texts which re-present the non-linguistic circumstances in which concepts were developed and experiences had.

But if we ask the somewhat different question as to why certain theorists, say, Machiavelli, are treated in depth here and not, say, Guicciardini his contemporary, then we must return to the reason I proposed as to why the Western canon of texts has come to look as it does. Like the philosophers or theorists of the ancient Greek and Roman worlds discussed in volume 1, the selected 'political theorists' to be found in this volume were not taken to be representative voices *of* their times. *Later* Europeans judged them to have been exemplary of the *best* of the past. For this reason the principle of inclusion of one as opposed to another thinker in this volume has been founded on a retrospective examination of which texts and thinkers Europeans, in the long course of their construction of their own identities and traditions, themselves deemed worthy of actively adopting and necessarily misinterpreting to serve their own present.

Past concepts for such Europeans in the pre-modern period were not antiquarian curiosities. They judged the texts, which expressed past concepts about values and institutions, to be usable, or else they ignored them and did not have them recopied for future generations to read and use. Indeed, there are periods where the sources for past conceptual usages are difficult for us to obtain, not least because those texts which do survive for us to look at are those that were allowed to survive by later rememberers of past usages deemed useful to them in a later present. Cultures preserve and destroy texts so that the history of texts is a history of their reception by later generations with other things on their minds. This is especially the case for medieval texts, many of which were lost, sold or burned after the Protestant Reformation. In general, we know that later generations actively destroyed texts from the past which did not suit their way of reading their present. Later scholars are dependent on earlier generations' 'retrospective nominations' – their decisions as to what they thought important to preserve for their own reconstructive and mediated uses. Subsequent orthodoxies actively kill off what they perceive to have been past heterodoxies which may not have been heterodox in their own times. Medievalists are especially dependent on the texts that were allowed to survive in dominant numbers often as a consequence of what much later librarians, operating within the post-Reformation confessional divide, thought important to preserve.

But no pre-modern 'political theorist' would have looked at the situation in this light. Unlike post-nineteenth-century historians, earlier Europeans looked for answers to what they took to be unchanging questions, and they thought they could engage unproblematically in dialogues with philosophers across time and re-use their solutions to what they took to be eternal problems about human governance. Of course, from our point of view, what they did was construct continuities with their selected pasts, while believing themselves to be able to learn from and, indeed, repeat the virtues of the past because they held that the past was filled with men who were just like them. Today, however, we would argue that they sustained this essential continuity by completely transforming past concepts to suit their own circumstances and experiences. They believed themselves to be living within a tradition but actually were in the extended process of constructing one. Where today some modern and post-modern theories insist on highlighting difference, pre-modern theories sought to mediate difference in order to transform it into an essential continuity of sameness.

Any modern historian of political thought necessarily works within the perspectives on and about the past that are current in modern Western culture. Therefore, below I have tried to identify certain conceptual configurations through languages used at the time in order to alert readers to, say, a notion of *ius* or right, whose meaning is perhaps related to some of our uses of the notion of 'right' but which, when situated in another context, implies a range of other and very different ideas, some of which may seem distinctly strange to us. Indeed, I hope to have revealed some of the numerous and simultaneous prejudices which were constitutive of ways of being in the world during the medieval and Renaissance centuries. The multiple pre-judgements were embedded and passed on in the languages people used and these prejudices lay behind such people's more reflective judgements as we read them in their 'political theory' texts.

All cultures are sustained by multiple prejudices which lie behind their more reflective judgements. More generally, I would suggest that there is a way of being in the world for humans which we may call 'understanding'. Understanding is an event, something other than, but inseparably achieved by means of, linguistic communication. It is less the case that we always possess our world linguistically than that we are possessed by language. In other words, our horizons are given us pre-reflectively by the languages we learn in a particular language community. But this does not mean that there is no way of mediating between different language games learned in different communities. This is because there is a reflexive dimension to human understanding that necessarily begins in an interpreter's immediate participation in a tradition of understanding, but such a tradition of understanding is only in part revealed in a present tradition of language use. Indeed, we shall see how earlier and later medieval thinkers, earlier and later Renaissance thinkers, integrated and fused language games from the past and their present in order to achieve *changed* socio-political concepts from within their traditions. Through interpretative effort they tried to bridge the gap between their own familiar world with its own horizons and that of strange meanings with other horizons, notably from ancient Greece, Rome and early Christianity. Medieval and Renaissance 'political theorists' enable us to observe men doing more than learning their own first language. We can observe them engaging in dialogues and learning other languages, expanding their original horizons – without ever losing them – by confronting and interpreting past texts and other voices. It is this reflexive dimension in which we are, ourselves, engaged when we read and interpret their writings. And this very activity of making texts intelligible to us when we read them ensures that what they had to say cannot be, and is not, completely lost to us. Not only has the past a pervasive power in the activity of human understanding, but all interpreters are, and always have been, within their own historicity.

Because we are readers of past texts, interested in the evolution of political theorizing as an activity, the philosophical questions and answers we confront in medieval and Renaissance texts, no less than in Greek and Roman texts, are transitory and historical rather than permanent. We shall need to become familiar with aspects of European history during what has been called the 'Dark Ages', succeeded by the 'high' Middle Ages and, thereafter, the Renaissance. Against this shifting historical backdrop we shall see that some questions and answers have none the less entered our own thought in an evolved state, mediated by the texts of the medieval and Renaissance thinkers we are about to read, who interpreted, made intelligible, and *changed* the meaning and use of even earlier ideas in order to accommodate them to their different intellectual and social contexts.[1]

---

1   For further reflections along these lines see J. Coleman, 'The Practical Use of *Begriffsgeschichte* by an Historian of European Pre-modern Political Thought: some problems', *Huizinga Instituut: History of Concepts Newsletter*, 2 (1999), pp. 2–9. See also the introduction to volume 1 of *A History of Political Thought* for how this does not mean that we can, any longer, think of these authors as 'just like us'.

1

Medieval Political Ideas and Medieval Society

The public triumph of Christianity in the fourth century (discussed in volume 1), established the context for the future development of that Latin, Western European political theorizing that we now call medieval political thought. In order to treat the centuries from the fifth to, say, the fifteenth as the *Middle* Ages, we are already complying with a later, retrospective, even pejorative perspective on this period. 'What is *middle* about the Middle Ages?' we might ask.

This view stems from the eighteenth century at least, at a time when history began to be seen as a story of humanity's progressive improvement and ultimate release from the illusions of religion and myth. The period from the fifth to the fifteenth centuries – a thousand years of European cultural and political development – was considered open to characterization as a monolithic hiatus, a decline from ancient philosophical reason, the dark ages, the 'age of faith', a period 'in the middle' between the particular reason of the ancients and that universal reason of the 'moderns' that putatively began in what is known as the sixteenth-century Italian Renaissance and reached its apex in the eighteenth-century Enlightenment. It was judged that medieval people wrote in a barbarized Latin and were oppressed by two forms of arbitrary rule: of feudal lords and institutionalized religious prejudices. It is the purpose of this volume to show that this long period in the Latin West was anything but monolithic, that there was no such thing as 'the medieval mind', that there are more difficulties than are usually acknowledged in distinguishing the end of the Middle Ages and the beginning of the Renaissance, and clearly, no one living at any time *between* the age of Augustine and the age of Machiavelli thought of themselves as a dweller 'in-between ages', which is what 'medieval' means.

These strange locutions, 'Middle Ages' and 'medieval', have none the less passed into our accepted academic periodization of the past. And there is a lively temptation to drop the 'middle' from examination and leap from the ancients to the moderns in university courses treating the history of political thought, following the misguided assumption that European political discourses and practices owe the Middle Ages very little. In fact, however, we owe the Middle Ages almost everything, and not only their very distinctive ways of reconstructing and passing on the ancient philosophical legacy of political theorizing. The Middle Ages established its own agenda and a collection of different political discourses which would either be absorbed, transformed or argued against until the early-modern period. But most importantly, Western Europe is overwhelmingly indebted to the medieval creation of institutions and practices which could never have developed either in ancient Greece or Rome.

Today the political *theory* of the ancients has survived for us, reinterpreted and reconstructed often as philosophically coherent discourses that have little to do with the cultures from within which they were generated, but the *practices* of the ancient Athenians (for instance, direct democracy where the *polis* was its men and not the modern state and its governing bureaucracy) were forgotten or rejected.[1] The Greek notion – found in Aristotle – that man is a political animal would be revived in the Middle Ages but rejected by many of Europe's early-moderns who thought that politics was the consequence of man's fear of death and aversion to pain rather than man's capacity for public deliberation and co-operative agency. If early-moderns sought an ancient society to emulate, they often chose Sparta and almost never Athens.

Rome, however, would play a larger role in the self-conscious construction of Europe's future. Not only did the Middle Ages emerge out of a late and declining Roman imperial reality; early medieval institutions and practices would be selectively saturated with the law of imperial Rome. But when the self-conscious, comprehensive revival of Roman law was undertaken in the twelfth century, it would be to the sixth-century Christian Emperor Justinian's codification of Roman law that they would turn. Very little of Cicero's Rome survives there and they did not possess the text of his *De re publica*. Therefore, even when during the Middle Ages and thereafter Europeans thought themselves to be the heirs of Rome, we will find them to have pieced together from disparate and fragmentary sources what they thought the Roman republic to have been, and then they reconstructed the Romans' republicanism in order to open up in practice something that might be seen as akin to a representative commercial democracy, where the people,[2] when gathered together, constituted the sovereign and made law by voluntarily and explicitly consenting to it. Medieval political theorists and practitioners were to take literally and then transform the maxim of late Roman law that 'what touches all should be approved by all' (*quod omnes tangit ab omnibus tractari et approbari debet*), wrenching it out of the context in Justinian's *Codex* where they found it, and thereby emphasizing a deliberative participation by the 'people' in consenting to the laws. Furthermore, the people would be declared capable of electing removable public officials as the executive government. Medieval governors would come to be described as directive functionaries, public administrators of a collective good which some interpreted as a peaceful, law-governed and self-sufficient life of which all men were equally aware, including those not considered experts in law and who had few possessions.[3] This was something of which the ancient Romans whom we have examined would never have approved because 'the people' for them were never to be considered a deliberative body.

Let us recall that citizenship in ancient republican Rome did not give every citizen the right to engage in government, but rather to be governed by those who were more than mere administrators. As Gruen has observed, 'a resplendent elite governed the Roman Republic'.[4] For ancient Romans, those who were most engaged in administer-

---

1   For a distinctive perspective see P. Rahe, *Republics, Ancient and Modern: classical republicanism and the American Revolution* (Chapel Hill, NC, 1992).
2   Or what they thought of as their representative: 'the weightier part', or the 'greater and sounder part', the *valentior pars*, or the *maior et sanior pars*.
3   See chapter 4 on Marsilius of Padua's *Defensor pacis (Defender of peace)*.
4   E. Gruen, 'The Exercise of Power in the Roman Republic', in A. Molho, K. Raaflaub and J. Emlen, eds, *City-states in Classical Antiquity and Medieval Italy* (Ann Arbor, MI, 1991), pp. 251–67: 'To be sure, the populace could make its needs felt – and not just as clients of individuals or factions. And Roman leaders had to take those needs

ing the *respublica* were also owners with a special *dignitas*, inherited or merited, indicating an acknowledged differential in what was due them: they differentially possessed more of the property that *was* the *respublica* and were likewise differentially obliged to engage in the maintenance of the state's law. Ancient Roman citizenship was a matter of degree.[5]

We recall that Cicero had made plain in his *On Duties* that social utility was the highest good and there were certain natural governors who recognize their duties of public service as an aspect of their own individual interest. And he argued that private property derived from custom but that the *rights* to private property were the creations of Roman civil law. The 'state' came into being through men's construction of an agreed means to preserve and stabilize customary agreements to what is differentially mine and thine, creating civic rights, enforceable in law. Where Cicero distinguished between all men as natural appropriators on the one hand, and on the other, men as legally entitled, unequal possessors under civil law, certain medieval theorists[6] would use these Roman arguments but transform them. By integrating Christian theological views concerning the nature of man and his duty to labour, theorists like John of Paris would alter Cicero's customary private property into a universally applicable labour theory of *natural rights* to ownership *prior* to the 'state'. John of Paris would argue that it was these prior rights which the 'state' was entrusted to serve and stabilize by fair administration and adjudication in property disputes. This medieval argument, significantly revising Cicero's, would be revived in the seventeenth century by Locke in his *Second Treatise of Government*.

As we saw in volume 1, ancient Roman magistrates consulted the aristocratic Senate on important issues and before introducing a bill to one of the popular assemblies magistrates were meant to set it before the Senate. This meant that the Senate was the only deliberative body and it had not only a firm grip on legislation but also defined the sphere of activity of the magistrates. When Cicero described his ideal republican mixture, he went even further than what appears to have been practice in order to eliminate any popular balance to his aristocratic republic: the people should maintain their sense of *libertas* while the *boni* retain their authoritative influence. But as we shall see, the practice of citizens collected together with a freedom of discussion and with the power to initiate business from the floor of the debating chamber would be a medieval institution based on *their* developed practices, especially in city communes. During the Middle Ages there would also develop a notion of rights that were other than acquired civic rights. The influence of Christian theology would be felt in discussions of a Christian liberty that

into account, at least on occasion. But the postulate that *nobiles* framed policies and actions to cater to that constituency misses the mark. It will be more fruitful to adopt a different mode of analysis: the exploitation of popular discourse to entrench the authority of the establishment' (p. 254). The aim of the Roman nobility 'was not to secure legitimation from the *populus* but to employ popular rhetoric to check challenges from *novi homines* or curb the ambitions of individual *nobiles*. Pressure by the populace played little part' (p. 267). See also W. Eder, 'Who Rules? Power and Participation in Athens and Rome', in Molho, Raaflaub and Emlen, *City-states*, pp. 169–96.

5   See W. W. Buckland, *A Text-book of Roman Law from Augustus to Justinian*, revd P. Stein, 3rd edn (Cambridge, 1975), pp.86–7 on privileged classes of citizens in relation to citizens with more restricted rights. Also T. J. Cornell, 'Rome: the history of an anachronism', in Molho, Raaflaub and Emlen, *City-states*, pp. 53–70, on both the artificial construct of the early Roman ideal of the integrated political community, the city-state, and the increasing separation of the aristocracy from the rest of the population.

6   John of Paris, *De potestate regia et papale* (*On royal and papal power*); see chapter 3, below.

could not be alienated or contravened, whatever freedoms were conventionally established by civil law.

One of the attitudes medievals did absorb from Romans rather than from Greeks was the notion of the city as open to outsiders who could be freely admitted and assimilated without the requirement of having been born a citizen. Citizenship could be acquired by service to the 'state'. How this was applied during the Middle Ages, however, and how the legal concept of citizenship was further defined beyond received Roman law came about through the medieval use of Roman law texts as little more than authoritative reference points for their own original solutions, and these emerged from the constant pressure on medieval civil lawyers to administer the law in practice, *de facto*, rather than simply to apply the rules *de jure*. As Quaglioni has demonstrated, medieval jurists gave preference to the substance of citizenship rather than simply to the abstract principles of Roman legal rules, and in so focusing developed new vocabularies as well as institutions to suit lived practice.[7] We shall see that it was the peculiar contractual genesis of medieval city communes, where the citizen was an active rather than passive member of the city (this activity resulting from *his individual will actually to contract with the commune*), that highlighted an un-Roman fusing of socio-economic principles and assumptions regarding authority and power that were typical both of feudal society and city communes, with forms of the Roman patrimonial system. There would be a spectrum along which the feudal *fideles* (the free vassal bound by oath to his overlord)[8] and the Roman *civis* (citizen) met. From medieval jurisprudence would develop the legacy to the early-modern and contemporary European world of the notion of acquired or naturalized *and* native citizenship as a *fictio iuris* (a legal fiction).[9] It was from the medieval jurists, responding to medieval practice, that our notion of citizenship as signifying merely the *juridical* status of those who are part of a state was to come.

In place of ancient Greek and Roman practices then, there emerged organized ways of life during the Middle Ages which came to serve, however unconsciously, as the foundations of some of the dominant attitudes that characterized the government of early-modern and modern cities and states. Indeed, Christianity as put into practice in monasteries from the sixth century onwards would emphasize a very unclassical attitude to work, favouring an ethic of toil in which labour was a form of prayer suitable both to fallen man as well as to God's only son, who on earth was a carpenter's son and his disciples workmen. Unlike ancient attitudes to economics, the medievals would give economy a central place in what they came to call 'practical moral philosophy' as well as in the constitutional organization of cities. Furthermore, medieval culture would reverse the ancient Greek journey from sacral kingship to politics by re-establishing a king–priest along a late Roman imperial model, who was at the head of a corporate endeavour, there to maintain peace, order and economic wealth. And the ancient philosopher, a theorist in the ancient city's midst, would with the help of a reinterpreted Cicero and Aristotle become the university-trained bureaucrat, actively engaged in policy-

---

7   D. Quaglioni, 'The Legal Definition of Citizenship in the late Middle Ages', in Molho, Raaflaub and Emlen, *City-states*, pp. 155–67.

8   See below, pp. 13ff.

9   E. Cortese, 'Cittadinanza (Diritto intermedio)', in *Enciclopedia del Diritto*, VII (Milan, 1960), pp.132–40. These were notions that went beyond a mere repeat of the Roman patterns. See Quaglioni, 'The Legal Definition', p. 165.

formation and dissemination in royal and ecclesiastical courts. While these developments occurred 'on the ground' as it were, we shall also see that during the Middle Ages
educated men continued to use the discourses of the ancient traditions with which we
became familiar in volume 1, applying both ancient philosophical and biblical insights to
their own distinctive conditions and experiences. Aristotle's *polis* would be reconfigured
as the medieval *civitas*, and Cicero's *respublica* would be applied to *any* well-governed
regime, be it a monarchy, a republic or the church itself, where the common, public
good was said to be served.

There is no doubt that in general 'medieval persons' would have thought of themselves as Christians and would have been aware to some degree that spiritual considerations played a role in helping to establish the aims and spheres of influence of temporal
power. Medieval political discourses would be forged out of the shifting relationships
between the thought and institutions which came to structure both the church and the
'state', giving substance and structure to the spiritual and the temporal spheres of life,
indeed to the very assumption that there *were* two such spheres where the church and
the state had separate but interlocking jurisdictions.[10]

Medieval Sources

Our sources for medieval political thought are very varied: they are the productions of
Christian theologians with teaching posts in universities or in the schools associated with
different religious orders, Christian philosophers who taught in the arts faculties of medieval universities, Christian historians, often attached to monastic centres, Christian
bureaucrats in the service of temporal or spiritual institutions, and Christian jurists, specializing in Roman and customary, or in church (canon) law. Indeed, we could add
poets, dramatists, local chroniclers, merchants, religious men and women, anyone who
acquired a sufficient degree of literacy and the standard genres of current, learned discourse to write about the ordered processes and ideals of their lives as they saw them.

But there are virtually no professionals whom we could call with any historical accuracy 'political theorists' during the Middle Ages. What is currently considered the autonomous discourse of politics is a development of the emergence of the early-modern
state in Europe. In an important and perhaps surprising sense, the autonomy of early-
modern political discourse developed outside the university and in opposition to what
the university milieu had become in the early-modern period. Hobbes's scorn for the
seventeenth-century university's slavish attitude to Aristotle and other 'authorities' led
him to develop a 'science' of politics, based on human experience, that was meant to be
autonomous in the sense that it drew eclectically on past thinking and yet owed nothing
to the university as an institution of learning with its settled categories of discourse. But
prior to the seventeenth century, politics was not a distinctive discipline with its own
subject matter and methodology. It had not yet disengaged itself either from the dominance of practical moral philosophy and theology as studied in medieval universities, or
from ancient rhetorical and ethical discourse as studied in Renaissance humanist schools.

---

10   See A. Black, 'Individuals, Groups and States: a comparative overview', in J. Coleman, ed., *The Individual in
Political Theory and Practice* (Oxford, 1996), pp. 329–40.

As we shall see, in the Renaissance humanist schools as in medieval universities, the discussion of the organization of human communities and of behaviour considered appropriate within communities of men, alongside analyses of moral right, of virtue and of personal responsibility for one's acts, be they the acts of ruler or ruled, were still tied to ancient authoritative discourses. In the early stages of a medieval or Renaissance student's education these discourses were first confronted in the process of learning to read and write a foreign language, Latin. Students across Europe were taught to read ancient Latin texts of holy scripture, Roman history, the Roman moralists and the Latin church Fathers. Using the texts of ancient Roman grammarians and rhetoricians (themselves translations and commentaries on ancient Greek theories of grammar and rhetoric), and supplementing these with Latin translations of Aristotle's rhetorical and logical treatises, medieval and Renaissance students absorbed theories about the relation between human thinking and language. They absorbed explicit and sometimes conflicting theories concerning the relation between reason and emotion and between persuasive speech and collective action. They learned how to distinguish between virtuous and vicious behaviour and between legitimate governance and its opposite. Medieval and Renaissance students were being prepared for professions in the non-academic world of 'state' and church bureaucracies in much the same ways. Education was vocational and for this reason we can regard Renaissance humanist schools as providing a very similar education, but in truncated form, to that provided by medieval university arts course programmes. Both were the heirs of ways of speaking about what we would call 'the ethical' and 'the political' that were inherited from the ancient Roman and Greek worlds, filtered through Christian perspectives. How they respectively reinterpreted and used these ancient masters and their 'classical' agenda is, in part, our concern here.

It will be seen that the specific historical milieux in which those men lived who wrote what *we* recognize as 'political theory' exercised an enormous influence on what they said about 'the political'. And they did not all say the same things, not least because the respective agendas of theologians, philosophers, bureaucrats and jurists were not the same. Furthermore, we shall see that when they wore different professional 'hats' they 'spoke' different languages: the language of the Latin Bible, the language of the theology of the church Fathers, of Christianized Platonism, of Roman civil law, of canon (church) law, of feudal and customary law, of Ciceronian rhetoric, and of Aristotelian ethical and political philosophy.[11] Latin remained the language of most political theorizing during the Middle Ages, broadly construed, and when the vernaculars came into their own, many of the earlier scholarly Latin terms and expressions would be 'translated' and put to new use. But during the medieval and Renaissance periods there was never a wholesale and self-conscious attempt, as there would be in the seventeenth century, to reformulate the ethical and political world 'from the beginning' and as though men were naturally non-social isolates who had to create politics as convention. Medieval and Renaissance Latin and vernacular texts always related back to the already formulated 'languages' of moral discourse that were found in a wide range of authoritative ancient texts which insisted that men were naturally embedded in the social. We shall see that Machiavelli, the so-called first modern, the so-called 'father' of what *we* mean by political science, was no exception to this. In short, when modern historians of political ideas approach the texts of the Middle Ages, they tend to study a range of discourses that collectively are

11   See A. Black, *Political Thought in Europe 1250–1450* (Cambridge, 1992), pp. 1–13.

called by them 'political thought'. But it is our aim here to show how, for the Middle Ages, 'political thought' is a rather messy and unstable category, not least because it is everywhere and it invaded all genres.

If the political thought of the Middle Ages begins in late antiquity with its particular reinterpretation of the legacy of ancient philosophy, it arguably extends to the middle of the seventeenth century, even beyond. The beginnings are clearer than the end. The beginnings of medieval political thinking are to be found in the rich mixture of Greco-Roman and biblical concepts which we have already seen to have been integrated into Augustine's *City of God*. But it is in the long period of transition from the world of Constantine's Roman Empire to a very different Western Europe in the eighth and ninth centuries that the context for the development of distinctively medieval political ideas was established.[12]

The Historical Context of Early Medieval Political Thought

Barbarian kingdoms emerged in the fifth and sixth centuries, peopled by heirs of those Germanic tribes who had settled within Roman borders and who eventually triumphed as the survivors of the collapse of the Roman administration. Barbarian kingdoms, with their own regional customs, gradually absorbed diluted remnants of Roman civilization, but their territorial rule would became the paradigm of medieval rule: *territorial kingship*. The slow decline and fall of the Roman Empire, from the later fifth until the eighth centuries, can be seen as the gradual replacement of a centralized Roman administration that had developed during the imperial period, with barbarian leadership in those Western European provinces previously captured and dominated by Rome.

The period from the end of the fifth to the eighth centuries has a character of its own. It saw the development of a strong ecclesiastical network of governance throughout Europe to replace the secular administration of old Rome. It saw the development of monasteries as alternative ways of living to those established in secular society and its social groupings. It saw the collection and final codification of Roman law by the Eastern Emperor Justinian in the sixth century which provided Europe with the *Institutes*, the *Digest*, the *Codex* and the *Novellae* of imperial Roman law, all collected into several texts for study. These collected texts are what are referred to as civil law, the law of the Roman civilian lawyers. This Roman law, originally based on precedent, then codified and to be appealed to by anyone interested in a *centralized* theory and practice of imperial Rome, would at first live in libraries and fall into relative disuse as barbarian kingdoms came to replace with their own laws – themselves influenced by Roman categories – the once centralized jurisdiction of the Roman Empire. Justinian's Roman law as a corpus would only be revived when in the eleventh century kings were made aware of this body of law that pre-dated the institution and law of the church and they saw it as a means to bolster temporal autonomy against the claims of the church.

With the flooding into Western Europe of peoples, some of whom were not converted to Christianity and who had their own customary laws suitable to warring,

---

12 The essential background text is J. H. Burns, ed., *The Cambridge History of Medieval Political Thought c. 350–c.1450* (Cambridge, 1988) (henceforth *CHMPT* (1988)), with its extensive bibliography. Also see the excellent J. Canning, *A History of Medieval Political Thought 300–1450* (London, 1996).

wandering and illiterate people, and with their infiltration of the Roman army and their partial Romanization, a once Mediterranean-led culture, dominated by antiquity, became a tribal, regionalized Europe, gradually left to its own resources. The kingdoms of Visigothic Spain, Frankish Gaul, the Lombards in Italy, and the Anglo-Saxon and Celtic kingdoms of the British isles emerged. The story of the sixth to eighth centuries is in part a story of the evangelization and conversion to Catholic Christianity of these barbarian successor kingdoms. This was spearheaded by missionaries sent by the Roman church and its first bishop, the pope of Rome. Western Europe during these centuries not only saw the conversion to Catholic Christianity of barbarian kingdoms within the limits of the Western empire, but also their progressive withdrawal from the sphere of imperial influence in Byzantine Constantinople. In the Byzantine East, a different history unfolded where this Greek-speaking part of the Roman Empire of antiquity more or less endured and the Eastern church never adopted the kind of independent ecclesiastical claims that would emerge in the West.

During the seventh century Palestine and North Africa had already been conquered by the armies of the new religion of Islam and by the eighth century Islam had conquered Spain, parts of southern France, and was only stopped in its advance northwards by the leader of the Franks, Charles Martel, at the battle of Poitiers. With the Mediterranean no longer the focus of what remained of Latin Europe, Gaul, parts of western Germany, Italy and the British isles became the theatre for the triumph of the Carolingian Franks who became masters of all of Western Christendom, excluding the British isles. But the influence of Islam, not least in having preserved much of the ancient Greek tradition of philosophy and science, would come to reassert itself on Northern Europe and, from the twelfth century onwards, would enable Western Europeans to reconnect with ancient traditions of speaking about the political.

In the year 800 the Carolingian Frankish king Charles the Great (Charlemagne) was crowned at Rome by the pope, a coronation of a king of the Franks as the heir to the Roman emperor. Charles the Great's empire left an enduring memory to later generations, although its own unity did not last long. During the ninth century the lands of the once united empire were divided among the different members of the Carolingian dynasty, with one of the family carrying the imperial title until the tenth century. During the ninth century Europe was invaded by pagan Vikings and central Europe by the Magyars. The collapse of the Carolingian empire made way for regional, territorial principalities whose rulers attempted to exercise the functions nominally belonging to the Carolingian king. Although after the disintegration of the Carolingian empire we begin to see Europe emerging as a congeries of territories ruled by individual feudal lords and princes, the legacy of a centralized rulership as established by Charles the Great served as a theoretical ideal which would be invoked in centuries afterwards as the model for organized government by a Christian king and emperor of a Christian people. From what is called the Carolingian Renaissance under Charles the Great, typically medieval concepts of rulership would remain fundamental to discussions of politics throughout the Middle Ages and beyond.

Beginning with the Carolingians, a variety of medieval ideas and attitudes – to custom and law, to institutional structure and purpose, to rule and subjection, to legitimate public power, to consent and mutual contracts of faithful agreement, to the sphere of religion and its relationship to the world of organized, secular institutions of collective protection and justice, to the relationship between the individual and the numerous collective agencies of which he was an incorporated member – would survive to be reinterpreted but not essentially obliterated well into what is now called the early-modern period. This is true despite the growing diversity of cultural and institutional structures that came to typify sixteenth- and seventeenth-century responses to local and more widespread public dilemmas. As we shall see, perhaps most fundamental was the notion of Christian kingship and a Christian people, laying the foundation for theories of monarchy which have survived into modern times.

Carolingian Christian Kingship and Feudal Society

Our aim here is to get some idea of the theory and practice of Carolingian kingship and sovereignty because these served as models for future emergent medieval 'states'. We also need to try to understand something about the economic and status organization of a society governed by Carolingian kings. Is it appropriate to call the Carolingian period one in which there was a feudal society requiring feudal government? Or was it the case that only by the late eleventh century were there truly feudal rulers who adapted a Carolingian legacy of political power and practice over defined European territories? These are not simply historical questions. They are questions the answers to which have guided the ideological construction of different European national states' histories into the twentieth century. There is a British tradition of historiography, for instance, which insists that feudalism was a foreign import, imposed on Anglo-Saxon society by the Norman Conquest in 1066.

Indeed, the first reference in English to 'the feudal system' occurs in Adam Smith's *Wealth of Nations* (1776). During the eighteenth century feudal*ism,* a word coined well after the supposed disappearance of the phenomenon it sought to describe, was taken to be a result of Roman decadence, Germanic arrogance or medieval brutality. Feudalism came to be used as a pejorative term. A distinction was then drawn between feudalism as describing a particular system of economic production on the one hand, and a legal system of governing the military organization of earlier society on the other. But scholars from the nineteenth century until today have investigated aspects of early feudal society and have discovered that its legacy was one that actually prevented absolutism and tyrannical rule, by passing on the notion of government as a kind of contract, and where there was a legitimate right of resistance to unjust or inefficient rule. Contract theory, rights of resistance, consensus politics, government as co-operative, were found to be central to the governance of a feudal society, especially when, as would later happen, feudal practices would be reframed in Roman law categories. A feudally saturated landscape could and did make use of certain key aspects of Roman law theory, especially from the twelfth century onwards.

None the less, there is a long-enduring scholarly debate about the general structure and significance of a feudal society and the period to which the term 'feudal' ought to be applied. Marc Bloch in his classic work *La Société féodale* (1939) distinguished two feudal ages. The characteristics of the first age were the personal bond between one man and another, often known as *vassalage*; a property bond was created by the granting of what later were called *fiefs* or land in return for military service; there was a distribution of governmental powers among numerous petty lords which led to a multiplication of jurisdictions. In time this led to immunities or exemptions from centralized law, and these immunities were granted by superior rulers or kings to lesser lords who then established their own systems of local justice, local tax collecting and military recruitment. The institutions of this first feudal age were held to be rooted in the folk practices of the early medieval West.

What has come to be called the second feudal age dates from the later eleventh century, a period in which the previous insecurities and the disruptive tribulations caused by Viking invasions had come to an end. Forest and wasteland clearances were undertaken to absorb the increase in population, extensions towards the east and south occurred, trade and an exchange economy developed with the use of money. With the re-establishment and growth of towns there were legal and intellectual attempts to improve and centralize authority. Older feudal practices and institutions were extended so that the lines of dependency formed networks across Europe.

Once feudal relations lost their original military characteristics they became stable contractual relationships between lords and vassals, where both parties to the contract were seen as free individuals, albeit of unequal status. The vassal was not seen as a mere subject of his lord and he had, by virtue of his consent to the contract, a certain individual standing which was enhanced by the grant of a certain local autonomy. The vassal could economically exploit the land he held in grant and he was further conceded immunities or exemptions from certain fiscal, military and judicial powers that were normally exercised by the superior lord over the said territory. In certain parts of Europe, and notably during the ninth and tenth centuries, the superior lord's ruling activities had become decentralized by the vassal's immunities and the latter took over as an economically self-sufficient exerciser of rights and duties within his own space. His amalgam of economic and political power was more potent than the old benefice in the days of the Carolingian empire. His public powers came to be known as *consuetudines*, customs, and he exercised them as the landlord with private jurisdiction and independent local power.

The population beneath the feudal relation was subjected: they were objects (or beneficiaries) of rule and not party to the feudal contract. Hence, a fief came to be equated with lucrative seignorial rights and this could shift effective power in a unified territory downwards, establishing private, local courts with autonomous systems of their own rules. This came to be further complicated not only by the different terms of grants by an overlord to individual vassals, but also by a system of subinfeudation in which a vassal of a higher lord was himself a superior lord to his own vassals.

Whether or not a strong monarch with a centralizing strategy was in place to manipulate feudal organization determined the different histories of European countries on the road to medieval 'state' formation. If a king were unable to claim to be considered sovereign and obeyed as the overlord of all other lords and vassals, then a regional fragmentation of authority ensued, with fiefs coming to be considered the divisible, inheritable and even alienable patrimony of a vassal's lineage. The initial, early feudal grant of public prerogatives, as immunities, over feudal land would become private and particularized. Such immunities came to be increasingly for sale, so that by the fourteenth century the European nobility had emerged from the feudalized landscape as an estate with a range of privileges, prerogatives, claims to honour and precedence along with responsibilities, all of which originated in the initial grants and liberties of a superior. The feudal language of 'rights' is, then, a language of privileges as concessions to individuals. We shall later see how it conflicted with another emergent language of rights as claims.

The fief and the vassalic relationship can be seen as having led to the rebuilding of a distinctive kind of monarchic 'state', when judicial reflection on feudal matters became prominent, especially by the thirteenth century. Some kings and territorial princes then began to attempt to regain control of what had become the hereditary transmission of fiefs in order to recapture for themselves various revenues and military service. Some kings and territorial princes were to be more successful than others in restructuring thirteenth-century feudalism in accord with the three emergent orders or estates of political society: clergy, nobility and labouring free men. What was to be left of feudalism when stripped of its original military and institutional significance was a form of land possession as a money fief, where the fief would normally be reserved for noble tenure. This proceeded hand in hand with a revitalization of the military nobility that was to be so prominent a characteristic of the end of the Middle Ages. We shall see that medieval 'state' formation by the later Middle Ages was, especially on the European continent, the consequence of emergent, centralized governments *checking* the resistance of individual feudal lords. They achieved this most notably by acknowledging freely governed and autonomous cities as the 'state's' new clients. From these new clients would arise some of the essential characteristics of the modern state: the universality and individuality of citizen allegiance to *it*.[13]

Across Europe, then, it would be concrete historical situations which determined whether a king or prince could minimize his feudal obligations and act 'absolutely' as an unopposed sovereign.[14] Some sovereigns were no longer to be considered the supreme lord (*seigneur*) but became, instead, overarching manipulators of feudality beneath their own public persons.[15] Hence, it has been argued that feudal institutions and practices ought not to be seen as *obstacles* to state formation. Rather, feudal practices should be seen as having been differentially deployed in order to enhance the centralizing strategies of kings and princes to provide them with a recovered monopoly over financial means and royal justice to support a hierarchical construction of power that would eventually characterize the modern state.

---

13   The literature on feudalism is enormous. For our purposes, the discussion by R. van Caenegem, 'Government, Law and Society', in *CHMPT* (1988), pp. 174–210 is a sufficient introduction. Also see J. R. Strayer, *Feudalism* (New York, 1965) and J. R. Strayer 'The Two Levels of Feudalism', in J. R. Strayer, *Medieval Statecraft and the Perspectives of History* (Princeton, NJ, 1971), pp. 63–76; D. Herlihy, ed., *The History of Feudalism* (New York, 1970); A. Black, *Political Thought* (see index under feudal ideas). A symposium on feudalism was published in *Past And Present* 73 (1978); W. Ullmann, *Law and Politics in the Middle Ages: an introduction to the sources of medieval political ideas* (Cambridge, 1975); C. Lis and H. Soly, *Poverty and Capitalism in Pre–industrial Europe* (Brighton, 1979), ch. 1; M. Bloch, *Feudal Society*, 2 vols (Paris, 1939/40) and English trans. 1961. See P. Anderson, *Passages from Antiquity to Feudalism* (London, 1974), pp. 150–1, 193–5 on communes in England contrasted with Continental urban autonomy and the oath of reciprocal loyalty between equals in communes, an early social contract, as opposed to feudal contracts between unequals. Also J. Coleman, 'The Individual and the Medieval State', ch. 1, and G. Dilcher, 'The City Community as an Instance in the European Process of Individualization', in Coleman ed, *The Individual in Political Theory and Practice*, the latter on the relation between feudalism and 'estates', the cities, citizens and subjects in Prussia until the eighteenth century. For an overview see M. Mann, *The Sources of Social Power: a history of power from the beginning to AD 1760*, vol. 1 (Cambridge,1986).

14   J. C. Holt, *Magna Carta*, 2nd edn (Cambridge, 1992), p. 29 discusses the demands for liberties on the Continent, aimed either at municipal independence (e.g. Lombardy in 1183) or at aristocratic immunity (German concessions 1220 and 1231 or French charters 1315), whereas in England demands for liberties were aimed at the control and subjection of the administrative functions of the Crown. By King John's reign in the early thirteenth century the sale of privileges became a final and permanent alienation of the rights of the Crown to the Barons; ibid., p. 57.

15   For an important reinterpretation see J. Giordanengo, 'Etat et droit féodal en France, xii–xiv's', in N. Coulet and J.–P. Genet, eds, *L'Etat moderne: le droit, l'éspace et les forms de l'état* (Paris, 1990), pp. 61–90.

Because feudalism is thought to have had such an overwhelming influence (whatever its contested interpretations) on the development of institutions and practices that are acknowledged aspects of the early-modern state, we can risk some oversimplification in order to grasp some of the characteristics of early medieval feudal society which endured and were transformed in the later period. We can point to the existence of a subject peasantry; the widespread use, by the ninth century, of what is called the 'service tenement or fief' instead of salary for military service – where the grant of seignorial rights included both the land and the dependent population dwelling thereon; the supremacy of a class of specialized warriors who constituted an aristocracy; the contractual ties of obedience and protection which bound one man to another; and the fragmentation of authority. It is thought that the Carolingian period provides evidence of at least the beginning of feudal relationships and most characteristic was the existence of a personal bond of sworn fidelity between the ruler and the free men or vassals who were ruled (*commendatio*). The *commendatio* established a degree of equality between an inferior vassal and the superior lord to whose protection he entrusted himself, and the vassal assumed duties of submission and personal aid. The vassal, not being considered a subject of his lord, had by virtue of his consent to the contract certain individual standing which was enhanced by the grant of a certain local autonomy (*beneficium*). Each party, however, acknowledged mutual companionship through a contract, each preserving the power to consent and to withdraw consent (*diffidatio*). This sworn fidelity consolidated the kingdom.

Charles the Great demanded a sworn oath from all free men in his dominions and placed special emphasis on the fidelity of lay and ecclesiastical nobles. It is this personal bond of mutual loyalty and affection between a free warrior and his hand-picked retinue of free close associates which came to be institutionalized by the Carolingians. The personal bond of fidelity presupposed some form of consent of the aristocratic faithful. Hence, early feudal government is defined as the exercise of power by kings or lords with the support of a military class, bound to their overlords by oaths of fidelity, where these *fideles* had the duty to give counsel to their king. A vassal was tied to his lord so that a mutual and life-long relationship was established between a lord and his man. In the Carolingian period, vassals constituted a large army of warriors, tied by contract to their overlord through personal loyalty, and the vassal was rewarded for his fealty by a grant, a benefice, of lands in return for the performance of his mainly military service.

The central importance of the feudal relationship, then, has been seen to be its contractual nature.[16] A general picture of early feudal society is a hierarchy in which Europe was divided geographically by means of spheres of influence and loyalty, based on land grants and military service. A contract of life-long mutual consent between a lord and vassal established normative limitations on ruler and ruled. This meant that the superior overlord could not require unconditional subservience from his *fideles*. Because the contract was mutual, any reneging on either side had consequences, and hence resistance was legitimate if fidelity on either side was breached.

If any vassal should wish to abandon his lord, he may do so only if he can prove that the lord has committed one of these crimes: first, if the lord should have unjustly sought to

---

16   Bloch thought the clearest legacy of feudalism to modern societies was its emphasis on the notion of political contract, where the contract presupposes individual contractees who are capable of individual consent. M. Bloch, *La Société féodale*, vol. 2 (Paris, 1940), pp. 258–60.

enslave him; second, if the lord plotted against his life; third, if the lord committed adultery with the wife of his vassal; fourth, if the lord willingly attacked him with drawn sword in order to kill him; fifth, if after the vassal commended his hands into his, the lord failed to provide defence which he could have done. ... We wish that every free man in our kingdom select the lord whom he prefers, us or one of our faithful subjects; we also command that no man abandon his lord without just cause, nor should anyone receive him, unless according to the customs of our ancestors.[17]

Anyone worthy of entering into faithful vassalage was a free man and not an unfree serf who was tied to the land like chattel. A faithful vassal was a noble, however insignificant his degree of nobility. What constituted nobility is hotly disputed but it appears to have had something to do with family origins, blood lines, distinguished ancestors going back to eponymous heroes of barbarian legend. German scholars have highlighted the associationist tendencies in this kind of society based on kinship bonding, blood lineage, unifying 'national' myths and oral customary codes. But there has been resistance to this interpretation on the part of other scholars because there is no secure evidence to demonstrate the link between the uniquely Germanic band of the king's warrior–companions mentioned by the first century AD Roman historian Tacitus in his *Germania* and the much later Carolingian *fideles*. What is clear is that early medieval societies rested on a diffused network of contractual agreements between relatively privileged individuals within larger groups, agreements which provided mutual aid and protection in relatively unsettled conditions, and that the oaths of allegiance which survive for these Christianized barbarian groupings were based on being made in the sight of God. The partnership between the king and his magnates who shared in his ministry as agents of the royal office was contractual, requiring some form of consensus. And it is notable that where Roman law ignored oaths, Carolingian professions of loyalty and mutuality of protection and order became the basis of virtually all kinds of bondings, and here it is thought that Charles the Great's ecclesiastical advisers played a foundational role.[18]

If feudal kingship rested on the consent of the king's free subjects, then in theory no succession could be allowed without some recognition of a king's fitness to rule. Consultation, at least among the more important of the magnates, both lay and ecclesiastical, was somehow required. Together such men determined in particular cases the extent to which a king was subject to the authority of law and custom in a contractual and collective community. A king who acted tyrannically or by whim, or who was negligent, was called *inutilis* or ineffective and his authority questioned and sometimes overridden.[19] The king's responsibility was to provide laws and perhaps more importantly to maintain the received laws and customs of the peoples within his domain. Under Carolingian kings documents known as *capitularies* represented both a theoretical and practical aspect by which royal reforms could be circulated and made known universally throughout the territory. Many Carolingian capitularies mention that they are the record of the deliberations and decisions on the part of an assembly. The capitulary of Herstal (779), for instance, states that its contents were agreed by the bishops, abbots and counts gathered

17 Carolingian kings' laws: *Capitularia regum francorum*, Monumenta Germaniae Historica [MGH] Legum II, no. 77, dated 802–3 and no. 104, dated 801–13.
18 See J. Nelson, 'Kingship and Empire', in *CHMPT* (1988), pp. 211–51.
19 E. Peters, *The Shadow King: rex inutilis in medieval law and literature, 751–1327* (New Haven, CN, 1970).

together with the king in one special council.[20] Decisions about secular and ecclesiastical organization that were recorded in the capitulary were subsequently made known to the people in the regions administered by the delegates.

The concern of kings in legislating and writing down laws seems to have been to fix custom rather than to bring in ostensibly new laws to change customary behaviour. Furthermore, Charles the Great showed himself concerned to surround himself at his court with learned clergy who could help him confirm custom with appeals to ancient texts and especially those of the Bible which spoke of kingship. Such councillors/counsellors were educated in monastic centres where theology and to some extent Roman law were studied. Most of Charles's advisers came from monastic centres in England or Ireland. And it was said that Alcuin of York not only taught Charles to read and write but he acted as his chief adviser.

Charles's royal enactments therefore have a strongly religious flavour where the idea of kingship as practised is rephrased in biblical terminology. Charles is described as the new King David and his ultimate authority comes from God. Carolingian kingship mixes early feudal seignorial along with theocratic notions of governance. The central idea behind theocratic monarchy was the divine origin of royal power and hence the king's relationship between those he ruled was based on *fides* in the sense of religious faith. But as a feudal, seignorial ruler this same king had with his *fideles* a contractual relationship of mutual fidelity. As Canning has noted,[21] such fidelity was not the source of his royal title but it might consolidate his actual power.

The dual theocratic–seignorial model of kingship was to become the distinctive form of monarchical secular government in Western Europe in the Middle Ages. But it would be the peculiarly constitutional solutions to the tensions between the two notions of ruling, theocratic and seignorial/feudal, that would help to set the boundaries of future European debates on the nature and practice of good government. It is important to realize that this dual theory and practice is thought to be particular to the Western European experience. Where we can find analogous feudal practices and institutions in other parts of the world, notably Japan, the tensions between central and local authorities have usually been resolved historically by a sacral monarchy as the *only* form of effective centralized government. As we shall see, however, the mixed inheritance of feudalism with the influences of Rome, Christian theological doctrine and the development of canon and civil laws to suit the evolving conditions of the medieval West's church and 'states', would produce a *constitutional* theory of the 'state' as a deliberate product of human reason and will. This would be the peculiarly European answer to the more universal problem of a tension between central and local authorities which was more usually solved by centralizing absolutisms.[22]

Translatio Imperii

With the help of learned advisers Carolingian emperors were able to claim to wield legitimate imperial authority since they saw themselves, after Charles the Great's coro-

---

20   MGH Cap. 1, no. 20, prologue, p. 47.
21   Canning, *A History*, p. 64.
22   B. Tierney, *Religion, Law and the Growth of Constitutional Thought 1150–1650* (Cambridge, 1982), p. 9.

nation as emperor in 800, to be the legitimate heirs of Byzantium. The 'translation of imperium' from East to West with imperium now lodged in the Carolingian line was pronounced along with an ideology that proclaimed a renewal and restoration of the idea of the Christian Roman Empire of Constantine. From Charles the Great onwards, the ideology of a Roman imperial restoration and renovation would continue to find champions. Indeed, poets at Charles's court proclaimed: 'Golden Rome renewed is once more reborn to the world', now geographically located in Northern Europe. And the bishops of Rome who sought independence from the Greek East increasingly looked to the Latin-speaking West for protection with the aim of consolidating a Western Latin Christendom that was divorced from a Greek-speaking Byzantine East, which the popes of Rome could not control. During the tenth century, when the centre of historical focus moves from Gaul to Germany and its Saxon kings, the Ottonian dynasty would once again seek to unite Germany and Italy under the rule of one Caesar. They too would be dominated by the notion of imperial *renovatio*, a Christian Rome renewed, with a reformed and purified church in the care of a German monarch and emperor. *Renovatio imperii Romanorum* would appear on Ottonian seals.

Theocratic Kingship

The Carolingian theory of kingship was effectively the work of Latin-speaking clergy, both at Rome and at the Carolingian court, hand in hand with the Carolingian aristocracy. With the Frankish appeal for the support of the pope in the election of their king over one they deemed *inutilis* – and this had established the Carolingian line in the first place – came the replacement of a Germanic kin-right with Christian principles. This has been seen as a conscious ideology on the part of Frankish clerical and lay aristocratic powers. Catholic Christianity was therefore a compulsory aspect of membership in the 'state'. Using the notion of the Roman imperial sacred kingship,[23] the Carolingians developed the religious element further. The Carolingian king and emperor was not only a convener of church councils, but he played a role in nominating bishops to ecclesiastical offices, and he was ultimately responsible for maintaining both clerical discipline and public morality. The Carolingian king ultimately pronounced on sound religious doctrine as it was to be taught in 'his' churches. Carolingian monarchy was theocratic not only in exercising legitimate intervention in church affairs but also in that the monarch himself was seen as sanctified, ruling as a surrogate of God on earth. Churches became literally the properties of the king's vassals and they were serviced by royal and lordly nominees. For the monarch to possess such powers he relied on the recognition of his royal and imperial titles by the pope in Rome. Furthermore, Carolingian rule depended extensively on the practical support received from bishops and abbots of monasteries within the domain, not least because bishops and abbots had been given vast tracts of land and they received, as feudal lords, payments in kind from serfs and lower vassals. Hence, the notion of Carolingian royalty was not only religiously sanctioned but it was also patrimonial. The king was patriarch, exercising authority over his household

---

23   Although it has been argued that in the Byzantine context the emperor had not been a priest nor had he been head of the church as an ecclesiastical body; see D. M. Nicol, 'Byzantine Political Thought', *CHMPT* (1988), p. 67.

and children, and in so far as the church was part of the realm, it no less than 'his people' were taken to have been committed to the king's care.

There was a spiritual and ceremonial aspect of Carolingian lordship where the king was viewed as a surrogate Christ. The clerical and monastic scholars at the Carolingian court developed a concept of kingship in the language of the Old Testament with David, Solomon and Melchisedek taken as both kings and priests of their people. The imperial crown, a combination of a royal crown and a bishop's mitre, publicly displayed the emperor's authority as both king and high priest. The ceremony of installing a king closely resembled an episcopal ceremony, and the king was more often viewed as a cleric than as a layman. Indeed, whatever the nature of 'original' barbarian kingship, once the tribes entered the Roman Empire they were directly influenced by and were assimilated to aspects of imperial government. And they understood that God was the source of royal authority, appealing directly to certain key texts both in the New Testament (1 Corinthians 15:10; John 3:27) and in the Old. Their formulation of a ruler as king by the grace of God (*rex dei gratia*) was widespread and by the end of the eighth century it became part of Charles the Great's royal title. This formulation was the distant ancestor of early modern divine right monarchy.[24] Furthermore, the Frankish people were identified with Israel under a theocratic kingship, an image of a 'chosen people' that would survive well into the seventeenth century in England and elsewhere on the Continent. In deriving his authority directly from God, the Carolingians said the king was God's vice-regent on earth, God's vicar, to whom the people were entrusted. In turn, the king by divine grace conceded governing offices and powers to those he governed, and hence his people were his subjects, subject to his superiority. On this theory, they seemed to lack any right of resistance to him.

But the office of kingship, being divinely instituted, had as its purpose the furthering of the divine will; hence the monarch was not to rule by absolute whim. His office, a duty, was that of Christian service for the common good of his people. In serving their good he was serving God. His office was a Christian ministry, exercised in his justice, mercy, humility, and in his serving, protecting and preserving the Christian religion. In Roman terms his was a tutorial role to his people, which in itself limited his freedom of action, as it required that he protect certain of their rights which were not necessarily derived as concessions from him. It is thought that 'the people' were conceived of as a separate entity, perhaps with certain inherent rights, separate from their ruler, even if in reality what was meant by ' the people' was the great men of the realm. 'The people', therefore, proved central even to this theocratic notion of monarchy. Crucially, theocratic kingship was not arbitrary absolute rule. And yet if the king was in theory limited both by his ministry and by customs, there were no means to enforce these limitations and no legal right of resistance: according to theocratic theory, his rule was not absolute but he was not controlled.

There is, however, a tradition of argument which goes back to nineteenth-century German scholarship that sees the limits on arbitrary rule having been inherent in the practices of Germanic tribes themselves. It has been asserted that Germanic peoples preserved a kind of popular kingship by election, thereby limiting a king's power by his need to answer to a popular assembly. But many scholars now think that there is too

24   Canning, *A History*, p. 17.

little evidence to demonstrate characteristics of Germanic practices *before* they were Romanized and Christianized.[25] There is no doubt, however, that practices of Romanized and Christianized Germanic kingdoms gave a place to popular involvement in the making of a king and part of the process of his legitimation was their recognition of the divine source of his authority. Furthermore, there was a popular aspect to the creation of customary law and royal law was meant to coexist with it, rather than replace it. The ruler caused to be written down the customary law which was given legitimacy and authority by his will. Since the different barbarian kingdoms were composed of different peoples with different oral customs, written codes which were often a mixture of Roman and Germanic elements came to be written down in Latin to apply to members of respective peoples (*gentes*). The most important and long-enduring barbarian code was the *Lex Romana Visigothorum*, a simplified Roman law code. Indeed, there survive other collections of 'national' laws of the different peoples in the regions under Carolingian rule, comprising the *Lex Salica, Lex Ribuaria, Lex Alamannorum, Lex Burgundionum* and the *Lex Baivvariorum*. Carolingian rulers were enjoined to judge wisely according to the written law, implying that judges as well as counts and royal agents were to know the different barbarian laws and have copies of them in their different regions to guide them in their day-to-day administration. There are documents which describe how Charles the Great assembled the dukes, counts and the rest of the Christian people, together with men skilled in the laws, and he had all the laws of his realm read out; each man's law was expounded to him and emended where necessary, and the emended law written down. Charles declared that the judges should judge in accordance with what was written and should not accept gifts; all men, poor or rich, should enjoy justice in Charles's realm.[26]

Theocratic Carolingian kings therefore worked within a legal tradition that was largely based on custom. Both the traditions of Roman law and Germanic law insisted that rulers governed within the legal structure of human laws rather than arbitrarily. And when law did not exist in written form, law was what experienced men declared it to be. Hence, despite the subjection of his people to his rule as God's vicar in theocratic theory, no monarch could rely solely on his theocratic claims for his legitimacy. The feudal, contractual partnership between the king and his aristocratic lay and ecclesiastical vassals underwrote his power. While the spiritual authority of his ecclesiastical magnates formally created him as quasi-divine monarch, once installed these ecclesiastics were subordinated in temporal matters to him. As a consequence, many scholars have argued that the contractual aspects of this kind of monarchy, based on bonds of sworn fidelity, in fact and practice superceded in importance the theocratic conception of his royal personality. Out of this bond of mutual faith would evolve not only notions of rights and duties of both ruler and ruled but even more abstract notions of rule over the corporate body of society, conceived as the *duties* of a public office.

The very notion of kingship as ministry emphasized a mixture of spiritual and secular power and capacities united in one person. But a distinction was also observed between 'the king's two bodies', his individual person by nature and his person by grace which raised him above natural men into a public, impersonal, official personality: a God-

25   See Canning, *A History*, pp. 16–17 for a summary view of the debate.
26   R. McKitterick, *The Carolingians and the Written Word* (Cambridge, 1989), p. 60.

man.[27] He governed a *regnum* or a *populus* comprised of Christian men, with a Christian liberty that acknowledged their freedom as sons of God but without otherwise destroying social ranks in a hierarchical *respublica*. Both Roman and feudal law equalized in a legal rather than a social sense. Society was governed by the person of the particular ruler and yet simultaneously was understood impersonally as a public realm, founded and structured by law in which *regnum* and *ecclesia* together comprised the commonwealth, the *respublica*, without implying a specific constitutional form of government. A monarchy could therefore be called a *respublica*. This way of speaking would continue well into the sixteenth century, so that any reader of medieval and Renaissance political theory texts must be careful not to confuse a specific reference to a republican constitutional form with the more general notion of a *respublica* as simply a law-governed community with the common good as its purpose.

The dual personality of the king, by nature an individual man and by grace and through ecclesiastical consecration a God-man, would also survive into the future. From the Carolingian period would also survive both the theory and practice of governance by consensus, whereby a realm is ruled with the counsel and consent of the faithful vassals in mutual contracts with their overlord, the king. In practice, 'consent' meant both an implicit general consensus and an explicit consent of a relative minority of important men, a notion that would later lead to the use of the term *maior et sanior pars*, 'the great and the good'. The language of much of this theory is Roman and legal. Its reality was often simply the rule of many Germanic peoples under one organizing principle. When linked with papal Rome, the language would be invested with ancient reverberations of empire and therefore continue a link with antiquity. The Carolingian period is important because it allows us to observe a period in European culture where sovereignty was construed as a faithful, religiously sanctioned sharing of power between a monarch, an aristocracy and the church, and where policies were based on the consultation and consent of these elite parties to policy.

The Origins of Papal Authority and the Gelasian Doctrine

It has often been observed that anyone wishing to throw light on the models that have influenced the formation of the European modern state cannot ignore the medieval Western church. The Latin church evolved a model of concentrated decision-making power and a pyramidal structure of institutional organization, what English-language historians often call 'papal monarchy', well before European states came into existence.[28] Hence, another language of legitimate authority was developed within ecclesiastical circles. Papal authority, the authority of the bishop of Rome, was understood to be founded in Christ's commission to St Peter as related in the Gospel of Matthew 16:18–19:

> And I say also unto thee, That thou art Peter, and upon this rock I will build my church;
> and the gates of hell shall not prevail against it. And I will give unto thee the keys of the

---

27   E. Kantorowicz, *The King's Two Bodies: a study in medieval political theology* (Princeton, NJ, 1957).

28   A. Padoa–Schioppa, 'Hierarchy and Jurisdiction: models in medieval canon law', in A. Padoa–Schioppa, ed., *Legislation and Justice* (Oxford, 1996), pp.1–15; K. Pennington, *Pope and Bishops: the papal monarchy in the twelfth and thirteenth centuries* (Philadelphia, 1984).

kingdom of heaven; and whatsoever thou shalt bind on earth shall be bound in heaven: and whatsoever thou shalt loose on earth shall be loosed in heaven.

This, along with Christ's command to Peter (John 21:15–17) to 'Feed my sheep', served as the scriptural foundations of papal legal claims to jurisdiction over European Christians throughout the Middle Ages.

Christ was to be understood as having built his church and he passed on governing jurisdiction to his apostle Peter and to Peter's successors. This is known as the claim to apostolic Petrine succession of the papacy. Each successive pope, many years after the age of the apostles, was to be seen as the 'unworthy heir of St Peter', as Peter's vicar, rather than as the heir of the previous incumbent. Each pope succeeded directly to the same legal powers of St Peter but not to his personal merits. A distinction had therefore been drawn between the office of pope on the one hand and the incumbent on the other, which enabled the papacy throughout the Middle Ages to claim that no matter how unsuitable a particular incumbent might be, he retained the full legal authority of pope 'in place of' St Peter. This notion of the duration of office, its impersonal indestructibility and its separation from the personal idiosyncrasies of an incumbent, was to remain fundamental to European political discourse on government in church and state.

Furthermore, by the mid fifth century the bishop of Rome was spoken of as head (*principatus*) of the church which was the Body of Christ. The church was seen as structured organically as a public corporation, a body (*corpus*) comprising a head (*caput*) and members. The head, the pope, was to be judged by no one and hence the pope was declared constitutional sovereign with a jurisdictional function as the final court of appeal in ecclesiastical cases. This was the culmination of the evolving hierarchical structure adopted by the church from the second century onwards where a system of functions and duties differentiated bishops, priests and deacons. There was also established a hierarchy between different episcopal sees, ranging from suffragan bishops to metropolitans and, the highest, patriarch. The empire's own institutional model, centralized and hierarchical, offered the church an example, but from the fourth century the church in the West began to evolve along its own road to claim Roman primacy. Thereafter, to the organic image of the church as the Body of Christ would be added a notion of hierarchy inherited from a sixth-century anonymous Christian neoplatonist who was erroneously thought to be St Paul's disciple Dionysius the Areopagite. This Pseudo-Dionysius wrote two works, *On the Celestial Hierarchy* and *On the Ecclesiastical Hierarchy,* whose core principle was that all powers emanate from above, from the principle of unity, God, in a succession of graded ranks and estates. The superior transmits capabilities to the inferior. By comparing a body politic with the human body, the hierarchy implicit in the organic analogy established that each part of the corporate, public unity was like a limb in a body and each had been assigned a specific task from which it must not default. Hierarchy expressed itself through a notion of differential participation in the origin and source of power, the one God, and it reinforced the view that each part must be content with its status. Appealing to this neoplatonist theory of infusion of differentials of power from an original, complete, divine source, led to the view that God transmitted the faculty of governing a whole body to its head. Both popes and kings would see advantages in this formulation throughout the Middle Ages, taking the institution of the graded hierarchy of lesser estates and their instruction in their respective tasks to be within their primary powers.

This hierarchical, organic theory, when applied to the pope as final, undisputed court of appeal in ecclesiastical cases, would not go unchallenged within the church itself. There was to be a major and enduring debate over the relationship of the pope's powers and those of his bishops throughout the Middle Ages, a debate which centred on biblical justifications for the scope of episcopal local autonomy and for the scope of the pope's centralizing authority. The passage in Matthew 16:18 which was read as expressly attributing to Peter and his successors the power to bind and loose on earth and in heaven was countered with Matthew 18:18 and John 20:23, where this power was accorded to all the disciples without distinction. Did bishops derive their local jurisdictional powers from the pope as St Peter's vicar or by being the successors to the other apostles, where Peter was simply to be seen as first among equals? Was the church organically structured as a governing, directing head over members or was it in origin a corporate collective, with local sites of episcopal autonomy, the pope being no more than an overarching, elected public administrator of the whole?

If there were these difficulties in interpreting the nature and limits of papal authority *within* the church, there would also emerge difficulties in determining the relationship *between* the functional scope and authority of temporal government and the functional scope and authority of spiritual government. The Carolingian relationship between temporal and spiritual authority, embodied in the exercise by one man, Charles the Great, of his imperial office as king *and* divinely appointed God-man, would gradually find competition from other theories and practices of public office in the Middle Ages.[29]

As early as the fourth century there was a view that clergy were superior to the laity, and we saw this already expressed by St Ambrose and others who contributed to the 'ascetic takeover' in the Latin West. By the end of the fifth century, Pope Gelasius attempted to define more precisely the relationship between the respective power and authority of empire and priesthood. He argued that the world was governed in two ways, one priestly and the other secular. Both spiritual and temporal rulers derived their authority and function from Christ's decree that they exist in parallel and observe their respective limits. Priests control religious matters and hence the emperor is the son, and neither teacher nor director, of the church where religion is concerned. The clergy is itself to recognize the primacy of the pope. However, in secular affairs, clergy obey and use imperial laws, the imperial power having been instituted by God. But in a hierarchy of authoritative power, the clerical was said to supersede the temporal. The priesthood was seen as bearing the heavier burden since clergy render an account before God for the kings of men.

Gelasian doctrine was read thereafter as — in theory at least — denying the Roman imperial possibility of uniting in one person headship of church and 'state'. Perhaps most significant and enduring was Gelasius's view that there was an ultimate duality of jurisdiction in the authorities over men. But in the Carolingian period it clearly was not maintained that a king was incapable of being both temporal ruler and in charge of his people's spiritual well-being. However, there would come to be developed a theory that sought to maintain in practice the authority of emperorship and kingship as exercised, but only through papal favour. Charles the Great did not himself appear to accept

---

29 But the Carolingian idea would survive, transformed, in the later fully blown doctrines of divine right monarchy that would enable post–Reformation rulers like England's Henry VIII to argue that in being heads of state they were also heads of the state's church.

this papal interpretation of his power. But out of this would later emerge an elaborate theory of papal supremacy over church and state with the temporal authority being graciously conceded to kings, without which kings could not legitimately function. It would lead to the possibility and eventuality of popes being able to depose kings.

Furthermore, the document known as the Donation of Constantine, a ninth-century monastic forgery, would be included in collections of church law and popes came explicitly to exploit it. It purported to be a constitution of the fourth-century Emperor Constantine in favour of the papacy, which said that Constantine had donated the imperial palace, the crown, and the very government of all of the Western Roman Empire to Pope Sylvester and his successors, in gratitude for his having been baptized and cured of leprosy. To the papacy was thereby accorded imperial power in the West; and the pope was recognized as higher than, and first of all, priests in the world.

By the eleventh century, during his conflict with the emperor Henry IV of Germany,[30] Pope Gregory VII would pronounce that kings and emperors were no more than lay members of the church and their first duty was to help the church provide for the spiritual well-being of their subjects. Bishops and the pope in particular were therefore the only ones in a position to judge of the spiritual suitability of such men. To the clergy alone had been given the powers to bind and loose in heaven *and* on earth (Matthew 16:18). Hence, an unsuitable lay governor could be both excommunicated from the church and his subjects freed from their oaths of loyalty to him. On this view, the king in the hierarchy of world governance was placed beneath the lowest of the orders of the clergy and well beneath the pope. The pope alone, then, not only can free a secular ruler's subjects from their oaths of allegiance, but he alone may judge and depose emperors. In line with the Donation of Constantine's assurance that Constantine had donated the governance of the Roman Empire to Pope Sylvester, the pope alone had the rightful use of the imperial insignia.[31] The church was now to be understood as autonomous and immune from all and any secular governance.[32]

These views had already begun to emerge during the tenth century, when there had been a call from enclosed monastic centres, notably in Burgundy and Lorraine, for a *renovatio* within the church itself.[33] Powerful men of noble feudal families had become abbots of monasteries that nominally adhered to the sixth-century monastic Rule of St Benedict. Now came a call from such enclosed 'cities of God' for a renewal of the Benedictine Rule, a more ascetic and rigorous application of its structure, and from within these centres emerged the radical reforming voices of a group of well-born and intensely spiritual men. At Cluny, a massive Benedictine monastery in Burgundy, came the demand that her foundations be established under the protection, not of neighbouring feudal lords, but of Rome itself. Cluny sought *libertas*, an immunity from feudalism's burdens and security for the church of God. The movement to purge the church of

---

30 This is traditionally known as the Investiture Contest. K. Leyser, 'The Polemics of the Papal Revolution', in B. Smalley, ed., *Trends in Medieval Political Thought* (Oxford, 1965) is still useful.

31 *Dictatus papae*, esp. 27, 12, 8.

32 See I. S. Robinson, *The Papacy 1073–1198: continuity and innovation* (Cambridge, 1990).

33 See P. J. Geary, *Phantoms of Remembrance: memory and oblivion at the end of the first millennium* (Princeton, NJ, 1994) on the extraordinary, selective use of earlier documents and traditions to suit the present perspectives of eleventh-century publicists and archivists engaging local conditions, as well as their wholesale destruction of inherited past documents and their importance in leaving a legacy from which twelfth-century views of the past would be constructed.

those clergy who had bought their offices, or who were dominated by feudal princes or local counts, or who lived with concubines and inherited their posts, had begun. Cluny, with the support of spiritually minded and Rome-centred German emperors who fostered the religious reform, would become the vanguard of the papal reform movement that, by the time of Pope Gregory VII, would come to argue against the reforming role of the empire itself.

By the mid-eleventh century it was argued that spiritual benefices and positions of power with land could not be conferred by a layman, a king, no matter how spiritual and concerned for the security of the church he may be. It was proposed that the church, as an ecclesiastical body, had a freedom from lay control and subjection, a *libertas ecclesiae*. This reveals a peculiarly feudal notion of negative liberty: the concession of an autonomous space of action and value, immune from the general rules and observances otherwise imposed by a superior lord on those ruled by him. But the claim was that this ecclesiastical immunity was not a grant or concession from secular governors but from Christ in the Petrine commission. The church was to be understood as autonomously structured as a hierarchy, with the pope as its monarch, indeed as emperor. And the liberty of the church consisted, in the first instance, in its own establishing of a *more than* feudal, hierarchical subjection of the clergy to the overlord pope. Not only was the pope the final court of appeal, but through his will alone could new legislation be produced. In the twenty-seven propositions expressed in his *Dictatus papae* and in his other letters, Pope Gregory VII attempted to establish a papal theocracy, curtailing the powers of bishops, and based on Roman primacy. He believed the Roman church (not specifically the pope) to be infallible and those not in agreement with this Rome-centred church were to be excluded from Catholicism. What was being attempted was a higher unification of Christendom over the particularism of organized feudalism throughout Europe.[34]

By only citing a part of the Gelasian doctrine, Pope Gregory VII gave the impression that royal power was not simply subjected to the priesthood in religious matters but in all matters. The powers of binding and loosing included the power 'to remove from as well as to concede to anyone, according to his merits, earthly empires, kingdoms, principalities . . . and the possessions of all men'. Augustine's understanding of a post-historical 'city of God' was being transformed into a realized community in this world, the institutional church, whose jurisdiction covered not only ecclesiastics but all of Christendom, since all men were the pope's sheep and Christ had commanded that Peter feed them all. On this view, monarchs were to function within structures evaluated by the clergy. In serving the 'state' they were serving the higher purposes of the Christian common good as defined and sanctioned by the church. And the church itself was to increase the numbers of its own *fideles* by increasing the number of kings and lords who were faithful to St Peter's vicar.

Pope Gregory VII's pontificate spawned the first pamphlet exchange of publicists engaged in what we recognize as perhaps *the* debate in medieval political theory over the relation between temporal and spiritual power. This set in motion the ongoing disputes that helped to define both in theory and practice the relative scopes of political and ecclesiological jurisdictions throughout the Middle Ages. But even among pious churchmen of the day there were many who refused Gregory's initiative and his programme,

---

34   For the *Dictatus papae*, 'Dictates of the Pope', in translation see B. Tierney, *The Crisis of Church and State 1050– 1300 with selected documents* (Englewood Cliffs, NJ, 1964 and reprints), pp.49–50.

since they held that the church's task was moral regeneration and not a reordering of the fundamental laws and principles of society. They were unwilling to forego the help that kings and emperors had already been giving to the reforming party within the church. Hence, Gregory set in train a scholarly movement that would lead to the establishment of a body of church law, the canon law which from the twelfth century onwards would establish the church as an autonomous, legal and governing institution, notably dominated by experts in canon law. Gregory had called upon monastic reformers who were familiar with the early councils of the church and the laws there promulgated to ransack the archives and bring together all decretals of former popes, the canons of church councils and passages from historians which set forth the power of the Holy See.

The German church, through the interest and power of German emperors, had actually been the most organized and reformed of Europe's churches, but as Gregory saw it the monarchy now had to be attacked at its theocratic heart in order for the papacy to liberate itself from the imperial system. To Gregory, a kingship with priestly powers along Carolingian lines, what he took to be a ruler who was both *rex et sacerdos* (king and priest), had to be destroyed, despite Charles never having claimed to be a priest in the sense of celebrating the eucharist. According to Gregory, Christ alone could give or take away *dominium* and this Christ-originated authority had passed directly to Gregory as Peter's successor. Either you are a king and layman, or you are a priest (*aut rex est laicus aut clericus*), not both. Gregory sought a real separation of church and 'state' with his interpretation of the king's so-called priestly character severely challenged. The king should instead be seen as a removable official. If he did not perform his official function, as determined by the pope, then he was to be regarded as a tyrant to whom obedience was not owed.

It has been generally observed that in establishing 'suitability' to rule as the test of lay kings, Pope Gregory VII further encouraged lesser lay princes to select and propose a candidate for papal approval. Kings should be chosen from below as a nominee, and this effectively favoured a theory of elective monarchy to an office that could then be filled by the elected nominee only upon papal approval of suitability. This implied to German princes that the authority in the realm was theirs to elect one of their number, and it served their particularist interests against the centralizing tendencies of German monarchs. Gregory's reading of church decrees led him to this theory of elective monarchy in order to destroy the sacred element in the king's person. But it was received as an appeal to that other structuring set of principles of feudal society: that legitimate government was based on a contract, consent to which was fundamental.[35]

During the fourteenth century papal publicists would take Gregory's theory even further, seeking to remove all autonomy from secular authorities. On their view, the pope was responsible before God for the whole Christian community, and was thereby taken to have the right to judge, depose and concede power to secular rulers, while being himself judged by none. As in Gregory's own time, such 'papal hierocratic' publicists would constitute only one side of the argument, and by the fourteenth century they would already be on the road to becoming a vociferous minority position in the medieval church itself. Their view would, however, continue to be sustained during the sixteenth century by canon lawyers and even adopted in reverse, by later monarchs with absolutist pretensions in their own realms.

---

35   H. Fuhrmann, *Germany in the High Middle Ages c. 1050–1200* (Cambridge, 1986), chs 3 and 4; A. Haverkamp, *Medieval Germany 1056–1273* (Oxford, 1988). part II, ch. 1.

Needless to say, in the medieval monarchical resistance to this doctrine of papal monarchy[36] alternative ideologies of legitimate temporal rule emerged.[37] Some would continue to maintain that the king was Christ's vicar and not merely a layman. They would
retain the Rome-centred focus on imperial kingship and either reaffirm a duality, but of
separate *and* equal co-operative spheres of power and jurisdiction; or they would reverse
the Gelasian and Gregorian hierarchy of church over 'state' altogether, and insist instead
on an overlapping duality where the church was a necessary but subordinate, non-
coercive, functional part of the 'state'.

Two Swords Theory

In Luke's Gospel, chapter 22, Christ, at the passover supper, distributes the bread and
wine to his disciples and warns that his betrayer is sitting at the table. After acknowledging those of his disciples who had continued with him in his temptations he says:

> And I appoint unto you a kingdom as my Father hath appointed unto me: That ye may eat
> and drink at my table in my kingdom, and sit on thrones judging the twelve tribes of Israel.
> (Luke 22:28–30)

> And he said unto them, When I sent you without purse and scrip and shoes, lacked ye any
> thing? And they said, Nothing. Then said he unto them, But now, he that hath a purse let
> him take it, and likewise his scrip: and he that hath no sword, let him sell his garment and
> buy one. For I say unto you, that this that is written must yet be accomplished in me. . . .
> And they said, Lord, behold, here are two swords. And he said unto them, It is enough.
> (Luke 22:35–8)

> Lord, shall we smite with our swords? One of them struck at the high priest's servant and
> cut off his right ear, but Christ said Suffer ye thus far. And he touched his ear and healed
> him. (Luke 22: 49–51).

In John's Gospel (18:11), after Peter has severed the servant's ear, Christ says to him:
'Put up thy sword into the sheath'.

We have two swords, they are 'enough' and they are used. We have Christ, appointed by his Father to a kingdom, and who appoints his disciples to the same kingdom, seated on thrones, to judge the people of Israel. Publicists elaborately interpreted
possible meanings. The monarchical resistance to the Gregorian case read Luke 22:38 as
referring to the church as possessing a spiritual sword, and the *regnum* or 'state' a carnal
sword. Some interpreted the priestly sword as encouraging obedience to the king as
God's vicar, since it was forbidden to clergy to shed blood, whereas the royal sword was
meant to enforce obedience. The two swords were to work co-operatively in bringing
about peace and unity in the Christian community. Pro-monarchists increasingly examined Roman law to provide material that would allow them to establish precedents for
secular rulers exercising jurisdiction in ecclesiastical as well as temporal matters. They

---

36   J. A. Watt, *The Theory of Papal Monarchy in the Thirteenth Century: the contribution of the canonists* (London, 1965)
provides a good analysis of 'papal monarchy'.

37   For the arguments against 'papal monarchy' from within the church, see B. Tierney, *Foundations of the Conciliar
Theory: the contribution of the medieval canonists from Gratian to the Great Schism* (Cambridge, 1955).

found that the Roman emperor had been the unifier of the church, and that imperial consent had been required to install a pope who had been chosen by clergy and people. It was argued that the king, standing in for Christ, was the head of the Christian community (*caput ecclesiae*). The pope was, after all, only Peter's vicar. Implicitly, the power of both swords was the king's.

French and English writers entered the debate either to argue that the two swords, spiritual and material, are the pope's 'to be drawn, perhaps at your command, if not by your hand'; that 'the pope has the plenitude of power [*plenitudo potestatis*] while others have been called only to a limited part of power and care';[38] or to argue that temporal power and jurisdiction is superior to sacramental power and jurisdiction, because Christ was king by virtue of his divine nature (as was indicated in Luke 22) and priest only by virtue of his human nature. The priesthood was therefore subject to the king as to Christ.[39] The authors on one or another side of the debate increasingly plundered 'authorities' to make their ideological cases by means of a selective use of the Bible, of Roman, customary and early church law, of history, and of the writings of the church Fathers. An investigation of the past, massively supported by institutions with a stake in the answers uncovered, was undertaken to justify the present.

If, in the earlier Middle Ages, government and its underlying principles were considered to be integral parts of applied Christian doctrine, then Carolingian theories of sovereignty and law-making were in many ways, as Ullmann observed, applied ecclesiology.[40] Biblical sources were interpreted and applied to Christian society as a whole. But in the twelfth century we begin to see an extension of medieval jurisprudence to the whole of society on the part of those who studied Roman and canon law. The governmental principles that were conceived, elaborated, applied and modified by medieval governments themselves were frequently first expressed by lawyers who, through legal practice, came to theorize about their own profession. An attempt to embrace the rules of social living of Christians *across* geographical boundaries was enhanced by an increasingly literate, bureaucratic group of men who uncovered ancient Roman and ecclesiastical documents. These revealed how, for instance, the Roman Empire was rationally governed despite its pluralistic differences across vast territories. Spurred on by the ambitions of monarchs and popes to collect into coherent systematic wholes the doctrines that would govern men in a centralized fashion, literate men sought to harmonize what looked like contradictions in the statements about society and the faith made by different church Fathers, earlier church councils, and ancient Roman authors like Cicero, all of whom wrote about a society that was in many ways unlike its medieval successors.

The Twelfth-century 'Renaissance': Canon Lawyers and their Heirs

The twelfth century was one in which practical and intellectual achievements in the arts and sciences across Europe combined to produce what has been called a 'rebirth and

---

38   St Bernard, *De consideratione*, 4.3.7.
39   Norman Anonymous.
40   W. Ullmann, *The Carolingian Renaissance and the Idea of Kingship* (London, 1969).

renewal', a renaissance.[41] New religious orders were established; new urban communes with increased numbers of organized merchants and artisans developed features of autonomous government. New ways of speaking about the different functional and professional orders or states of life were elaborated to take into account the proliferation of different roles and obligations in a society that was developing more complex institutions. The expansion of urban schools, soon to develop into the earliest universities, and a multiplication of monastic foundations, increased the scope for discussion of the themes of the goal of human life and the government of society that had been found in the authoritative writings of the Bible, the church Fathers and the ancient philosophers. More men were acquiring literate skills. New approaches were found to the old texts of grammar, logic, poetry, philosophy and theology which had been the mainstay of monastic education for centuries, inspired by the rediscovery of further ancient texts. New texts of authority were discovered, traditional texts were reorganized, and modes of interpretation were more sharply defined. Everywhere, there appears to have been a need to organize knowledge in a comprehensive, rational manner. Everywhere, there were quests to understand the universal order that was thought to exist behind the often fragmentary remains of the past. One such quest resulted in a new jurisprudence, 'reborn and renewed' with the rediscovery of Justinian's *Digest c.* 1070 which supplemented the relics of Rome's laws that existed in barbarian adaptations.

The claim in the twelfth century for a *renovatio imperii* was far from new. But we must be aware that both the German monarchy and even the city commune of Rome took as their principal model the period of late antiquity and the empire of the Christian emperors from Constantine to Justinian, but not the empire of Augustus and certainly not the republic of Cicero.[42] What was being 'reborn and renewed' from the twelfth-century renaissance and its aftermath comprised an appropriation of selected forms of antiquity which were then grafted on to contemporary institutions, the form of Roman law in particular, being imposed on the substance of life . Thus began the attempts at creating an intellectually coherent, rational discipline to guide legal thinking. Conflicting authorities had to be harmonized to provide guidance to present agents, and a literary methodology, developed first among theologians, was adapted to reduce contrary arguments to agreement (*solutio contrariorum*). This is what is called the scholastic method of debate that would endure for centuries in learned circles, and in the twelfth century it was in the process of emergence.[43]

It is thought that the so-called Gregorian Reform movement began the revival of Roman law categories and added to civil law the pronouncements of several centuries of church councils and various popes, enshrining these in a body of church law. Church lawyers had to create their authoritative book first since, unlike Roman lawyers, they had not inherited a closed corpus. During the twelfth century, canon law was collected into one textbook by the monk Gratian and it was known as the *Concordance of Discord-*

---

41   See R. Benson, G. Constable, C. Lanham, eds, *Renaissance and Renewal in the Twelfth Century* (Oxford, 1982) for excellent discussions and important bibliographies; for a very useful overview see D. E. Luscombe and G. R. Evans, 'The Twelfth–century Renaissance', in *CHMPT* (1988), pp. 306–40; and J. Canning 'Development: *c.* 1150–*c.* 1450, politics, institutions and ideas', in *CHMPT* (1988), pp. 341–66.

42   R. Benson, 'Political *Renovatio*: two models', in Benson, Constable and Lanham, *Renaissance and Renewal*, pp. 339–86.

43   See below, chapter 2 on Aquinas's method.

ant Canons, or simply as the *Decretum* (1139/40). The *Decretum* comprises one authority set against another, one text against another, side by side with technical juristic materials from all the periods of the church's past. A not always successful attempt is then made to reconcile apparently opposing positions. Commentaries on the *Decretum* by jurists known as decretists[44] and further compilations of papal decretals, themselves commented upon by jurists known as decretalists,[45] proliferated.

By the end of the twelfth century, papal centralization had already extended beyond the field of judicial decisions and gradually engaged the field of legislation; papal decisions in certain specific cases that reflected the conditions of medieval life came to exert influence as authoritative precedents for similar cases. Many of the popes of the twelfth and thirteenth centuries had trained as lawyers and they became increasingly aware of their role as legislators and creators of new laws for the church. Because the creation of new law in the church was an ongoing process, popes provided answers to specific problems within their judicial authority and sent them as decretal letters (not unlike late imperial rescripts) to bishops in order to answer enquiries on difficult points of law. Or they had made decisions on cases that had been directly submitted to the apostolic see by appellants or aggrieved parties. By the thirteenth century unsolicited papal rulings established new law. Consequently, there was an expansion in the roles of professional decretists and decretalists in interpreting juridical doctrines. But it is not simply that they were fascinated by earlier authorities that could confirm papal sovereignty; they also examined early Christian texts which focused on community and collective organization, the life of the early church, the activities of early councils. Consequently, Huguccio, the greatest decretist wrote that the church is the aggregate of the faithful and exists wherever the faithful are.[46] Canonists, always looking for reconciliations, did not necessarily see this as opposed to papal sovereign headship. Some came to teach that the papal sovereign will was expressed in its highest form when the pope acted in and with the gathered church or its representative council. They went further and simultaneously drew on the Roman law of sovereignty to defend a doctrine of papal headship of the church as well as defending the structure of the church in terms of Roman corporation law.

Hence, much of what we call political theory, because it discussed the inviolable, fundamental law framework in which sovereign rulers and legitimate communities operated, emerged from the interpretations of these learned canon law commentators and interpreters. Most notably it was in their recognition of a need to find solutions to two competing problems, the overriding right of a sovereign to rule and the overriding claim of a community to defend itself against the abuse of power, that they made their mark and developed a range of original and influential perspectives on constitutional thinking. As a consequence, it has rightly been claimed that the canonists probably had a greater impact over a wider spectrum of what we regard as important issues in political theory than did the civilian lawyers, who at least initially were more tied to the authoritative Roman law texts of Justinian.[47]

From 1150 to 1250 a series of clashes between the papacy and the Hohenstaufen

---

44   The most distinguished was Huguccio, *d.* 1210.
45   The most distinguished were Pope Innocent IV, *d.* 1254, Hostiensis, *d.*1271 and Bernard of Parma, *d.* 1266.
46   *Summa* ad C. 24 q. 1 c. 9.
47   Canning, *A History*, p. 117. Tierney, *Foundations of the Conciliar Theory* is the classic text.

dynasty of German emperors, most notably Frederick Barbarossa and Frederick II, was marked by theoretical discussions that were overtly political and couched in increasingly legalistic terms. To the heated debate over the relation between temporal and spiritual jurisdictions, the tremendously active Pope Innocent III, in a series of decretals,[48] made a lasting theoretical contribution to the notion of papal monarchy. Although some have questioned the extent of his actual power, whether he was a lawyer or a trained theologian, and whether he should be viewed as a papal hierocrat or a dualist,[49] there is little doubt that Innocent made various ad hoc claims to ultimate power in secular matters. Faced with specific historical situations, he claimed to have the power to choose between claimants to the imperial crown, and that his was the right to examine and reject, if necessary, candidates elected by the German princes. Because it was the pope who *instituted* the emperor, Innocent III argued that he was also the *source* of imperial authority. Furthermore, he argued in general that the pope could exercise temporal jurisdiction incidentally and that he could perform the office of secular power sometimes and in some things himself, while in some things through others. He appeared to go so far as to make the general claim of the pope's jurisdiction in civil *and* ecclesiastical cases, and certainly that in civil cases where sin was involved (*ratione peccati*) the pope had a right of intervention. Royal power was a derivative of papal power, and papal power, in deriving from divine authority, could transcend canon law usage itself.[50] During the thirteenth century, popes and decretalists actively realized what was once perceived to be the mere potential of royal power in Christ's commission to Peter that he bind and loose in heaven and on earth. And the canonist Hostiensis would go so far as to argue against the lawyer Pope Innocent IV that pagans and infidels could not be recognized as ruling validly at all.[51]

Whatever the success of papal claims in the sphere of temporal jurisdiction (and the emerging territorial monarchies during the thirteenth century resisted them vociferously both in theory and practice), when canon law was applied in matters of church administration we can observe the medieval church thinking and behaving as a proto-state. It has been argued that those institutions destined to play important parts in state formation, such as the impersonal, hierarchical and specialized structure of the office, were first realized in and through the classical canon law of the twelfth century. The legal instruments that created centralized authority in the church, such as the power of a higher judge to summon cases, the right to lodge appeals, the notion of office, the concept of a juridical person, inquisitorial proceedings, forms of collective decision-making, and in particular the majority principle (*maior et sanior pars*), rules on the legal efficacy of agreements and rules relating to the power of dispensation and the granting of privileges, were all in some way to be imitated by medieval 'states'.[52] In practice, the legal and judicial apparatus of the Roman church's *curia* became increasingly elaborate in

---

48   Especially *Venerabilem* and *Per venerabilem* (both 1202) and *Novit* (1204).

49   See the collected articles in K. Pennington, *Popes, Canonists and Texts 1150–1550* (Aldershot [Variorum], 1993).

50   Differing interpretations in M. Maccarone, *Vicarius Christi. Storia del titolo papae* (Rome, 1952), esp. pp. 110–16; and Pennington, *Pope and Bishops*, pp. 67–74.

51   See J. Muldoon, *Popes, Lawyers and Infidels: the church and the non-Christian World, 1250–1500* (Liverpool, 1979), esp. pp. 29–48, and who takes the story up to the debate over the treatment of Native American Indians in the New World; also see below, p. 103 on Aquinas's view.

52   See the summary in A. Padoa –Schioppa, *Legislation and Justice*, p. 342.

order to deal with what was becoming an overwhelming workload. The officials at the Roman *curia* dealt with church organization across Europe, the administration of ecclesiastical property, the establishment of procedures for the decisions of collegiate bodies of churches or monasteries, the development of the scope of jurisdiction and the procedures for ecclesiastical lawsuits, the placing of the sacrament of marriage within the jurisdiction of canon law,[53] the church's intervention in contracts and legal institutions deemed relevant to the spiritual well-being of Christians,[54] and the establishment of penal canon law including secular and spiritual sanctions against those deemed to have broken church laws. By the thirteenth century, Roman primacy had been realized in practice by legal means, in the universal jurisdiction of the pope and in papal legislation which developed from his jurisdiction. The legal means of this realization were largely the same as those to be used by European states in the process of their own formation: through imitation, differentiation or opposition. But if the church appeared 'first' in applying its canon law theory in practice, especially in the domain of its own governance, the scientific study of Roman law jurisprudence on the part of jurists known as Glossators was not far behind. In the course of the thirteenth century civilian jurists established reasons to support the view that a king was an emperor in his own kingdom, recognizing no superior in temporal affairs, *de facto* if not also *de jure*.

The Twelfth-century 'Renaissance' and the Civil Lawyers

Indeed, the church's body of canon law and commentary came to vie with the twelfth-century revival of purely secular, civil Roman law as they found it in the full text of Justinian's sixth-century *Corpus iuris civilis*. The revived study of Roman law was further inspired by the German emperor Frederick I (Barbarossa) when he saw his rights being whittled away by the encroachment of the church in matters of sovereign rule. In Bologna, where civil law studies had already been undertaken, he formally established the first civil law school in Europe to study and enshrine civil law and the ruler's legitimate rights to constitutional rule. Germanic customary laws, as these had evolved in different parts of Europe, along with feudal law and the civil law of the Romans with explanations and commentaries by Glossators,[55] followed later by more philosophically orientated but also practical-minded 'post-Glossators', combined to provide a stock of ideas for civil lawyers engaged in determining the kinds of institutional structures that were seen as acceptable to communities throughout Europe.

Justinian's *Corpus iuris civilis* (comprising the *Code*, the *Digest* (or *Pandects*), the *Institutes* and *Novellae*) is not without its ambiguities, especially when men sought to apply its principles to an evolving medieval society. As Kuttner noted, 'any "continuity" of Roman jurisprudence between the sixth and eleventh century in the West remains a dream, if by "jurisprudence" we understand an intellectually coherent discipline, a

---

53   J. Coleman, 'The Owl and the Nightingale and Papal Theories of Marriage', *Journal of Ecclesiastical History* 38 (1987), pp. 517–68.

54   J. Coleman, 'The Two Jurisdictions: theological and legal justifications of church property in the thirteenth century', *Studies in Church History* 23 (1987), pp. 75–110.

55   Most notable was the Bolognese jurist Azo *c.* 1208–10, and Accursius whose *Glossa Ordinaria* on the *Corpus iuris civilis c.* 1230 provided the standard commentary until the seventeenth century.

mastery of the sources which can give rational guidance to legal thinking – as distinct from professional routine'.[56] But this sixth-century compilation establishes additional major problems for historians of Roman law itself. We should try to grasp what this collection really is and what kind of society it reflects.

The *Code*, which was rapidly revised to take account of new legislation, consolidated imperial enactments, correcting or omitting what was, by the sixth-century, out of date. It includes a great number of Justinian's own constitutions and deals, among other things, with church law, functions of high officials, private law and criminal law. The *Digest* committee that was established to study and abridge the writings of those jurists (*prudentes*) to whom emperors had given the authority to interpret the law, were directed to eliminate contradictions and choose what they thought were the best views. Conflicts were, however, left standing and certain obsolete doctrines retained. Justinian instructed that the *Digest* was to be the sole authority for the *leges* and the writings of jurists and there were to be no objections raised on the ground of differences from the originals, nor commentaries made. Most of the material comes from few writers, and in particular, the jurists Ulpian (*d.* 223) and Paul (early third century AD). Very few are from Rome's republican period. Although the *Digest* contains earlier material, it is in essence the chief authority for *Justinian's* law: modern students of Roman classical law are warned to use it with caution because a great deal of Roman legal history was concealed by Justinian's compilers. Justinian said he intended to restore classical law doctrine, but much of what was done could be thought of as new doctrine under the guise of ancient authority. The *Institutes* was meant to be a book for beginning law students and its committee of compilers used, in particular, the writings of Gaius (first half of the second century AD). The *Institutes* was meant to have the force of law, but it does not always agree with the *Digest*. The *Novellae* includes new imperial enactments and demonstrates not only reforms but absolute changes of principle.[57]

In the sixth century this collection of law was meant to apply to the whole empire, but in its own times it was soon found incapable of dealing with the variety of custom in the provinces. Furthermore, it may be recalled that Justinian was an emperor established in the East and it is thought he was much influenced by local conditions in the Greek-speaking part of the empire. There was no Western jurist in any of his councils. In short, his compilation is that of an Eastern potentate. Should we be surprised, then, that the principles of absolutist, theocratic, imperial rule stand shoulder to shoulder with principles that reflect older republican and classical practices? Should we be surprised that in drawing on Gaius in the *Institutes*'s treatment of the private law notion of citizenship (*civitas*), Justinian, for reasons relevant to his own times, has hardly anything to say that reflects the older Roman notion of differences in citizenship status? In the sixth century the question of citizenship was not important because practically every free man, by then, was a citizen (*civis*).[58] Therefore, when the whole of the *Corpus iuris civilis* was made available to twelfth-century students and thereafter, they were certainly not being provided with a detailed account of Roman republican law. They were being provided with a late imperial compilation and it was soon discovered that the *Corpus iuris* could be

56   S. Kuttner, 'The Revival of Jurisprudence', in Benson, Constable and Lanham, *Renaissance and Renewal*, pp. 299–323.

57   See Buckland, *A Text-book of Roman Law*, pp. 39–47.

58   Ibid., p. 61; Quaglioni, 'The Legal Definition', pp. 156–8.

scrutinized for authoritative statements to support either monarchy or constitutional government by the people. There were sufficient statements to be found that affirmed both divine and popular sources of rule. Medieval jurists were not averse to citing passages out of context to suit their needs.

Justinian's *Corpus iuris civilis* demonstrated to twelfth-century jurists how Roman jurisprudence was the knowledge of things divine and human, the science of the just and the unjust. Its dominant perspective is theocratic with imperial authority deriving from God: the emperor is the lord of the world (*dominus mundi*). It also showed them that the study of Roman law comprised two branches: public law, concerned with the welfare of the Roman 'state', and private law, of advantage to the individual citizen. Most of what Justinian's compilation provides is private law. But there are also statements that speak of the possession of authority by the Roman people, who then transfer their power to the emperor. And they could find in the *Digest* 1.3.32 the survival of the republican idea that the will of the people makes both written law and custom; laws can be abrogated not only by the vote of the legislator but through the tacit consent of all through disuse.

Furthermore, from the unclear story presented by Gaius and Ulpian on the relation between natural law and the law of nations (*ius naturale* and *ius gentium*),[59] Justinian's compilers presented two contradictory views: Ulpian said that the law of nature (*ius naturale*) was shared by all living creatures, but this was different from the law of nations (*ius gentium*) which is known by each and every individual human through reason. Gaius, on the other hand, held that *ius gentium* and *ius naturale* are the same thing: the law which nature has instilled into all nations. Twelfth-century thinkers would be inspired by these contradictions to examine what was meant by 'nature'. Some would develop a natural law theory well beyond the texts in Justinian, with profound consequences for political theory and practice. Notably, some came to insist that civil law could not contravene what was natural, and that rulers themselves were obliged to act in accordance with the *ius naturale*, that is, reason. The civil law, those laws created by a state for its own members, *added* to, but could not conflict with, those more general statutes and customs prescribed by reason that were common to all humankind.

They would also thread their way among the contradictory statements on slavery and select those texts which argued that captivity and slavery were contrary to the law of nature (*ius naturale*) by which all men from the beginning were born free. But they discovered passages confirming that the universal law of nations (*ius gentium*) served as the source of almost all contracts and allowed for slavery as utility conclusions in the circumstances. Furthermore, they pointed to those passages where the emperor was described as having his authority and power to make and enforce law, the *lex regia*, conferred on him by the people who voluntarily gave him their authority so to act for the common welfare. The Roman notion of a *pactum* between a ruler and his people, along with the emphasis on a natural law which prevented arbitrary government, appears to have made sense to a Europe with feudal characteristics. If feudalism could restrict a ruler's claims to a plenitude of power, despite his increasingly centralized legislative omnipotence, then the feudal contract could be situated within the Roman law analysis of natural law and the law of nations to which all parties of contracts were subject. For this reason both Roman and canon law commentators focused increasingly

---

59 Buckland, *A Text-book*, pp. 52–5.

on the role of the ruler's will in the making of law, a will that was limited by divine law, by natural law and by the law of nations.[60] These 'limitations' would receive much greater treatment at the hand of medieval commentators than they ever did in classical Roman law.

Furthermore, the legislative capacities of a monarch were balanced by an acknow-ledgement of the role of the people in the creation of law. Medieval Roman lawyers explicitly discussed whether or not the *lex regia* was irrevocable by the people. It was recognized that a ruler could not exercise unlimited power, despite the Roman law principle that 'law is that which pleases the prince'. And Glossators discussed whether custom could abrogate imperial laws. They agreed that it could. Law, for twelfth-century jurists, had to be consonant with reason and by the thirteenth century they were to go beyond the text in the *Digest* where it said that law could be abrogated by the people's *tacit* consent, evidenced in the customary disuse of the law. They invoked the yardstick of reason and men's *explicit* consent to what was reasonable.

If, by the twelfth century, European medieval society had increasingly come under the sway of written custom and promulgated, written law, then written custom required rational discussion. Custom was to be judged against the criterion of reason, and law had to embody what was deemed reasonable. To clarify the nature of human reason, lawyers originally gave way to the arguments of another group of professionals: theologians. But lawyers also established a distinctive kind of discourse of their own which by the mid thirteenth century was seen as turning many of them into the mere bureaucratic spokes-men of increasingly centralizing monarchs in church and 'state'. Some of them came to argue what can be called the positivist line, that the ruler's will, in being held to *be* reason, *is* law. Canon lawyers like Laurentius Hispanus applied this to the pope so that he could change what was previously held to be just to what is now deemed unjust. This seemed to argue that the pope's will was distinct from the rational content of law, and hence law is simply what is legislated by legitimate, sovereign authority. French canon lawyers employed the terms *ius positivum,* although the law-maker was still viewed as operating within the terms of the common good. But there was opened the possibility of a ruler having an extraordinary power to transcend and even suspend ordinary, objec-tively rational principles. Some lawyers would coin the terms *potestas absoluta* to extend the scope of sovereignty of the ruler's will, even if in ordinary circumstances the ruler was not meant to deviate from accepted norms.[61]

The appeal to a plenitude of power, first associated with the terms *potestas absoluta* to express the jurisdictional primacy of the pope, would come to be adopted by thirteenth-century secular rulers as well. It is not simply that they read the tracts of the opposing 'camp', but rather that the frequent interchanges of bureaucratic personnel occurred between the spheres of ecclesiastical and secular government. The very word that is used for the royal personnel, king's 'clerks', tells us that these men were 'clerics', holders of ecclesiastical benefices, and literate in Latin, ready to put their skills to work in the service of church and/or 'state'. Especially in the twelfth century many of the same men served both (e.g. Thomas Becket). And many such men would not allow the rift be-tween law as rational and law as will to go unchallenged.

60   See chapter 2 on Aquinas.
61   Canning, *A History*, p. 118.

Civilians and Canonists

Both civilians and canonists built up a rational jurisprudence which provided them with a recognizable methodology to interpret and harmonize apparently contradictory authoritative texts. Their rational jurisprudence also provided them with a distinctive perspective on the world, a perspective that would come to be resisted by those trained either in the liberal arts or theology faculties in universities. Out of the legal perspective on the one hand, and out of the philosophico-theological perspective on the other, would emerge some of the major treatises of medieval political theory to be discussed below. For both perspectives, at the heart of the discussion of law as rational was the distinction between the two jurisdictions of church and 'state' over the different spheres of Christian lives. It became clear both to lawyers as well as to philosophers in the arts faculties and theologians in theology faculties that the instrument that expressed the shape of society was law as a set of binding rules:[62] law determined property ownership, rights (or their lack) of individuals and groups, the curriculum content of higher education in newly developed universities across Europe, even the intimate relationships between men and women before and after marriage. Law came to be seen as the means to legitimize reasonable practice; law was the justly enforceable acknowledgement of customary structures and relations judged reasonable.

Let us pause for a moment and consider this: local custom, when judged reasonable, is legitimately binding. This may at first sight appear surprising, since there is no doubt that Justinian's *Corpus iuris* contains strong absolutist statements, and civil lawyers in the service of a king, following the language developed from Roman law by canonists which they then applied to the plenitude of power of the pope, often referred to the absolute power of the 'prince' who 'is not bound by the laws' or 'who gives the force of law to whatever pleases him'. In some cases, European monarchs tried to impose a written codification of the law based on Justinian's law, but it is noteworthy that these attempts either failed completely or succeeded only in part.[63] There were always various social groups who were determined to defend their own customs and privileges which Roman law either denied or invalidated. In the practice of defending certain of their traditions, they rejected some Roman law principles in favour of others. The ambiguity of Justinian's Roman law, especially when applied to societies that were different from ancient imperial Rome, allowed men to seek support for their own ways of living, reconstructing the meaning of Roman law to suit their needs: they found support for individual rights to private property against the claims of the 'state', or references to the individual's power to dispose what he owned by will, or support for the individual's freedom in shaping contracts. Certain rights could be defended against individuals as well as against public authority. Furthermore, medieval society was comprised of numerous corporate groups: there were religious collectivities inspired to imitate what they took to be the collective life lived in common by Christ and the apostles, and there were merchant and craft guilds, voluntarily set up for mutual support. Collective bodies, such as city communes or leagues between cities, rural communities and professional and urban trade guilds, appealed to Roman legal texts concerning *universitates*, the generic term which

---

62   See chapter 2 on Aquinas.
63   See the various contributions to A. Padoa–Schioppa, *Legislation and Justice*.

described the various kinds of corporative associations already constituted in practice.[64] The law was to recognize their *already-constituted*, and now guaranteed, group legal status.

There is no doubt that in Roman law there are corporations. During the republic there were three types: the *populus Romanus*, municipalities and private corporations. But 'as the Emperor waxed the *populus* waned'.[65] There was nothing corporate about the emperor and the *populus* was to lose all importance when the imperial officials were to become the real state officers. Municipalities, on the other hand, during the republic were mainly subjugated communities which received or at least were not deprived of corporate character, but their power of acting as legal persons was variously restricted. During the empire similar corporate rights were conferred on local communities and the very foundation of such a community was an act of state. Such a corporate community could not act for itself. Persons were appointed to it to act for it. There were numerous kinds of private associations such as trade guilds and burial clubs. During the empire private *collegia* could not be founded without state authority and it is not clear that *collegia* had corporate capacity.

After the adoption of Christianity by the state, Constantine had authorized gifts by will to Christian churches, and from here church property was thought of as that of the church as a whole, although each community regarded its property as a separate patrimony under the administration of its bishop. Under Justinian, legislation secured the right of bishops to the general supervision of gifts to various charitable establishments, and these charitable establishments were regarded as corporate juristic persons. The power which resided in the corporation came to be delegated to an official representative who acted on the community's behalf. The representative's power was derivative, revocable and could be modified. But to Romans, the state preceded private corporations which were then partly modelled on it. Their status was a civic creation of state law. *Corpus habere* required a state concession. This does not appear to be the genesis of many of the collective bodies of medieval society which often emerged as local responses to particular ideals or needs in given circumstances, without 'state' recognition, since there was no 'state' to offer the concession. In studying the medieval jurists scholars sometimes tend to associate the emergence of medieval collegial practices with their juristic description and hence give the jurists more of an originating role than they actually had (doubtless following the model of ancient Rome, which gave so much power of legal development to the jurists).

Individual and Collective Liberties

England is an interesting case in point, but is not unique in demonstrating that prior to legal description and prescription there was presumed to be a royal art of governing which consisted in persuading lords and gentry that there was a close coincidence of interest between them and the crown. This was what was called the common good and it was served in different ways by independent local gentry and self-governing local

---

64   P. Michaud-Quantin, *Universitas. Expressions du mouvement communautaire dans le moyen âge latin* (Paris, 1970); A. Black, *Guilds and Civil Society in European Political Thought from the Twelfth Century to the Present* (London, 1984).
65   Buckland, *A Text-book,* p. 175.

communities on the one hand, and the king on the other.[66] Without this coincidence of interest, threats to the established order, be they from foreign invasion or from popular insurrection, would ensue and be threats to them all. The king no less than the commons would come to be seen as exercising their respective liberties as means to the common good. The king's liberty was not an absolute power because it was thought to be constrained by the goals of the collective *regnum*. Hence, in practice and theory, the royal art of governing, *when successful*, proved to be a management of personal liberties and political autonomies at the local levels where a centralized state's authority could not hope to establish itself in the manner of much later, early-modern absolutist governments.[67]

If we ask what was thought to be the origin of these personal liberties and political autonomies, we can uncover the answer by observing first that medieval liberty is everywhere in medieval charters and legal records. The words *libertas* or *franchise* mean a power to act in affairs of the community and to exert influence on one's fellows, free from the interference of sovereign government.[68] This kind of liberty is a political liberty, a privilege granted by some higher authority which acknowledges a capacity to engage in independent action, to exercise power and authority. We have already seen that in the early Middle Ages, following Roman and feudal traditions, certain men were the recipients of rights as privileges, granted to designated landowners to act autonomously in territories immune or exempt from extraordinary taxation, official duties and burdens. In Frankish Gaul, lay aristocrats were granted franchises as military vassals of a superior lord, by means of which they held free tenure and were free from private obligations of a servile nature to their superior landlord. In England, franchises developed to signify jurisdictional powers either of a rural aristocracy or of urban corporations. Such jurisdictional powers acknowledged the active capacity to act as a holder of a court or to be a judge, free from official interference within a defined territory or over a specified group of people.

Some historians understand liberties granted by charter to remain, by definition, privileges, even when the recipients were communities; they were not the rights of individual citizens. For liberties claimed as individual rights, they say we have to look at the records of royal justices and parliaments where many of the cases brought are concerned with personal liberty in the most basic sense, i.e. complaints against arbitrary imprisonment and extortion of money for release. Royal courts allowed what had been those rights of feudal lordship to be reduced to civic and economic rights of individuals. The creation of new legal systems and the elimination of intermediate feudal lordships led to the equal subjection of everyone to the sovereign king in territorial communities that established medieval 'states'.[69]

The example that is often given, but it can be applied elsewhere in Europe, is King

---

66　See J. Gillingham, 'Crisis or Continuity? The Structure of Royal Authority in England 1369–1422', in R. Schneider, ed., *Das spätmittelalterliche Königtum in europaischen Vergleich* (Sigmaringen, 1987), pp. 59–80.

67　J. Coleman, 'Structural Realities of Power: the theory and practice of monarchies and republics in relation to personal and collective liberty', in M. Gosman, A. Vanderjagt and J. Veenstra, eds, *The Propagation of Power in the Medieval West* (Groningen, 1997), pp. 207–30.

68　A. Harding, 'Political Liberty in the Middle Ages', *Speculum* 55 (1980), pp. 423–43; J. Coleman, 'Medieval Discussions of Human Rights', in W. Schmale, ed., *Human Rights and Cultural Diversity* (Goldbach, 1993), pp. 103–20.

69　See A. Harding, *England in the Thirteenth Century* (Cambridge, 1993).

John's signing of Magna Carta with his barons in 1215. Article 39 insisted that 'no free-man shall be captured and imprisoned or disseized [of his property] or outlawed or exiled or in any way harmed except by lawful tribunal of his peers and by the law of the land.' As the private feudal contract shifted into the public domain by virtue of the king being party to the contract, the king was to be seen as the head of public government and his legislation circumscribed by the customary law of the land. By the thirteenth century it seemed perfectly consistent to assert that the king was supreme lord in his own realm and also to say that his judicial and legislative authority was limited, not only by divine and natural law but also by his need to obtain counsel and consent, as well as by the licit rights of his subjects. If King John conceded this right as a privilege to his rebellious barons, the concession was originally devised in the interests of aristocratic 'free men', an estate cre-ated by royal prerogative, and it confirmed the traditional rights of the Crown within the law. But from the fourteenth century onwards[70] the very words which spoke of free men's rights to trial by peers were changed by parliament so that 'no free man' became simply 'no man' (1331 and 1352) and 'due process of law' was added. By 1354 we have: 'no man of whatever estate or condition he may be' shall be captured, imprisoned and so on, except by a tribunal of peers and due process of the law of the land. An assertion of law that was originally conceived in the interests of one exclusive estate had been reinter-preted and widened to become a fundamental law concerning the equal rights of subjects before the law and against arbitrary sovereign authority.

But other historians have argued that charters of liberties may be read as providing evidence of two things: they conveyed or simply *acknowledged* already exercised freedoms of even larger numbers of people, for instance, borough communities to which lords granted free burgage tenure and also liberties and free customs of a more active kind, these being obtained as communal privileges but were often enjoyed as individual rights. Susan Reynolds has argued that such charters, rather than offering or conceding legally such 'new' liberties, actually merely reflected in written law the *de facto* collective and individual freedom of action.[71]

All of these liberties, once acknowledged by charter or in some other legal regulation, became by definition privileges granted as concessions by some higher authority. There is no concealing the fact that the growth during the thirteenth century of more central-ized governments and their respective academic and legal experts, be they national mon-archies in France and England or city-states in Italy, each with its respective attempt to *replace* the diffuse feudal principalities or local *signori* of an earlier period with centralized republican or national law, enormously reduced the real freedom and power of *earlier* franchise holders. Across Europe, in both national monarchies and emergent city repub-lics, liberty as an aspect of lordship suffered a decline from its earlier meaning of autono-mous power, to being an acknowledged legal right. In fact, liberty and custom were coming to be detached from, even opposed to, traditional, feudal lordship and instead were coming to be linked with customary 'constitutional' practices.

---

70   As Holt, *Magna Carta,* has shown, pp. 9–16.
71   S. Reynolds, 'The History of the Idea of Incorporation or Legal Personality: a case of fallacious teleology', in S. Reynolds, *Ideas and Solidarities of the Medieval Laity, England and Western Europe* (London, 1995), esp. ch. vi, pp. 1–20; and G. Post, *Studies in Medieval Legal Thought: public law and the state, 1100–1322* (Princeton, NJ, 1964), p. 69 on the application of Roman law principles to already existing communes and craft guilds with their own institutions and officers.

The importance of understanding that medieval professional law, especially but not exclusively of the civil variety, did not in most cases create but rather acknowledged and confirmed evolving practices, cannot be overstated. The law itself thereby developed creatively to suit new and changing circumstances. Social reality was not the only source of their ideas but the ideas, whatever their source, when put into practice had to apply to the particular problems of life they were meant to solve. Legal practitioners found themselves to be confirming in law *de facto* practices rather than imposing *de jure* Roman law categories and principles on temperaments and in circumstances that could not see the *de jure* rules as reasonable. Civil lawyers recognized and articulated what less learned people took for granted when they said that the *populus* of a city was, in Roman law terms, a *collegium* under the *ius gentium* (the law of nations). This meant it did not need permission from any higher authority to be one. In practice the degree to which towns and other communities were allowed to run their own affairs depended more on their political relations with local superior authorities than on being able to produce written evidence of some formal, legal delegation of authority. The word *universitas* like the word *commune* was often used in documents without implying some new and special kind of unity in the sense of a newly created legal power or corporate personality of the group which, upon such formal legal recognition, suddenly was empowered to act in ways its members had not been free to act before.

There is no doubt, however, that with the increasing deployment of academics and professional lawyers from the thirteenth century onwards, consistent rules about group responsibilities were framed, but these did not consist in newly representing groups or corporations as legal persons so much as turning already known and exercised moral norms into legal rules. In an overwhelming number of cases the *law followed practice*. The strong assumption of medieval community meant that it was taken for granted that everyone had a right to associate with fellows provided that the actions of their association were lawful and did not exceed the customary restriction on their freedom of action as individuals with whatever status they had.[72]

Precisely because it was no simple issue for a king to legislate arbitrarily, the central question for professional civil lawyers, funded by monarchs, concerned the very nature of created law and the clarification of who was entitled to create it. It may be surprising for modern sensibilities to accept that a major topic of medieval discussion was not whether irrational tyrannical rule was possible, but what to do about it. Should a king, whose office was to represent his subjects by bearing the personality of the public corporation, not rule for the common good, as determined by the consent of his subjects or at least his aristocratic counsellors to this representation, he was declared a tyrant. Hence they asked: was such a ruler removable? Under what conditions is there a right of resistance to him? And what is the precise role that consent plays in the development of law? Whose consent is required? In the twelfth century John of Salisbury, England's Henry II's Chancellor and friend of the ill-fated Thomas Becket, famously and influentially put the argument in favour of tyrannicide in his tract called *Policraticus* even if, in the end, he

---

72   The concern to define the essential nature of a group with legal capacity, what we now mean by the modern corporation, was not a medieval concern. Rather, as Reynolds has shown, it was a concern of nineteenth-century German lawyers who looked back on medieval records to find precedents for trends in their own professions within a nineteenth-century monarchical state, the *Rechtsstaat*, when the free and autonomous behaviour of groups could only be realized, indeed created, through prior legal definition.

appears ambiguous as to whether or not an undoubtedly justified reason for the killing of a tyrant could or should be translated into legitimate action. His argument would be well known to early-modern Europe.[73]

It is not therefore as surprising as perhaps we might think to find that from the twelfth century on, discussions of the natural shape of society frequently used natural, organic metaphors. What was natural increasingly came to be aligned with what was rational. The propagation of power was taken to be a natural process no less than the 'state' was increasingly seen to be a natural phenomenon. What was natural was also increasingly aligned with God's intention for men living according to ordered reason in an organic society. The head and members had distinct functional and natural duties to the well-being of the whole, referred to as the Christian body public, the *corpus rei publica*, the public corporation. By the mid thirteenth century the church itself would be referred to as the *corpus mysticum reipublicae*. Some spoke of the body of the *respublica* as having a head, the king, but that its soul was the clergy. The king's counsellors could then be imagined as the body's heart, judges as the eyes and ears, soldiers the hands, farmers the feet. No part could be removed without the whole deteriorating.[74] Similarly, Roman law's interest in society as a collective entity was selectively put to use in favour of collective associations, especially in towns, that groups of men had themselves established, for instance, as guilds which they set up in order to pursue their trades, or as teachers with collective interests and whose identity was itself represented by the very word university (*universitas*). These discussions filled in the details of what were taken to be the undoubted responsibilities to the common welfare of official individuals at different levels of the socially structured whole.

Sovereignty and Corporations

European state formation was to emerge progressively, often but not exclusively from the theoretical and practical appropriation by the 'centre' of the task of administering the law in its various manifestations: some medieval nation-states accomplished this through establishing central lawcourts (and schools for national law: the Inns of Court) to control non-royal courts (England); others by establishing a monopoly of royal justice and thereby controlling customary law (France). While the objectives set by secular political power were often the same across Europe, the means to achieving the objectives varied. Europeans, in practice, displayed a set of differentiated but interconnected legal traditions. As Tierney has amply demonstrated, the growth of what we think of as Western constitutional thought can only be understood through a consideration of the simultaneous growth of the theory and practice of both church and 'state' governance because each borrowed from the other from the twelfth to the seventeenth centuries. Indeed, the juridical culture of the twelfth- and thirteenth-century Roman and canon lawyers con-

---

73   John of Salisbury, *Policraticus*, ed. and trans. C. J. Nederman (Cambridge, 1990); J. van Laarhoven, 'Thou Shalt *Not* Slay a Tyrant! The So–called Theory of John of Salisbury', in M. Wilks, ed., *The World of John of Salisbury* (Oxford, 1984), pp. 319–42; C. J. Nederman, 'A Duty to Kill: John of Salisbury's theory of tyrannicide', *Review of Politics* 50 (1988), pp. 365–89; R. H. and M. A. Rouse, 'John of Salisbury and the Doctrine of Tyrannicide', *Speculum* 42 (1967), pp. 693–709.
74   John of Salisbury, *Policraticus* (1159), vi, 19–21, 25.

tributed to the seedbed from which grew the forest of early-modern political theories, most notably exemplified in the writings of Hobbes, Locke and Rousseau.[75]

The competing and complementary traditions of canon and civil law tackled many of the same issues in order to justify their respective understandings of the nature and source of sovereignty, by which was meant the power to judge, legislate and command. Canonists and civilians treated many of the same themes as they tried to find a place for spirituality and the church's administrative hierarchy in a society that saw its major conceptual and institutional debt to be Roman institutions and law. Often, a text of Roman private law was assimilated into canon law, where it was adapted and altered to establish a principle of constitutional law, whereafter it was reabsorbed into the sphere of secular government in its new constitutional form.[76] Or royal administrators, curial bureaucrats and organizers of new religious orders selectively dipped into the common pool of available legal doctrines to justify certain practices or encourage certain developments. Both treated the following themes: the meaning of the Roman law dictum *maior et sanior pars* in order to clarify how the will of a corporate group was expressed; the meaning of *plena potestas* on the part of the pope, the corporate church and the prince, in order to explain a theory of representation where a group was obliged by the acts of its representative agent with full power, even if the group had not previously consented to the representative's specific acts; the meaning of the Roman law dictum *quod omnes tangit ab omnibus approbetur* (what touches all is to be approved by all), a doctrine of consent applied to corporate bodies where the approval of the whole was required and not that of each individual member. It is this doctrine that came to support the notion that representative assemblies, acting on behalf of the whole who are touched by decisions taken, bind the whole; the distinction between *dominium* and *jurisdictio*, the right to govern one's own and the right to administer what was not one's own.

The notions of consent and representation were as important to ecclesiastics who were concerned to define the role of bishops in the church, the role of the congregation of the faithful, the role of monks in electing their abbots, all in relation to the pope, as they were important to men of different rank and status in the nascent 'states' of Europe who sought to define the origins and source of princely power, the role of a prince's counsellors, his administrators and his subjects. Likewise, members of church and 'state' hierarchies were concerned to define the nature of membership in corporate structures. The church was seen as a corporation just as were the new universities, the trades guilds in towns and the very 'state' itself, made up as it was of corporations with limited rights of self-direction and abilities to delegate powers to a representative in their name.

Tierney has shown how the period from 1250 to 1350 saw these juristic ideas assimilated into an increasing number of political and philosophical writings on the nature, rights and duties of church, 'state' and the members of each. And he has shown that what is most distinctive about these works, whether penned by theorists who were pro-papal or pro-secular monarchy, was their concern for the origins of government. They asked: was it in the people's consent or was it in God's authority? These discussions would be enormously stimulated by the rediscovery of Aristotle's ethical and political writings and their translation into Latin during the thirteenth century. But the reason

---

75 Tierney, *Religion*; see also K. Pennington, 'Law, Legislative Authority and Theories of Government, 1150–1300', in *CHMPT* (1988), pp. 424–53.
76 Tierney, *Religion*, p. 25.

that Aristotle seemed so relevant was because of real-life circumstances during the thirteenth century where, especially in northern Italy, in Flanders, in France and England, towns were demanding charters of liberties which acknowledged their abilities to run their own economic and political affairs.[77] Aristotle also provided university philosophers and theologians with another discourse about man and the political which bypassed juristic discourse and demonstrated that ethics and politics were disciplines that underpinned positive law. The debates over the origins of government took Augustine's ideas much further, as it was no longer viable to suggest that government was a necessary evil. Rather, it was now being viewed as something natural, something that even existed in Paradise before man's fall and expulsion from the Garden of Eden. Rightful jurisdiction over men's lives on the part of princes and town councils, or parliaments comprised of the various functional estates, were seen as the natural consequences of man's reason rather than as the inscrutable imposition of arbitrary rule on an essentially unruly and irrational human nature.

If we look at the theories of sovereignty maintained by civilians we see a concern to define the nature of supreme jurisdiction over men living socially and collectively within defined geographical boundaries. By 1200 a distinction is already drawn between ruling and owning, between, in other words, the right to act as judicial arbiter and the right to own property. It would later be argued that the prince is not the owner of his subjects' property but he is an arbiter in property disputes which arise among his subjects who are owners. Likewise, within the church there was a distinction between jurisdiction and property rights. A prelate may have jurisdiction over his church but he does not own its property. He is an administrator of what is not his own but of that which is held collectively by, say, all the monks of a monastery or the canons of a collegiate church, or even of Christendom taken as a whole corporation, a congregation of the faithful, which collectively owns church property which the ecclesiastical hierarchy administers.[78] Thus a bishop and even the pope, some argued, could not alienate or sell church goods because they did not belong to them.

Furthermore, in the *Decretum*, Gratian had argued that however superior in wisdom a man may be, his decisions had no juridical force unless he had first acquired public authority. How then is public authority acquired?[79] This question concerning the origins of government as legitimate jurisdiction would remain central to European political theorizing well into and beyond the early-modern period. It lies at the heart of the corollary issue of political obligation of subjects and citizens who unite to confer or convey power to a representative whom they have agreed to obey.

Well before 1300 jurisdiction rather than ownership was seen in both church and 'state' to be the characteristic of rightful power inhering in a ruling office. From where, then, did this rightful jurisdiction arise? Some argued from the consent of the governed; others from God's authority. From here there emerged a further distinction between legislating and judging. Some argued that the people or their representatives legislate, the ruler judges according to the laws set out. Furthermore, we see a distinction being drawn between the allegiance that may be owed by subjects – as members of a 'state' or

---

77   R. Celli, *Pour l'histoire des origines du pouvoir populaire: l'éxperience des Villes–Etats Italiennes (xi–xii siècles)* (Louvain–La Neuve, 1980) and see below, chapter 6.

78   See chapters 3–5 on John of Paris, Marsilius of Padua and William of Ockham.

79   See chapter 2 on Aquinas.

of a corporation – to the person of the prince, and the allegiance to his office or public personality. If a prince does not act in accordance with reason and the laws legislated, his office is not impugned although he may well be. Similarly, canonists worried about what was to be done with a heretical pope. Although it was claimed that the pope could be judged by no one, it was conceivable that the *status ecclesiae* may be threatened by a particular incumbent who engaged in scandalous crimes and heresy. The need for the offices of prince and the pope is presumed: the need for this particular prince or pope, should he turn respectively tyrant or heretic, is not assumed.

The various hypotheses on the origins of government as legitimate jurisdiction and the nature of political obligation were posed when they were precisely because medieval corporative structures had developed out of custom and sought legal justification in canon and Roman civil law. Canon lawyers in particular argued that men had certain rights prior to government by natural law, and lawyers understood these rights as active and claimable with material consequences, once men had become incorporated into some group like the church or a craft/professional guild. The way men united corporatively and thus defined their joint identity was through the voluntary consent of a gathering of men into a unity, a consent to incorporate themselves as a religious or secular community. Practice spurred theory. Tierney is therefore right to note that government as legitimated by consent is not at all an obvious conclusion for most of the human race during most of its recorded history. The medieval concern for government by consent was an extraordinary development out of the medieval conditions of living from at least the twelfth century onwards. It is a different view from the one we examined in volume 1, in the writings of Augustine, where legitimate government is divinely sanctioned order to keep the peace in history, and it is different from St Paul's understanding of legitimate government as simply the powers that be, which are ordained by God. It is also different from much that they found in Justinian's *Corpus iuris civilis*. If consent figures in these older pronouncements at all it is to an order already imposed, often for inscrutable reasons.

From at least the thirteenth century onwards some began to speak of consent as the *cause* of legitimate government, a consequence of medieval society being saturated with consensual practice. Especially in the towns of Europe, corporate groups, especially craft guilds, chose their leaders by consent, leaders who were representatives and spokesmen for the collective will.[80] Civilians like Azo mirrored this when he argued that the people conceded power to their representative and thus do not transfer it in the sense of totally alienating it irrevocably to a ruler. If a Roman example were needed, they cited the maxim that 'he who rules over all is to be chosen by all'. The Roman people created the emperor by conferring their own authority on him, said the civil law. So too from the thirteenth century, kings summoned assemblies and parliaments in order that members would consent to his taxation. By consenting frequently they won the right to consent: the monarch was justified in his expectation that they would continue to consent and this in turn led kings to continue summoning parliaments. Even Augustine was eclectically read to be in favour of consensual authority when he wrote that a true people, a political community, a *respublica*, was a multitude associated by consent, to that which they loved, God in common. From the later twelfth century and during the thirteenth, then, there were canonists and civilians who argued that governing power ultimately came from

80   Black, *Guilds.*

God as a remote first cause, but through the people's choice and natural reason, which delegated or conferred power on an office holder with what amounted to derived juris-diction. It is this medieval constitutionalism, through the sovereign people's consent, that would play a role in the writings of the Dominican theologian Thomas Aquinas. It is fundamental to realize that this discourse emerged in a range of milieux and prior to anything we can recognize as a distinctive Italian pre-humanist or humanist discourse of the supposed preference for republics over monarchies.[81]

We have already indicated the counter-tradition in both church and 'state', that of papal and royal theocracy. For proponents of these positions the source of power was God and this power was then delegated either to the pope from whom kings derived their portion, or else God's power was separately rendered to the pope or church for spiritual rule, and to the monarch who stood as Christ's vicar in the temporal world. For these theorists the people had no constituting power granted to them; they passively had im-posed on them secular and spiritual rule. An examination of practice, however, indicates that this theory was almost invariably resisted because it did not often match the facts.

Natural Law, Rights and the Lawyers' Concern for Individual Autonomy

The language of developing theological doctrine in the twelfth and thirteenth centuries focused on the baptized Christian individual who is judged to have his or her own personal soul which is endowed with liberty and is, therefore, responsible for its acts, barring the cases of madness, delirium or hypnosis. Those damned were said to have individually merited their damnation and were to be deprived of the vision of God, having actually sinned by reason of their individual consent to evil. In theological and pastoral texts, the individual is treated *per se* as well as in relation to religious and secular authorities. Both men and women are seen as morally responsible for their acts, although women are deemed weaker vessels than men; penitential remedies were devised to correct both practices and the individual intentions behind acts.[82] Twelfth-century theo-logical texts, in particular, speak of an area of human liberty in which the individual is considered an agent without in the first instance any historically specific political and contingent restraints placed on his own will.

Canon lawyers similarly defined this sphere of agency and we shall focus on their taking up of the theme of *ius naturale* in order to stipulate certain natural, psychological capacities in men which enable them to make claims to certain natural rights that are independent of the civic order in which they may live. Some have argued that the canonist notion of *ius naturale* may already be seen to imply a subjective right of indi-viduals.[83] Without at first making any direct appeals to explicitly subjective rights, canonists discussed a personal sphere of inalienable, individual, moral autonomy where the *ius naturale* is defined as a faculty or ability or power of an individual agent, a power associ-ated with reason and moral discernment that is intimately linked with this person's

---

81   See chapter 6 on Machiavelli and humanism in the Renaissance; further evidence is in Post, *Studies in Medieval Legal Thought.*

82   Coleman, '*The Owl and Nightingale*', with discussion of the penitential remedies of Burchard of Worms.

83   B. Tierney, *The Idea of Natural Rights: studies on natural rights, natural law and church law 1150–1625* (Atlanta, GA, 1997).

nature, prior to his incorporation into any political structure. Gratian's *Decretum* had taken over from the seventh-century bishop and scholar Isidore of Seville the notion that natural law is that instinct of nature which is common to all peoples. Through the gift of reason to the individual human soul and, in addition, through the teachings of the Old and New Testaments, the law of nature as God's supreme moral law is known to each and every man. This *ius naturale* defines an area of liberty where the individual is free to act as he pleases. This liberty leads to specific claims and powers on the part of humans as humans. The assumption here is that any representative human individual is defined in terms of his capacities as a member of the human species and not as a unique self. Rather, the individual is an example of a class of beings with normative capacities. These views were widely diffused in the law schools of Europe by the end of the twelfth century and were thereafter transmitted in the *Ordinary Gloss* to Gratian's *Decretum*. *Ius naturale* is spoken of as a psychological power or capacity which defines an area of liberty for an individual who acts or not, as he pleases, within the context of other actors.

Gratian also referred to *iura libertatis*, rights of liberty that can never be lost no matter how long a man may be held in bondage. He noted that the human race is ruled in two ways, namely by *ius naturale* (natural law) and by custom.[84] *Ius naturale* is what is contained in the law and the gospels by which each is commanded to do to another what he wants done to himself and is forbidden to do to another what he does not want done to himself. *Ius naturale*, he says, is the *ius* common to all nations, in that it is everywhere held by instinct of nature rather than by human enactment.[85] His examples of *ius naturale* are the union of man and woman, the free generation and education of children, the possession of all things in common, the one liberty of all, the acquisition of those things taken from air, land and sea, the return of a thing deposited or money entrusted, and the repulsion of force by force. These examples comprise a substantive list of 'claims' any human as human may make. The more general principle sustaining a man's rights is: do unto others as you would be done by. And Gratian added that any customary or human law that stipulated something contrary to this *ius naturale* was to be held null and void.[86]

In general, canon lawyers said that the necessity of an individual's defence against injury and force was a principle of natural law, known by reason in man.[87] Some extended this right of self-defence, which was categorized in Roman law as private law, to the public law of the 'state'. States, too, had a right of self-defence from natural law by analogy and extension from the private individual right. Indeed, gradually, in the thirteenth century, we see the growth of the idea that the social contract derives from natural law which gives individuals the right to defend themselves, and the 'state' is the best means of collectively so doing. Where the 'state' was conceived as a corporation, a fictive legal person, it neither existed apart from, nor had rights of its own above, those of its individual constituent members, arranged hierarchically and understood as a gathered collectivity.[88] *Sui generis*, this corporative 'state' had no rights and no interests apart from the common good. It is the public 'reason of state', conceived in this corporative manner, that can be seen at times

---

84 *Decretum Gratiani . . . cum glossis* (Venice, 1660), C. 16.9.3 *dictum post* c. 15; Dist. 1, *dictum ante* c. 1 and c. 1.

85 Dist. 1, c. 7.

86 Dist. 8, *dictum post* c. 1.

87 R. Weigand, *Die Naturrechtslehre der Legisten und Dekretisten* (Munich, 1967); S. Kuttner, *Repertorium der Kanonistik* (Vatican, 1937).

88 K. Pennington, 'Law, legislative authority', pp. 424–53; J. Canning, 'Law, Sovereignty and Corporation Theory 1300–1450', in *CHMPT* (1988), pp. 454–76 .

to have hindered the development of the individual and his rights. But where Roman law preferred the public welfare to the private, canon lawyers stepped in to argue that should public interest endanger an individual Christian's private salvation, then private right must be asserted first. 'Reason of state' obliged no individual Christian absolutely.

Twelfth-century theological and philosophical texts had already begun to emphasize a kind of ethical personalism by focusing on the sphere of private individual intention behind acts. As the theologian Peter Abelard had proclaimed early in the twelfth century, it was the moral value of a person's intention that gave value to his acts rather than their consequences.[89] Out of this concern for private intention arose the extended practice of private confession as stipulated in the decrees of the Fourth Lateran Council of 1215. On this view, intending, moral, social and rational individuals were considered to function best in corporate groupings, be they guilds, city corporations, universities or religious orders. But such collectivities were constituted by individual consent and individual will.[90] With the elevation of marriage to a church sacrament during the twelfth century, the marriage contract was seen as a typical expression of two consenting individuals, male and female, to a binding relationship which could only be cemented at the age of reason, the age of consent. No marriage would be recognized by the church without an explicit consent of both parties, in words and before witnesses. A doctrine of what we would later call subjective rights was already implicit in marriage law.[91] It is clearly explicit in the writings of the great canonist Huguccio.[92] For Huguccio, the primary meaning of *ius naturale* is a subjective force or power that is inherent in the soul. In a secondary sense he claimed that *ius* could be used to refer to moral laws known through reason, such as the scriptural injunction to do not to others what you would not have done to yourself. But he insisted that such moral precepts *derive* from, are the *effects* of, a prior natural *ius* or right, so that subjective rights should be seen as giving rise to objective rights. His is an analysis of human nature as rational, self-aware and morally responsible before it acts in ways that confirm rationality and responsibility.

It appears that the natural law of the Stoics and of Cicero, by which men's reason could discern a cosmic rational law as objective, and which according to Cicero was an *innata vis* (innate power) in man,[93] came to mean a subjective force, a faculty or power inherent in human beings. It was the twelfth-century lawyers who made this clear in theoretical writings and practical decisions. But it was also a view inherent in the discourse of theologians who were concerned with what we might call human psychology, the functions and capacities of the soul. We shall see that the concern with human psychology was integral to the most elementary education a medieval student might receive, and that students who never even finished their university degree would have become familiar with ways of speaking about human psychology when they studied grammar, logic and rhetoric and what was called practical moral philosophy. The next step was to specify what consequences of possessing such an inherent psychological

---

89   P. Abelard, *Ethics: Scito te ipsum*, ed. and trans. D. Luscombe (Cambridge, 1971), p. 45.

90   See Black, *Guilds and Civil Society*.

91   Coleman, '*The Owl and the Nightingale*'.

92   R. Weigand, *Die Naturrechtslehre*, pp. 215–16; B. Tierney, 'Origins of Natural Rights Language: texts and contexts 1150–1250' in Tierney, *The Idea of Natural Rights*, ch. 2; and B. Tierney, 'Origins of Natural Rights Language: texts and contexts 1150–1250', *History of Political Thought* 10 (1989), pp. 615–46.

93   See volume 1, chapter 5 of *A History of Political Thought*.

power could be observed in those laws that had to be obeyed or those rights that could be licitly expressed. Theologians like Aquinas would provide one view, canonists another. Both were related. Canonists, for instance, divided natural law into commands, prohibitions and demonstrations that men know prior to the 'state's' positive enactments. Some described the primeval state of affairs and others expanded on an original area of permissiveness, a right of nature, when rights could be licitly exercised.

From here arose discussions of whether private property was a natural right or whether it was simply a creature of positive and public law. In general, where positive law was held to be created by the sovereign, all sovereigns were to be conceived as bound by a prior natural law and hence by reasonableness. And prior to sovereigns and 'states' was the individual as a social being, living in a society with fellowship that came before particular, constitutional orderings of men in historical *regna*, as Cicero had also maintained.

Origins of Property Rights

The debate over the natural or conventional origins of property took the discussions of individual rights further.[94] According to the canonist Huguccio, private property is a social institution which involves a natural obligation to others. While property should be private, he thought there was a sense in which it should also be common, so that ownership and administration of property is the responsibility of individuals, but worldly goods had to be shared with others in times of need.[95] Huguccio did not use this Ciceronian doctrine to assert a natural right of the poor to the superfluities of the rich. But other canonists and theologians did. They argued that the poor man who stole in times of necessity had a right to what he had taken, even without the explicit consent of the owner. Alanus specifically argued that in such circumstances what the poor man takes is really his own *iure naturali*, by natural right. Others argued that the poor man took what he needed 'as if he used his own right and his own thing'. This position became enshrined in Hostiensis' *Lectura on the Decretals*. Canonists, thereafter, insisted that a person in need had a rightful power to do what was necessary to stay alive. While it was realized that a secular judge would not recognize the poor man as having a rightful claim, it was stated that 'many things are owed that cannot be sought by judicial procedure. They can, however, be sought as something due mercifully'.[96] Hence, natural rights were to be considered more extensive than a state's legal and positive systems of justice, indicating that a natural equity was still to be recognized over and above more narrowly conceived systems of positive law. And it was thought that in such a system where a civil judge would not recognize an extension of rightful claims to include equity beyond the strict letter of the law, a bishop could use ecclesiastical courts' jurisdiction to compel a recognition of such a claim.[97] Clearly, this was an argument that accepted the sphere of civil jurisdiction of 'states' but allowed for a more universal, moral correction by

94 Coleman, 'Property and Poverty', *CHMPT* (1988), pp. 607–48.
95 Tierney, 'Origins of Natural Rights Language', *History of Political Thought* 10 (1989), p. 641.
96 Ibid., p. 642; this is different from classical Roman *aequitas* which was meant to be fairness, but in post–classical texts it is used to mean indulgence in favour only of a weaker party; see Buckland, *A Text-book*, p. 55.
97 J. Coleman, 'The Two Jurisdictions'; G. B. Flahiff, 'The Writ of Prohibition to Court Christian in the Thirteenth Century', *Mediaeval Studies* 6 (1944), pp. 261–313; G. B. Flahiff, 'The Use of Prohibitions by Clerics against Ecclesiastical Courts in England', *Mediaeval Studies* 3 (1941), pp. 101–16.

ecclesiastical authority. However, it would also be developed by some to the effect that certain natural moral principles simply could not be contravened by positive law.

As seventeenth-century critics like Robert Filmer would observe, natural law theory leans toward universal equality with the result that women, children and servants can be considered on the same level as adult independent males. A subjective conception of rights means that the community is not the assigner of due, because each person advances claims for him or herself.[98] He was not impressed.

Medieval Education: Practical Moral Philosophy of Ethics, Economics and Politics

Today a student might ask: how educated did one have to be in order to gain familiarity with the above rather difficult and complicated discussions and issues? Precisely who was involved in these discourses on governance and natural rights, and how vigorously were they disseminated to a wider audience beyond professional theological and legal experts?

During the twelfth century, urban cathedral schools – the precursors of universities – took on the task of educating young men who were not monks for the increasing number of positions in the bureaucracies of emergent 'states' and self-governing cities and in the expanding bureaucracy of the church hierarchy. The requirements of their studies, along with the increasing pastoral needs of the church and the demands of bureaucracies, led to a quite remarkable degree of conceptualizing about government. If we ask where a student might learn how to speak about ethical and political matters, well before he went on (if he ever did) to study the higher disciplines of law or theology, we need to turn to the curricula of twelfth-century schools to provide the answer. It was in the study of the liberal arts, notably in what was called – since antiquity – the *trivium* of grammar, logic and rhetoric that he would come across reference to *ethica* and *politica*. He would learn that ethics and politics were categorized as practical arts or practical virtues. He would be using extracts from an introductory school text, a commentary on Porphyry's *Isagoge*, written by the late fifth-century Roman Boethius (*In Isagogen Porphyrii commenta*), where he would read that the 'science of politics' was part of practical philosophy which aims to treat virtue and is to be distinguished from theoretical philosophy which aims to treat the truth. He would be taught that the good life on earth is conceived of as the virtuous life and it leads on to the heavenly life.

Boethius had said that the 'science of politics' belongs to moral philosophy, which he divided into ethics, economics and politics. In using the terms 'political science' (*scientia politica*) we must be careful not to understand their use of the word 'science' in nineteenth- and twentieth-century terms, thereby implying some kind of empirical, objective, universally applicable, law-bound and value-free method of investigating 'facts'. To medieval thinkers, following Aristotle, 'science' meant a way of knowing that emphasized normative, *human ideas* about a distinct subject matter or object of knowledge. When the term 'science' was modified by 'political' it was taken to be a branch of the wider field of practical *moral philosophy* that was necessarily invaded by value and was concerned with appropriate *human acts* in the world. What they knew about reality was

---

98   R. Filmer, 'The Anatomy of a Limited or Mixed Monarchy', in P. Laslett, ed., *Robert Filmer: Political Works* (Oxford, 1949), p. 287.

a consequence of what they first knew about human knowing. They theorized about mind and language first in order to get at the extra-mental and the extra-linguistic.[99]

Twelfth-century teachers like Hugh of the Augustinian abbey of St Victor in Paris, in writing a treatise on the appropriate methods a student needed to learn in order to read and interpret scripture, history, grammar and poetry texts, also spoke about the three practical arts of ethics, economics and politics.[100] Hugh placed the study of ethics, as part of practical philosophy, between the study of logic (which included the *trivium* of grammar, dialectic and rhetoric) and theoretical philosophy (by which he meant theology, physics and mathematics). Hence, after a student studied logic he would go on to study ethics. Hugh went on to say that practical moral philosophy, in being divided into ethics, economics and politics, concentrated on the individual (ethics), his private economic relations with others, that is, those acts considered under Roman private law (economics), and public, civil acts (politics).[101] Practical moral philosophy was in effect Hugh's way of describing that part of the liberal arts curriculum pursued by students in his care, which came after their having spent time on grammar, dialectical logic and rhetoric. This means that after students had learned to read Latin texts and write Latin by imitating ancient Latin texts in the curriculum, they would be asked to treat ethics, economics and politics. In dealing with ethics, they would read and discuss ancient texts that treated personal moral conduct; then they would study economics, looking at texts which dealt with the sphere of private household affairs and the relations within the family unit; and then they would study politics by examining texts which treated conduct in the 'city'. Hugh equated the words *publica* with *politica atque civilis*, and he says that *polis* is the Greek term for what in Latin we call the *civitas*. His students would have been rather younger than most university students today.

We can name the texts that twelfth-century students read or heard expounded by their teachers.[102] They learned Latin composition from two ancient Latin textbooks by Donatus (*Ars Minor*) and Priscian (*Institutiones*) and the latter, in particular, includes many quotes from Cicero's *De inventione* and from Marius Victorinus's fourth-century commentary on this work.[103] The educational focus was initially on the art of composition and this was taught by formally analysing the great Latin literature of the past. The increasingly utilitarian application of rhetoric to letter-writing, essential to governmental bureaucracies, brought forth textbooks known as *dictamen* or *ars dictandi*, taught by teachers known as *dictatores*. But the imitation of other literary works was at least as significant, if not more so, in the teaching and learning of composition to acquire elo-

---

99   See volume 1, chapter 4 of *A History of Political Thought* on Aristotle's logic.

100   *Disdascalion de studio legendi*, 2.19.

101   Solitarium, privatam et publicam, vel aliter ethicam, oeconomicam et politicam, vel aliter in moralem et dispensativam et civilem.

102   See the contribution 'The Twelfth-century Renaissance' by D.Luscombe and G. R. Evans in *CHMPT* (1988), ch. 12; also J. Coleman, 'The Science of Politics and Late Medieval Academic Debate', in R. Copeland, ed., *Criticism and Dissent in the Middle Ages* (Cambridge, 1996), pp. 181–214, and J. Coleman, 'Some Relations Between the Study of Aristotle's *Rhetoric*, *Ethics* and *Politics* in Late Thirteenth- and Early Fourteenth-century University Arts Courses and the Justification of Contemporary Civic Activities (Italy and France)', in J. Canning and O.-G. Oexle, eds, *Political Thought and the Realities of Power in the Middle Ages* (Göttingen, 1998), pp. 127–58.

103   It is worthy of note that discussions of grammatical *regimen* (government) and the ideas of force and government in syntactical relations derive from Priscian's discussion of verbs governing various cases. The notion of concord (*congruitas*) was also initially a grammatical term meaning agreement and was discussed with respect to the section in Donatus's *Ars Minor* on concord (*congruitas*) in syntactical relations.

quence. The rules of *dictamen* were often spoken of as too limited and formal.[104] Hence, more detailed classical works on rhetoric continued to be influential, particularly Cicero's *De inventione*, the anonymous *Ad herennium* attributed to him, and Horace's *Ars poetica*. They read Cicero's *De inventione* to learn how to write and argue logically, Boethius's Latin translations of Aristotle's logical works (including the *Categories* and the *De interpretatione*), and numerous other Latin poets, historians and orators. Perhaps the most influential rhetorical legacy was Augustine's *De doctrina christiana*, book 4, which radically adapted Cicero's theory to the needs of the Christian orator and writer. All were studied in an attempt to acquire what was called 'eloquence', so that they could write correctly, pronounce correctly, argue satisfactorily, and persuade or dissuade in a language that initially had to be learned: Latin.

In the process of acquiring eloquence through studying grammar in the first instance, they absorbed the views of Roman moralists and historians, like Sallust, from whom they learned that the Roman people had flourished and won their most striking victories during the pre-imperial period, that of the republic, when they had shaken off the yokes of their early kings. Students learned how to imitate the speeches found in Sallust's *Catilinarium* and *Iugurthinum* to inspire soldiers. And they learned from Sallust and other Roman historians a variety of proverbs – on friendship, on the contrast between the natures of different peoples – which they then used out of context. The texts of Roman historians were taught to students learning grammar as moral commentaries on Rome's history and as stylists to be imitated.[105]

William of Conches, associated with the cathedral school at Chartres, even insisted that no one could call himself an expert in grammar if he was not also a logician and an orator. What he called the complete doctrine of eloquence (*doctrinam omnis eloquentie*) was the whole *trivium* which he believed was fundamental to anyone who wished to grasp both ethics and physics, making possible the investigation of the very nature of things.[106] The inherent vocational nature of this education is obvious. These skills, William insists, are for the common utility. If you cannot read and write, and furthermore speak, argue and persuade, then the subsequent study of substantial matters in ethics, economics and politics will be to no avail. Once the student had some of the skills of 'eloquence', he focused on ethics, economics and politics, and here Cicero's *De officiis* in particular would become familiar to him.[107]

The liberal arts of the monastic and urban schools of Europe were based on Roman pedagogy which aimed to produce men of letters and culture. Quintilian's *De institutione oratoria* told them that every teacher of oratory was concerned with the moral development of his students. They held Cicero's *De inventione* to be a moral classic, especially book 2 where virtue is discussed. More advanced students read his *De officiis* to discover the relationship between friendship, duty and virtue, and reflected on his discussion of

---

104   J. Martin, 'Classicism and Style in Latin Literature', in Benson, Constable, and Lanham, *Renaissance and Renewal*, pp. 537–68.

105   B. Smalley, 'Sallust in the Middle Ages', in R. R. Bolgar, ed., *Classical Influences on European Culture AD 500–1500* (Cambridge, 1971), pp. 165–75.

106   The text is in M. Gibson, 'The Early Scholastic *Glosule* to Priscian, Institutiones grammaticae: the text and its influence', in M. Gibson, *'Artes' and Bible in the Medieval West* (Aldershot [Variorum], 1993), p. 251.

107   See K. Fredborg, 'Speculative Grammar', pp. 177–95, and M. Tweedale, 'Logic (i): from the late eleventh century to the time of Abelard', pp. 196–226 and K. Jacobi, 'Logic (ii): the later twelfth century', pp. 227–54, all in P. Dronke, ed., *A History of Twelfth-century Western Philosophy* (Cambridge, 1988).

justice as that which maintains the common bonds of society. Not only did they adapt his view 'that men are not born for themselves alone' to a Christian context, but they also commented on his notion of duties to friends and country. Beginners read Cicero's scheme of virtues, adapted from his *De officiis* in a mid twelfth-century anonymous collection of snippets (an anthology called a *florilegium*), the *Moralium dogma philosophorum*. The subject matter was held to be part of civic studies but students were first introduced to it in their study of grammar and logical argument.

They also became familiar with the notion in classical authors that the ideal of the virtuous life was both private and public and that the individual could not be truly virtuous unless he was also a good citizen. With the twelfth-century revival of urban life and the expansion of city communes, particularly but not exclusively in northern Italy, sovereign communities governing themselves by law were ready to adapt Cicero's teachings to the active life in the *civitas*. The Ciceronian definition of a *civitas* as a union of persons possessing a common view about justice, which they could read in Augustine's *City of God*, was a practical confirmation of their life. Augustine's *City of God* also drew on Sallust's moral view of how peace and security were corrupted by Roman wealth, ambition and discord. Clearly, they accepted that there were many views that were common to both ancient philosophy and Christian doctrine, so that teachers in urban schools, like Peter Abelard, could claim that ancient teaching on the *rei publicae status* and about the conduct of its citizens was not only similar to the teaching of ancient moral philosophers like Plato in his *Timaeus* and in Aristotle's *Categories*, but was in accord with the gospel. Abelard, in his own work called the *Scito te ipsum* (know thyself) or *Ethica*, would draw not only on the Bible and the church Fathers but also on Aristotle's *Categories* for his discussion of virtue as a habit. Abelard would note how Aristotle says that a habit is not simply a disposition of character but a quality acquired by effort. This, he says, is what a virtue is.[108]

John of Salisbury, whom we may regard as an example at the extreme end of the spectrum of twelfth-century, highly educated familiarity with the moralist teachings of classical Latin authors, was well known and much admired for having been greatly influenced by the Roman moralists and especially Cicero. He quoted from them in his *Policraticus* more frequently than he quoted from the Bible or the church Fathers. In his *Metalogicon* he entered a plea for logic to be conceived as an art, as an education in the art of thinking, reasoning and speaking in order that practical wisdom as well as theoretical knowledge may thereafter be acquired.[109] At the other end of the spectrum, where students were beginning their education in literacy and argument, they too were becoming familiar with the ideals of personal conduct and social behaviour as discussed by the ancient classical moralists and philosophers. But we must be aware that they were deriving these views from Roman moralists and not least Cicero, as well as from Latin translations of Aristotle's logical writings, *Categories* and the *De interpretatione* (*Perihermenias*), and *not* from either Plato's *Republic* or Aristotle's *Nicomachean Ethics* and *Politics*, Latin translations of which they as yet did not possess, nor from Cicero's *De republica*, the entire text of which was only rediscovered in the nineteenth century.

108   *Ethica*, book 2 on prudence and the virtues, ed. Luscombe, pp. 128–9; see C. J. Nederman, 'Nature, Ethics and the Doctrine of 'Habitus': Aristotelian moral psychology in the twelfth century', *Traditio* 45 (1989/90), pp. 87–110.
109   *Metalogicon*, ed. C. C. J. Webb (Oxford, 1929), II, 1–3.

The Contribution of Arabic and Jewish Thinking to the Twelfth-century 'Renaissance'

Until now we have said nothing about the extension of the political boundaries of Latin Christendom from the end of the eleventh until the thirteenth centuries. And there is no time here other than to acknowledge that European 'states' and the universal church engaged in a series of brutal Crusades to regain control of the Holy Land in the Middle East. On the way, Christian armies engaged in pogroms against European Jewish communities and plundered Greek–Christian Constantinople. Latin conquests brought northern Europeans into closer contact with the culture of the Muslims in Spain, Sicily and the Holy Land. This was to be a crucial turning point in the intellectual development of the West, because Arab culture had inherited a wide range of the works of Aristotle and his ancient Greek commentators along with the works of Plato and Greek medical science which were not available in the Latin West.[110]

In Muslim Spain, Islamic, Jewish and Latin culture had intermingled and ancient Greek texts in Arabic and Hebrew translations were avidly discussed. From the twelfth century, Latin translations of the philosophical and scientific writings of the ancients with translations of their Arabic and Jewish commentators began to arrive in Northern Europe. But the story of the Islamic transmission of ancient Greek thinking begins much earlier, in Persia (modern Iran) and Iraq. The Syriac-speaking peoples of the Near East had cultivated the art of translation from as early as the fourth century and they provided Syriac versions of ancient Greek writings on science and philosophy which were then to be translated into Arabic. Especially during the eighth century, Baghdad had been particularly receptive to Hellenistic and Jewish influences and ninth-century Baghdad became a centre where Syriac versions of Aristotle, Ptolemy, Euclid and Galen were rendered into Arabic. The first Muslim philosopher to head a school and who was considered the second Master after Aristotle, Al-farabi (d. 950), studied in Baghdad and wrote commentaries on Aristotle's logic, physics and metaphysics. He also recovered the significance of Plato and introduced him to the Muslim community as the supreme authority on political philosophy and the investigation of human and divine laws. He wrote commentaries on Plato's *Republic* and *Laws*. In his *Enumeration of the Sciences* (*De scienciis*) he was to write the earliest and most comprehensive account of the basic themes of political science in Islamic philosophy, where he argued that lawgiving, philosophy and rulership should be linked in one person, a philosopher–king who is also the prophet–lawgiver. Substantial extracts were to be translated into Hebrew and eventually into Latin.

Ibn Sina, known in the west as Avicenna (d. 1037), also a Persian, was a physician and a courtier who was to exert an even stronger influence on Islamic, Jewish and Christian thinking, especially because he discussed the ideal state in his book called *The Healing,* which was divided into four parts: logic, physics, mathematics and metaphysics. Book 10, chapter 4 of his metaphysics contains his important discussion on the establishment of the city, the household and the general laws. It would be translated into Latin in the mid twelfth century.

The Jewish thinker Moses Maimonides (d. 1204), born in Cordoba in Muslim Spain

---

110   For a full discussion of translations and bibliography see M.-Th. d'Alverny, 'Translations and translators', in Benson, Constable and Lanham, *Renaissance and Renewal*, pp. 421–62.

and writing in Judaeo-Arabic, was a disciple of both Plato and Al-farabi. He too out-lined the scope of the study of ethics, economics and politics and added a fourth class of practical philosophy which corresponded to the religious law of both Muslims and Jews. But in revering Aristotle, as did Arabic philosophers especially in Spain and the Maghreb, he explained in his major work, the *Guide of the Perplexed*, that scripture and the Talmud, when correctly interpreted, fully conform with the ethical and metaphysical teachings of Aristotle. One of his major themes is the rationality of the divine Law's commandments and the limits to that rationality. To Maimonides, Aristotle represented the extreme of human intellect, 'if we except those who have received divine inspiration', and the highest ambition of rational man is to understand him.

Another Muslim philosopher who lived most of his life in Cordoba in Spain, and perhaps the most influential on the Latin West, was Ibn Rushd, known in the West as Averroes (*d.* 1198). To the West he would become 'the commentator', no one needing to refer to him by name. He had studied Islamic jurisprudence and theology and then went to Marakesh where, under the Almohad princes, he was given the task of creating a coherent paraphrase of Aristotle's works. When he returned to Spain he became a judge and composed commentaries, probably the most important for the Latin West being his middle commentary on Aristotle's *Nicomachean Ethics*. His writings were trans-lated into Hebrew and Latin. His ideal state, however, was crafted under the influence of Plato and he wrote a commentary on Plato's *Republic*. Aristotle's *Politics* was not available to him. In fact, there appears to have been no Arabic version of the *Politics*.

This classical period of Islamic philosophy, and the names of only a very few of the many luminaries who contributed to it have been mentioned here, produced a vast amount of literature on Plato's and Aristotle's writings. While a good deal of this litera-ture interpreted both ancient Greek philosophers as capable of being harmonized one with the other, meaning much the same thing but saying it differently, Plato was the thinker to whom many turned for reflections on human society and law. For Ibn Sina (Avicenna) Plato's philosopher–king and lawgiver was assimilated to the Muslim prophet in a 'state' that saw no distinction between church and state. Aristotle was, largely, the philosopher they read for his logic, metaphysics, psychology and ethics.

In the Latin West, however, the overwhelming influence of Plato on Islamic political thinking was to be overlooked in favour of Aristotle. Aristotle was the logician they already knew, in part, and increasingly he became *the* natural and moral philosopher. From the late fifth century, Europeans had already incorporated Aristotle's *Categories* and his *De interpretatione* in Boethius's Latin translations into their education system. These works came to be called the *logica vetus* (old logic) as soon as other Aristotelian works, now called the *logica nova* (new logic) began to be translated from the Greek by James of Venice and other anonymous translators, probably in Italy, including his *Prior* and *Posterior Analytics*. To these were added Aristotle's writings on natural philosophy, notably his treatises *De anima* (on the soul)[111] and the *Physics*. It would be the Greek-speaking East and the Greek-speaking parts of southern Italy which would, thereafter, provide the Latin West with what they needed of Aristotle on ethics and politics. Northern Europeans were prepared for Latin translations of these Greek texts by their developing

111 Also known in an Arabic version and translated by Michael Scot; the archdeacon of Toledo in Spain, Dominic Gundisalvi, collaborated with Jewish scholars to translate Avicenna's commentaries on Aristotle, and Gundisalvi wrote his own *De Anima*.

interest in nature. Aristotle, as an expert on natural philosophy, along with other ancient Greek authors on medicine were being translated first for use by physicians in twelfth-century medical schools, such as the ones in Salerno and Montpellier, and they were coming north to Bologna, Paris and England.[112]

Aristotle in the Universities

By the thirteenth century, when many universities were established, including Paris and Oxford, Europeans' knowledge of more of Aristotle's works on logic and natural philosophy had expanded and was to have a decisive effect. We can understand this if we realize what a university's vocational course of study, meant to prepare its students for future careers in the church or 'state', had become. We have already seen that the great impetus to scholastic development in the twelfth century, and the emergence of universities in the thirteenth century in which scholasticism flourished, came from a practical need for clear, authoritative solutions to practical questions about collective 'governance' relating to things both personal and public: marriage, baptism, authority in secular society and church, the legitimacy of self-founding groups and their autonomous organization within a social hierarchy of organizations like religious orders, guilds and city governments. Medieval universities like Paris, Oxford and Bologna owed their success to their development of *methods* to answer what we would call moral and political questions. They were set up as 'think-tanks' which serviced church and 'states'. They developed techniques for accumulating, arranging, reorganizing and interpreting a vast body of written materials from the past and present so that answers could be given to those questions it was thought important to ask, with consequences outside the university itself as well as within it.

It is here within what would become a *conservative methodology* for answering questions, the scholastic method, that *scholastic critical freedom* lay. The wide range of substantive questions and arguments within what undoubtedly became a tight, academic, argumentative format, allowed not only for the emergence of numerous personal and regional differences, but also for the growth of 'schools' of interpretation or 'circles' with recognizably distinct 'perspectives' on current issues. All served the same end: to answer questions convincingly and authoritatively from an ever-expanding agenda of practical moral and political issues. That the questions and answers kept changing as the agenda in church and 'state' changed meant that the universities needed to teach rules of analysis and debate, that is, a procedure by which problems could be brought to light and solved. They learned these procedural rules from the ancients and then developed them to serve their own needs. The scholastic *quaestio*, for instance, posed a problem the solution to which was found in apparently conflicting authorities. We have already observed this among the lawyers, both canon and civil, but it was taught prior to legal training in the liberal arts course. Laying out authorities on both sides, they distinguished among meanings of terms with the view to discovering how conflicting authorities

---

112   See D. Luscombe and G. R.Evans in *CHMPT* (1988); R. Lerner and M. Mahdi, eds, *Medieval Political Philosophy: a sourcebook* (Ithaca, NY, 1963) part 1: political philosophy in Islam, and part 2: political philosophy in Judaism; O. Leaman, *An Introduction to Medieval Islamic Philosophy* (Cambridge, 1985); C. Sirat, *La Philosophie juive médiévale en pays de chrétienté* (Paris, 1988); J. Jolivet 'The Arabic Inheritance', in Dronke, *A History of Twelfth-Century Western Philosophy,* ch. 4; J. Coleman, *Ancient and Medieval Memories*, pp. 328–31.

could be used to bolster one favoured position or another, and at the same time do justice to the authorities themselves.[113]

Ethics and Politics in the Liberal Arts Course

At the turn of the thirteenth century exactly how much moral and political discourse could be obtained from the texts heard and read in a university's liberal arts course where one studied grammar, the *logica vetus*, then *nova*, to say nothing of the study of *philosophica moralis* or *practica* which came after the study of language and logic, all in the pursuit of learning to argue well? It turns out that in addition to the citation of Ciceronian displays of eloquence in service of civic studies, and well before Latin-reading Europeans had translations of Aristotle's *Ethics* and *Politics*, the new logical and scientific works of Aristotle were mined, not only for moral and political topics but also for modes of argument that were seen as appropriate to moral as opposed to other 'scientific' or epistemic subjects. Most notably, as Arabic works in Latin translation were increasingly read, especially the works of Avicenna (*Metaphysics* X.4) which included excerpts from Al-farabi's *De scienciis*, early thirteenth-century scholars became familiar with ancient discourse on the ethical status of the *civitas* and the degree of human 'happiness' achievable through the right relationship between ruler and ruled. As Aristotle's complete *Organon* was introduced into the arts curriculum they became aware that he had written a *Rhetoric* and a *Poetics* which as yet they did not possess but, following Arabic commentators, they thought of these works as the seventh and eighth books of the *Organon* and therefore classified them as instruments of logic. They could read in translations of Alfarabi's catalogue of the sciences that Aristotle's *Topics* teaches dialectics, which is concerned with probable or contingent things such as ethical matters, the purpose of which is to bring about strong opinion, employing syllogisms which follow from generally accepted premises. Al-farabi also mentions Aristotle's *Rhetoric* and says it seeks to persuade by employing the enthymeme and the example. Western Latin readers would have to wait more than half a century to possess a translation of this work.

Even Robert Grosseteste, one of the earliest and perhaps the first serious Western student of Aristotle's *Posterior Analytics* (as well as of the *Physics*), and well before he set to providing a full translation and commentary on Aristotle's *Ethics*, had a subject index arranged systematically as well as a bibliography where he listed under each subject the authors and the places in their works where important subjects could be found. Aristotle's *De animalibus* is referred to with reference to the unlikely ethical and political topics of education, the law of war, just kingship and honouring one's parents. Grosseteste's Index says Aristotle's *Metaphysics* provides information on electing church officials!

Aristotle's logical works and especially the *Posterior Analytics* (translated *c.* 1140) were undoubtedly difficult,[114] but these texts provided those students who stayed the university arts course with a theoretical account of general reasoning based on observation and

---

113 As Southern has rightly pointed out with reference to the later twelfth century onwards, 'the remarkable developments of this time in government and society in theology and law and in the application of rational discourse to ordinary life would not have taken the form they did if the schools of Paris and Bologna had not existed'. R. Southern, *Robert Grosseteste: the growth of an English mind in medieval Europe* (Oxford, 1986), p. 50.

114 According to fourteenth-century university statutes, a student by the end of his second year would have heard the *Topics* and the two *Analytics*.

leading to a body of 'scientific' knowledge. In this work students confronted questions concerning the degree of certainty in the acquisition of different kinds of knowledge, along with principles for the systematic organization of human knowledge. The limits of human knowledge were exposed in the specification of *demonstrative* knowledge, where the demonstrative syllogism corresponds to the direction of the process of reasoning regarding necessary matters. Aristotle discussed the logical structure of argument and proposed rules for studying the data that were available to the human senses. And in the final chapter of the *Posterior Analytics* he had made a very un-Platonic point. He asked: how are humans able to obtain the primary knowledge of *principles* which are necessary to *demonstrative* argument? He answered by saying that such principles are not innate, nor are they acquired from pre-existing knowledge. Rather, first principles must come from some capacity of the soul for recognizing general truths which then fit the evidence of the senses.[115]

Grosseteste was not alone in finding in the *Posterior Analytics* a theoretical account of the roles of observation and general reasoning in the building up of a body of scientific knowledge. Since primary knowledge that was necessary for valid demonstration was neither innate nor acquired from pre-existing knowledge, Grosseteste was able to argue that despite the Fall, which overthrew man's natural powers of the higher faculty of reason, man *could* acquire general principles and build up a true image of the universe through sense perception and observation. What, then, might be the relation between these general principles derived from sense perception and observation, and an individual's behaviour according to ethical norms? Students had been taught from the *Topics* that in contrast to the demonstrative syllogism, the topical syllogism corresponds to the direction of the process of reasoning regarding contingent, rather than necessary matters. Indeed, Aristotle had asked in the *Posterior Analytics*, not only how can we know and what can we know about the structure of events which we experience in the world, but what degree of certainty can we achieve in what we know? Aristotle had argued that there were degrees of certainty, dependent on the subject matter under investigation. He was therefore understood as having provided a critical analysis of demonstrative knowledge in every area of science from biology to psychology to ethics and it became clear that demonstrative knowledge and its certainty could not be had in all domains of enquiry. A study of his *Topics* had already indicated that demonstration in matters of probable or contingent circumstances could only attain the probable certainty of strong opinions through syllogisms which followed from accepted, general premises.

As we shall see, when later thirteenth-century scholars had Aristotle's *Ethics* and read book 6 on the nature of 'political science' as *distinguished* from other 'sciences' and arts, they were already prepared to interpret Aristotle's distinction between 'sciences' or kinds of thinking and to accept his classification of political 'science' or prudence as *distinct* from scientific demonstration (as discussed in the *Posterior Analytics*). By this time they were also familiar with a conception of learning that linked, rather than divorced, the soul and the body so that it was now natural to speak of men learning from the particulars of sense experience from which, by induction, they generalized to moral rules of behaviour. Thereafter, prudence, or political 'science' was a way of thinking, a consequence of particular experiences in contingent circumstances, rather than a revelation

115   See volume 1, chapter 4 of *A History of Political Thought* on Aristotle.

from on high. Hence, where dialectical demonstrative logic was seen as appropriate to confirm necessary and unchanging truths, a separate part of logic – rhetoric – would come to be seen as appropriate to ascertain what was plausible in particular and contingent circumstances. The 'science' of politics or prudence would be linked with rhetorical persuasion as its methodology, rather than with demonstrative logic.

The consequences were startling. There was a shift away from Cicero to Aristotle as the educator in *philosophia moralis et politica*, along with the categorization of rhetoric as a distinct, indeed separate part of logic which seeks to persuade an audience of beliefs rather than to prove necessary truths. The shift appears to have begun with the influence of Arabic commentaries on Aristotle, notably Averroes's 'Middle Commentary'. Aristotle's *Rhetoric*, when translated from the Arabic by the monk Hermannus Alemannus in 1256, provided a method for teaching persuasion from the *rhetorical* topics. Around the same time Hermannus translated into Latin that part of Averroes's 'Middle Commentary' in which he interpreted Aristotle's *Poetics*. Hermannus appears to have had difficulties with the text of the *Poetics* and turned for help to Averroes and translated him. Hermannus made clear that although Cicero had made rhetoric a part of civil philosophy and Horace had treated poetry rather as it pertains to grammar, the correct view was that both rhetoric and poetics are to be considered parts of logic.[116]

It was henceforth made clear that the method of rhetoric was distinct from dialectic and rhetoric used its own types of argument based on a psychology of the emotions and the habitual formation of character. From then into the fourteenth century the scope of rhetoric would be linked more closely with the moral sciences of ethics and politics, taking into account the limitations of the audience being addressed, and whether it was educated or not. Rhetoric would be discussed and taught not only in terms of its status among the other arts and sciences, but also as to its practical usefulness within moral sciences and, most significantly, in terms of a psychology of the emotions and their guidance by a practical intellect that had been persuaded by certain kinds of arguments that inspire to action.

The Purpose of Aristotelian Rhetorical Persuasion

By the late thirteenth century in the liberal arts regimes of medieval universities it had come to be thought that logic was made complete by teaching the method whereby the faculty of desire might be guided by reason. It was said that man acts as regards both himself and others through an understanding that combines imagination and the faculty of desire. The persuasion of rhetoric or rhetorical logic relates to the act of the intellect in respect of the faculty of desire in so far as it is directed towards others. Rhetoric is the kind of persuasion that is addressed to a large number of people and therefore uses the example and the enthymeme.[117] Because men live with each other through mutual trust,

---

116 W. F. Boggess, 'Hermannus Alemannus's Rhetorical Translations', *Viator* 2 (1971), pp. 227–50. There are more than 90 manuscripts of Aristotle's *Rhetoric*, many of which, including the earliest, have substantial marginal and interlinear glosses. *Aristoteles Latinus*, 696, 433, 1782, 746 for the thirteenth century and 961, 962 for the beginning of the fourteenth century; Hermannus Alemannus, *De arte poetica cum Averrois expositione*, ed. L. Minio–Paluello, *Aristoteles Latinus,* xxxiii (Brussels, 1968), p. 41.

117 See below, pp. 65ff, on Aristotelian Rhetoric.

that is called persuasion which is intended to produce trust in others, whereas poetic persuasion relates to that act of intellect in respect of the faculty of desire through which a man guides only himself. The anonymous author from whom these Aristotelian views are taken noted that because all things which relate to the life of a community have to be watched over by judges and rulers, and those things are concerned with the act of justice – an act which in a sense is judicially dispensed, with some degree of compulsion, to inferiors by superiors – therefore, rhetorical persuasion is said most of all to have its place in the sphere of judicial acts. On the other hand, in his own private domain any person is his own judge and master, providing that he does not annoy those with whom he lives, and therefore poetic composition (which need not be in verse) relates to private and voluntary acts, poetic discourse being concerned with the praise and blame of voluntary acts that are not acts obliged by law. Poetics deals, then, with practical reasoning relating to the acts of man concerning himself and is considered a part of logic, a logical procedure relating to the acts of the practical intellect which fall within ethics. But rhetoric, similarly a part of logic, deals with the acts of practical reasoning which pertain to others and such acts fall within politics. This writer goes on to distinguish the other parts of logic from poetics and rhetoric, emphasizing that poetry and rhetoric attain lesser degrees of certainty. Rhetoric, however, not only aims to teach the pursuit of virtuous ways and the avoidance of evil, but it lays down guidelines in relation to actions which are subject to justice and to compulsion, precisely because it concerns itself with ways of living with special reference to others. The common good, which is aimed at by means of rhetoric, is judged to be more important than the good of the individual, which is poetry's aim. Indeed, citizens have to be drawn away from injustice by means of judicial acts, and this 'drawing away' is achieved by rhetoric, that part of logic which guides a collective morality to serve the utility of the common life of the populace. In true Aristotelian fashion, the author emphasizes that among ordinary people error arises more often from a perversion of desire, and hence from bad habits, than from a naivety of understanding.[118] Among those parts of logic which can be applied to morality, then, rhetoric is judged the more worthy and divine for it concerns itself more closely with the common good.

The author makes plain, however, that the more basic parts of logic, starting with the books of the *logica vetus* and continuing through the *logica nova*, must be studied first and are more applicable to speculative objects, before a student reaches the stage where he engages with practical, moral realities by means of the methods of rhetoric and poetry. He believes that the practical arts of ethics, economics and politics, as the constituent parts of practical philosophy, come after the study of grammar and dialectic in the liberal arts curriculum of the university because he represents a generation that had come to see grammatical studies themselves as under the control of speculative rather than practical philosophy. Grammatical and dialectical studies at university level had come to be linked less with literary style and Ciceronian civil philosophy and more with a theory of reality and a psychology. Logic had come to be studied without regard to its practical applicability, and hence as a 'science', as a theory with its own purpose, rather than as an art. The rediscovery of more of Aristotle's writings had led during the thirteenth century to a perceived intimacy between the reality of things and their conceptualization by the human mind. The interdependence between language and the structure of things, me-

---

118   Compare Marsilius of Padua, pp. 155–6 below.

diated by the human mind's psychology with its ability to perceive, signify and functionalize these things in language, led to considerations of the relation between those kinds of logical arguments that could demonstrate certitude about the world on the one hand, and those kinds of arguments that could achieve only true-for-the-most-part, or plausible statements about experiences, on the other. The 'sciences' and their respective status, in consequence, had been reclassified.[119]

We can observe this reclassification of the 'sciences' and their respective applications to different kinds of discourse in terms of the degrees of certainty that each 'science' achieved in another way. Just before Hermannus translated Aristotle's *Rhetoric*, Grosseteste and his team completed the translation of Aristotle's *Ethics*. He also assembled and translated ancient commentaries and provided a new commentary *c.* 1250. Grosseteste understood the subject of ethics in an Aristotelian fashion: the subject of ethics was none other than the constitution and operations of the passions and the powers of the soul. Hence, the university treatment of practical philosophy, of ethics and politics, supplementing the speculative insights gained earlier from Aristotle's logical and natural science works, had become by the mid thirteenth century increasingly Aristotelian in focus. Ethics was related to the psychology of motivation and in turn was linked to a certain kind of non-demonstrative, contingent and plausible discourse, that of rhetoric, which affected psychological motivation to action.

If the *Posterior Analytics* had enabled Grosseteste and men like him to argue that men could acquire at least the general principles and build up a true image of the universe through sense perception and observation, then the *Ethics* taught him that the operations of human capacities as they responded *inwardly* through emotions and reason to particular events and situations required that the 'sciences' of ethics and politics be *inexact*. Grosseteste was therefore able to argue that general positive laws could never take account of all the individual circumstances. He invoked Aristotle's notion of equity as an inward quality, a virtue or habit, which needed to be developed by rulers to supplement the law. Grosseteste argued that *epieikeia*, equity, 'is a word with many meanings. Inwardly it expresses a quality which shows itself in thoughtfulness, grace, modesty and love of self-knowledge. Outwardly, it expresses moderation in applying the rules of positive law and in softening the rigours of the law according to the circumstances in unusual cases'. It was these qualities, as discussed by Aristotle, which Grosseteste urged the members of the ecclesiastical hierarchy, even Pope Innocent IV, to exhibit.

The Thirteenth 'Aristotelian' Century

It can no longer be thought that Europeans were taken by storm when Aristotle's *Nicomachean Ethics* and *Politics* were translated into Latin. The *Ethics* was translated by Grosseteste *c.* 1250 (the *ethica vetus* was available in the twelfth century – books 2 and 3) and the *translatio antiquior–ethica nova* which comprised book 1 and a few fragments

---

119   The above derives from an anonymous *Quaestio* on the nature of poetry, Paris, BN lat. 16709, transcribed in G. Dahan, 'Notes et textes sur la poétique au moyen âge', *Archives d'histoire doctrinale et littérarie du moyen âge* xlvii (1980), pp. 214–19, and adapted from the translation in A. J. Minnis and A. B Scott, eds, *Medieval Literary Theory and Criticism, c. 1100–c. 1375, the Commentary Tradition* (Oxford, revd edn, 1991), pp. 307–13; this contains an excellent bibliography on all the above issues.

was already available in the early thirteenth century. Book 1 and part of book 2 (the *translatio imperfecta*) of the *Politics* were translated by the Dominican William of Moerbeke in 1260 and by 1265 he provided the rest – the *translatio completa*.[120] The reason usually given for the readiness of Christian Europeans to 'accept' Aristotle's ethical and political observations is that they were in fact impervious to his distinctly ancient Greek political convictions and simply 'translated' what they saw in the texts to bolster what they already believed about their own society, which was constructed in very different ways from that of Greece in the fourth century BC. But by now it should be evident that what by mid century they believed was *already* in large part Aristotelian, once translations of the Arabic and Greek texts and commentaries on the logical and natural science works became incorporated into university studies. By the mid thirteenth century, particularly in Oxford University statutes, Cicero is not even mentioned. Indeed, it is difficult to know how far Cicero was read in universities in the thirteenth and early fourteenth centuries because of the lack of information in the early university statutes, along with the apparent scarcity of thirteenth- as opposed to twelfth-century commentaries either on Cicero's *De inventione* or on the pseudo-Ciceronian *Rhetorica ad herennium*.[121] What had happened during the thirteenth century is that the 'sciences' came to be reclassified and rhetoric was not only taken to be a part of logic, as was poetics, but it was linked increasingly to an analysis of the passions and therefore to the motivating springs of ethical and political agency. Aristotle's writings had provided them with a theory of reality and a series of analyses of how different kinds of arguments might confirm what was to be held as necessary and what was to be considered as plausible about the world of experience. Cicero and the other Roman guides to eloquence, who had been for centuries the teachers of *styles* to be imitated in speech and writing, were replaced with a doctrine that explained the psychology of how and why eloquence was successful, or not. It was this doctrine of how and why rhetorical persuasion succeeded, itself based on a theory of reality and an analysis of human psychology and human modes of argument in relation to that reality, that would become fundamental to men of prudence who governed monarchies or republics.

We have seen that by at least the end of the twelfth century the general question concerning the object of 'scientific' knowledge, belief and opinion had been formulated as an epistemological problem by men whose learning was sufficiently advanced for them to be recognized as teachers of grammar and logic. Debates over the object of scientific knowledge had become central to the arts course curriculum early on, focused as it was on logic, and related to this was the classification of the different kinds of science and their subjects on the basis of the degree of certainty achieved by different kinds of argument, applicable to different subjects of discourse. This guided medieval teachers as to where and when various subjects were to be studied in the university's

---

120   See C. Flüeler, 'Die Rezeption der 'Politica' des Aristoteles an der Pariser Artistenfakultat im 13. und 14. Jahrhundert', pp. 127–51, and Tilman Struve, 'Die Bedeutung der aristotelischen 'Politik' für die naturliche Begrundung der staatlichen Gemeinschaft', pp. 153–71, both in J. Miethke, ed., *Das Publikum politischer Theorie im 14. Jahrhundert* (Munich, 1992); and C. Flüeler, *Rezeption und Interpretation der Aristotelischen 'Politica' im späten Mittelalter*, 2 vols (Amsterdam/Philadelphia, 1992). Also G. Wieland, *Ethica–scientia practica. Die Anfange der philosophischen Ethik im 13. Jahrhundert* (Munster, 1981).
121   K. Fredborg, 'Buridan's *Quaestiones super Rhetoricam Aristotelis*', in J. Pinborg, ed., *The Logic of John Buridan* (Copenhagen, 1976), pp. 47–59.

liberal arts curriculum. As we have seen, among the different sciences were those called *practica*. Now, with Aristotle's *Rhetoric* and his *Ethics* to hand, *scientia politica* was confirmed as being the most sovereign of the practical 'sciences'. Linked to politics was rhetoric, defined by the end of the thirteenth century as that science of discourse which moves both the intellect and the emotions, and it is distinct from dialectic which moves only the intellect. Rhetoric is now taken to be part of moral science and it has a subject matter that is different from dialectic. Rhetoric is about human affairs and man, and deals with particular circumstances where one judges the more or less good. Dialectic, on the other hand, is now a speculative 'science' and deals with the truth *per se*.[122]

By the later thirteenth century, then, Aristotle had come to replace Cicero in the university as the master in the 'science' of politics and its related rhetorical strategies of public persuasion. Cicero continued to be cited but mainly for those areas of moral philosophy known as *ethica* and *privativa* , that is, the government of the self and the government of the household.[123] It was Aristotle who became the source not only for a substantive analysis of the public sphere by the end of the thirteenth century; he also became the guide to the form of argument which such a substantive analysis should take. Cicero and other Roman moralists would still be read and cited, indeed increasingly so, in advice on personal conduct and conduct among friends and family (*solitarium* and *privatam*), but many university-trained authors who were engaged in *political* theorizing would simply integrate and harmonize Cicero's views with Aristotle's when their concern was the government of a community (*publicam*). We shall see later how the political theorists under consideration below used these two great but often opposing ancient minds to confirm a synthetic medieval vision of the nature of good politics and its purpose, Cicero supplementing but never replacing the Aristotelian conception of the public realm as it was understood in university milieux.[124] Indeed, once poetry was recognized as the discourse to be linked with the individual's ethical behaviour, and rhetoric linked with moral public behaviour for the common good, practical philosophy and its two kinds of persuasive discourse, as they took Aristotle to understand them, began to structure much of the political theorizing addressed to princes and citizens. This is most obvious in those texts of education and instruction known as 'mirrors for princes'. One of the most widely influential medieval example of such a 'mirror' was *On the instruction of princes*, the *De regimine principum,* by the Augustinian Giles of Rome (Aegidius Romanus) (post 1285). Machiavelli's *Il Principe* (*The Prince*) will provide us with an early sixteenth-century Renaissance version of the same genre.[125]

---

122   K. Fredborg, 'Buridan's *Quaestiones*, p. 50 on the anonymous literal commentary on Boethius's *De differentiis topicis* [possibly by Kilwardby?] lectio 9 and Nicholas of Paris's commentary, both influenced by Aristotle's treatment of rhetoric; O. Lewry, 'Grammar, Logic and Rhetoric, 1220–1320', in J. I. Catto and R. Evans, eds, *The History of the University of Oxford*, vol. 1: *The Early Oxford Schools* (Oxford, 1984), pp. 401–34; O. Lewry, 'Four Graduation Speeches from Oxford Mss (c. 1270–1310)', *Mediaeval Studies*, xliv (1982).

123   K. Fredborg, 'Buridan's *Quaestiones*, p. 50 on the shift of interest from the Ciceronian–Boethius doctrine of the 'art' of rhetoric to the Aristotelian 'doctrine' of rhetoric.

124   See Aquinas, John of Paris and Marsilius of Padua, below, chapters 2, 3 and 4.

125   See below, chapter 6.

The Later Thirteenth-century Understanding of Rhetoric's Service to a Prince: Giles of Rome

Giles of Rome (*c.* 1243/7–1316) is the earliest Parisian master whose name is associated with a commentary (*c.* 1280) on Aristotle's *Rhetoric*, using the Dominican William of Moerbeke's recent translation rather than that of Hermannus.[126] Here he argued that rhetoric serves the need of the practical intellect, specifically of the man who uses his reason to discover and practically promote the common good of society. Rhetoric is therefore the proper instrument of a statesman in carrying out his task of persuading those under his government to perform those actions which serve the common good. The orator must be able to deal directly with particular and practical issues and his concern is to use arguments to arouse the passions of his readers/auditors. He must speak in a way which will appeal to the capacity even of the simplest and most uneducated listener. Indeed, the audience of rhetorical orations is presumed to be *grossus* and for this reason enthymemes and examples most suit the capacity of the minds of such people. Giles omits all references to Ciceronian material.

Giles began his enormously popular *De regimine principum* after 1285[127] and dedicated it to the future king of France, Philip the Fair. Book 1, chapter 1 poses and answers the question: what is the mode of procedure in the instruction of princes? Citing Aristotle's *Ethics* and his own commentary on the *Rhetoric*, Giles says:

> In the whole field of moral teaching the mode of procedure, according to the Philosopher [Aristotle] is figurative and broad. For in such matters one should make one's way by use of types and figures, for moral actions do not fall completely within the scope of narrative. The subject matter itself, along with the end purpose of an art of princely government, as well as its intended audience all confirm that the mode of procedure should be figurative and broad. Since the body of knowledge which relates to princely rule is concerned with human actions and is included within the moral sphere, and the subject matter of morals does not admit of detailed and thorough scrutiny but concerns individual matters, because of their variable nature the individual actions which are the subject matter of this work show that we must proceed by way of figures and types. If we look at the intention of this art of princely government, then as Aristotle says in the *Ethics*, we undertake moral study not for the sake of abstract contemplation, nor to gain knowledge, but in order that we may become good. Hence, the end of the science of princely government is not to gain true knowledge concerning its own matter but rather, moral activity. Since subtle arguments are more effective in illuminating the intellect while those that are superficial and broad are more effective in stirring and firing the affections . . . in moral matters, where the goal is an upright will and that we should become good, one must proceed by persuasion and the use of figures. . . . As to the audience which is to be instructed in this art: although the title of this book is 'on the instruction of princes', all of the populace is to be instructed by it. Although not everyone can be a king or prince, everyone ought to do his best to see that he becomes the sort of person who would be worthy to be a prince or king. And this

---

126   *Rhetorica Aristotelis cum Egidii de Roma commentariis* (Venice, 1515; photorepr.: Frankfurt, 1968); K. Fredborg, 'The Scholastic Teaching of Rhetoric in the Middle Ages', *Cahiers de l'institut du moyen-âge grec et latin*, 55 (1987), pp. 85–105; Ubaldo Staico, 'Retorica et politica in Egidio Romano', *Aegidiana* 3. *Documenti e studi sulla tradizione filosofica medievale*, III, 1 (1992), pp. 1–75.
127   Rome, 1607, repr. Aalen, 1967.

cannot be achieved unless the tenets which are to be related in this work are known and observed. So, in a sense, the populace as a whole forms the audience for this art. But only a few are endowed with acute understanding. Hence, the remark in the third book of the *Rhetoric* that the larger the population, the farther are they from understanding. So the audience for these moral matters is simple and unsophisticated as I showed in my commentary on the first book of the *Rhetoric*. Because the populace as a whole cannot understand subtleties, one must proceed in the sphere of morals in a figurative and broad way. According to the Philosopher in his *Politics*, the subject ought to know and do what his lord ought to know and command. [*Politics* III, 4, 1277a25–b7]. If, by means of this book, princes are instructed as to how they should conduct themselves and how they should govern their subjects, this teaching must reach out to the population so that it knows how it ought to obey its princes. Since this cannot be achieved except by arguments which are superficial and appeal to the senses (*rationes superficiales et sensibiles*), then the mode of procedure in this book ought to be broad and figurative.

We are being told that this famous 'mirror for princes', perhaps the most famous medieval tract to establish the political theory genre known as 'instruction on princely government', is a work of oratory, following the prescribed form as well as the substantive content of Aristotle on rhetoric, with references to Aristotle's *Ethics* and *Politics* to confirm the arguments Giles himself wishes to make on princely government. He has not written a commentary on Aristotle's *Ethics* or *Politics*; he has his own agenda but draws on quotations or paraphrases from the *Ethics* and *Politics*, and cites numerous worthies including the recently deceased Dominican philosopher and theologian Thomas Aquinas,[128] merely as relevant support or explanatory example.

Aristotelian Rhetoric

What is implied in the use of Aristotelian techniques of rhetorical persuasion and figures?[129] Aristotle's *Rhetoric* is a curious work when compared with Cicero's *De inventione*, for instance. Aristotle's is a detailed psychology of the human emotions, which can be moved by a kind of informal reasoning and a kind of prose style. It seeks the roots of persuasive discourse and the reasons for its success in the nature of human character and emotion. Its method is that of a kind of demonstration in the absence of deductive certainty. Aristotle describes rhetoric as a counterpart to dialectic (I, 1, 1). And rhetoric, like dialectic, is a 'tool subject' in contrast to politics, ethics and other 'sciences'. Sciences are forms of knowledge of underlying 'facts'. Rhetoric, like dialectic, however, is an art rather than a 'science' in the sense that the art of rhetoric can be taught, it is a skill, but it is one that is a productive activity of the orator rather than a feature of language and argument.

Aristotle speaks of rhetoric as a kind of offshoot of dialectic and of ethical studies (I, 2, 7). As an art, rhetoric is a combination of analytical knowledge and the knowledge of men's characters (I, 4, 50). Its successful use can only be achieved by an orator's grasp of the most important features of human nature, emotional and intellectual. The orator must be a logician in order to understand the principles of his arguments, and a

128   See chapter 2 on Aquinas.
129   Text: G. A. Kennedy, trans. and notes, *Aristotle On Rhetoric: a theory of civic discourse* (Oxford, 1991).

psychologist in order to understand the basis of character and emotion. His audience need be neither. Because rhetoric as a skill is not a field of theoretical knowledge or speculation but a praxis of practical reason, it takes self-evident premises as its starting point and then proceeds by a syllogistic method, aiming at finding the persuasive aspects of a *particular* subject matter in order to motivate rational agents to action. The orator looks to persuade people of a certain sort of what is plausible, so he needs to know of what sort his audience is. Rhetoric is defined as an ability to see the available means of persuasion in *each case* (I, 2, 1). And persuasion occurs through the argument when an orator shows the truth or the apparent truth from whatever is persuasive in each case (I, 2, 6). The orator's task is to find *(inventio)* those aspects of his subject that can be employed in his arguments which are designed to stress certain features which can induce the appropriate emotional state in his given audience. *He* needs to discover the correct premises, where to begin, in order to persuade. Once he has his premises, he argues by means of 'proofs common to all' and these are what are called either the rhetorical enthymeme or the example. The enthymeme, a kind of rhetorical syllogism, contrasts with the logical syllogism, because it uses premises and conclusions that are ordinarily probable, not necessarily logically valid, and sometimes the very premise is omitted if it is thought to be assumed by the audience (I, 2, 8–13; II, 22, 1–17). Furthermore, an orator's premises are not indubitably true or necessary (unlike those of dialecticians using demonstration) (I, 2, 14). Rather, his premise is something considered true for the most part and produces true-for-the-most-part conclusions. He derives his enthymemes from such probable starting premises and the enthymeme is tied to a particular subject matter, applicable only to it, and is not applicable generally (like topics) to any possible subject matter. He may also persuade by using examples (para-digms), either by speaking of things that have happened before (historically) or by making up a fictional illustration (II, 20, 1–9).

Who needs to learn this skill? The prudent man. In the *Nicomachean Ethics* Aristotle had insisted not only that the 'science' that studies the supreme good for man is politics, but that under political science come those arts most highly esteemed: the arts of war, of property management (economics), and public speaking.[130]

Aristotle outlines three species of persuasive oratory: (1) *deliberative* oratory, which offers advice by exhortation or dissuasion and concerns future events, aiming to illumi-nate the advantageous or the harmful; (2) *judicial* oratory, most common in the lawcourts, which proceeds through accusation or defence and deals with the past and what has been done in order to arrive at a decision concerning the just or the unjust; and (3) *epideictic* oratory, which praises and blames existing qualities in the present, reminding the audience of the past and projecting the course of the future; it aims to illuminate the honourable and the shameful (I, 3, 1–6).

Deliberative oratory aims to establish the advisability of a given position or decision. This final objective is what is called the deliberative objective and is that which is the most worthy and important, indeed the finest form of rhetoric, for Aristotle, because it deals with political judgement. It seeks to persuade by the enthymeme (rhetorical syllo-gism) and the example, and examples from history are more useful than the fictional variety since generally, he says, future events will be like those of the past.[131] He provides

---

130   NE I, 2, 4–6. See volume 1, chapter 4 of *A History of Political Thought* on Aristotle.
131   II, 20, 8; compare Machiavelli, chapter 6, below.

political topics that are useful in deliberative rhetoric where advice is offered in public, notably on finances, war and peace, 'state' security, and the framing of laws (I, 4, 7). Here he makes it clear that 'state' security, the safety of the 'city', is in its laws and he advises the orator offering advice to know how many forms of constitution there are and what is conducive to each and by what each is naturally prone to be corrupted (I, 4,12). Furthermore, it is useful when engaged in constitutional revision, not only to know the constitutions in effect in other 'states' but to observe what constitutions are suitable to what sort of people (I, 4, 13). Although these subjects belong, he says, to politics rather than rhetoric, they are the subjects which comprise the agenda of the orator and he needs to have propositions dealing with these subjects if he is going to give counsel by his deliberative oratory. Furthermore, in his effort to demonstrate that a course of action is in the best interest of his audience, a deliberative orator needs an understanding of the objectives and values of human life, and these, in addition to the previous political propositions, provide additional premises for his argument (I, 5, 1ff.).

Because deliberation in public councils and assemblies is designed to promote the happiness or at least the utility of those on whose behalf it is conducted, the orator has first to grasp the constituents of human felicity or 'happiness' in order to understand how certain subjects may appear relevant to an audience seeking plausible proofs. Hence, where the *Nicomachean Ethics* gave a conceptual analysis of human well-being (*eudaimonia*) based on moral and intellectual virtues and their means of acquisition, the *Rhetoric* simply identifies those constituent components of human felicity and then studies (book 2) the human emotions which he wishes to produce or control.

In book I, 6 Aristotle provides some extraordinary definitions for the orator, especially if he has already considered the character disposition of his audience. He indicates a list of what are the more or less agreed upon goods for most men who are of the rather conventional kind. There is no urgency here to explain why a man needs to know and then do the morally right thing as there was in the *Nicomachean Ethics*. Instead, he emphasizes here that the good is simply what all desire and the *many* resembles *all*; in general, things that are deliberately chosen are to be taken for good. He says that ordinary people prefer to do a range of things: evil things to their enemies, good things to their friends, and generally things that are possible. They value things easily done, for since easy, they are possible. And things are good if they turn out as people want; but they want either nothing bad or an evil less than the accompanying good, and the latter will be the case if the cost is either unnoticed or slight. Furthermore, people value things that are peculiarly their own and that no one else has or does and that are exceptional, for in this way there is more honour. And people value things that are suited to them and such things as are befitting their family and power. And people value things they think they are lacking in, even if small, for none the less they choose to get these things. And most of all, each category of people values as a good that to which their character is disposed, and the range of values comprises victory, honour, money (I, 6, 21–30).[132]

Aristotle is making clear that it is no part of the orator's task to preach values that are not shared; rather, it is his task to discover, in given circumstances and in the light of a particular audience, what all desire and he is to begin with this as 'the good' and 'the advantageous' (I, 7, 28). Indeed, the greatest and most important of all things for an orator is an ability to persuade and give good advice by achieving an understanding of

132   Compare Machiavelli, *Prince*, chapter 6, below.

each form of constitution and to distinguish customs and legal usages and the advantages of each. This is because all people are persuaded by what is advantageous and preserving the constitution is advantageous. A constitution reflects the character of a given people and an orator should become acquainted with the kinds of character distinctive of each of the four forms of constitution: democracy, oligarchy, aristocracy and monarchy (I, 8, 1–5). It is significant that Aristotle defines monarchy in accordance with its name, as that in which one person is sovereign over all; of these, some are a kingdom with orderly government, some a tyranny where power is unlimited. The orator, therefore, is to know the aims of each constitution and why choices are made in light of these aims, by the characters of persons that are formed by different constitutions. The skilled orator simply adapts his persuasive speech to the character of his audience.

If he is successful, and his deliberative oratory is preserved in writing, a disinterested reader of another time and place would have no way of determining the personal preferences of the orator. He would simply have revealed the values and characters of those whom he has successfully addressed and advised!

The orator is meant to be able to come up with recognizable, exemplary archetypes of agents' characters and how they were formed by social and material conditions, or age, and he addresses them in ways that would appear most convincing to them. In this way he is able to provide types of proofs or conclusions, be they logical (for the educated), emotional (for the many) or ethical (for all who are part of a given community with established conventions). The conclusions of proofs are suited to the character who is the recipient of his speech. His style is functional: it aims to secure the conviction of the audience, and Aristotle emphasizes clarity (book 3) without excluding ornate embellishment, imagery and metaphor. Indeed, he speaks of the style of deliberative oratory as like shadow-painting, providing an outline without detail as it is intended to be seen at a distance; the greater the crowd, the further the distance of view, and exactness is wasted effort.[133]

If rhetorical argument in general proceeds by enthymeme and example, Aristotle believes that deliberative oratory, which deals with the possible and the future, best uses populist arguments which employ examples, either narrating a version of the facts of past events as the speaker sees them, or inventing similar stories. It is in narration that clarity and descriptiveness are most important, but the orator is no mere narrator.[134] In persuading by enthymeme and example, the orator is using a kind of induction, or he is using a kind of dialectical syllogism, but it is a syllogism that is formally imperfect. A medieval university student would have studied the species of enthymeme, not least when he treated Aristotle's *Prior Analytics*.[135] What is sought in the use of Aristotelian rhetorical persuasion, then, is the construction of plausible arguments that sway the emotions of a given, large audience to conclusive opinions that appear true to it, or at least plausible for most similar cases. There is no recourse to universal conclusions because the orator only argues his particular case with particular conclusions. If the audience is, in general, the

133   III, 125; compare Machiavelli's dedicatory letter to the *Prince*, where he compares his method to landscape painters who station themselves in the valleys in order to draw mountains or elevated ground, and ascend an eminence in order to get a good view of the plains.
134   For parallels with this method, see chapter 6 on Machiavelli.
135   II, 27, 70a 30.

uneducated people who understand only rhetorical enthymemes that *prove consequences*, then it is assumed that they cannot understand the *causes* of things or else have no interest in causes.[136]

Returning to Giles of Rome's Rhetorical *De regimine principum*

This, then, is the rhetorical method that determines the substance of Giles of Rome's *De regimine principum*. The work was a product of the arts curriculum of the later thirteenth century, following Aristotle's *Rhetoric*, and the tract's divisions follow the division of *philosophica practica* as *solitarium/monasticum/ethicam* (book 1: on the government of the self); then *privativam/oeconomicam/dispensativam* (book 2: on the government of one's household); and last, *publicam/politicam/civilem* (book 3: on the government of the city or *regnum*). If Giles holds this to be the method of the orator, he also holds it to be the method of the prudent man, the king, so that his argument is that kings must learn how to be orators.

This is a conclusion that most of us have been taught could never have emerged from university scholasticism and the arts course of Paris, or elsewhere; indeed, that we would have to await the humanists, especially from the city-states of Renaissance Italy, to hear it.[137]

We can take one interesting example of how Giles puts this method to use when in book 3 he discusses the government of the city or *regnum*. He describes the *regnum* as a concrete, territorial state, rather than as an abstraction, and he gives examples of cities which have several neighbourhoods in which men practise various crafts and arts. The *regnum* is defined functionally as a great multitude in which there are many noble and free men, living virtuously, according to institutional arrangements (*ordinati*) under an optimum regime, as under a king: *multitudo magna in qua sunt multi nobiles et ingenui, viventes secundum virtutem ordinati sub uno vivo optimo, ut sub rege* (book III, pars 1, c. 9).[138]

On the question of whether a king who is elected is preferable to one who inherits his office (book III, pars 2, c. 5), Giles first presents a rhetorical argument to be used to convince princes, *ex parte regentis*, of the benefits of being concerned for the common good if they have inherited their office, and then another to convince the people, *ex parte populi,* of the merits of hereditary monarchy. These are arguments from differential emotional motivations on the parts of different social ranks in a monarchy that already operates with the hereditary principle, as did France. Giles, following Aristotle, knows the character of his audience. His argument to convince a hereditary prince of the merits of serving the common good starts with the emotional self-interest of a father: he notes that it is natural for a king to feel a love for his own, and naturally he cares more for his own kingdom when he believes its well-being to be consonant with his own good. He

---

136 Compare Marsilius of Padua, chapter 4, below, on ordinary men not seeking the causes or principles behind the laws but having enough sense to judge the consequences of laws proposed to them; the above considerations should be kept in mind when we come to discuss Machiavelli's *Prince* (chapter 6) and Machiavelli's debt to this tradition.

137 See chapter 6 on Renaissance humanism.

138 Compare below with Machiavelli's understanding of *vivere politico*, *Discorsi* 1, 18 and his statement in *Discorsi* 1, 25: 'e questo . . . debbe osservare colui che vuole ordinare uno vivere politico, o per via di republica o di regno'.

wishes therefore not only to be the ruler during his own lifetime, but to rule through his own sons, and since the future hope of the country resides in his sons, he must be convinced that the good of his country is his own good, so that he is moved to love his country as he loves his sons whose good depends on the good of the realm after he dies. Thus, those who wish to achieve the good of the realm (*ad procurandum bonum statum regni*) that is governed by a hereditary monarchy must rhetorically motivate a king to love his realm by showing him that his natural and ardent love for his sons will be best achieved if he provides well for the realm that they will inherit.

The argument *ex parte populi* is based on a given tradition of behaviour: he says that when it is the case that the people are used to obeying the descendants of the king, then they are of a certain disposition to follow the rules of one person who has already received respect as the designated successor.[139] Giles, however, goes on to argue that *election* of a king is valid absolutely (*absolute*), that is, theoretically and speculatively,[140] but in practice, and in France, he prefers hereditary kingship here because when one considers the concrete condition of men (*experimentaliter*) hereditary succession is best in these circumstances. He has started with given and particular cultural premises, and then argued that if and when men have become used to living under kings, then hereditary kingship is most likely to be accepted. Giles has not presented a general truth but a rhetorical particularity using the enthymeme and the example, given his knowledge of his audience, the future king of France and his people.

He goes on to argue that right reason (*recta ratio*) is *always* decisively superior to positive law and tradition, but that it is plausible that where there is an *optimus rex* (the best king) there will be *optima lex* (the best law). And for this reason he thinks that the king must take up the lessons taught by the orator because only then will his own right reason coincide with the natural law which God impresses in the mind of man, the consequence being that the king will then be able to direct the positive law but be above those laws himself (not above either natural law or right reason). He will be the prudent man who has acquired virtues and whose desires, when guided by practical reason, will issue in those exterior deeds, justified by effective good reasons (*boni rationis effectiva*), that will enable him to be seen as justice itself in action.

Indeed, previously (book II, ch. 1, 14) Giles had distinguished between what he calls a *regimen regale* and a *regimen politicum*. The distinction refers to those who are seen as the authors of the laws of any *civitas,* be it the ruler who governs according to his own will and according to those laws he has himself instituted (*regale*), or the ruler who governs according to laws instituted by the citizens according to their own traditions and customary agreements (*regimen politicum*). He expresses no preference. Rather, he is distinguishing between what these respective types of regimes are called (*est denominandum*) and the distinction rests on who institutes the laws. As Aristotle had noted in *Rhetoric* (I, 8, 1), the edict of the central authority is authoritative and central authorities differ in accordance with constitutions. For Giles, both the *regimen regale* and the *regimen politicum* are orderly governments. The *regimen regale* is not what Aristotle referred to as a tyranny, where power is unlimited, but rather, a monarchy where one person is sovereign over all and where there is orderly government. Someone who governs and deploys oratori-

139   Compare Machiavelli's *Prince*, chapter 6, below.
140   *Contra* M. Viroli, 'Machiavelli and the Republican Idea of Politics', in G. Bock, Q. Skinner and M. Viroli, eds, *Machiavelli and Republicanism* (Cambridge, 1990), pp. 143–72.

cal persuasion had better know which kind of regime he is addressing. An *optimus rex* instituting *optima lex* is as much bound by natural law and right reason as would be the citizens who, in a *regimen politicum*, institute laws.

Rhetoric outside the University and Aristotle within the University

If we turn briefly to what has been called the pre-humanist rhetorical culture that began to flourish in the Italian city-republics of the early thirteenth century,[141] we find what has been called a new and distinctive form of political literature emerging, a literature of advice-books devoted to explaining the duties of a city official known as the *podestà*. These works were the compositions of *dictatores* who prepared model speeches to be imitated, like Guido Faba, as well as the more specialized treatises on city government.[142] All demonstrate a heavy reliance on the views of the Roman moralists. These were most often available to them in the same florilegia that were available to cathedral schools and students in the university arts courses. Cicero's *De officiis* was known to them from the twelfth-century *Moralium dogma philosophorum* and from the thirteenth-century compilation by Guillaume de Peyrault, *Summa virtutum et vitiorum*. The writings of these Italian *dictatores*, even before that moment when Aristotle's *Ethics* and *Politics* were made fully available in Latin, were engaged in integrating Ciceronian and Aristotelian insights, as we shall see below when we discuss the twelfth- and thirteenth-century experiences of Italian cities.[143]

Doubtless, the ideology of self-governing republican city-states of the early thirteenth century pre-dated the recovery of Aristotle's moral and political works. But of course in the twelfth- and early thirteenth-century schools and universities, what was understood as practical moral philosophy, comprised of ethics, economics and politics, also predated the recovery of Aristotle's *Ethics* and *Politics*. Aside from the Roman moralists like Cicero, we have seen that the logical and increasingly known natural-science works of Aristotle were studied for their teachings on moral and political topics. And we should not think that the teaching of Aristotelian philosophy was limited to the universities of Paris and Oxford; it was also pursued on a very large scale in thirteenth-century Italy.[144] In Italy, Aristotelian philosophy was especially connected with the study of medicine and law. The older Italian universities like Salerno, Bologna, Padua and Naples had no theology faculties, but where there were isolated courses and chairs of theology they were usually part of the faculties of arts. The teachers of Aristotelian philosophy in Italian universities were laymen and lay Aristotelianism continued to dominate philosophical teaching in Italian faculties of art until and throughout the Renaissance, well into the sixteenth century.

---

141   See further below, chapter 6.

142   For instance, the anonymous *Oculus pastoralis c.* 1220s, Orfino da Lodi's *De sapientia potestatis* (1240s), Giovanni da Viterbo's *Liber de regimine civitatum* (*c.* 1253) and Brunetto Latini's famous encyclopedic *Li livres dou trésor* (*c.* 1266, written in French).

143   Q. Skinner, 'Ambrogio Lorenzetti: the artist as political philosopher', *Proceedings of the British Academy* LXXII (1986), pp. 1–56 has argued, on the contrary, that there was no such integration, as well as that Aristotle did not come to replace Cicero and other Roman authorities.

144   As P. O. Kristeller long ago showed in *Medieval Aspects of Renaissance Learning: three essays*, ed. and trans. M. P. Mahoney (North Carolina, 1974), esp. 'Thomism and the Italian Thought of the Renaissance', pp. 29–94.

In universities across Europe, then, it appears that Aristotle came to replace Cicero as the analyst of the public sphere among arts faculty students and lecturers studying practical moral philosophy who were increasingly interested in the psychology of motivation behind political agency. But as we will see, the familiar texts of Cicero that had once been studied for eloquence would be re-read with a view to his teachings on the legitimate origin of government – like the *De inventione*, book 1 – and integrated back into an Aristotelian framework by university graduates who had entered the employ of diverse patrons to serve as their 'political theorists'. Cicero would be used by political theorists to supplement the ammunition already provided by Aristotle in order to establish normative proposals for the arrangement of secular political communities that seek not only the peaceful and self-sufficient communal life but the life which could be described as a *vivere politico*. An ongoing familiarity with Roman law and an interest in rediscovering Rome's historical legacy to a Europe experiencing increasing turmoil would ensure that Cicero *and* Aristotle could be integrated in texts that sought to justify the natural origins of government and the *de facto* arrangements of popular sovereignty.[145]

Despite the early thirteenth-century alarm on the part of church authorities that the pagan Aristotle was coming to dominate university discourse, by 1255 all the known works of Aristotle were placed on the arts faculty lecture programme at the University of Paris. The study of the 'authentic' Aristotle, as translated into Latin, was increasingly pursued by arts faculty philosophers who were concerned primarily to 'read' the texts literally to an audience of scholars, most of whom would never proceed to a higher faculty of law or theology, or even obtain a BA. Most students went to university in order to qualify for lucrative employment within the established orders of the church, government service or one of the organized professions. Their skills were meant to be utilitarian, enabling them to compose propaganda on behalf of papal, imperial or royal and civic patrons. Rigorous training in the logical analysis of texts and adversarial argument underlay all the university disciplines and the techniques of disputation were taken to be foundational for later occupations, not least for those allied to the law. The Parisian ruling that no theology should be taught in the arts faculty enabled arts faculty philosophers to read Aristotle 'literally' and allow him to speak for himself, as it were, without in the first instance trying to determine whether or not what he said was true. As we have seen, by 1255 the works of Aristotle that were read in lectures were largely translations of his logical and natural-science/philosophy books that had flooded into Europe from the later twelfth century onwards. Then to the works of logic were added not only Aristotle's *Nicomachean Ethics* (*c.* 1250 onwards) and to a much lesser degree his *Politics* (*c.* 1260 and 1265 onwards) but also his *Rhetoric* (1256 Hermannus and *c.* 1269 + Moerbeke), which seemed to follow on directly from his *Topics* and other related works of commentary by Boethius.

It appears, then, to have been the *Topics*, the *Rhetoric* and the *Ethics* rather than Aristotle's *Politics* which taught arts students of the later thirteenth century and increasingly throughout the fourteenth century, what kind of 'science' politics was meant to be. There are very few mentions or surviving manuscripts of commentaries from arts facul-

---

145   See below, chapters 3 and 4 on John of Paris and Marsilius of Padua. This argument modifies C. J. Nederman, 'Nature, Sin and the Origins of Society: the Ciceronian tradition in medieval political thought', *Journal of the History of Ideas* 49 (1988), pp. 14–24; also see C. J. Nederman, 'Nature, Justice and Duty in the *Defensor Pacis*: Marsiglio of Padua's Ciceronian impulse', *Political Theory* 18 (1990), pp. 615–37.

ties on Aristotle's *Politics* until the late fourteenth and the fifteenth centuries.'[146] But as we have seen, students in the arts faculty had already become familiar with Aristotle's different logical works where he analysed the diverse kinds of argument and proof required by different subjects, with their attendant discussions of degrees of certainty attainable in each, supplemented with his ethical and political observations in these very works. And by the end of the thirteenth century a student would know, for instance, that rhetoric was a kind of *dialectica moralis*, a kind of science whose conclusions were true in *most* cases. He would see that the rules of logic and rhetoric, which he had spent so much time acquiring, were tightly allied to the kind of 'science' Aristotle understood politics to be in the *Nicomachean Ethics* book six, on which he would by now have heard lectures. Aristotelian discourse concerning the nature of 'scientific' thought and the place of ethics and politics within an intellectual frame of practical moral philosophy was already known from his works on logic and rhetoric, so that lectures on his *Ethics* would seem like a furtherance of a perspective students had already adopted. University statutes tell us that from the later thirteenth century and during the fourteenth century, familiarity with the *Ethics* was increasingly required for BAs who had just graduated (determined) and who were then to proceed as more advanced students, lecturing to younger undergraduates but still going to the lectures of their masters. What would such a student have heard and studied?

Aristotle's *Ethics* for Medieval University Students

In book 6 of the *Nicomachean Ethics* Aristotle discusses five different 'states of mind/soul' by which the soul arrives at truth 'by affirmation and denial'. Aristotle classifies each mind-state in relation to the kind of truth each may attain, and each mind-state has a different mode of proceeding and a different object. His five mind-states are art or technical skill, scientific knowledge, prudence, wisdom and intelligence. What kind of mind-state is political thinking? The third mind-state, or mode of thinking, Aristotle calls prudence (*phronēsis*). He says that we call someone prudent if he is able to deliberate rightly about what is good and advantageous for himself, not in particular respects as, for instance, what is good for health or physical strength, but what is conducive to the good life (for man) generally. A prudent person calculates successfully with a view to some serious end, and since one deliberates about variable things and about things that can be done by oneself (this is what deliberation is), one is not in the sphere of 'scientific' thinking *per se* which deals in the realm of the necessary. Aristotle had already discussed how scientific knowledge (*epistēmē*) implies the ability to demonstrate and he refers back to his treatment in the *Posterior Analytics*.[147]

Furthermore, he distinguishes between art and prudence, saying that the class of things that admit of variation includes both things made and actions done. For Aristotle, *making* is different from *doing*, and therefore the rational quality or mind-state that is concerned with doing is different from the mind-state or rational quality concerned with making. This distinction between making and doing will reverberate throughout the later Middle Ages and find its recapitulation in Machiavelli's distinction between founding or making a state, on the one hand, and maintaining it, on the other.[148] All art, says Aristotle, deals with bringing something into existence and to pursue an art means to study how to bring into existence a thing which may either exist or not. Since art does not deal with things that exist or come into existence of necessity or according to nature, there is a sense in which art and chance operate in the same sphere. The efficient cause of such making or production lies in the maker and not in the thing made. In short, the kind of reasoning that is engaged in founding a state is not the same as the rational quality or mind-state that is required for governing it. And the kind of mind-state required for governing is called prudence, which he goes on to call a virtue rather than a science or an art.

Since it is impossible to deliberate about things that are necessarily so, prudence is not a 'science' (*epistēmē*); nor is it an art. Prudence is concerned with action whose end is doing well. Prudence is a reasoned state of mind that is capable of action with regard to things that are good and bad for man. The prudent man deliberates about means to an end, and the end is itself a practical good that can be attained in action; he *calculates* about means to the best of goods attainable by man. Prudence, then, is a *quality* that belongs to those who can envisage what is good for themselves and for people in general. One is not born with this quality but acquires it from experience. Prudence is a *virtue* rather than an art, and it is the virtue or excellence of that part of the soul that is susceptible to reason, and there are two parts of the soul so susceptible. It is the virtue of that part of the soul that deals with the variable and contingent. The part of the soul that deals with the necessary, however, is engaged in 'scientific' thinking. Prudence, however, is the virtue of that part of the soul that forms opinions. Opinions are formed with regard to the sphere of possibles or variables where something can be or cannot be, can be done or not be done. Although prudence *is* concerned with universals, that is, with the *principle* that the end of all deliberation is the good for man, prudence *as a virtue* takes cognizance of particulars. It is practical: a prudent man needs to have *some* theoretical knowledge, but to be effective in action he needs experience and practical knowledge. Hence, prudence as a virtue is concerned with conduct whose sphere is particular circumstances. And the 'science' that *co-ordinates* prudence is the 'science of politics'.

The prudent man will find it useful to acquire the art of rhetorical persuasion. But Aristotle does not identify rhetorical excellence with prudential excellence because rhetorical invention is an art or skill associated with a different, productive mind-state or rational quality from the mind-state or rational quality that engages in deliberative calculation and doing. Governing is, at best, either supplemented by productive arts or the consequence of an 'artistic' first founding.[149]

The kind of prudence that is confined to the daily administration of public affairs and deals with particular circumstances is practical and deliberative. It is called deliberative because it considers a course of action that is not yet decided and, therefore, is not necessary. A prudent man acts as the result of the deliberating process. Therefore, politics cannot be a demonstrative 'science'. It is, none the less, a kind of thinking, a state of

---

148   See below, chapter 6.

149   *Politics* I, i, 1253a30: the impulse to form a partnership of this kind is present in all men by nature; but the man who first united people in such a partnership was the greatest of benefactors. See volume 1, chapter 4 of *A History of Political Thought* on Aristotle and below, chapter 6 on Machiavelli.

mind. Aristotle implies that to be involved in deliberating for the collective good of men is a different species of knowledge from that deployed in deliberating about one's own good. Then he says something crucial to link an individual's prudence with a kind of collective prudence or political 'science'. Although people tend to call prudent those men who are concerned only with the self and the individual and therefore seek their own good, he says it is impossible to secure one's own good independently of domestic and political 'science' which seek the collective good, in family and in the 'state'. Politics, that is, political thinking about the collective human good is, then, the full realization of prudence, the latter being found also at the levels of household and individual. Political thinking or prudence is, however, an intellectual virtue, and since thought by itself moves nothing, deliberative calculation of means to a moral end must be supplemented by an agent's choosing to act in one way or another. It is here that Aristotle links thinking with desire, in so far as man as an originator of action is a union of desire and intellect. Acquiring the art of rhetorical persuasion will enable the prudent governor to motivate men to action with a view to the common good.

Aristotle mentions how people tend to speak of prudence when they discuss the collective entity 'the state'; the implication is that men tend to generalize in speech from personal prudence to deliberation about collective well-being. Hence, one aspect of 'generalized' prudence or political 'science' is controlling and directive and is called legislative science. But the other, indeed primary, aspect of prudence deals with particular circumstances and, he says, bears the name that properly belongs to both aspects: 'political science'. This is because, without the virtue of deliberative reasoning about particular circumstances and conduct, a virtue learned from experience and with a moral end in view – the good for man – the controlling and directive aspect of political science, legislating, would be inadequately carried out. One cannot legislate for a collectivity unless one has first developed virtues and learnt to be prudent from experience of particulars and deliberation on these with a moral end in view. Prudence belongs to all the forms called domestic, legislative and political 'science' and the latter may be divided into deliberative 'science' on the one hand, and judicial 'science' on the other. Prudence, in dealing with enactments, the last step done as a consequence of deliberation in particular and variable circumstances, apprehends the *ultimate* particular which cannot be apprehended by epistemic, 'scientific' knowledge.[150]

A student who had heard lectures on the *Ethics* would recognize the divisions of practical moral philosophy into individual, domestic/economic and political/civic. He would also be told that if he followed a career in the 'state' or in the church bureaucracy, and hence deliberated about means to the general, collective human good, he would find his logical and rhetorical training useful, especially if his audience were educated men in *parlement* or the papal *curia*. If they were uneducated and vulgar, he would be told that experience would count more to them than ornate and closely argued syllogisms because such an audience would want to know the consequences of actions rather than the cause of things, and hence would be satisfied with the enthymeme and example, with plausible reasons.[151] He would know that lawyers and legislators needed to be trained first in the difference between demonstrative reasoning, on the one hand, and deliberative reasoning with a moral end in view, on the other, before they took up roles

150   See volume 1, chapter 4 of *A History of Political Thought* on Aristotle.
151   See Fredborg, 'Buridan's *Quaestiones*'.

as law-makers. Most of all, he would know that a student who had not studied university 'logic' in this wide sense with its moral underpinning, would not be suitably trained to advise legislators or be able to take up judicial posts in church or 'state' hierarchies. Furthermore, Aristotle's *Rhetoric* (I, 13, 1374a–b) would have made it clear to him that legal statements, being universal and therefore general, are not applicable to each and every case but only to most. Hence, actions which should be leniently treated are cases for prudent judgement and equity, looking not to the letter of the law but to the intention of the legislator; the prudent man's judgement of particular cases according to his own developed sense of equity is what enables him, in the circumstances, to pardon human weaknesses.[152]

Lawyers versus the Arts Faculty Philosophers

But it was not accepted by everyone that the sciences called *practica*, the most sovereign being *scientia politica,* were to be taught only in the arts course curriculum, followed by the theology faculty. Disputes arose, which would last for centuries, between arts and theology moralists on the one hand, and the law faculties on the other.

Already in the thirteenth century civilian lawyers were calling themselves *politici*; but philosophers who dealt with the *science of politics* as practical moral philosophy insisted that lawyers knew nothing of the moral virtues and hence were no more than Sophists. Hence, they argued that the appropriate place to study practical moral philosophy, divided into ethics, economics and politics, was, in the first instance, in the university's arts course. There a student would read and analyse the texts of the ancient philosophers and church Fathers and from these texts he would learn how to rule himself, his family and the city. The academic argument over the 'science' of politics that was to have most effect on the future of the university itself was with respect to which expert, in arts or law, was best able to influence legislators and princes. Who was best able to apply himself to the significations of events as written down in authoritative texts from the past in order to render such texts of use to the present: someone knowledgeable in language theory, logic and modes of argument, someone familiar with human psychology and the effects of persuasive speech on men's motivations to act morally and for the collective good, or those who had lost all their morals and simply went into the employ of bureaucracies and massaged the law to suit their patrons? Academic philosophers and theologians joined forces especially against the civil lawyers in a battle for power inside and outside the university that would run from the thirteenth to the sixteenth centuries with increasing virulence.[153]

This contest would have important effects on the kinds of political theory written especially during the thirteenth and fourteenth centuries. It would affect what was said

---

152   It is also important to realize that Masters in the higher faculty of theology were also treating some of these same texts, linking them notably to other texts that dealt with the soul and with metaphysical issues. The point is that some of Aristotle's writings were doubly treated.

153   For the course of this debate in England see J. I. Catto and T. A. R. Evans, eds, *The History of the University of Oxford*, II: *Late Medieval Oxford* (Oxford, 1992). G. H. M. Posthumus Meyjes, 'Exponents of Sovereignty: canonists as seen by theologians in the late Middle Ages', in D. Wood, *The Church and Sovereignty, c. 590–1918: essays in honour of Michael Wilks* (Oxford, 1991) [= Studies in Church History, Subsidia, 9], pp.299–312, provides a useful discussion and bibliography on the opposition between theologians and lawyers.

about universalist conceptions of rule by German emperors, by monarchs, and by the papacy on the one hand, and on the other, about self-governing corporations and representative institutions. By the fourteenth century, theologians would observe that the lawyers who circled round kings like France's Charles V were bad counsellors because their vast influence on public policy was through flattery. It would be claimed that they treated Roman law as dogma rather than interpreting law in relation to the common good. They did not understand the moral principles behind the law and consequently it was the lawyers who led states into tyrannies by attributing to princes a *plenitudo potestatis*, showing themselves in favour of tyrannous absolutism.[154] Lawyers were said to be turning the prince into a God on earth (*Deus in terris*). This anti-jurist opprobrium would continue well into the future.

The New Mendicant Orders: Franciscans and Dominicans and Political Theory

We have spent a good deal of time examining the nature of the university arts curriculum. However, thus far we have not been sufficiently specific about a certain group of scholars whose interest, especially in Aristotle, would far surpass the average arts faculty lecturer or his students, with enormous consequences for the future of political theorizing. These were members of what are known as the mendicant orders, namely the Franciscans and Dominicans. The impetus for their foundation in the thirteenth century goes back to the rise of new religious orders and movements during the twelfth century, which may best be described as a reformation from below.[155] A new emphasis had come to be placed on the literal interpretation of the gospels and the Acts of the Apostles as codes of behaviour to be imitated through literal observance, in order to purify and revive what were taken to be the practices and ideals of the primitive church. For centuries, centres of religious life in medieval Europe had been monastic communities, specially endowed and set apart from secular life. To the Benedictines had been added other monastic orders such as the Cistercians, living according to St Benedict's sixth-century Rule, and the Augustinian Canons. But a new lay piety put particular stress on material poverty, and the withdrawal and contemplation that was so fundamental to the ideals of older monastic orders came to be replaced by an engaged ministry and an active apostolate that preached to the faithful. The process of adjusting the religious life to the social and economic changes that had occurred during the twelfth and thirteenth centuries was brought to a culmination by the papal establishment of the mendicant orders, namely the Franciscan and the Dominican friars.

St Francis, the founder of the Franciscans, had grown up as the son of a cloth merchant in the flourishing Italian town of Assisi. He established a Rule (*c.* 1209) for his followers in which he avoided reference to social hierarchies in an attempt to level social degrees by means of a vocabulary that raised to spiritual prominence all the social

---

154   See Coleman, 'The Science of Politics', pp. 204–6; J. Krynen, 'Les Légistes "idiots politiques": sur l'hostilité des théologiens à l'égard des juristes en France au temps de Charles V', in *Théologie et droit dans la science politique de l'état moderne* (Rome, 1991), pp. 171–98.

155   B. Bolton, *The Medieval Reformation* (London, 1983), chs 3 and 4; R. I. Moore, *The Origins of European Dissent* (Oxford, 1985).

inferiors of his day. He called upon his followers to associate with and be considered poor, feeble, vagabonds, beggars, labourers, illiterates, the powerless and the dispossessed. They were to own nothing and beg for daily subsistence in cities. He and his movement soon became enormously popular and influential.[156] There is a revision of his Rule, dated 1221 (*Regula prima*), in which his followers are admonished that they are to have no property.

> Franciscan candidates should sell all possessions and give the money to the poor; friars may not meddle in the candidate's property affairs; no one is to be called 'prior' for there is no distinction amongst friars minor; they may not accept positions of authority in houses of their employers; friars who have a trade should remain at it; their payment is never in money; otherwise, they seek alms; they may not claim ownership of any place. In general, they should have neither use nor regard for money, considering it as dust.

The *Regula prima* clearly condemns the action of brethren arrogating to themselves as an individual corporation any goods which should remain the common property of all men. The friars were voluntarily to refuse both ownership and possession of temporal goods because they believed themselves to be imitating the spiritual perfection of Christ's poverty. But Francis died without clarifying the legal aspects of the friar's relation to property, and the final version of his Rule (1223) would be revised through reinterpretation with the help of juristically minded brethren and a cardinal protector who would become pope. By the third quarter of the thirteenth century, the true owner of goods and property offered to the Franciscans was legally determined to be the papacy in lieu of Christ.[157]

About the same time, the Dominicans were established by their founder, an Augustinian canon St Dominic. His aim was to combat heresy, especially in southern France, through preaching. To succeed in preaching, Dominic thought it vital to be seen as setting an example by living a simple, more apostolic life than that of the church's ecclesiastical dignitaries. Like the Franciscans, Dominicans set up in cities, but unlike the early Franciscans, Dominicans showed an immediate appreciation of the role which universities were to play in the recruitment and development of their Order. Poverty was merely a channel of communication for Dominic, whereas for Francis it was the very purpose of his order. If the two orders were in principle very different, they rapidly borrowed aspects of organization from one another. The Franciscans, in particular, followed the Dominicans into the university. By the middle of the thirteenth century, wherever there was a town, there were friars who lived by begging for alms, and wherever there was a university, the friars established their own *studia* and then entered the university's theological faculty, against much opposition from the secular clergy who had previously established themselves as university teachers.

Although both the Franciscans and the Dominicans were mendicant orders with distinctive views on the nature of apostolic poverty, their attitudes to ownership and use of property would gradually become formalized and noticeably divergent. In this diver-

---

156   The classic study in English is M. Lambert, *Franciscan Poverty: the doctrine of absolute poverty of Christ and the apostles in the Franciscan Order, 1210–1323* (London, 1961).
157   See Coleman, 'Property and Poverty', in *CHMPT* (1988), pp. 631–37 and further bibliographical citations therein.

gence lay the foundations of two fundamentally opposing strands of political theory whose differing attitudes to property led to different doctrines about ruling. It was initially through the in-house debate between the Franciscans and Dominicans themselves, over the relationship between jurisdiction, ownership (*dominium*) and use, and their respective views on the legitimacy of ecclesiastical wealth and its relation to so-called apostolic poverty, that some of the most powerful, more general political theories would emerge to influence the remainder of the Middle Ages and well beyond. The Franciscans would argue the theocratic line that the pope had supreme jurisdiction and *dominium*, whereas ecclesiastics and kings exercise a delegated jurisdiction alone.[158] The Dominicans, on the contrary, would argue that the use of material goods could not be separated from their ownership, but that proprietary right and ownership over property was not the same as having jurisdiction over it, so that neither princes nor popes were owners of the property over which they exercised jurisdiction.[159] The Dominican Thomas Aquinas would contribute to this debate and establish foundations on which his later fellow Dominican, John of Paris, would erect a theory of individual rights to property, where he argued that the origin of property rights was in the labour of individuals, and that the 'state' was established by owners as a fiduciary power to protect these rights.

A good deal of what is recognized as later medieval political theory, to say nothing of the distinctive influence of developments in fourteenth-century philosophy and theology on European political thinking well beyond the sixteenth century, was the consequence of the intellectual efforts of Franciscans and Dominicans. Indeed, if we look to thirteenth-century Dominican *studia* and to university theology faculties where the mendicant orders had numerous distinguished masters, we see a much greater influence of Aristotle's ethical *and* political discussions penetrating their various treatises where they compared the organization of secular society with that of the church. If we cannot find many widespread or influential arts faculty commentaries on Aristotle's *Politics*, we can certainly see them proliferating in the *studia* of Dominicans where they produced literal commentaries on the *Ethics* and *Politics* as soon as these works appeared in translation.[160] Even before the Dominican William of Moerbeke had translated the entire *Politics* (*c.* 1265), Dominicans seemed interested in what he provided in the imperfect translation of book 1 and part of book 2 (*c.* 1260). And they rapidly expressed an interest in the *Politics*'s analysis and evaluation of different constitutions – monarchies/tyrannies, popular versus aristocratic constitutions – its discussion of citizenship, and its emphasis on political agency. When Thomas Aquinas, whose works we will examine in chapter 2, returned as a master in theology to the University of Paris in 1269, he worked not only on the second part of his encyclopedic *Summa Theologiae* but also on literal commentaries on Aristotle's *Ethics* and *Politics*. His teacher, the Dominican Albertus Magnus, had previously lectured at the Dominican *studium* in Cologne on Aristotle's *Ethics*. Aquinas's notes and questions on these lectures have survived. But it would be in Aquinas's theological works, for example his *Summa contra gentiles* and the *Summa Theologiae* as well

---

158   See below, chapter 3, on John of Paris. See also Coleman, 'The Two Jurisdictions'.

159   J. Coleman, 'The Intellectual Milieu of John of Paris, OP', in J. Miethke, ed., *Das Publikum politischer Theorie im 14. Jahrhundert* (Munich, 1992), pp. 173–206.

160   For a more sceptical view on the importance of the *Ethics* before the second half of the fourteenth century see G. Wieland, 'The Reception and Interpretation of Aristotle's *Ethics*', in N. Kretzmann, A. Kenny and J. Pinborg, eds, *The Cambridge History of Later Medieval Philosophy* (Cambridge, 1982), ch. 34.

as his commentary on the arts faculty core text, the *Categories*, written for Dominican students, that he would specifically refer to Aristotle's *Politics*. Many other citations from the *Politics* appear, as we might expect, in his only strictly political work, the fragmentary 'mirror for a prince', *De regno, ad regem Cypri*, written for the young king of Cyprus. In being able and willing to cite from the *Politics* books 1–3 of the complete translation in *c.* 1268 and from books 5–8 by 1271, Aquinas brought Aristotle into a scholastic synthesis that insisted that political engagement in the city was a natural goal for rational men seeking the good life, and this goal was related to man's final end, his salvation.

Well into the fourteenth century Dominicans continued to write political tracts on the powers of the pope (*De potestate papae*), comparing them to powers exercised by kings, each drawing notably on Aristotle and firmly Thomistic in their theology, but differing in their aims, emphases and methods, to provide a wide range of theories of government in church and state. They would be matched by Franciscans who likewise drew on Aristotle in distinctive ways for their range of theories. After we examine the works of Aquinas, we can observe the different uses of Aristotle in the works of the Dominican John of Paris, the Franciscan William of Ockham, and the former University of Paris arts faculty lecturer turned political ideologue, Marsilius of Padua.

2

St Thomas Aquinas

St Thomas Aquinas (1225–74) was in his own times considered neither the most important nor the most influential philosopher and theologian. There is no doubt that during the sixteenth century the Jesuits developed his many insights and these would proceed to influence the political theories of Grotius, Hooker and Locke. And in 1879 his teachings were declared the official philosophy and theology of the Roman Catholic Church by Pope Leo XIII. Any specialist who studies his writings in the context of works penned by his contemporaries might well wonder why he was not more universally revered at the end of the thirteenth century, if only because he amply shows himself to have possessed the most synthetic mind of his generation, a mind that was intimately familiar with nearly all the intellectual developments in the university and to some extent outside it, not least concerning the logic of the arts course, natural philosophy, psychology and metaphysics, ethics and politics, law and theology. And he provided, especially in his *Summa Theologiae*, a comprehensive reading of the divine and human order of things. But he was a Dominican, and in his times produced some exceedingly controversial views, not all of which were the consequence of his masterly synthesis of Aristotle's works. Some of his views, including on the material nature of human individuality, were to be condemned by the bishop of Paris, Stephen Tempier in 1277.[1] Similarly, after his death, the Franciscans brought out lists of corrections to his teachings. The attitude of Aquinas and the Dominicans to the relation between property ownership and political rule found less favour in papal circles at the time than did that of the Franciscans.

The great translator of the works of Aristotle and other ancient Greeks, the Flemish Dominican William of Moerbeke, outlived Aquinas by twelve years and when he died (1286) the translation of Aristotle into Latin was almost at an end; only the 'Economics', translated by Durand d'Auvergne in 1295, was to come.[2] By 1271 Aquinas had the complete *Politics* to add to the *Ethics,* as well as all the other Aristotelian works that had been received into the arts and theology faculties, to enable him to shape what has often been called the Christian Aristotelian world view. But it should be clear by now that Aristotelianism, from logic to metaphysics, had already provided a methodology and a perspective that had become integral to university discourse in general. The scholastic

---

1   These are listed in translation in R. Lerner and M. Mahdi, eds, *Medieval Political Philosophy* (Ithaca, NY, 1963), pp. 335–54.
2   J. Brams and W. Vanhamel, eds, *Guillaume de Moerbeke* (Leuven, 1989).

development of, for instance, Aristotle's psychology (from his *De anima*) and the distinctive scholastic explanation of the processes of human cognition by means of a theory of intellective abstraction,[3] was adopted by Aquinas. Aquinas did not suddenly discover it: he worked within it and then went beyond it.[4] Was Aquinas simply intellectually in the right place at the right time to be able to do this by reflecting on a mass of texts?

As a Dominican friar, his life was not spent in cloistered seclusion but in cities; he had contacts with princely courts (he wrote his *De regno* for the King of Cyprus and his *De regimine judaeorum* for the Duchess of Brabant); he attended ecclesiastical councils, he lectured in Dominican *studia* and in universities, and he spent time at the papal *curia*. Indeed, prior to his entry into the Dominican Order he had started his education in the liberal arts at the Benedictine monastery at Montecassino. Not only had he seen monastic life at first hand, but he then went to study the liberal arts at the University of Naples, which had been founded by Emperor Frederick II. He was born into a family belonging to the lesser nobility in Aquino near Naples, a part of the kingdom of Sicily where Muslim, Jewish and Latin cultures mingled. His family had hoped for his future in the Benedictine Order and his brothers actually imprisoned him for a year when they learned of his desire to join the Dominicans. But they relented and Aquinas made his way to Paris to study with the German Dominican Albert the Great. Thereafter, he went to Cologne with Albert, then returned to Paris to study theology, subsequently made his way to the Dominican house in Naples, was assigned to the Dominican priory in Orvieto, then Rome, Viterbo, back to Paris, then Naples, and, when on his way to attend the Council of Lyons, he died. Over the years he spent a tremendous amount of time on the road travelling from Italy to Germany to France and back.[5] His massive literary output is all the more remarkable. It testifies not only to his own practical involvement in disputes concerning his own Dominican Order but also to his concern to establish a more enduring, indeed, universal theory of the political.[6] His theory re-establishes a natural and rational mode of organizing social living so that men would be justified in actively affirming their commitment to achieving their natural ends in the public arena.

There is a sense in which one needs to know nothing about his own life and times to understand his philosophical and political arguments.[7] But truly to understand why he argued the ways he did, one needs to know some of the alternative contemporary views available to him, not all of which appear as contrary arguments requiring resolution in his *Summa Theologiae*. Alternative perspectives were not simply views that floated above the realities of lived life. They were crucially embedded in ways of living it. In becoming an astute commentator on virtually all of Aristotle's works, Aquinas made a choice that some contemporary theologians had not explicitly made. In matters that concerned the nature of the human soul and its modes of access to the truths of reality, Franciscans in particular favoured aspects of a Christian Platonism that was by far the more fundamental and long-lived underpinning of Christian philosophy and theology from the time of

3   See below, p. 87.

4   J. Coleman, *Ancient and Medieval Memories* (Cambridge, 1992), pp. 328–460.

5   J. A. Weisheipl, *Friar Thomas d'Aquino* (Oxford, 1974; revd edn Washington DC, 1983); more briefly, A. Kenny, *Aquinas* (Oxford, 1980), ch. 1.

6   See J. I. Catto, 'Ideas and Experience in the Political Thought of Aquinas', *Past and Present* 71 (1976), pp. 3–21.

7   See P. T. Geach, 'Aquinas', in G. E. M. Anscombe and P. T. Geach, *Three Philosophers: Aristotle, Aquinas, Frege* (Oxford, 1973), pp. 65–125; B. Davies, *The Thought of Thomas Aquinas* (Oxford, 1992); J. Finnis, *Aquinas: Moral, Political, and Legal Theory* (Oxford, 1998).

the early church Fathers, especially Augustine, until Aquinas's own time. But Aquinas and his Dominican Order chose Aristotle. The condemnation of 219 propositions by the bishop of Paris, Tempier, in 1277, more than fifteen of which are generally regarded as reflecting Aquinas's teaching, initially checked the spread of Thomism.[8] As a Dominican, Aquinas also made certain choices as to how, for instance, reason and law should be seen as playing themselves out in human society under the aegis of God's will, and his conclusions were not mere intellectual exercises in philosophical coherence. Those more influenced by Christian Platonism found his views intolerable. Furthermore, in writing a defence of mendicant poverty and of the rights of mendicants to teach in the universities of Paris and elsewhere (*Contra impugnantes cultum et religionem*), his views affected his order 'on the ground'. Many of his ethical and political views directly favoured the rational authority behind constitutionalism rather than theocratic/absolutist perspectives on government and human nature, and a contemporary who read them would know in which ideological camp such a mind could be enlisted.[9]

But he was also of his times and many of his views, for instance his attitude to Jews, his belief in the natural inferiority of women, his belief in a natural social hierarchy, his defence of burning heretics, do not immediately endear him to liberal, Western sensibilities any more than do Aristotle's 'little local prejudices' make the ancient Greek a desirable neighbour in a pluralistic society. But Aquinas, like Aristotle, presented much larger ethical and political theories which, when applied to different times and evolving attitudes, find room for the *historicity* of many practices and prejudices. In insisting that humans should use their critical, rational intellects in a bid to resolve problems of individual and social behaviour, Aquinas's optimism about the human capacity to identify goals and pursue them to some degree of satisfaction places politics centrally on the agenda.

Aquinas's writings provide a true *summa* of nearly one hundred and fifty years of medieval intellectual enquiry and practical developments in the sphere of politics, but what this means for him is much larger than the modern term ' political' often connotes. Hence, what he says about sovereignty, constitution-building, elections, popular representation, legislation and adjudication, public and private authority, property, taxation, the common good, is always and often explicitly tied in with his wider philosophy of man, his methodology for discovering truth, his attitude to nature including the inanimate, and of course, his faith in that which transcends the natural: God. We are asked to deal not only with a philosophy of humankind but also with a philosophy of natural order in the entire universe.[10] We are not asked to deal with a series of proposed positive laws backed by more or less enduring positive institutions somehow divinely sanctioned. We are asked to deal with a metaphysics of the political.

It is always pointed out how immensely influenced Aquinas was by the writings of Aristotle.[11] This is true. But he was also influenced by Latin translations of distinguished Arabic and Jewish commentaries on Aristotle, and especially by the writings of both

---

8   On the early fourteenth-century defence of Aquinas by Dominicans against his critics see J. Dunbabin, *A Hound of God: Pierre de la Palud and the Fourteenth-century Church* (Oxford, 1991).

9   See A. Black, *Political Thought in Europe 1250–1450* (Cambridge, 1992), ch. 1 on Aquinas compared with others.

10   See Kenny, *Aquinas*, esp. chs 2 and 3.

11   J. Dunbabin, 'The Reception and Interpretation of Aristotle's *Politics*', in N. Kretzmann, A. Kenny and J. Pinborg, eds, *The Cambridge History of Later Medieval Philosophy* (Cambridge, 1982), pp. 723–37.

Avicenna and Averroes. He is therefore heavily indebted to a kind of neo-platonized Aristotle, and by his own debates with arts faculty Aristotelians who were even more willing than he was to adopt, for instance, Averroes' various interpretations of Aristotle. At the very end of his life Aquinas was intensely engaged in sorting out an acceptable Aristotle for Christians against more radical 'Averroist' opponents who proposed the view that the world was not created and that religious faith and rational enquiry could produce two, irreconcilable truths.[12] Furthermore, he had to accommodate the neoplatonism of perhaps the most important Latin church Father, St Augustine, to his own rather different understanding of the consequences of the Fall for human reason.[13]

Philosophy of Man

During the thirteenth century, the question 'what is reality like and how do humans know it as it is?' constituted one of the major scholastic set questions with which every university student and teacher had to deal. Such questions and answers received even more sophisticated examination in theology faculties, so that when Aquinas wrote his *Summa Theologiae* as an encyclopedic exposition of questions and answers, he did not set his own agenda. Here he systematized the questions and answers given by others and himself in a more thorough way than did most of his contemporaries, and in that systematization he was able to include more interlinking answers, fitting them into a metaphysical whole, than anyone else in his generation.[14] He was helped in this by having become a tremendously sophisticated Aristotelian. In terms of man's purpose and the means to its achievement in this life, Aristotle had provided a full analysis in the *Nicomachean Ethics*, preceded by relevant compatible insights in his various works on logic, natural philosophy, psychology, epistemology and metaphysics, and Aquinas absorbed this completely.

Reality and Metaphysics

When Aquinas, like Aristotle, speaks about reality, he assumes that nature, that is, the natural world, the cosmos, and man as part of that natural whole, is somehow ordered to natural ends. Aquinas, therefore, accepts Aristotle's teleology. Human beings are part of a reality that is given, ordered, not chaotic or unknowable, and humans think about it and communicate their thoughts to one another. Aquinas follows the 'old logic' school text, Aristotle's *Categories*, in saying that it makes no difference to the reality or occurrence of a thing whether one person has affirmed that it will happen and another denies it. As Aristotle explained in his *Categories*[15] and as every student studying the liberal arts would have known:

---

12   This is what used to be called the doctrine of double truth; see F. Van Steenberghen, *Thomas Aquinas and Radical Aristotelianism* (Washington, DC, 1980).

13   In general, see the useful collection of essays in N. Kretzmann and E. Stump, eds, *The Cambridge Companion to Aquinas* (Cambridge, 1993). Some of my analyses below differ from views expressed in this collection.

14   The analysis below takes further J. Coleman, 'MacIntyre and Aquinas', in J. Horton and S. Mendus, eds, *After MacIntyre* (Cambridge, 1994), pp. 65–90.

15   See volume 1, chapter 4 of *A History of Political Thought*; also Aquinas, *In perihermenias* 1 *lectio* 14.4–15.1.

things will be the same whether this has been affirmed or denied since the course of reality or something's existing or not existing does not change just because of our affirming or denying it. This is because it is not the truth of our indicative sentences that causes the reality but rather, *reality causes the truth of our statements*. So that it makes no difference to what is happening now whether somebody affirmed or denied it a thousand years ago or indeed ever.

Aquinas interprets Aristotle as having argued correctly *from the truth about things to the truth about indicative sentences*; truth in expressions is related to the ways things are or are not in reality. Humans have certain cognitive powers which enable them to transform their sense experience of the world into thoughts. They not only take in information by means of sense perception but they also deduce conclusions from logical premises. Truth is the conformity of human cognition to reality. But there are degrees of completeness and certainty we can attain through our various modes of thinking. Reasoned accounts of reality may be given in our propositions but, following Aristotle, Aquinas too holds that there are different degrees of epistemic justification: both hold that there are premises of which we, as humans, are absolutely and necessarily certain, and there are others of which we are less certain and which only hold true for the most part. There are certain truths which strike humans everywhere as foundational, as first principles known in themselves (per se).[16] And there are others which depend on contingent circumstances where we either generalize from particular experiences and assert a probable truth that holds for now and in like circumstances, or we examine whether a theoretical premise actually meets our experience of the 'facts'.

From the logic of the *Posterior Analytics*, Aquinas argues that there are certain premises which cannot be demonstrated or achieved through inference (drawing a conclusion deductively from premises) but are simply known by humans, and these first principles, known *per se*, are then the causes of our conceptual conclusions. This constitutes both Aristotle's and Aquinas's foundationalism. But first principles are not floating about up there and beyond us. They must arise in us through the way we experience and think about the world. Hence, our logical ways of arguing and our ways of knowing what there is, rest on what is called a metaphysical realism, a set of first principles, the truth of which humans cannot logically prove but which they accept as the starting point of whatever else they can logically prove. Indemonstrable propositions or first principles express the most basic, metaphysically immediate facts about reality for all humans. Because they are not specific to cultures, humans everywhere cannot fail to see their necessity and they are graspable by everyone. Both Aristotle and Aquinas hold that such first principles or immediate indemonstrable propositions are not obvious to everyone in their daily living of life. To be directly aware of them as necessary truths takes effort, and living side-tracks most of us or most of us cannot be bothered.

Aquinas, like Aristotle, assumes there is some kind of unconscious metaphysics that humans as humans share and use when they know things and that this is presupposed in our subsequent descriptive theories of knowing. Epistemology and the logic of thinking and speaking rests on a prior unconscious metaphysics. Aquinas explains this by saying that there is a notion of actual existence that is more basic than logical existence. Whenever we say that something exists in the sense of 'is true' or 'is the case', or that there is

16 See below, pp. 105–6, on natural law, e.g. the precept: pursue the good and avoid the evil.

something that belongs to the kind we are talking about, there is for us a *prior sense of being* implied which is akin to 'is there or alive'. Aquinas notes that the Latin verb *esse* can be used to express existence in many ways. For both Aristotle and Aquinas, actual existence is intuited as a first principle that is indemonstrable, or, as Aristotle put it in that other 'old logic' arts faculty school text the *De interpretatione*, 'the necessary and not necessary are first principles of everything's either being or not being and it is clear that what is of necessity is in actuality, so that if things which always are, are prior, then also actuality is prior to capability (possibility).'[17] What kinds of things always and necessarily 'are' and therefore are actual existents in their own right?

Naming, Natures and Actual Existents

It must be clear to anyone reading this, that our own education today provides almost no help in penetrating this kind of discourse. To understand where Aquinas is coming from we would need to study Latin grammar and logic in the ways students did in the medieval arts faculties. Their education began with a theory of language and its relation to the ways humans conceptualize reality and speak about their ideas. Anyone who had studied grammar and logic based on late antique Latin grammarians and Aristotle's logical writings would be aware of the argument, used by Aquinas, that naming does not have signification by nature. Nouns or names are conventionally imposed, thinking came before grammars, but conventional signification *does* fit the natures of things.[18] Every name (where a name or noun like 'man' is predicated as a universal, of many) signifies some determinate nature, for instance, human being, and there needs to be an individual in the mind as a concept to which the name or noun refers, the concept in the mind itself referring to something in the world which does not have to be present at the time of the concept being thought of or it being named. Nouns first signify our concepts and thereafter the world, and such signification is without time, so that it makes no difference to the truth of a sentence at what time a name or noun is applied. Nouns or names are conventionally and historically imposed but they are *ahistorical* in their signification. They signify something as if it were something that exists in its own right.

What exists in its own right is an actual existent, not merely a logical existent. Such an actual existent is a genuine individual, a human being or any other individual substance that is a something. According to Aristotle and Aquinas, nothing can just be, it must be a something, even though something that exists actually can come to exist in another way: a stone as a something can become a statue when sculpted, as a something else. Like Aristotle, Aquinas distinguishes between that which exists potentially and that which exists actually. For a particular something to be a something it must have the universal nature of all somethings named by the noun. Universal natures are actual existents. To think them or speak them does not mean that upon opening one's eyes, the thing is there, present and existing. But for one to be able to think them, and for the thought to be true, at some time or other one had to experience the individual as present and existing which has the universal nature of all somethings named by the same noun.

---

17 Aquinas, *In perihermenias* 1 *lectio* 14.8 and 14.11. In general, see C. Martin, ed., *The Philosophy of Thomas Aquinas: introductory readings* (London, 1988), with extracts and discussions, esp. pp. 153–77.
18 Aquinas, *In perihermenias* 1 *lectio* 4.11.

Otherwise, the thought would be a chimera, a mental fiction without being capable of conforming to the real world.

When nouns as conventionally established signifiers of the natures of things are employed, what kind of 'thing' are they signifying to be a thing's nature? Aquinas, like Aristotle, starts from reality rather than from language. He says that there is something in virtue of which Socrates or any other named individual is a human being. The essence or nature of man, human nature, is not a Platonic form that is separable from individuals: natures do not float separately in or above the world. Aquinas insists that it is useful to speak of the nature of a thing but not as a something which we extract and display and point to as a thing, but rather the form or essence or nature of a thing is a functional expression signifying, for instance, what being a man is.[19] Human natures are actual only when they exist in an individual who actually exists and acts in a peculiarly human way. We can speak of human nature as a consequence of observing the capacities of and tendencies in human behaviour. This specifically human behaviour is not simply moved by unconscious drives that men share with other animals. It is behaviour that is voluntarily undertaken, deliberated upon, thought of and actively chosen to achieve certain goals or ends.

Natures and Definitions

It is by observing human tendencies, acts, 'practices', that *we* grasp the nature of what it is to be human and therefore are able to give a definition of what is human. In terms of cognitive psychology, Aquinas speaks of mentally stripping the sense-perceptible aspects of external things from their original matter in order to produce what is called the intelligible species, which are the primary contents of the mind. Things outside the mind are potentially intelligible to us but they must be processed by the soul to become actually intelligible, the process being described in terms of the reception of forms abstracted from sense perceptibles. This is a kind of cognitive encoding that we engage in to make something actually intelligible to the intellect. In this way we arrive at the natures of corporeal things, and natures are abstractions which are referred to in our definitions. The definition does not change over time. As for Aristotle, so too for Aquinas, a definition is 'a set of words (*logos*) which indicates the essence or nature (of a subject)'.[20] Definitions mirror, in conventional language, the nature or essence. Definitions have no history, and when one gives a definition, say of man or doctor, one is predicating a genus of a subject, one is placing the thing to be defined in a genus and adding the differentiae. For Aristotle, as for Aquinas, genus and differentiae are among those things that are without qualification more intelligible and so absolutely universal; therefore, the elements of a definition must be prior to and more intelligible absolutely than any subject whose essence is thereby expressed. This is a realist (and not a materialist) understanding of definition and it is fundamental to Aquinas's way of thinking. There can only be one definition of a subject, and in describing the fixed and universal nature of a thing which is timeless and not open to historical alteration, we are allowing definition to function by providing us with unitary subjects of discourse.

19   Aquinas, *Commentary on the Metaphysics* VII, *lectio* 2 .
20   Aquinas, *Commentary on the Metaphysics*, V *lectio* 10.4.

When we observe human capacities and tendencies in order to define human nature, we are doing something more than passively observing what happens in acts. Aquinas says we are observing tendencies or intentions that are there and not only created in our minds from some constant repetition of the conjunction of events. The nature of something is not to be confused with a thing's accidents, whether someone has a snub or red nose, and accidents are not existents at all and certainly not in their own right. To speak of human nature we are referring to what is essentially human according to a definition of human being and this definition includes a person being a material thing. Humans are composite beings, as a species they have what he calls souls joined to bodies. The essence or nature of human being includes matter but not *this* matter. The nature or essence of the human being is a combination of a life force that is subject to mortality; a set of unconscious natural, biological drives which keep each alive, fed, procreating; a capacity to desire and to reflect rationally or consciously on experience and deliberately to make choices concerning various means to achieve what are recognized as peculiarly human ends; and even a capacity to think beyond ourselves and to conclude that we are not the centre of the universe. This understanding of human nature will be fundamental to our understanding of Aquinas's discussion of the natural law in his famous 'Treatise on Laws' in his *Summa Theologiae*.[21] All this is actualized, put into active life, when we are born as individual bodies which are constantly changing. The essence or nature of the human race is made individual in Socrates whose material body is constantly changing as he grows older. Socrates' individual essence, the nature of his humanness, cannot be defined to include *this matter now*, but matter or body in general.

Anything of a certain kind or essence or nature has, by definition, the properties, powers and tendencies which belong to that essence. From these follow the thing's specific or essential activities. Aquinas, like Aristotle, says that the only way *we* can describe or think of human capacities or tendencies to act in certain ways is by observing specific performances or practices and therefore tendencies are described teleologically by means of a series of causes leading to an end which is implicitly or explicitly grasped by the agent, prior to the performance.[22] For Aquinas, the capacities of an agent as a certain kind of essence or nature are determined by the *way* it has actual existence.

Substantial Form and Corporeal Individuation

Following Aristotle, Aquinas explains that matter is not anything specific and separable and different from made-up substances. Matter is not a kind of thing and *we* cannot properly be aware of matter in itself except by considering change.[23] Matter is simply that in anything which can become something else. At any time matter will be some substance in virtue of what Aquinas calls some *substantial form*. The substantial form is defined as that in virtue of which this lump of matter is a substance of this kind and not of another kind. According to Aquinas, the substantial form of humans as well as of animals is the soul or psyche. Aristotle, in the *De anima*, had called the soul the *entelechy* of the body, the entelechy being the formative principle of the body. For Aquinas, each

21   See below, pp. 105–6.
22   Aquinas, *Commentary on the Metaphysics*, VII *lectio* 2.16–36 and *De veritate*, 10.4.
23   Following Aristotle, *Physics*; Aquinas, *Commentary on the Metaphysics* VII *lectio* 2.16.

of us is a human being in virtue of the substantial form or soul. What individuates one person from another, what makes one human different from another, is that each is a different lump of stuff but with the same human form. The form in virtue of which each human is human is an individual, too, when individualized in a single person. Each person has an individual substantial form in a distinct lump of matter. The human soul should be understood as the actuality of its body, identical in its essence and potencies, so that the soul of each man is immattered in this or that particular body. Each man's intellectual capacities are to be considered as part of the soul–body complex. Anything that humans may know, even in the most abstract of terms, depends in the first instance on a particular man's body's sensible response to the world of particular things. Souls are differentiated *per corpora* and the degree of perfection in that supreme factor of the soul, the intellective, depends on the degree of perfection in the *complexio corporis*.

This is Aquinas's radical theory of corporeal individuation. Each human knows that of which he is capable by sensually experiencing the world and coming to general conclusions through sensed experience. Matter, then, for Aquinas, is the principle of individuation.[24] As a form, the substantial form is formally identical with all others of the kind so that in so far as we are human we are not different from one another; our difference is in the fact that we are different lumps of matter that are informed by a human psyche which has no gender as such.

Aquinas discussed how each person's individuating intelligence, each person's unique understanding, must be retained as individual even though each man is considered as part of the human species with universally shared characteristics. He asked[25] how, when we speak of the act of understanding, do we make this act the act of a particular person? Not only does he argue, radically for his time, that there must be as many individual souls as there are individual bodies; he also argues that my intellectual activity might differ from yours thanks to our different sense images, so that the image of stone in my imagination is one thing and its image in your imagination, another. But the sense image of stone is not what informs our recipient understandings. Rather, what informs our understanding is what he calls the intelligible species[26] which is abstracted from the particular sense image. This means that it is the nature, the intelligible idea of the stone that all of us understand in the same way, even though we each perceive individual stones by means of their sense images. The very natures of things we experience are constant, there to be abstracted by the activity of minds acting individually on the basis of their images derived from such experiences. Hence, the knower is an individual and his knowledge is an individual piece of knowledge, but this does not preclude what he knows from being something universal or general, that is a nature. We *understand* natures but *sense* particulars.

To recapitulate: matter is not a *this* something except in virtue of its form by which it comes actually to exist. Because nothing in the world can just be (it always must be a something), what the something is, is a substantial form immattered in this individual.

But note that the substantial form of a distinct lump of matter which is Socrates, is *not* the same as the nature or essence of Socrates. The nature functionally defines what his being a human is, which includes Socrates having a body but not *this* body now. Nor is

24 ST Ia 75–6.
25 ST Ia 76.
26 See below, p. 94.

the nature or essence of being human the peculiarly human soul. The nature of 'man' is a certain way of acting and tending in the world which is encapsulated by the definition of the nature of man.

Being and Essence

Aquinas goes beyond Aristotle by emphasizing in a way that Aristotle did not the *distinction* between natures or essences and existence. Aquinas appears to have filled in Aristotle's oblique references to the operations of *Nous* both at the beginning and at the end of human cognition. At the beginning, Aristotle spoke of an intuitive awareness we have of the existence of something as present but not, as yet, of a *knowledge* of what it is as a something. *What* it is will come from induction. At the beginning, *Nous* is an intuitive perception of particulars that grasps the *infimae species*, the lowest or earliest universal or class by which individuals can be known to us,[27] indicating that we are aware that a something is present, and then induction enables us to have a concept of what it is. At the other end, *Nous* apprehends definitions which cannot themselves be proved by logical demonstration, and at this end the activity of *Nous, theoria*, is a mental observation that Aristotle thinks is more perfect than demonstrative and deductive reasoning. Aquinas, however, spends much more time precisely distinguishing between essences or natures on the one hand, and the act of being or existence of things, on the other, and he explicitly claims that in all creatures there is a *real distinction* between a thing's nature and its being. It is this real distinction between essence/nature and being/existence which distinguishes God from his creatures.[28]

For Aquinas, natures do not have existence except in individuating matter. The composite of form and matter is made actual by existence and therefore existence is the ultimate actuality of every finite thing and is always distinct from the thing's nature. We engage different mental activities when, on the one hand, we apprehend a thing's nature, and on the other, when we apprehend its existence. Here, it is the influence of the religious beliefs of Muslim and Jewish commentators on Aristotle, and neo-platonist theories of participation, that conditioned many scholastic theological discussions of the divine cause of the world's existence. For them as for Aquinas, the world received its existence from God. For Aquinas, God is the first efficient creative cause and as the first instance of Being, the divine nature is that to which all other beings refer. No created thing could have Being as its nature, since every creature's being is other than its nature. This is reflected in the way humans come to have a knowledge of a nature, on the one hand, and of existence, on the other. Aquinas starts from the existential actuality that all sensible things receive from something else. All naturally created things are linked in a hierarchy of existential being, and to Aquinas, existence is the highest actuality.

Existential 'being' is, for Aquinas, an analogical concept, by which he means that it can be applied in different ways to mean different things. Things exist in different modes which are somehow proportional to one another. To say 'God is' and 'the world is' takes 'is' to mean different but related things. There is an *analogy* between the way an uncreated

---

27   NE VI, ii, 1143b1–5.
28   See the somewhat differing discussions of N. Kretzmann, 'Philosophy of Mind' and S. MacDonald, 'Theory of Knowledge' in Kretzmann and Stump, *The Cambridge Companion to Aquinas*, chs 5 and 6.

first cause exists and the way a created universe exists, but they are not identical. As we shall see, Aquinas develops a natural theology which is based on analogical thinking where humans predicate attributes of God that pertain to things known in the created world. He argues that by natural reason, humans conclude that there must be a first efficient uncaused cause and a being that is necessary rather than contingent. Nature is shown to our reason as guided towards goals *by* something whose being/existence is uniquely united with its understanding – outside and above natural change. This, for Aquinas, is an agent *extrinsic* to nature, that is pure actuality and not mixed with matter or potentiality as are all creatures. From experience and rational reflection, Aquinas thinks it is possible to derive a being that is not caused or moved by another, and this would be an eternal, unqualified, necessary, purely and wholly existing being which is identical with its self-understanding. Subsistent entities in the created universe are linked in a hierarchy of actualized being: the lowest member of a higher genus is always found just above the highest member of a lower genus so that, for instance, animals are found above plants. By thinking analogically, humans are able to reason from diversity to unity, from actual existences arranged hierarchically to that whose essence and existence are not distinct. The one Necessary Being has no essence or nature except that it be necessary being, and this is its existence, without potentiality, unchangeable, and unified. This is God. But things in the world exist according to their own natures and their natures are found to be ranked.

Cause and Effect

In his *Metaphysics* Aristotle had spoken of a Prime Mover as a separate substance and as an efficient cause, originating motion rather than bestowing existence on creatures. But for Aquinas, God is the first efficient creative cause, the first instance of being to which all other beings are referred; hence, finite beings move towards a pure perfection, an infinite, what is called God. Existing is the effect of the first and most universal cause, God. In having created a universe of diverse beings, each moving towards its own end or perfect state, God can be understood as having established a hierarchy based upon the degree of perfection that each nature can attain. Creation in hierarchy is an idea, the result of an internal development of *our* thinking, a philosophical insight: it is not a result of external revelation. Human reason discovers this but it also discovers that it cannot achieve its perfection through reason alone. Aquinas takes the observation that we experience the world and then think about what we experience in terms of cause and effect, to be evidence that we are enclosed in a meaningful whole which extends *beyond* our intellectual capacities to grasp the whole solely through the efforts of self-motivated thinking. Following Aristotle in book 1 of the *Nicomachean Ethics*, Aquinas agrees that we start by knowing what is knowable to *us* as the kinds of beings we are, but what is known absolutely is, at least initially, hidden from us. There are limits to our cognitive access to reality and through natural reason we come to be aware of this limitation.[29]

29   The distinction between Aristotle and Aquinas is evident here in that Aristotle can be read as understanding man's ultimate end as an intrinsic good, whereas for Aquinas it is clearly extrinsic. For interesting modern interpretations of Aristotle as thinking of *eudaimonia* as an extrinsic good, or as either a dominant or inclusive doctrine, see T. Nagel, 'Aristotle on *Eudaimonia*', pp. 7–14 and J. L Ackrill, 'Aristotle on *Eudaimonia*', pp. 15–33 in A. O. Rorty, ed., *Essays on Aristotle's Ethics* (Berkeley, 1980).

But there is no limit to our natural *desire* to know. In contrast to Augustine's complaint about man's vice of curiosity, his vain desire, cloaked in the name of knowledge (*Confessions* X), to seek knowledge for its own sake, Aquinas does not think that God and the human soul are alone worthy of being known. For Aquinas, and for the entire scholastic tradition that had developed from the twelfth century onwards, philosophy is both legitimate and praiseworthy, originating in[30] human nature itself and its desire for perfection. As Aristotle had said, all humans marvel at things and desire to know the causes of what they see. And for Aquinas, it is only by the human intellect, by man's rational nature, that he has the capacity to turn to his origin and cause. Man's search to know the cause of all, ends in the first cause and in perfect knowledge, but philosophy cannot attain this end. Man's history shows him to have made only a gradual progress in the knowledge of causes, and with Augustine Aquinas holds that we can only know God's effects in the world and *that* there is a universal cause.

Grace Added to and Perfecting, Not Destroying, Nature

But because the way humans come to know anything depends on sense experience, and God is not perceptible by the senses, to know God *as* the ultimate good or end is not open to self-motivated intellectual achievement. To attain man's perfect end, the vision of God, requires supernatural grace. Intellective powers need fortification, grace added to nature. Hence, Aquinas's famous dictum that grace does not destroy nature. But grace *presupposes* nature, and faith *presupposes* natural knowledge, which turns Augustine's perspective on its head.[31] For Augustine, and those medievals influenced by him, *credo ut intelligam*, I believe *in order that* I may know. For Aquinas, 'the truths about God which St Paul says we can know by our natural powers of reasoning – that God exists, *for example* [and there are others] – are not numbered among the articles of faith, but are presupposed to them. For faith presupposes natural knowledge, just as grace does nature'.[32]

Sense Origin of Knowing

Both Aristotle and Aquinas accept that reality is fixed and ordered and is as it is, and also that humans share a particularly human way of thinking about what there is, so that there is a species-specific uniformity in how we know what there is to know. At the level of conceptualizing reality, human thinkers know the same universals and this demonstrates to both Aristotle and Aquinas that there is a universal language of thought that is species-specific, prior to any conventionally established language, be it written or spoken. And for both, all human conceptualization, all our general knowledge, has its origin in sense experience. Both insist on the importance of 'observation' by the senses as the origin of knowledge. In accepting this, Aquinas was rejecting Muslim neo-platonism, which argued that the intellect of the human soul needed to have what was intelligible

---

30   Following Aristotle's *Metaphysics* I, 1–4.
31   See volume 1, chapter 6 of *A History of Political Thought* on Augustine.
32   ST Ia. 2.2 ad 1 and 1.8 ad 2.

to it impressed on it from some extrinsic and separate, higher (divine) intellect. He was also rejecting Plato's view of innate 'ideas' in the human soul whose cognitive awareness of these forms was darkened by the soul's union with the body.

Aquinas's discussion of human nature in relation to how each of us lives our lives, a discussion which is elaborated especially in the central parts of the *Summa Theologiae*, shows him to be engaged in a massively impressive recapitulation of themes and variations on Aristotle's *Categories, De interpretatione, Topics, Metaphysics* and the *De anima*. As a consequence of a discussion of the soul, he shows it functioning in the world of Aristotle's *Nicomachean Ethics*. Aquinas wrote the middle parts of the *Summa* about the same time as he wrote his commentaries on the *Ethics*. He goes beyond Aristotle especially where certain issues were left undecided in the final tenth book.[33]

Aquinas provides a coherent re-presentation of Aristotle's discussion of perception and conceptualization in the *De anima* when he treats the question: how can we ever think conceptually of our sensual experiences?[34] How do we intellectually respond to what we feel? It is not a question of how sense data get into our heads from the outside, but rather a discussion of what has to happen *in us* when we are affected by the world. Following the by-now traditional scholastic analysis of cognition, he describes what is called the sensitive part of the soul which is caused to change by objects which it apprehends or perceives. The cause is outside but the alteration is inside. In response to the material characteristics or external accidents of external things, the soul's internal senses and imagination set up an outline or image of the thing. As Aristotle explained, sensing and imagining are re-presentations according to the capacity of sense perception. It all happens within the soul/mind and an image is set up which is *like* the things sensually experienced out there. Aquinas says, as does Aristotle, that it is not necessary that a likeness have the same manner of existing as that of which it is a likeness. Through the soul's sense powers we are aware of an individual thing through our sense organs having been affected by something's determinate dimensions, colour etc., but these are not *in* the sensitive soul *as* colours etc., but as their cognitive encoding representations.

But to say that someone has an image or likeness in his imagination of what his sense organs have experienced is not to say he *knows* what he experiences. To know or be intellectually aware of a something is to have a concept, a thought, a form which is universal, like the concept 'man'. When we think intellectually we think in terms of the inmost nature of that kind of thing which is to be found in the individuals sensed. We think about natures of things and we sense particulars. When we think we have an immaterial awareness of material things. Our thoughts are *of* the world by means of representative likenesses; the intellect comes to be aware of the nature or essence of a thing by means of its likeness which is its own medium of awareness, a creation of intellect in response to what there is beyond itself. Our cognitive faculties are in a state of receptive potentiality with respect to their proper objects. Although the intellect depends for its data on the operation of our sense organs, the processing of the data does not use any body at all in a direct way.[35] The internalization process of sensory cognition

33 See A. Donagan, 'Thomas Aquinas on Human Action', in Kretzmann, Kenny and Pinborg, *The Cambridge History of Later Medieval Philosophy*,ch. 33.
34 Aquinas, *De veritate* 10.4–6; ST Ia 75–83.
35 ST Ia 78.4 ad 4 and Ia 84.6, 84.7; 85.1; in modern terminology, this is equivalent to arguing that mind as function is not the same as the brain, the bodily organ that functions in the ways it does.

therefore 'detaches' the sense perceptible aspects of external things from their original matter. And when we think of the nature, the form, the essence and its tendencies, we do so as something existing in flesh and bone but not in *this* flesh or in *these* bones.

Aquinas describes the intellect as having two distinct but interrelated powers.[36] There is what he (and other scholastics) called the *agent intellect*, which is active and productive, acting on internal sense images to produce intelligible species or natures. Then there is the *possible intellect*, a receptive 'part' of the soul, which functions by receiving forms that have been abstracted from sense perceptibles and are made actually intelligible by the light of the active intellect. The possible intellect receives the forms as actually intelligible in virtue of the agent intellect, but they are as likenesses of determinate things and it cognizes them as natures. But, as we have already seen, natures do not have existence except in individuating matter. With Aristotle (and *contra* Plato), Aquinas insists that it is natural for us to have cognition of natures but not as they are in individuating matter; rather, as they are abstracted from matter by intellect's consideration. Intellection, then, is a cognition of things in their universality.[37] As for Aristotle, the only way that we can be aware of anything and think about it is by first having sensed it; but thinking is not sensing, although they are related. The intellect's way of cognizing something is also different from the thing's own way of existing. This does not mean intellect's cognition is untrue and not in conformity with reality. Intellect considers specific natures of material things but without their individuating principles, their matter, having a part in the specific nature. The intelligible species, our concepts, are intellect's means of accessing individuals. Intellect knows individuals *through* their natures existing in particulars.[38]

When the intellect forms natures (intelligible species) as conceptual likenesses of things (the result of induction), it then goes on to judge the thing it has grasped 'by affirmation and denial' and this logical judgement is its own activity. In its first apprehension the intellect does not acquire a complete cognition of the thing, only a something as present or not. It then acquires intellective cognition of the thing's properties, accidents and dispositions associated with it. The first judgement made is as to whether something actually exists or not. Intellectual judgement, thereafter, is characterized as the correct or incorrect application to reality of definitions, which decides whether the definition is true or false. The truth is a match of thing and intellect.[39] But we must remember that there is a difference between the way things exist and the way we, as humans, come to know them. *We* have to start from the senses, reasoning inductively, and then we engage in deductive inference: that is simply how we operate in the world. But the real, as actual existents, already is, whether or not we perceive it or affirm it or deny it. Reality comes before us.

Aquinas then places the things of nature as existents before the divine intellect, that is, the creator cause of there being the kinds of existents that there are. Existents are true according to their match first with the divine intellect, by which is meant that they fulfil what is ordained for them by a first ordering cause of what there is. Hence, if we then go on to ask whether our thoughts are congruent with the world, the answer for Aquinas is that they certainly can be, but the truth of existents does not depend on their relation to

---

36   ST Ia 79.11 ad 1.
37   ST Ia 12.4c and Ia 13.9c.
38   ST Ia 84.7c; also see ST Ia IIae 55.1c.
39   Aquinas, *De veritate* 1, 1 resp.

the human intellect and its ways of coming to know. Aquinas and Aristotle both insist that all our knowledge arises originally from our knowledge of the first unprovable, somehow intuited principles concerning existence, and it is an awareness of these principles that arises in us from the senses.[40] We are part of what there is, not outside it or over it, and we exist in a manner that is peculiar to being human in a world in which other things exist according to their own natures.

Aquinas believes, as does Aristotle, that our awareness starts with the senses, so we are more easily aware of the things that are more available to the senses. But, by nature, things are more easily *known* which are by nature more fit for our (cognitive) awareness, and these are the things that are most existent and most actual.[41] These are less available to our senses. Naturally, we think in universals but we sense particulars, and what links these parallel but interrelated capacities to sense and to think is the soul's representative likenesses, from corporeal images to universal concepts or natures (intelligible species), which are judged existent and actual by reason.

Reason and Will

Aquinas's philosophy of mind is related to his account of the will; intellect and will are both central to his ethics because moral issues concern acts of will. The will is a faculty of the rational soul and it is a necessary concomitant of intellect.[42] The parallel here is with Aristotle's discussion in the *Nicomachean Ethics* (I chapter 13 and II chapter 3) of that not altogether irrational 'part' of the soul that is amenable to reason. Aristotle says we can speak of the appetitive 'part' of the soul as rational too. The appetitive part of the rational soul Aquinas calls the will.

Every nature has a tendency or inclination which is associated with it and this inclination is called appetite. Some natural things act without judgement, as when a stone falls to the ground. Those natural things (like plants) which do not have cognition have *necessitated* inclinations or natural appetites, i.e. to preserve themselves. Animals, however, act from judgement, but without freedom. Animal life has natural appetites *and* sensory cognition and with the latter comes goals that are dependent on contingent circumstances and what is desirable to an animal's senses. Through natural inclinations and sensory cognition an animal seeks what is suitable to it and flees from what is harmful, and also actively resists things that deter access to what is suitable. A lamb, for instance, by natural judgement which is not free, perceives that a wolf is to be fled, and it does this by natural instinct rather than by deliberation. But the human soul not only has necessitated inclinations as well as sensory appetites. It also has rational appetites. A man acts through judging that something is to be shunned or sought after through his ability to know. This particular practical conclusion proceeds not from natural instinct but from reasoning from experience; he acts freely, being open to several possible courses of action. Following Aristotle, Aquinas notes that in contingent matters, reason can go either way, as is obvious in dialectical and rhetorical arguments, and it is because man is rational that such decisions must be free. And it is free decision which is the cause of

---

40   Ibid., 10.6.
41   Aquinas, *Commentary on the Metaphysics* VII *lectio* 2.32–3.
42   ST Ia 19.1c and see ST Ia IIae 6–21.

man's self-determination. This free decision does not mean that man is his own first cause, since God is. But a first cause does not prevent voluntary action from being voluntary, since God works in each according to its nature. The nature of man is to be a moral deliberator, freely choosing to will what is rational or not. But he is not free to choose whether or not he tends towards his ultimate fulfilment, his happiness. His freedom is with respect to means to that end.[43] How much control does reason have over sensuality?

In humans, Aquinas says that external sensation requires the impact of external sense objects and reason cannot supply these. But, as with Aristotle, *that* we can feel is not what makes us human, that is, capable of acquiring virtue and thereby achieving peculiarly human excellences. Aquinas says that the (soul's) interior powers both of knowledge and desire do not need external stimuli and they come under the rule of reason, which can both excite and temper the feelings of sense appetite. As with Aristotle, it is whether you feel pleasure or pain rightly or wrongly, it is your disposition or frame of mind in virtue of which you are well- or ill-disposed in respect of feelings, that matters. We are not praised or blamed simply for having feelings. We are praised for virtues and blamed for vices. Human acts are those which are voluntarily ordered to an end, thereby being objects of choice, and they are the subject of praise and blame. Human acts, whose source is the reason and the will, and which follow from virtuous or vicious dispositions, constitute the moral order. Moral philosophy deals with these and, as with the earlier arts faculty tradition we have examined, Aquinas holds that moral philosophy is subdivided into ethics, household economics and politics. Moral philosophy distinguishes between individual prudence, domestic prudence and political prudence.[44]

Humans as substantial forms have essential inclinations and as rational animals they seek their well-being. What Aristotle called *eudaimonia*, Aquinas calls *beatitudo*. Although they are not in control of the achievement of their ultimate end (this is implicit in what they are), their choices concern means to that end.[45] The means are particular goods that are not *necessarily* connected with their end. All human agents *necessarily* pursue the same ultimate end, the human good, by living their lives differently, performing a plurality of more or less virtuous practices, and even making mistakes about what is good for them in individual actions. But as humans they cannot fail to seek their good. In being capable of making free choices about the means to their end, humans rationally deliberate and then desire in accord with their deliberation. In rational cognition, humans think universals and the will, as an intellective appetite, is then moved by this array of particular goods of one sort. The will chooses with regard to particular goods that have been collectively presented to it by the intellect.[46] The act of choice by which the will, as an intellective appetite, tends towards something proposed to it by reason as good is, for Aquinas, materially an act of will but formally it is an act of reason because it is directed towards its end by reason.[47] Reason motivates: it is not the slave of the passions; nor are the passions slaves of reason.

For Aquinas, the *cause* of freedom of choosing is reason, although the subject of

43   ST Ia 80.1, 83.1 resp. and ad 3.
44   ST IIa IIae 47.11c.
45   ST Ia 82.2c.
46   Aquinas, *Summa contra gentiles* III.3 and 25.
47   ST Ia IIae 13.1c.

freedom is the will. He speaks of man's rational activity, common to many acts, analogously in the sense that an activity can be called rational, but not because it is the act of
reason as such, but because it comes under the sway of reason. Since good is the object
of intellectual appetite, the will, then the virtues perfective of rational activity are those
feelings that are directed by reason. As with Aristotle, the moral virtues, as habits that help
to constitute a person's character disposition, are primary. Moral virtues are stable dispositions that love the good. These moral habits dispose one to *use* the intellectual virtues
well.[48] And to use the intellectual virtue of prudence, the practical intellect, well, depends on already acquired moral virtues. 'Moral virtue, which makes the appetite right,
is a precondition of prudence.' To calculate well about the means to the private and
common good, one must already have acquired the stable disposition that loves the
good for man. And no one acquires this by living alone; character disposition is acquired
through habits in law-governed political communities.[49]

The Will's Relation to Justice as Universal Principle and as Historically Contingent Conclusion

Justice, therefore, has the will (the intellective appetite) for its subject. Justice is concerned with voluntary choice in actions that reveal that emotions have *consented* to reason. Moral virtues need to be joined with right reason. Justice in general, then, is concerned
with the due measure of right external acts, giving what is due to another. Justice in
general, then, operates according to the universal conclusion: do unto others as you
would be done by. Given that one's own good must take place within common fulfilment, the *civitas* as the perfect community is the setting in which one comes to have an
interest in the good of others of the species for their own sake and *as* members of the
species.[50]

But there are conclusions that may be drawn from this principle which take into
account the contingency of historical circumstance. Here, the Middle Ages intrude,
backed by a Ciceronian understanding of desert according to rank. Aquinas notes that
the function of justice is to establish the right measure in various kinds of exchanges and
apportionments.[51] He thinks that all moral virtues share in common that general characteristic of justice: giving what is due to another. However, he is no egalitarian democrat,
and like Aristotle – but read through Ciceronian eyes – he holds that the word 'justice'
is also extended analogously to external actions where a rational, legal order has been
instituted to direct men's actions to the common good. Here, what is due depends on
the status of the recipient, and it is not clear, as it is in Aristotle, that status is ideally a
consequence of moral merit. Rather, there is a whiff of the feudal, backed by Ciceronian
views of friendship in the city according to rank, when Aquinas says: 'A thing is due to
an equal in one way, to a superior in another, and to an inferior in yet another; likewise

48   ST Ia IIae 57.1 resp. and 57.2.
49   ST Ia IIae 57.4 resp., ad 3; 58.5 resp.; see Aquinas's discussion of Socrates as falsely believing that every virtue
is a kind of prudence, i.e. an intellectual virtue, so that if a man possessed knowledge he could not sin. ST Ia IIae
558.2 resp.
50   ST Ia IIae 90.2.c.
51   ST Ia IIae 60.3, 3.

there are differences between what is due from a contract (*ex pacto*), a promise, or a favour (*ex beneficio*) conferred'.[52] This appears to go beyond Aristotle's notion of proportional equality; Aquinas specifies particular social status and public responsibilities as the determinants of just desert.[53]

Aquinas does not present the reason as coercing the will's choice; he follows Aristotle in saying that reason commands the appetitive part by a *political* rule, like that of a ruler over subjects who are free and reserve the right to set up some opposition.[54] Again, the passions are not the slaves of reason, nor is reason the slave of the passions. He describes reason as a final cause, moving the will, just as an aim moves an agent. But he also thinks we can speak of the will as moving the intellect and all powers of the soul as an efficient cause, coercively. And he provides the example of a ruler concerned with the common good of the entire society, making decisions which control the local governors responsible for particular provinces.[55] Reason, however, has an absolute primacy and an act of knowledge precedes every movement of the will. 'The source of decision-making and understanding', Aquinas says, 'is an intellectual principle above our intellect, and this is God, as Aristotle says in the *Eudemian Ethics*' (vii, 14. 1248a24)![56]

According to Aquinas, human beings are naturally appreciative of human good and evil as a natural consequence of their rationality, by which he means our being able to think in the way he describes. Hence, the object of reason is the true universally, and we say that the true expresses a relation between an existent and some thinking mind.[57] When we reason, we move from principles naturally known, which does not mean innate but does mean universal natures, to particulars, that is, we think deductively. We can conceptualize and then think deductively in the first place because we first experience things sensually. Once we have thought, we turn back, just as Aristotle said we did, from the concept to the world as we have sensually cognized it, to test our theories against the 'facts'.[58]

Eudaimonia/beatitudo: Immortality and the Completion of Desire

When the intellect conceptualizes, it does not perceive of our existence only under the aspect of 'now' as do the senses; rather, it conceptualizes existence absolutely, without qualification, existence in general. When humans grasp existence without qualification, Aquinas says there is then set in motion a desire to exist without qualification.[59] Hence, we can define complete human well-being, *beatitudo*, as continuous and perpetual existence. Taking Aristotle's definition of *eudaimonia* as the human end for which all other things are done by man, the ultimate object of human desire to be achieved through a

---

52   ST Ia IIae 60.4 resp., ad 1.
53   Following Pseudo-Dionysian hierarchies, Aquinas notes that no multitude would be properly organized unless it were arranged into different *ordines* to which were attached different activities and functions. ST Ia 90.3; 106.3; 108.2; 112 .2.
54   ST Ia IIae 58.2 resp.
55   ST Ia 82.4c.
56   ST Ia 82.4 ad 3.
57   Aquinas, *Summa contra gentiles* II.25; ST Ia 83.1.
58   Aquinas, *De veritate* 10.5 resp.
59   Aquinas, *Commentary on the Nicomachean Ethics* 1 *lectio* 10.12.

series of means ordered to a given, species-specific end, Aquinas says that because of the way intellect thinks, humans conceive of and then desire immortality. But this desired end is not achievable as we are mortal and mortality is part of the definition of human nature. In our present life, complete well-being, *beatitudo*, is impossible; we cannot live forever. But there is, as there is for Aristotle, a well-being which *is* possible in *this* life and which is distinctly human and therefore, mortal, and it is realized only when a human being actively engages in good performances or practices as a human being throughout his whole life.[60] Well-being in this life, then, is a series of end-related, rationally guided, moral performances that are specific to human beings; these are judged in accord with a completely human life. A completely human life is not one lived by lurching from one impulse to another, one unconsciously determined preference to another. Nor is it a life lived alone, no matter how contemplative. But a completely human life is, according to Aquinas, simply not enough for us. We want to live forever and we want all our desires to cease.

Hence, for Aquinas, human souls or psychologies can be spoken of in two ways, one of which emphasizes our capacity to be intellectually aware, and the other of which emphasizes our capacity to desire.[61] Aristotle had defined the good in the *Nicomachean Ethics* as that which all things desire so that the object of our desire is simply the good. But the object of our awareness is defined as the true, by which is meant that we become aware when the thinker creates mental representations, universal likenesses, of what he or she has sensually experienced. The existent should match the intellectual conception of it for it to be true. Those things not perceived by the senses cannot be grasped by the human intellect in the way it grasps things through universal thought, and this means for Aquinas that God cannot be grasped essentially, in his nature, by human minds operating normally.

Rationality and the Freedom of the Will

As Aristotle said, everything in nature moves and acts for an end that is its good since, by definition, the end of something acting naturally is the result of natural appetite. Humans have a natural appetite for their good. But their appetites for those things which serve as means to that good need training and guidance. And as we have seen, Aquinas affirms that we cannot desire something before we have some intellectual grasp of its nature. It is the intellect which moves appetites by first proposing their objects to them. Thereafter, the intellectual appetite (will),[62] in turn, moves the sense appetites of passion.[63] Free will is simply choice (*vis electiva*) among desirable alternatives.[64] We have to want or will to obey either our reason or our passions; we do not, as humans, simply act on passionate impulse alone. And the object proposed to us as desirable is first grasped by intellect. Once the will *consents* to its proposed object, the sense appetites then move the body.

---

60 Ibid., 1 *lectio* 10.13.
61 Aquinas, *De veritate* 1.1.
62 Aristotle's *prohairesis*.
63 Aristotle's *orexis*.
64 ST Ia 81.4 resp.

The Will and the Doctrine of Original Sin

There is no doubt that through a life of persistent bad habits a man can pervert his intellectual understanding of his human end, just as Aristotle had said. As we shall see when we discuss Aquinas's understanding of natural law, Aquinas shows how the Christian doctrine of original sin can explain that a man's will can freely choose not to fulfil the principles of natural reason that he knows. He understands Aristotle's akratic man, the man with an inconsistent will, to be a possibility for all men who suffer the consequences of the Fall by having open to them the possibility of not fulfilling natural reason. But he does not understand the consequences of the Fall as a loss of natural reason and the principles of action known by it. There simply are starting points of human thinking that are accessible to all men, and these are basic principles of morality that are not tied to specific cultures. But since the constraining power of the moral law that obliges us to obey it comes from our knowledge of our human end, certain habitual ways of living can obscure this end and thereby the means we choose to it.

And so in order to act in a way that is fully human, it is not the sense appetites that require training, but the intellective appetite, the will. This is where a collectively lived life in a law-governed community finds its place: in the education of the will through rational laws that suit the kinds of beings we are. This also means that training unconsidered habits, becoming acculturated to any old tradition, is insufficient for one to act truly humanly. One must be intellectually and critically aware of what one does, what one desires and its purpose. It matters that humans become acculturated to *rational* traditions because these are the only ones to which they ought, if they are truly to act humanly, voluntarily to consent.

This is quite a startling thing to believe. But we have seen that the very notion of customs and laws being held up to the standard of reason was central to scholastic and legal arguments in the thirteenth century. And as Aristotle had said, social laws that are rational can be considered coercive in the training of the young, but someone who voluntarily does what a rational law commands actually does something that is natural to what being a man fully means.

Aquinas puts this in the following way. Only those actions of man are properly called human which are characteristic of man as man (and not man as animal). The difference between man and irrational creatures is that humans are masters of their actions, through reason and will, through thinking and desiring and acting on these in a peculiarly human way, that is, through free judgement of choice. Actions deliberately willed are properly called human, and actions are willed because their end or purpose has been thought of.[65] Indeed, man is free to make decisions, for if this were not the case, counsels, precepts, prohibitions, rewards and punishment would be pointless.[66] Every agent acts for an end, even non-intellectual agents. An agent does not move unless it intends an end and the determination of an end by rational agents is made by the rational desire or will, rather than by biological impulse or instinct. Men apprehend an end, they grasp what they are aiming at, and they direct themselves there, doing this rather than that, as means to that end.[67] Hence, acts are called human since they are deliberately willed.[68] The capacity

---

65   ST Ia IIae 1.1 resp.
66   ST Ia 83.1 resp.
67   ST Ia IIae 1.2 resp.
68   ST Ia IIae 1.3 resp.

deliberately to will something is what Aquinas means by man being a morally responsible choice-making agent. When a man has a grasp of what it means to be human, not acting on impulse but on reasoned desire, whose natural object is the good universally and absolutely, he acts with an unchanging and timeless rational end in view. Through thinking and experiencing, he discovers an already existent truth about ordered reality, a truth that has no historical dimensions.

Natural Theology

Reasoning towards what is universally and absolutely true is not an alien command imposed on recalcitrant human nature. Rather, it is a consequence of what Aquinas insists is a natural desire in all humans to know the cause of what they see; thus, man by nature desires to know the first cause of all that there is and why it is so. This is God. Not only does experiencing and then reasoning from effect back to cause lead the human mind naturally on a search to find out about the beginnings as the ultimate end of all intellectual search. Just as Aristotle had said that all men possess *Nous*, *all* are natural theorizers, so too Aquinas says that this knowledge of the ultimate end of all enquiry is actually available to all men who are sufficiently reflective to think of the world order as a whole and wonder how it came to be and how it is sustained.[69] Knowledge of the ultimate end of intellectual enquiry, knowledge of the first cause of all the effects, is not a knowledge of an innate idea. Rather, the first cause is the *extrinsic* end or goal of all rational enquiry. A natural theology which reasons from effects back to cause can show us some of the main attributes of what Aquinas calls God, our ultimate end, the first cause of all, but for Aquinas, this is just the necessary and natural beginning. Natural theology must be supplemented by revelation in scripture. Furthermore, a serious study of natural theology requires a rigorous philosophical training which includes the study of logic and epistemology, and their metaphysical underpinnings, namely the studies of the arts faculty. This is a study for which Aquinas says most men have neither leisure nor inclination, but for which they all have the potential as humans because all have a natural appetite to know what is true.[70]

Given their human natures, humans *are* capable of being perfected. But they can come to know God as the first cause *in his very nature* only through divine assistance and not through an intellectual search. This is because all man's thoughts have their origin in the senses and God essentially, in his nature, cannot be sensed. True happiness as man's ultimate end, therefore, exceeds created nature. But in actualizing himself as a deliberating agent with a natural end in view that is given, then, intellectually, a man naturally seeks the true and naturally desires his good. By definition, an end must absolutely satisfy man's natural desire so that there is nothing left for him to desire or know. Aquinas insists that there is, *by nature*, one ultimate end for all men: to know all the answers and to achieve the satisfaction of all desires.[71] All humans agree in desiring the ultimate end, since all humans desire their good to be complete. That in which this is realized, of

---

69　See P.Geach, 'Aquinas', in Anscombe and Geach, *Three Philosophers*, pp. 67–125.

70　Aquinas, *Summa contra gentiles*, III.25; III.63; IV.54; *De regno* I.1, 4 and 6; ST Ia IIae 1.4 resp. and ad 1 and ad 2.

71　ST Ia IIae 1.5 resp.; 1.7 resp.

course, differs from human to human, but there is a suitable good for humans as such which is their happiness or human well-being. This essentially brings desire to rest. A desire for such a complete end is first apprehended by the intellect. It is conceived as the possessing of an essential and present knowledge of God, the cause of all, which man as man cannot achieve through his own limited cognitive powers.[72] For Aquinas, then, all men are naturally religious in the sense of developing a natural theology, but they come to realize this by living in political communities comprising rational deliberators.

If man *were* his own ultimate good, then the consideration and ordering of his actions and passions would be his happiness, and ethics and politics would be his end, consisting in the cultivation of virtues that enabled him to live a satisfying private and public life. But Aquinas insists that with some effort, humans are capable of grasping, although not fully, that ultimate human happiness is an *extrinsic* good, something beyond themselves and their own creations, where intellectual searches to know, and continuous desiring, cease.[73] Man's ultimate perfection has to be through a knowledge of something like, something analogous to, but *above*, the human intellect. And Aquinas interpreted Aristotle as thinking that man's ultimate end – permanent, continuous and pure contemplation – could not be realized by human agents either. Aristotle had said in book 10 of the *Ethics* that 'the activity of God which is supremely happy must be a form of contemplating and among human activities, that which is most akin to God's will be the happiest. The life of the gods is altogether happy and that of man is happy in so far as it contains something that resembles the divine activity'.[74] Aquinas develops this further: 'In man's present state of life, his ultimate perfection is in the activity whereby he is united to God, but this activity cannot be continual because we are human, not divine'.[75] Hence, the good we can achieve by ourselves is mixed with sadness and worry that it will be disturbed. Humans cannot have complete and continuous happiness in this life because of what they are, souls 'in' bodies, mortal, rational animals. They have no choice as to their natures but they do have a choice as to how they live. 'Hence, the Philosopher [Aristotle] when considering man's happiness concludes "we call men happy but as men".'

State and Church: The Consequences of Natural Theology

Aquinas interpreted Aristotle as having realized that our conceptual reach exceeds our practical grasp, and this enabled him to go on to speak of the complementarity of the philosophical and theological ends of man. Hence, as a Christian theologian, Aquinas finds a place for the role of the church as well as the 'state' and he adds: 'But God promised us complete happiness when we shall be like the angels in heaven'. If Christ had not appeared, according to Aquinas, men would simply have to accept that they die at the end of all their intellectual and appetitive effort; that after politics was simply death. Without God's promise, Aquinas seems to suggest that humans will never be completely at peace because their minds will always be thinking and their wills desiring infinitely. Under such conditions, and with intellectual effort, imperfect social and po-

72   ST Ia IIae 2.6 resp; *Summa contra gentiles* 1.8.
73   ST Ia IIae 2.8 resp.
74   NE X, 1187b7–29.
75   ST Ia IIae 3.2 ad 4; Ia IIae 2.5 and 2.8 resp.; ST Ia IIae 3.4 resp; *Summa contra gentiles* III 63.

litical happiness is man's lot. Even here, however, there is a general good that all men can naturally see and then seek (if not completely attain) because that is what conceptualization and willing are: the activities of thinking a mind's natural object – the unqualified and universally true – and the activity of desiring the will's natural object – the universal and unqualified good.[76] Conceptualizing and willing are not engaged in a void and men can only be moral deliberators and agents within moral communities. As we shall see, the promise of the extrinsic good comes through the teachings of the church, whose office is to educate in the faith and to keep an eye on the practical realization of goods that are *means* to the completely good and true, as promoted by a rational, law-governed 'state'. In this way, the natural and supernatural ends of man are harmonized. There is, for Aquinas, a harmony of human and religious values, of reason and faith.

For Aquinas, men are so constituted as to be capable, through deliberative choice, to follow through on their reasoning by means of intentional acts. And human acts are judged by their ends. Aquinas says the same act, e.g. killing a man, can be ordered to diverse ends, for instance, upholding justice or satisfying anger. In the first way it will be an act of virtue, in the second, of vice.[77] Human acts which are deliberately willed, by definition, have as their natural ends or objects the unqualified, universal good.[78] If someone acts for an end that is not the good, he acts against his nature and is to be held morally responsible for so doing, effectively, for being wilfully ignorant of what human nature is, thereby harming himself and others.

In the language of the two swords theory, the ideal state's rational laws punish the vicious and irrational by coercive or rehabilitating means. But behind the function of the 'state' as directing and co-ordinating the common good is the church that guards the vision of men acting to secure the unqualified, universal good and the natural order of reason. Positive civil law, as we shall see, is trumped by natural law. Since, through virtuous living, man is further ordained to a higher end which consists in the enjoyment of God, then temporal government is subject in spiritual things to priests, most importantly to the successor of St Peter, the vicar of Christ, the pope, as to Christ.[79] It pertains to the office of public authority and therefore political rule, to promote the good life of the multitude in such a way as to make it suitable for the attainment of salvation.[80] Since what pertains to *beatitudo* is learned from God's law, scripture, the church is universal educator, and the 'state' is charged with finding the means to secure the end taught. Aquinas does not, thereafter, indicate that should a 'state' not function in ways that suit its role of directing men to their ultimate goal, the institutional church has coercive ways and means of responding. Nor does he think a ruler can impose on individual subjects or citizens a legal duty to pursue their ultimate ends. But he does imply that a multitude that is church-educated and 'state'-governed will itself be capable of judging that its ends are not being adequately pursued, and it will devise the ways and means of removing public officials who do not serve the common good in its ultimate, salvific sense.

76   ST Ia IIae 4.3c and resp.
77   See J. Barnes, 'The Just War', in Kretzmann, Kenny and Pinborg, *The Cambridge History of Later Medieval Philosophy*, ch. 41.
78   ST Ia IIae 1.3 ad 3; 1.1 resp. and ad 1 and ad 2; 1.2 ad 3.
79   *De regno* II, 3, 102–10.
80   Ibid., 115.

The nature of man realizes itself through action. To possess one's end, the perfect good by definition, without movement, belongs to one who has it by nature and this belongs to God alone. No creature can attain its natural end without some activity natural to it by which it tends towards its ends. Deeds on the part of man are therefore required for happiness, says Aquinas, not because of any inadequacy of the divine power that bestows happiness, but for preserving the order of things, that is, for maintaining reality. If humans do not act to natural type, it will be because they have chosen not to be comfortable with their natures. And there is a crucial role for a 'state' that is devoted to the common good to play in enabling them to conform to their natures and act according to reason.

Free Will and Responsibility

When commenting on Aristotle's *Categories*, Aquinas insisted that whatever we choose, we as humans are the initiating and controlling principles of our individual and collective futures, precisely because we deliberate and act in whatever ways we do. As far as human affairs are concerned, Aquinas says that Aristotle shows that it is obvious that human beings are the originating principle of those things in the future they do as the controllers of their own acts, and that they have in their powers to do or not to do.[81] They do not only act by natural instinct but by deliberating and judging what is to be done. He says that if you deny this originating principle, you remove the whole structure of human intercourse and all the principles of moral philosophy. If you deny this, Aquinas says, 'there is no point in persuasion, or threats, or punishment or reward, by which people are encouraged to do good and discouraged from doing evil, and so the whole science of society becomes vain'. 'People who do what they do not want to do', he says, 'may not have freedom of action but they do have freedom of choice.'[82] And Aquinas makes it clear that 'if one lives in a society whose customs and traditions are not in accord with what a reasonable nature would consider appropriate, then by deliberating, a person who is accustomed to do something can, indeed should, act against custom and tradition'.[83] Humans are not obliged to obey irrational laws, which, he argues, are not even worthy of being called 'laws'. In this life, humans are obliged by reason. We shall see how far he takes this theory of resistance to irrationality.

Aquinas on Law and Politics[84]

In his treatise on the laws[85] Aquinas discussed the four laws that govern an individual's ethical behaviour and the community's political practices. Instead of sacralizing public

81   Aquinas, *In perihermenias* 1 *lectio* 14.5.
82   Aquinas, *De malo* 6 ad 22.
83   Ibid., 6 ad 24.
84   A useful text in translation is Paul Sigmund, ed., *St Thomas Aquinas on Politics and Ethics* (London, 1988), with numerous extracts from various works including *Treatise on Laws* and *On Kingship (De regno)*. Also see *On Kingship*, trans. G. Phelan, revd T. Eschmann (Toronto, 1982).
85   ST Ia IIae 90–108.

power as had some contemporary theologians who followed an Augustinian tendency, Aquinas emphasized the autonomy of the natural order in a universe of secondary causes that leads, ultimately, to the primary cause, God. Hence, he showed no interest in empires as products of force and conquest, nor was he concerned with a notion of government as the product of human artifice. Government is natural. Philosophically, he showed very little interest in historical kingdoms or republics, although he provides examples of current practices or he cites (especially) Roman history, to illustrate his philosophical arguments. He is directly interested in the common good and the means to its realization by a multitude of men who, as free subjects,[86] find themselves together with common interests which require direction. It is from his analysis of what man is and how he behaves with others, collectively, that he then proceeds to a discussion of the proper means to administer, direct and care for the needs of the multitude.[87] He does something unusual for his time, however. He puts humans back into the natural order by recognizing 'irrational' natural instincts to be parts of their natures.

Natural Law beyond Cicero

There is no doubt that Cicero's understanding of true law as right reason in agreement with nature, universally applicable, unchanging and everlasting, had been absorbed into medieval thinking, not least through their reading of many of the Latin church Fathers who had cited his views.[88] Roman lawyers also took up the appeal to a universal, natural reason when they discussed the forces which prompted men to live in society and establish good government. And Justinian's *Institutes* had defined justice as the set of constant purposes which gives every man his due. A constant standard of equity and justice was said to reflect the divine reason by defining what is just and what is reasonable. Jurisprudence was to be understood as the science of things divine and human. As we have seen, in distinguishing between private law that deals with advantages to the individual citizen, and the public law that has the welfare of the state as its goal, Justinian's texts emphasized that the private citizen was bound to observe three different laws: the *ius naturale* or natural law (the precepts of nature); the *ius gentium* or the law of nations (devised by man, common to all humankind and prescribed by natural reason in all societies, e.g. trading with money, contracts); and last, the *civil law* of Rome (man-made and specific to a particular community with its own problems and customs).

But we have already seen that Justinian had included two not easily reconcilable Roman jurists' understandings of natural law: Ulpian's and Gaius's. According to Ulpian, three laws could be distinguished: a natural law, separate from the law of nations, which could be described as that which nature teaches all animals, and it therefore applied to man's as well as animals' instincts. He then described the *ius gentium*, not as a general natural law but as a contrived common law, universally applicable to humankind, which men developed in order to maintain international relations. Last, he described Roman civil law (*ius civile*). Gaius, however, had written that the laws of every people governed

---

86   ST Ia IIae 96, 4.
87   ST Ia IIae 90, 3.
88   See C. J. Nederman, 'Nature, Sin and the Origins of Society: the Ciceronian tradition in medieval political thought', *Journal of the History of Ideas* 49 (1988), pp. 3–26.

by statutes and customs could be divided into two groups: *ius gentium* and *ius civile*, the law of nations being a law that was natural to humankind. He made no mention of a separate more fundamental *ius naturale*.

Gratian's collection of canon law, the *Decretum*, had taken up some of these Roman law understandings and had said that humankind is ruled by two laws: natural law (*ius naturale*) and custom. He also said that man is ruled by divine and human law. What he appears to have meant by natural law is that which is contained in the Mosaic law and the gospels. Natural law then, is the moral law of God, an instinct of nature that is common to all *peoples* (similar to the law of nations of Gaius) which, in its highest sense, is the *lex divina* of scripture. Gratian emphasized the divine character of natural law and its identity with the commandments of scripture so that a natural ethics and the natural-ness of human society were thereby read as divinely sanctioned. By the time that Aristo-tle's explicit statements in the *Ethics* and *Politics* were available, the 'state' had already become, through the work of the commentators on Roman and canon law, a supreme moral entity itself, and a product of man's reason.

Thirteenth-century theological works also began to include a distinct section 'on the laws'. When Aquinas included his own 'treatise on the laws' in his *Summa Theologiae* he drew on the canon and Roman law tradition in a selective way. Aquinas preferred the understanding of Ulpian, for whom three laws could be distinguished: a natural law, separate from the law of nations, which could be described as that which nature teaches all animals, and it therefore applied to man's as well as animals' instincts. Aquinas adapts Stoic principles, Aristotle's teleology, and a neo-platonized Christian metaphysics of participation. In an age when the rational aspect of the natural law had become domi-nant, commentators have observed the distinctiveness of Aquinas's position in his wish-ing to accommodate irrational instinctive aspects of natural behaviour in his understanding of the natural law. He would emphasize an intrinsic natural instinct or principle in men, which consists in the dictates of natural reason in matters common to man and animals. This enables irrational animals as well as humans to participate in their respective ways in the eternal law or reason, an extrinsic principle with a divine purpose. Rational creatures participate in a distinctive way – intellectually and rationally – in the divine purpose, but they also participate by natural instincts in that purpose, just as irrational creatures par-ticipate in the divine purpose by natural instinct. There is, then, a generic sense of natural law which is common to all creatures, and a specific *lex naturalis* which is com-mon to rational men alone. The law of nations, the *ius gentium*, he sees as the conclusions of rational applications of the rational *lex naturalis* and having the force of natural law.

Natural Human Community

As a Christian Aristotelian, Aquinas was interested in community (*civitas*) as a system of relations between individual men and groups thereof. The relationship is based on the naturalness of linguistic communication. He underlined the communitary dimension of political groupings, especially when he commented on Aristotle's discussion of lan-guage. In his unfinished *Commentary on Aristotle's Politics*[89] he absorbed William of

---

89   Which breaks off at book 3 chapter 8 and was to be completed by Peter of Auvergne.

Moerbeke's words *communicatio, communitas, communio politica* and its synonym *civitas* to correspond to Aristotle's *polis*.[90] He says that language (in general, not any one conventionally established language) has been given to men by nature, which does nothing in vain, and it is designed for what men communicate between one another regarding the useful and not useful, the just and the unjust. It therefore follows that since communication on these points constitutes the domain of the city, man is an animal, naturally domestic and political.[91] Thus man, a speaking being by nature, is also naturally social, that is, political, and this demonstrates the natural character of, literally, 'the political communication' or the political community, this resting on the natural character of linguistic communication.[92] Indeed, unlike Augustine's view of the extraordinary lack of success in linguistic communication, for both Aristotle and Aquinas communication presupposes stable, shared assumptions about the way things are and the kinds of agents we are. Embedded in human thought come to be foundational moral truths that are made explicit in linguistic communication under the pressure of circumstances. Human speech reveals that foundational moral principles are not culture-specific.

Elsewhere,[93] Aquinas argued that a society is called public when people communicate and deal with each other in constituting a *respublica*. All of the people of one *civitas* or of one *regnum* are associated in one *respublica*, so that the *respublica* is a generic type of political *communitas*, and not a specified constitution. Kings can directively govern the *respublica*.[94]

In his *Summa Theologiae*'s 'treatise on the laws' Aquinas calls natural law those stable, underlying principles of moral practices that always lie beneath the more plural variations that emerge in cultural living. Behind the customs and civil laws that are particular to historical communities, lies a moral perception that to engage in certain behaviour is right or wrong, whatever the independent sanction in the civil or customary law. These primary practical principles are arrived at by induction and are naturally known ends, prior to the development of any virtue as means to them.[95] Human moral discourse, then, is constructed on a set of foundational principles which may be encapsulated as: 'the good is to be pursued and done and the evil avoided'. Thereafter, whatever things prudence, or practical reason, naturally grasps to be particular human goods as means to the human end, fall under the already known precept of the natural law as to what is to be done or avoided. But note that *all* those things to which a man has a *natural inclination*, his reason then naturally grasps as 'goods' to be pursued and done. As with Aristotle, humans do not know which inclinations are natural prior to an understanding of what the human good is. Upon reflection, humans recognize that along with every other

90   Moerbeke, *Politica*, I.1.22: 'Diki enim civilis communitatis ordo est. Diki autem iusti iudicium'.
91   *In octo libros Politicorum Aristotelis expositio*, para. 37.
92   *Communicatio politica* is closer to the Greek, more organicist vision of political groupings; *societas civilis* is further from the Greek. D. Colas, *La Glaive et le fléau, généalogie du fanatisme et de la société civile* (Paris, 1992), pp. 34–7, rightly argues that it was Bruni who used *societas civilis* in his translation of the *Nicomachean Ethics* (1416–17) and *Politics* (1438), and in substituting for *communitas* a humanist, civic understanding of Italian cities, the communitarian notion that is in Aquinas had become, rather, an associative dimension, modeled on Cicero. Bruni explicitly wanted to replace Moerbeke's translation which he found barbarous with its many transliterated Greek words, and replaced Moerbeke's 'Hellenism' with Rome. See below, chapter 6.
93   *Impug*. II.26.
94   ST Ia IIae 100.5c.
95   ST IIa IIae 47.6c.

created thing, they have inclinations to preserve themselves in existence as the sorts of beings they are. Like animals, humans have sexual inclinations, and inclinations to care for their young. But to humans alone belong the further inclinations to know, converse and to live in society together.

None of these inclinations is a matter of choice. They are the natural law, and the human species has its own mode of participation in the divine ordering of things, the eternal law. The whole community of the universe is governed by divine reason, which Aquinas calls the eternal law, and the rational guidance of created things on the part of God has the quality of law. *All* created things, and not simply humans, participate to some degree in this eternal law. Humans participate in it in a mode proper to them, which is through reason, being capable of making choices to control their own acts and those of others. The natural law is man's participation in the divinely created order of things.[96]

Hence, as a species we cannot choose whether or not to preserve ourselves, mate and as a consequence of procreation, rear children, live in society and search for the causal source and answer to all the effects we experience. But humans need morally to shape their natural inclinations to live as they were intended to live and to pursue their good, well. Practical reason, made positive in civil law, regulates natural inclinations to enable humans to make choices for the achievement of their comprehensive good. Natural justice is, then, a series of rational principles which follow upon the inclinations of nature.

In sum, all laws, eternal, divine, natural and civil are interlinked.[97] Every species has its own nature or end, and man achieves his specific end, his characteristic virtue or excellence, by acting according to reason. Through a rational consideration of his natural instincts man comes to learn the general principles of the law of nature, and hence this knowledge is not the consequence of Christian revelation: natural reason is a sufficient guide. But the law of nature is also to be found in divine law, scripture, and, for Aquinas, there is no contradiction between the positive law contained in scripture (such as the commandments) and the law of nature as it applies to man. The foundation of human morality is the natural law, and in grace not abolishing but perfecting nature, revelation is joined to nature. But it is the natural law, and hence natural reason, that is the standard by which all civil, positive laws of any 'state' may be judged. In the particular circumstances of a historical community, human law-makers are allowed a certain latitude to establish in detail, and according to changing circumstances, what is ordained by the natural law.

Aristotle had spoken of legal justice as conventional, based on no original reason why it should take one form or another, but it is obligatory once agreed upon and laid down. Aquinas, however, speaks of legal justice or positive justice as enshrining rational principles which establish its obligatory validity. It is here that we see the civil law being

---

96   ST Ia IIae91.1 and 2.
97   It is these interconnections which came to be denied by early-modern political theorists who sought to establish natural law upon rational and secular foundations; natural law came to be spoken of as whatever conforms to right reason, natural law being deduced by reason simply from the nature of things. This position would be developed in the writings of Grotius, Pufendorf and Montesquieu. The problems with this purely rationalist account soon emerged: what does reason mean? intuition? the observation of nature as 'fact'? mathematical non-contradiction? self-evident truths based on history and precedent? simply the positive law as established by governments?

trumped by natural law. Civil laws must be rational and conform with foundational principles which cannot be gainsaid.[98]

The Consequences of the Fall

But even if the civil law conforms to the rational precepts of natural law, it still is possible for a free individual to contravene both the civil and the natural law. Humans are the only creatures with capacities to choose to shape their natural inclinations in distorted ways. This is because the doctrine of original sin allows for almost the total loss of natural law's precepts through sin and perversity, the consequences of persistent bad habits which can obscure the intellectual understanding of human ends. Aristotle similarly had argued that consistent bad habits could obscure one's reason and the view of one's human end. But where Aristotle had spoken of a remarkable indeterminacy that was essential to the human condition, allowing us an autonomy to shape the quality of our lives, Aquinas sees the indeterminacy as a consequence of Adam's first sin, but where there still remains enough of a rational ability to shape our moral dispositions and actions and so conform to our natures as divinely intended. Furthermore, where Aristotle was explicit about the corrupting effects on habits that acculturation to the norms of bad societies may have, Aquinas places less emphasis on cultures as promoters of moral perversity, and places more emphasis on individual responsibility to reject irrational norms. For Aristotle, it was exceedingly difficult to change one's habituated character disposition, however one's reason observed it with dismay. This is why it made all the difference in what kind of society one was educated from the beginning. Aquinas, however, takes for granted that a Christian moral education is in place under the guidance of the church, whatever the nature of the 'state'. Consequently, for Aquinas it was not only possible but imperative that men reject irrational norms and shape their natural inclinations under the guidance of their reason.

But he was more obviously an Aristotelian, despite the influence of Augustine on his thinking, in finding it impossible to believe that man's will is wholly corrupt and that government is a necessary evil. For Aquinas, government is a necessary good and even in paradise society was law-governed. In distinguishing between human nature before and after the Fall,[99] he says that before the Fall men could have perfected themselves to the point of performing works of justice and other virtues without special divine grace. Man could therefore obediently fulfil all the commandments of the law in paradise. And his dominion over other created things was directive rather than coercive. But even before the Fall, Adam did need special supernatural 'elevating' grace to fulfil commandments with the right disposition, in the spirit of charity. After the Fall, man needed yet another 'healing' grace to fulfil commands of law even in an external sense of obedience. This healing grace, according to Aquinas, heals the *mind* of those to whom it is granted that they will commit no sins arising out of *reason*, which is the source of all mortal sins leading to damnation.

But those venial sins which arise out of man's bodily appetites and instincts cannot be

98   See A. Black, *Political Thought in Europe, 1250–1450* (Cambridge, 1992), pp.37–40, for a brief but interesting discussion of Aquinas's theory of law.
99   ST Ia IIae 109.2.

corrected by grace. Man cannot, therefore, live a wholly sinless life after the Fall, even with God's grace, and thus man can never be 'perfect' in so far as perfection means being 'like God', free from all sin. And yet, quoting Aristotle's *Ethics*, Aquinas says that man's ultimate perfection consists in the contemplation of the highest object of contemplation – the good – and by means of this rational contemplation, man can become most like God analogously, for it is his *intellect* which makes man God-like. Human perfectibility, in so far as it is possible within natural limits, consists of an act of intellect. For Augustine, the divided will could only be perfected by grace and there was no route to human perfectibility within natural limits.

Aquinas's emphasis on the rational capacities of men to overcome 'lower nature' is linked with his Aristotelian emphasis on the perfectibility of man and society through reason. There is an opening up of the sphere of action of the free will guided by reason, so that man is *not* regarded as morally helpless without grace. He can do some particular good, naturally. And as Aquinas said in his introduction to his *Commentary on Aristotle's Politics*: 'The state is in fact the most important thing constituted by human reason . . . for politics as the most important science treats of the most perfect things and thus, it treats of the highest and perfect good in human affairs'. The 'state' then has a role to *enforce* reason through law in order to realign habits and their resultant practices to the right end, the common good. Law, to be effective in promoting right living, must have compelling force, and Aquinas notably insists that this power of compulsion belongs either to the community as a whole, or to its official representative whose duty it is to inflict penalties.[100]

Individual Rights and the State's Law

What does this tell us about the relation between prudence as enshrined in civil laws and the individual's rights and responsibilities? It has been argued that Aquinas does not take his analysis of individual knowing and individual responsibility for acts any further to develop a doctrine of subjective, individual rights to be exercised in the public sphere.[101] But it can be argued that his analysis of the four laws which rule men and creation – eternal, divine, natural and positive/civil – does emphasize a sphere of moral autonomy of the individual which has specific consequences for the 'state'.[102]

In discussing the law of nature, he speaks of men sharing a natural inclination to good with all creation. Specifically, all seek self-preservation automatically. Men also have inclinations in common with animals, such as the sexual instinct and the rearing of offspring. But most important and unique to men is their natural inclination to know the truth about God and to live in society. Men are social and political animals, as well as naturally religious. The natural law applies to them alone as conscious, rational, moral, social creatures. Its foundational precepts arise in them as the result of experience and such foundational principles cannot be demonstrated. 'The good is to be pursued and done and the evil avoided' is an indemonstrable foundational principle from which all

---

100 ST Ia IIae 90. 3 ad 2.
101 Although some sixteenth-century Thomists like Vitoria thought he had; see B. Tierney, 'Origins of Natural Rights Language: texts and contexts 1150–1625', *History of Political Thought* 10 (1989), p. 638.
102 ST Ia IIae 90–7.

other conclusions are thereafter deduced, such as: 'do unto others as you would be done by'; even 'love thy neighbour as thyself'. The natural law, therefore, teaches humans to avoid ignorance and not to give offence to or harm others with whom they must associate.[103] This standard of truth and rightness for all men is known naturally and equally by all, but note, it is not innate as an idea or precept, but rather, it necessarily emerges in thought through the experience of living a human life. Note also that it does not imply any equalization of status in society or politics, because in coming to the historically and contingently particular conclusions that are drawn from such universally and equally known moral principles, although the standard of truth remains fixed (the good is to be pursued and done and the evil avoided), the specific historical circumstances of its application vary. As history changes, the secondary precepts or conclusions drawn from immutable, naturally known, moral first principles also change in particular cases. The natural law is not altered but added to and these additions are judged by practical, prudential reason in contingent circumstances.

Like Aristotle, Aquinas believed that man's natural inclination to virtuous actions could, by a certain education and discipline, be converted to virtuous habitual behaviour. Both the divine law, namely the commandments of scripture, and the positive law of the 'state', act in such an educational manner, preventing men from doing evil in order to provide a peaceful life for the community. Where scripture, encountered through the church (and notably through the preaching of his own Dominican Order), instructs, educates and persuades, the civil law commands. Civil law regulates man's conduct with respect to his fellows with whom he has to live. But the necessity of enacting positive, rational, human civil laws still requires that human law has the quality of law in that it proceeds according to reason. Law is defined as a rule or measure of action in virtue of which one is led to perform certain actions and restrained from the performance of others, and the rule and measure of human action is reason.[104]

But to Aquinas this means that a prince or anyone else in charge of directing the means to the achievement of the common good is subject *voluntarily* to reason and to natural law, as is any man.[105] Does this mean that a ruler as a public authority is not bound, except in conscience, to obey the civil laws? Morally, the public person is obliged but can he also be obliged in and under law? It is important to realize that, as with Aristotle, law governs a community, not a man as an individual. For Aquinas, the person(s) charged with public authority, directing men by law to the common good, are unifying and co-ordinating functionaries, representatives of the corporate will of a community. When viewed as a public official, he is not a private person in an office but the office itself. The acts of a ruler as director and the acts of other public authorities as 'delegates' are to be considered acts of the group. Public policy is then the actualization of the potentials of the group, the *civitas*. And acts are understood by asking and answering 'what are they done *for*?' According to Aquinas it is the *ruled* especially, the group or *civitas*, who need a practical understanding and prudential judgement concerning the group's common good, and whether or not those directing them towards this end are doing their job.

---

103 ST Ia IIae 93.1.
104 ST Ia IIae 90.1.
105 Compare Giles of Rome, above.

In the fragmentary *De regno*, Aquinas says that it is not even legitimate for the direct-ing ruler of a multitude to deliberate *whether* he shall establish peace in the multitude subject to him, just as a physician does not deliberate whether he shall heal the sick man encharged to him, for no one should deliberate about an end which he is obliged to seek, but only about the means to attain that end.[106] But are the practices of public office under law? The answer is that they are under moral law which is consonant with right reason; this includes, for a ruler, the possibility of legitimately dispensing equity with mercy, in individual cases, beyond the strict letter of the positive law. Practices of public office are not simply under the positive law of lawyers, because for Aquinas lawyers cannot define things authoritatively. And if they are unfamiliar with the moral under-pinnings which legitimate positive law, they are simply enforcers of convention that may well be irrational.

The Contrast with Augustine

In the *De regno* Aquinas says that a king who is concerned for his own well-being and not for the common good is a tyrant, by definition. And he says that a scheme should be carefully worked out which would prevent the multitude ruled by a king from falling into the hands of a tyrant.[107] In particular, once the king is established, the government of the kingdom must be so arranged that opportunity to tyrannize is removed. Further-more, his power is to be tempered.[108] The details are not elaborated in these fragments. Should the king stray into tyranny, but if not to excess, then he is to be tolerated; but if to excess, then the multitude maintains the right to depose him, for he has not kept the covenant with his subjects and did not act faithfully as the office of a king demands.[109] Public office is a fiduciary power, and its incumbent is open to removal if the common good is not pursued.

Aquinas is theorizing in the midst of a society with a multitude of consensual prac-tices. Hence, he says that to order affairs to the common good, by law, is the task either of the whole community or of some one person who represents it. And the promulga-tion of law is the business either of the whole community or of that public person whose duty is the care of the common good.[110] Not only should all have some share in sover-eignty in order to maintain peace and stability, but all should have some share in sover-eignty *because* of the principle that every man, in so far as he is rational, participates somehow in government according to the judgement of his reason. Human laws are never infallible since they are not the conclusions of demonstrative science, but rather, deal with contingent things that are possible.[111] Hence, human laws are continuously open to rational scrutiny and change. If it is discovered that positive law, enacted by a public authority, is at variance with natural law and reason, it is not legal but rather a corruption of the law. The validity of the civil law depends on its being just, that is,

---

106   *De regno* 1, 2, 17.
107   Ibid., 1, 6, 41.
108   Compare ST Ia IIae 105.1.
109   *De regno*, 1, 6, 49.
110   ST Ia IIae 90, 3.
111   ST Ia IIae 91ad 3.

reasonable. And an irrational 'law' is not obliging on the individual. However, the consequences for the *individual* who judges that promulgated law is not rational and therefore not binding, are not always clear.

In his early *Commentary on the Sentences*[112] Aquinas argued that irrational laws established by self-seeking tyrants rather than by community-minded sovereigns are not obliging and that the overthrow of such government is praiseworthy and not to be considered seditious. But he added in the later *Summa*[113] that unjust positive laws do not oblige in the forum of reasonable conscience, *in foro conscientiae*, unless, perhaps, to avoid scandal or riot; on this account a man may be called to yield his rights (*homo iuri suo debet cedere*). And if the disorder and scandal that resulted from the toppling of a tyrant by the community were likely to lead to even greater harm and disturbance than already existed, then overthrowing the government is not advisable. There is never, for Aquinas (or his contemporaries) a *private right* to depose or kill tyrants. There is, however, a public right to perform such action, a deed that may only be carried out by public authority. This is an idea with an important future in Western political theory.[114]

Aquinas is clear, however, that should one be commanded by public authority to commit sin, one is obliged *not* to obey the command, and he cites the Acts of the Apostles: 'we must obey God rather than men'. The kinds of unjust laws he has in mind here are laws of tyrants which promote idolatry or something else against divine law. Such laws exceed the power of public authority and are to be resisted.[115]

The Mixed Constitution

It seems that Aquinas modified his idea of public duty with the notion of utility, but a doctrine of subjective, individual rights exercisable in the public sphere is not elaborated. Yet he insisted that all human law must be directed to the common welfare of the city or 'state'. Human law is promulgated by the ruler of the community according to the particular regime (i.e. be the constitution a monarchy or a republic) that has been established. He is most in favour of monarchy, but one which has the characteristics of a mixed government that is constituted by and takes advice from the feudal nobility and reflects the opinions of the wise, the wealthy, and the entire people. The law of this 'state' must achieve the common consent of nobles and people.[116] Aquinas therefore revises the contemporary neo-platonist support for 'feudal, absolute' monarchy. He looks to a 'state's' unification in a sovereign who directs the common good as a public official with jurisdictional and law-making powers. These powers are derived from the represented will of members organized in and by a *mixed constitution*. The mixed constitution is Aquinas's interpretation of Aristotle's *polity*, but its characteristics conform more to the operations of medieval communities, legally redefined in Roman law terms.[117]

---

112   II Dist. 44, 2, 2.
113   ST Ia IIae 96.4 resp.; ST IIa IIae 42.2 ad 3.
114   Much of the above will bare comparison with the discussion of resistance in Locke's *Second Treatise of Government,* including *De regno* 1, 6, 51 where Aquinas says that should no human aid whatsoever against a tyrant be forthcoming, recourse must be had to 'God the King of all, Who is helper in due time in tribulation'.
115   Compare Augustine in volume 1, chapter 6 of *A History of Political Thought.*
116   ST Ia IIae 105.1 ad 2.
117   See J. M. Blythe, *Ideal Government and the Mixed Constitution in the Middle Ages* (Princeton, NJ, 1992), ch. 3 for a full discussion but with minimal reference to Aquinas's ethics or theology.

Following Aristotle, but also confirming Aristotle's views by experience, he notes that where popular governments existed, they were prone to disunity and dissension. Government by the multitude (democracy), in practice, is not itself a tyranny but is more likely to *lead* to tyranny than rule by one man, although oligarchies are even worse than democracies. It is therefore more expedient to live under a king, but it belongs to the right of the multitude to provide itself with a king. And it is not unjust that the king be deposed or have his power restricted by that same multitude.[118] Ideally, as he argues in his *De regno*, the best ordering of power in a city or kingdom is obtained when there is one virtuous commanding head, but where those under him actively participate in the election of those who rule, and such rule must be rational and publicly minded rather than according to a ruler's individual whim. He calls this kind of limited monarchy, in city or kingdom, 'political rule' (*regimen politicum*) rather than the full and *un*limited power of 'regal rule' (*regimen regale*).

Indeed, a human group with its own customs can, he says, be in one of two conditions, self-governing or not. Where there is custom, that is, when anything is done again and again, Aquinas notes that it is assumed that it comes from the deliberate judgement of reason. On these grounds custom has the force of law. And

> if it is a free country, where people are able to make their own laws, their common consensus about a particular observance expressed in custom, is more important than the authority of the ruler who has the power of making law only in so far as he represents the people; a whole people can make law, not a single individual. If, however, people are not free to make their own laws or to put aside a law laid down for them by superior authority, then all the same a prevailing custom among them obtains the force of law when it is allowed by those whose office it is to make laws for them; by this very fact authority seems to approve what has been brought in by custom.[119]

A *regimen politicum*, the public, political sphere, *either* where free men make their own law through common consensus about customary norms, *or* where they are ruled by a public authority which makes laws for them, that is, for the common good, is ideally characterized by the deliberations of reason. The constitutional mechanisms can make clear whether or not they are self-governing in practice, i.e. whether they are institutionally structured as republics or monarchies. For the sake of expedience, Aquinas has already argued his preference for a mixed and therefore limited elected monarchy, but the principle behind the *regimen politicum* is not a constitutional type so much as deliberative reason which informs the law. If a *regimen politicum* is what the public, political sphere ought to be, however, Aquinas does not clarify how any individual moral agent, or any self-constituted collectivity, may act to bring it about if it, as yet, does not exist.

---

118 *De regno* 1, 6, 41–9. Numerous parallels may be drawn with historical practice in the city-states of Aquinas's native Italy. His king has characteristics of the *podestà*. See below, chapter 6.

119 ST Ia IIae 97.3. resp. and ad 3. Compare Marsilius of Padua, below, chapter 4. This raises an interesting issue about the potential for the view of a majority to obscure and 'tyrannize' over that of a minority within the community, which Aquinas says nothing about (nor does Locke), the reason apparently being that established majority custom is assumed to be the consequence of deliberate judgement of reason.

Private Property Rights

According to the standard view, by nature all things are common,[120] but Aquinas asks whether natural law can be changed. He argued that many things over and above natural law have been added, by divine law and by human laws, which are useful to social life. Common possession and universal liberty are said to be of natural law but private possession (*distinctio possessio*) and slavery (*servitus*) exist, not by natural law but by rational human contrivance for the utility of human life. The natural law is, therefore, not changed but is added to. Indeed, he argued that the private and individual *possession* of material things is natural to man in his circumstances.[121] Private property according to civil law is therefore *permissible* and is a *conclusion* of natural law. The division of the community into spheres of private property is, for him, no more than a utilitarian conclusion of reason in the circumstances to further peace and commerce. It results from human agreement which, thereafter, is enshrined in positive law.[122] But beyond the satisfaction of limited human needs and modest profit, the superabundance possessed by any individual is *owed* to the poor by *natural right* and it is to be used for the common welfare. It is left to individuals to make provision for the poor from their own wealth, except in cases of urgent necessity when a starving person may take what legally belongs to another and not be considered to have obtained such through robbery. For what is taken by God's command, God being the owner (*dominus*) of the universe, cannot be against the owner's will, and hence cannot be considered theft.[123] Private property is therefore circumscribed by a prior natural necessity and morality, which reads Aristotle's argument through the spectacles of canon lawyers and the Dominican Order.

Indeed, Aquinas speaks of a moral urgency that all individuals know, or have a duty to come to know. His emphasis is on the development of an individual inner freedom from avarice, an internal control that is more significant than external legal regulations and sanctions of the 'state'. For without this internal freedom, this inner moral responsibility,[124] social disorder becomes the norm and it is then that men take things that rightfully belong to others. An inner transformation is required which thereafter leads to public virtue and the good society. The public sphere of the 'state' is the outer reflection of moral individuals who have individually conquered inordinate desire for excessive wealth and dominance over others. This conquest is evident in the moral virtues as habits of individual citizens. This means that the 'state' and its good government is a *consequence* of and reflects the moral autonomy of rational individuals. The 'state' is not a means to the achievement of human moral autonomy through the 'state's' positive recognition, in law, of individual subjective rights. Moral autonomy is not something the 'state' can offer because men already have it, by natural law. The 'state' can only create 'the conditions in which' men pursue their end, a system of those rational laws which guide the choices that men are already capable of making, towards the achievement of a collective

---

120 ST Ia IIae 94.5.
121 ST IIa IIae 66.1–2.
122 Compare Cicero.
123 ST Ia IIae 94.5 resp. 2.
124 ST Ia IIae 19.5; the act by which reason applies universal principles of morality to particular cases is called conscience, *conscientia*.

good. Aquinas understands the order of the *civitas* – as an interrelationship between its parts and a co-ordination of those parts – in terms of its purpose or goal as a moral association.

If Aquinas does not develop a doctrine of subjective, individual rights that are capable of exercise in the public sphere, we have already seen that there was a juristic language of natural, individual rights which had grown up among civilian and canon lawyers. But even they, it can be argued, were not creating human moral autonomy by legislating it onto the statute books or by insisting that one or another constitutional form (republic or monarchy) offered men this autonomy. They were recognizing that zone of natural, moral autonomy, that psychological power, which civil laws of whatever constitution are obliged by reason to confirm.

Is Aquinas's political theory new? It certainly is a Dominican reading of the operations of contemporary community, in society and in the church. And it is penetrated by Aristotelian insights which were not, as yet, taken up by all theorists, so that Aquinas would, for some time to come, be of immense influence largely within his own order alone. While there also is a Ciceronian legacy that has been absorbed into Aquinas's perspective, it is not as pure or pervasive as is Aristotle's overall influence. Cicero and other Roman moralists are, in Aquinas's writings, always filtered through canonist and civilian discourse, where they are given either a Christian or an Aristotelian 'spin'.

Cicero's condemnation of a 'state' that redistributed property was rejected not only by radical fringe groups in medieval society. Aquinas in particular understood there to be a natural claim on anyone's superfluity of property, not least, the claim of a poor man who ought not to be considered to have stolen from a legitimate owner what he needs to keep himself alive. For Aquinas, this indicated that the particular conclusions of primary moral law were to be taught both by church and 'state', and were meant to be a part of the moralizing perspective of 'state' government. Although, like Aristotle, he did not think the 'state' could legislate for private generosity, he is, much more than Aristotle, implying that the 'state' has moral responsibilities in actively creating an ambience where men do choose to share their possessions with others. 'Love thy neighbour as thy self' was intended to be realized in communal relations. The church's teachings on morals and religion were meant to be actualized by good 'state' government. State law was meant to induce citizens to choose to act virtuously, so that personal morality depended on communal morality. But, as we noted above, Aquinas took this further through Christian doctrine by insisting that ultimately, personal morality and one's responsibility for exercising it is to be judged according to the value of one's intentions in the eyes of God, rather than according to communal values.[125] The biblical commandments of the divine law not to intend to commit crimes against persons and property were universally obliging on Christian consciences. Although what was to count as murder and theft, and how they were to be punished, were to be determined by each 'state', the individual's intention – towards the good or evil – was most finally judged by God's moral law, to which man has rational access.

The newness in Aquinas's approach to ethics and politics, then, is the newness of the twelfth- and thirteenth-century naturalism. It is the newness of the scholastics' recogni-

125   ST Ia IIae 21.4 ad 3.

tion of the comprehensive perspective of Aristotle, brought into a systematic whole for Christians by Aquinas's efforts. But it goes beyond contemporary naturalism by reinstating rational man in the order of nature and thereby finding a place for man both as body and mind, as a creature of natural instinct and rational deliberation. Consequently, it affirms that man, as *that* kind of being, is to be actively involved in shaping and sustaining the polity as a means to his final end.

3

John of Paris

From at least the last decade of the thirteenth century to the middle of the fourteenth, a remarkable range of political theories was aired which proved to be profoundly influential, to some extent in their own days but even more so for posterity. One crisis after another faced European territorial states and the city republics of northern Italy, from increased population growth, famines and warfare. There developed increasingly centralized 'state' machinery that was required to secure the finance to maintain social order. Although the old, universal claims of the German Roman Emperor on the one hand, and the universal claims to power of the papacy on the other, were maintained, the political theories of the time showed these claims to be contested in the defence of national sovereignty. Perhaps the most notorious conflict between the church and state arose between France's King Philip IV the Fair (1285–1314) and Pope Boniface VIII (1294–1303).

Philip IV was not any different from other European monarchs in his seeking to tax the French clergy in order to pay for his war with England, but he did so without papal consent. In 1296 Pope Boniface VIII, a member of the powerful aristocratic Roman family the Gaetani, issued a papal bull *Clericis laicos* to reaffirm that clergy could only be taxed upon licence from the Apostolic See. Boniface asserted that temporal rulers, be they emperors, kings, princes, dukes, earls, barons, *podestà*, officials or rectors, in *regna,* cities or universities, had no jurisdiction over clergy and their property. Therefore, even kings supported by representative assemblies did not have absolute authority in their own realms. Boniface intended that the French clergy should disobey Philip IV.

In 1301 Philip IV had the bishop of Pamiers arrested and tried for blasphemy, heresy and treason. This breached the canon law principle that bishops could only be tried by the pope, and Boniface called the French bishops to a council in Rome not only to discuss the church's liberty but also to correct France's king and ensure the good government of his kingdom. In his letter to Philip, *Ausculta fili* ('Listen, son . . .'), Boniface maintained that Philip was subject to the pope as head of the ecclesiastical hierarchy, but he was taken to have implied that the king was subject to the church in both temporal and spiritual matters. Thereafter, in 1302, Boniface issued *Unam sanctam* where he laid out the official papal line on the subordination of the 'state' to the church, and indeed, asserted that the earthly power was instituted, and meant to be judged by, the spiritual. Much debate in the scholarly literature has been about the degree to which anything that was stated in *Unam sanctam* was new.[1] But it was this conflict that spawned a mass of

---

1   These documents may be examined in translation with brief commentary in B. Tierney, *The Crisis of Church and*

political tracts, and perhaps most notable for its long-lasting influence on other like-disputes in other times and places was the *De potestate regia et papali* (On Royal and Papal Power) by the Dominican John of Paris (*d.* 1306).[2] In particular, John's tract would later influence fifteenth-century conciliarists and seventeenth-century republicans.[3]

John has been judged a major advocate of the royal position and his treatise has been taken to be a principal literary weapon in Philip's arsenal against the pope.[4] But *On Royal and Papal Power* is *not* a single-issue treatise; it is a series of tracts written possibly over several years, and although it may well have been used by Philip, its origin is in the cumulative series of issues with which John's Dominican Order had to deal.

These events finally came to a head in 1295–7 when Boniface VIII became pope and his election was contested by two rebellious cardinals, Peter and James Colonna, members of a powerful, rival aristocratic Roman family to that of Boniface. The college of cardinals had chosen Boniface after the previously elected pope, Celestine V, had resigned. Because there had been no clear precedent in church history for papal resignation, an academic debate ensued over whether a pope could licitly resign his office. John of Paris does, briefly, deal with this issue. But it was in the initially narrower debate between the Franciscans and Dominicans over their respective relation to property, and papal jurisdiction and *dominium*, that John of Paris developed his most famous arguments, making use of distinctively Dominican positions from canon and civil law, as well as distinctively Dominican theological arguments.[5] He would draw much more specific conclusions than did Aquinas from the Dominican distinction between property ownership and its administration (*dominium* and *jurisdictio*) in the church and the state.

In elucidating the proper relationship between spiritual and temporal powers on the one hand, and the proper relationship between church rulers and temporal rulers to their respective subjects on the other, John spent more time treating these issues within the church than within the *regnum*. But his real claim to fame is in having narrowed the definition of *potestas* in both church and 'state' to mean, specifically, *potestas* as *dominium*, lordship over material property: *dominium in rebus*. This understanding of *potestas* would have great influence, not only on justifications of property ownership and the inalienable private rights of individual men over things in the world,[6] but also on the separate notion of constitutional government, established by a people to be a fiduciary,

---

State, 1050–1300 (Englewood Cliffs, NJ, 1964), pp. 172–92. For the Latin texts and German translations see J. Miethke and A. Bühler, *Kaiser und Papst im Konflikt, zum Verhältnis von Staat und Kirche im späten Mittelalter* (Dusseldorf, 1988).

2   Text and German translation in F. Bleienstein, *Johannes Quidort von Paris über königliche und papstliche Gewalt (De regia potestate et papali)* (Stuttgart, 1969); English trans. A. P. Monahan, *John of Paris on Royal and Papal Power* (New York, 1974) and J. A. Watt, *John of Paris, on Royal and Papal Power* (Toronto, 1971).

3   J. Coleman, 'Dominium in Thirteenth- and Fourteenth-century Political Thought and its Seventeenth-century Heirs: John of Paris and Locke', *Political Studies* 33 (1985), pp. 73–100.

4   For a review of the past literature see J. Coleman, 'The Dominican Political Theory of John of Paris in its Context', in D. Wood, ed., *The Church and Sovereignty c. 590–1918: essays in honour of Michael Wilks* (Oxford, 1991), pp. 187–223; also J. Coleman, 'The Intellectual Milieu of John of Paris OP', in J. Miethke, ed., *Das Publikum politischer Theorie im 14. Jahrhundert* (Munich, 1992), pp. 173–206.

5   For the earlier debate between the two orders see J. Coleman, 'The Two Jurisdictions: theological and legal justifications of church property in the thirteenth century', *Studies in Church History* 23 (1987), pp, 75–110; J. Coleman, 'Property and Poverty', in J. H. Burns, ed., *The Cambridge History of Medieval Political Thought c. 350–c.1450* (Cambridge, 1988) (henceforth *CHMPT* (1988)), pp. 607–48.

6   This would come to influence the seventeenth-century John Locke in his *Second Treatise of Government*.

administrative, public power acting as judge, not owner, of the just proportion owed by each to the common good. He applied this notion of constitutional government, responsible to its constituency, to the church as well. Furthermore, John argued for a separation of politics from theology by insisting that civil authority was autonomous, sovereign in the realm of temporal property, and free of ecclesiastical coercion, because the origins of the 'state' were natural and the origins of property were prior to the 'state'. We shall see that his argument – that the community, through explicit consent, has the ultimate sanction of authority – was to be further developed by Marsilius of Padua. Marsilius would also go further with John's argument that the best form of government for both church and 'state' was one in which the people regularly participated through their chosen representatives in the preservation of government.

Biographical Details

There is little doubt that John, as a Dominican at the convent of Saint-Jacques in Paris, was a member of an order that was favoured by French royalty and that he was intellectually antagonistic to the hierocratic views of lawyers and theologians who wrote for the papal cause. But we know very little about his life, other than that he seems to have been a combative man in combative times. His name is found among those Dominicans who signed a petition in 1303 for a council, launched by King Philip, to judge Boniface VIII. But he never names Philip in his *On Royal and Papal Power* and only mentions Boniface once, with respect to his contested election after the resignation of the saintly pope Celestine V. This occurs exclusively in the final chapters of the tract, which appear to have been added later in order to treat specific problems that illustrate the more general thesis he had already sought to maintain. Following the practices of lawyers, John speaks generally and impersonally of popes, kings and emperors. And the conflict between Philip and Boniface was a specific instance of an already ancient conflict over the respective limits of papal and royal power.[7]

On Royal and Papal Power contains twenty-five loosely connected chapters. Chapters 1–10 deal with specific arguments largely made by Franciscans and Dominicans from 1270–81. Chapter 11 lists opponents' views and widens the debate beyond the position of the Franciscan opponents to take in the views of papal hierocrats who argued similarly. Chapters 12–13 are preliminary general remarks before a point-by-point refutation of opponents in chapters 14–20. Thereafter, chapter 21 seems to be a separate treatise on the Donation of Constantine and on the powers of the Roman emperor, drawing on traditional Roman law arguments. Chapter 22 deals with whether one is permitted to debate and judge issues concerning the pope and has the form of a determination in a university debate, possibly as a contribution to the debate on such issues that was held at the University of Paris *c.* 1295. Chapter 23 treats 'frivolous' arguments put forward largely, but not exclusively, by radical Franciscans, that the pope cannot resign. This debate was occasioned by the resignation of Celestine V in 1294. Chapters 24–5 answer these arguments, drawing on the treatise by the Augustinian Giles of Rome, *De renuntiatione papae* (1297), which favoured papal resignation and mentions the specific

---

7   See further, J. Coleman, 'The Two Jurisdictions' and 'Property and Poverty'.

problem of Celestine V and Boniface VIII's subsequent accession (1294–5).

John of Paris's arguments reflect his Dominican milieu. He maintains Dominican positions as these were developed between the 1270s and 1290s, and this means that it is no longer certain that John's tract was written in direct response to Boniface VIII's *Clericis laicos* (1296), *Ausculti fili* (1301) or *Unam sanctam* (1302). The tract presents a Dominican perspective on the relationship between the pope and the church, the pope and temporal rulers, the relationship between the church and its collective property, and the relationship between temporal rulers and the private property of their subjects. The heart of John's theory is an examination of the different modes by which individuals and corporations may legitimately acquire and hold property, and the consequences for the secular and spiritual administration and dispensing of such property that is held in different ways.

These views emerged initially out of the property–poverty debate between secular and mendicant churchmen of the mid-thirteenth century, a debate which continued at least until 1290 when the University of Paris debated, and the cardinal legate Gaetani, the future Boniface VIII, found in favour of the mendicants and their privileges against the secular clergy. The property–poverty debate had then taken a turn in which the mendicant orders themselves came to disagree with one another; the Franciscans established a perspective on property ownership, its use, and jurisdiction which differed from that of the Dominicans. Franciscans tended to conflate jurisdiction and ownership (in order to establish that the pope, standing in for Christ, was the rightful owner of all Franciscan property and therefore that the papacy had jurisdictional powers over the said property); but they separated ownership from use (so that the Franciscans had the right to use what was not owned by them, and hence were able to maintain their commitment to voluntary apostolic poverty, thereby *legally* owning nothing, like Christ). The Franciscan perspective on their own order's property had been shaped earlier in the thirteenth century by Pope Gregory IX and even more so by Pope Innocent IV, who had created the legal fiction of papal *dominium* of goods used by Franciscans. Although it appears that St Francis had interpreted poverty to mean primarily the renunciation of material goods in excess of the barest necessities, after Innocent IV had decided that the order should renounce all *dominium* into the hands of the papacy, poverty came to be interpreted as a reununciation of all rights to ownership. The Franciscan Bonaventure argued in his *Apologia pauperum* (1269) that possession of temporal goods was to be treated with regard to *dominium* on the one hand and *usus* on the other. The nature of evangelical poverty is to renounce earthly possessions in respect of *dominium* and *proprietas* but not to reject *usus* utterly. The profession of perfect poverty is the rejection of *dominium* in common and in particular, since the life of Christ and the apostles showed the pattern of a rejection of individual and common ownership of things. Indeed Christ's royalty, his kingship in heaven and on earth, is the basis of ecclesiastical property, but Christ voluntarily chose to give up those aspects of his royalty which would make him *de facto* king on earth and in heaven. Christ refused royal dignities in order to be an example to men and he condescended to become poor and a beggar, so that poverty is an individual and voluntary profession, just as Christ assumed poverty for humankind.[8]

---

8   Gregory IX: *Quo elongati* and Innocent IV: *Ordinem vestrum*. M. D Lambert, *Franciscan Poverty: the Doctrine of the Absolute Poverty of Christ and the Apostles in the Franciscan Order 1210–1323* (London, 1961) is the classic account. See J. Coleman, 'The Two Jurisdictions', esp. pp. 77–85.

The papacy's acceptance of the *dominium* and jurisdiction over Franciscan property was thereafter widened, not least in the arguments by the Augustinian Giles of Rome,[9] to *all* property relations in both the church and in secular society. But Giles, writing in 1301–2, was not the first to claim that *dominium* or any kind of possession can only be justly maintained through man's baptismal regeneration within the church; like John of Paris, he too argued that *potestas* as *dominium* was to be narrowed to *ius in rem*, rights in things, but to Giles, even civil law may only be justified through its foundations in the church which establishes *communicatio*, the linking of men with one another in the first place; it is the church's *ex*communication which casts a man from all society, so that without the church there would be no property partitions, sales, donations, and no laws which enabled anyone to be able to say 'this is mine'. For Giles of Rome there is no rightful *dominium* over temporal things unless one has these by being subject to and through the church. Giles of Rome's argument[10] that it was not sufficient for anyone to be considered a legitimate owner *unless* he was a member of the church, was already foreshadowed in Franciscan views. That Giles, a formidably knowledgeable Aristotelian, could make this argument indicates the degree to which he followed his own rhetorical advice to suit your oratory to its recipient, in this case the pope.[11]

The Franciscan Position

The argument advanced by Franciscans was that all members of ecclesiastical and lay communities have no fundamental (as opposed to legal) rights of ownership as individuals or collectively; they are only administrators and stewards of wealth. In effect, God gave the world in common to humankind for men's use (not ownership). This position came to be developed out of the narrower application of this principle to Franciscans alone: in voluntarily following Christ's absolute poverty, what Franciscans use is in the free gift of the pope and the cardinals of the church, so that friars are cut off from dispensation, that is, from selling property even to maintain their own lives. Cardinals dispense things for Franciscan use. Indeed, the property offered to Franciscans always resides in the giver and it can be recalled whenever the donor chooses. Franciscans are not entitled to own the property that pious men may offer to them because these offerings are actually to God; and even here, God already owns what, in civil law, is recognized as private possessions offered for Franciscan use. Ultimate ownership as well as jurisdiction are God's. Hence, in the world, ownership and jurisdiction were claimed from God rather than from any temporal king, and the pope as Christ's vicar merely tolerated as a (legal) concession various kings' claims to exclusive jurisdiction in actions *ratione materiae*. St Peter, or his vicar the pope, stands in for Christ as owner; he is the overseer of all the apostles, bishops and Christians. Franciscans, therefore, went beyond

---

9   In his *De ecclesiastica potestate*, dedicated to the pope.

10   'Non sufficit quod quicumque sit generatus carnaliter nisi sit per ecclesiasm regeneratus quod possit cum iustitia rei alicui dominari nec rem aliquam possidere.'

11   Aegidius Romanus: *De ecclesiastica potestate*, ed. R. Scholz (Leipzig, 1929, reprinted Aalen, 1961), esp. pp. 70–8, 103 – 5. For a fuller discussion of Giles of Rome's (Aegidius Romanus) position in *De ecclesiastica potestate* see J. Coleman, 'Medieval Discussions of Property: *ratio* and *dominium* according to John of Paris and Marsilius of Padua', *History of Political Thought* 4 (1983), pp. 209–28, esp. pp. 213–15.

their own status as mendicant users of goods and argued against a recognition of *natural* rights to property ownership *tout court*. For them, the pope's *plena potestas* meant that he alone had supreme jurisdiction and *dominium*, and ecclesiastics within the church hierarchy as well as kings simply exercised a conceded, delegated jurisdiction. As the Franciscan archbishop of Canterbury Pecham would come to argue, a temporal king's very crown, his rights and prerogatives are dependent on those of the crown of Christ and Christ's royalty, his *dominium* and *jurisdictio*, are the sources of the church's liberties. Indeed Moses, as God's lawgiver, ordained that whoever disobeyed the priest should die.[12] There is never a hint either of natural law arguments for the legitimacy of private ownership or constitutionalist conceptions which limit absolutist policies of popes, as there is in contemporary Dominican theories. For Franciscans, all questions fall under the rubric of the spiritual and the pope is the adjudicator with powers to bind and loose on earth as well as in heaven.[13]

John of Paris's *On Royal and Papal Power*, presenting the Dominican stance which opposed that of the Franciscans, therefore reflects a view that was at the time not the one that the papacy favoured. He rejected the view which asserts that Christ's absolute *dominium* in the world as well as in heaven means that the' pope is a universal owner. And he rejected the Franciscan understanding of a necessary obedience to the pope who legitimates the binding nature of all human constitutions.

The Dominican Position

The Dominicans separated jurisdiction from ownership, arguing that public office did not imply that the official, in either church or 'state', owned what he administered. And they argued that if one owned property, it was illogical to separate ownership from its use. The Dominican position was that to have proprietary right and ownership over property is not the same as having jurisdiction over it, and neither princes nor popes are owners of the property over which they exercise jurisdiction. Governing did not include the capacity to own that over which a governor exercised jurisdiction. John of Paris's argument concerning the origin of private property rights on the one hand, and the origins of the 'state' and the church on the other, was to be one of the strongest statements of the Dominican position and it took Aquinas's argument much further. Aquinas had maintained that the ownership of a moderate amount of private possessions, over and above the barest necessities, was both natural in man's circumstances on earth and just, serving as it did the higher end to use them well. For Aquinas, private property was a natural conclusion of natural law precepts known by all, and on this view, temporal goods have a certain good in themselves.[14] John of Paris was one of the early great defenders of Aquinas's views and he was, in his own time, better known as an articulate supporter of Thomas than for his more political work. He composed a series of corrections to the Franciscans' list of corrections of Aquinas's views. And his earlier,

---

12   D. Douie, *Archibishop Pecham* (Oxford, 1952), pp. 129–30; *Registrum . . . Pecham* I, pp. 240–4 (Lambeth, 1281); J. Coleman, 'The Two Jurisdictions', pp. 107–8.
13   For the full argument, especially from the Franciscan archbishop Pecham, see J. Coleman, 'The Two Jurisdictions' and 'The Dominican Political Theory', pp. 201–2.
14   ST IIa IIae 66.1–2.

negative views on the Franciscan so-called 'perfection of poverty' would resurface in his *On Royal and Papal Power*, when he challenged the Franciscan view that the pauper who, like Christ, *voluntarily* assumed poverty is more perfect than the rich man. If this is the case, John would argue, than how is the pope, who they say is owner of their property, evangelically perfect?

This complicated argument would achieve a resolution beyond the time of John of Paris, when by the early 1320s the pope at the time, John XXII, would decide in favour of the Dominican stance and elevate Thomas Aquinas to sainthood as having maintained a more acceptable defence of the impossibility of dividing ownership from use. John XXII would finally insist that the Franciscan doctrine of Christ's absolute poverty was heretical. This debate over the nature of jurisdiction and ownership typified not only the dispute between the two mendicant orders but served as a microcosm of what was occurring in the wider world. It helped to define the distinct and separate roles of church and state by drawing a line between their respective jurisdictions and their distinctive relationships to property and wealth, both within the church and in secular 'states'.

The Origin of Government

John begins his *On Royal and Papal Power* by citing Aristotle's *Politics*, which he reads not only through the mediating interpretations of Aquinas, but also through the institutions of Rome which survived somewhat transformed in the governance of medieval cities, not least in Italy. He is concerned to begin with definitions and he defines the nature of the *regnum* as the government of a perfect multitude for the sake of the common good and regulated by one.[15] He clarifies further that, in general, *regimen* or 'government' is to be taken as a generic term to which is then added the multitude (*regimen multitudinis*) in order to differentiate this human community from the kind of government appropriate to animals, which are governed by natural instinct, and also to differentiate it from government by reason, which, he says, applies to those who live a solitary life. John follows the division of the practical arts or practical philosophy into *solitarium, privatam et publicam*, or ethics, economics and politics, developed from the twelfth-century onwards. Government by reason deals with personal moral conduct, that is, *solitarium* or ethics. He understands 'perfect' in the phrase 'the government of a perfect multitude' to be that which distinguishes between a perfect community and the domestic community which is not perfect because the family is not self-sufficient for anything more than a short period of time and not for all the needs of life as is the city (*civitas*). Neither the family (*communitas domus*) nor the village (*vicus*) can achieve what is sufficient to living as can the city or kingdom (*civitas seu regnum*) (chapter 1).

He accepts that the common good may be served by one man, as well as by an aristocracy, which is rule by the few more virtuous men[16] and which, he says, some call rule by decisions of the prudent or of a senate, and also by what he calls *polycratia* where the people rule by plebiscite. We see here a mixture of Aristotle's best constitutions – monarchy, aristocracy and polity – actualized in Roman institutions, and John contrasts

---

15 'Regnum est regimen multitudinis perfectae ad commune bonum ordinatum ab uno.'
16 'Id est principatus optimorum . . . ubi pauci dominantur secundum virtutem.'

them with their deviant versions in tyranny, oligarchy and democracy, each of which governs for sectional interests rather than for the common good. But like Aquinas, John thinks that the government of a perfect multitude by one man according to virtue is more expedient (*utilius*) than government exercised by many or a few virtuous men. A single ruler better upholds the unity of the perfect multitude and hence better achieves peace and concord in the governing of a multitude. It is important to emphasize that the single ruler's purpose, according to John of Paris, is to serve peace and unite the multitude in harmony in order that a city or kingdom may achieve self-sufficiency. He takes this to be the meaning of the common good.[17] Hence, John concludes that it is necessary and advantageous for man to live in society such as a city or a territorially defined region which is self-sufficient in everything that pertains to the whole of life, and under the directing government of one who rules for the common good and is called a king.[18]

We are next told that this government (*regimen*) of a perfect multitude, thus defined, derives from natural law and the law of nations. John of Paris here cites Aristotle's *Politics* book 1, but he also knows his Cicero (especially *De inventione* I, 2) and he uses him to supplement what he reads in Aristotle. Hence, he says that it is also clear that this kind of kingly government for the common good has its roots in natural law, in that man is naturally a civil or political and social animal.[19] Indeed, prior to the first kings who exercised government, men lived without rule like beasts. Their common speech brought them together, and as Cicero had said, certain men who were better able to use their reason, applied persuasive arguments to get them to live an ordered life in common under one ruler.[20] Once brought together they were bound by definite laws to live communally. These laws are called the law of nations (*ius gentium*). We note that original community is *prior* to any common agreement about *civil laws,* and persuasive rational arguments themselves establish a community under natural law and the law of nations (chapter 1).

John says (in chapter 3) that men learn from natural instinct, which comes from God, that they should live in communities; consequently, in order to live well communally, they should elect *rectors* who are of such a kind that they are appropriate to the community in question. There is no divine commandment that all laymen should be subject in temporalities to one king. Neither man's natural tendencies nor divine law commands a single, supreme, temporal monarch for everyone and there is no natural reason to have a universal unifier, i.e. an emperor. He presents a general argument for the natural existence of diverse communities, and explains that secular powers are diverse because of the variation in climate and the differing physical constitutions of men. One man, he argues, could not possibly rule the world's *temporalia* because his authority, ultimately, is his sword and he cannot be everywhere at once.

John (chapter 2) is concerned to recognize that aside from this natural end of man in

---

17   Compare Marsilius, below.
18   'Ex quibus praedictis patet homini necessarium et utile in multitudine vivere et maxime in multitudine quae sufficere potest ad totam vitam, ut est civitas vel regio, et praecipue sub uno principante propter bonum commune qui rex dicitur.'
19   'Quod homo naturaliter est animal civile seu politicum et sociale.'
20   'Et cum per verba communia ad vitam communem naturaliter eis convenientem . . . ad vitam communem sub uno aliquo ordinatam rationibus persuasoriis revocare conati sunt, ut dicit Tullius, et ita revocatos certis legibus ad vivendum communiter ligaverunt, quae quidem leges hic ius gentium dici possunt.'

community there is also a supernatural end of man: life eternal. Rulership here belongs to a divine rather than a human king: Christ, who is not only man but also God. But because the obstacles on the path to man's desired supernatural end must be cleared, in order that remedies and necessary helps be provided if man is to achieve salvation, Christ as *priest* offered himself as a sacrifice, removing that universal obstacle which was the injury done to God by man's original sin. The church and its remedial sacraments, therefore, were established to remove the obstacle to man's supernatural end. Where the rule of diverse men in a community is achieved through the authority of the ruler's *coercive sanction*, his sword, the spiritual unity of Christians is achieved through the *verbal sanction* of the church.[21] But John (chapter 4) goes on to demonstrate by means of biblical texts as well as arguments from Augustine's *City of God* the chronological priority of society and government to this spiritual remedy. He builds on his earlier observation that society and government are to be seen as natural, having been established through reasoned persuasion, binding men through natural law and the law of nations to live the ordered communal life of self-sufficiency (chapter 2).

John compares the structure of the church and that of secular governments: all priests are ordered in a hierarchy to one supreme head, Peter's successor, the pope, and this pyramidal ordering of the ecclesiastical hierarchy came from Christ's own mouth, rather than as a decision of a council, when Christ said 'feed my sheep'. Christ decided that there was to be a subordination of church ministers to one head, and this is to be contrasted with the lack of divine commandment that the ordinary faithful be subject in temporalities to one single supreme monarch. The need for one supreme head in the church, as we shall see, is to maintain, through final verbal adjudication, a unity of orthodox faith and the detection of heresy. The need for diverse monarchs is to settle disputes through impartial adjudication in private property disputes through civil law backed by coercive sanction.

The Thomistic Underpinning of *dominium in rebus*, Lordship and Ownership of Things

Recall from the previous chapter that Aquinas and his Dominican supporters argued that the human soul should be understood as the actuality of its body. The soul is identical in its essence and potencies in all men, but the soul of each man is immattered in this or that particular body. Each man's intellectual capacities are to be considered as part of the soul–body complex. Although in man there is only one substantial form, intellective soul, souls are distinguished one from another in virtue of their bodies. This distinctive and controversial Thomist theory of corporeal individuation leads John of Paris to an understanding of human effort and labour in the world of things as a distinguishing feature of human potential when it is actualized as human existence. He presents a theory of human acquisition that is natural and which is the means by which men not only survive but are individually who they are as a consequence of their actions. Humans know their capacities by sensually experiencing the world and coming to general conclusions through sensed experiences. The external world to be experienced acts on

---

21   Compare Marsilius, below.

the soul's sense faculties to produce our thoughts, the intelligible species. In order for humans to know anything, the soul cannot operate by itself, but requires actualization by objects which are sensible species or similitudes of external things. In this life, then, the proper objects of the human intellect are material objects which are known through their intelligible species. John of Paris concludes that matter, what might be seen as potential property, remains potential until it is informed by use, by man's intention to actualize matter through human labour and acquisition. Private property, acquired through an individual's labour, is the natural process by which man achieves his actualization, converting use to ownership. Thomistic metaphysics is at the base of John of Paris's labour theory of natural rights to private property.

He argues that the clergy do have ownership (*dominium*) and jurisdiction in temporalities, but this power is not theirs because of their ecclesiastical status or because they are vicars of Christ and successors of the apostles. Ecclesiastics have *collective ownership* and jurisdiction of church property in virtue of the concession and permission either of rulers who endow them, through piety, or of other lay donors. The property of the church belongs to the *communitas personarum*, to the corporative community of persons, as a consequence of pious donations. Ecclesiastics therefore have collective ownership and jurisdiction of church property in virtue of concessions made by temporal rulers.

The Justification of Private Ownership

How do rulers and other individual donors come by their property which they then may offer to the church? In taking up Aquinas's thesis of corporeal individuation, John of Paris argues that among men there is a great diversity of bodies while they share the same species-specific soul. All men are constituted in the same essential degree according to the unity of the human species. This expresses the Thomist doctrines of the unicity of substantial form and of matter as the principle of individuation. Furthermore, each individual is *dominus* or owner of his own property, which is acquired through his own industry. Each individual is, therefore, the administrator of what is his own, to do with as he wishes (chapter 3). Exterior lay goods are acquired by individuals through their own skill, labour and industry and as individual persons they have in this property, right and power and true ownership (*dominium*) (chapter 7). Consequently, each person may order his own property, dispose of it, administer it, hold or alienate it, as he wishes without injury to any other person, since he is the owner. Furthermore, such goods or property, once acquired through the labour of the individual, have neither interconnections with other men nor are they mutually inter-ordered; in other words, they are no longer held in common (chapter 7). Once property is acquired through labour and industry an individual's rights to his own property are inalienable. Neither in the original community that is formed through persuasion, nor in that community which elects rectors and establishes a 'state', are the temporalities of laymen communal. Therefore, each remains master of his own property as it was acquired through his own industry. There is no need for administration of *temporalia* in common, for each is his own administrator. In the language of Aquinas, this means that human nature is actualized in the circumstances of life on earth by the act of labour and acquisition which constitute a particular man's existence, where existence is the actualization of a thing's nature.

But John must show what function is served by a community of private owners coming to agree to establish a 'state' and elect 'rectors'. John develops the position that each individual person may dispose of his own things as he wishes, except in times of necessity, when the prince may dispose of private goods in the interest of the common good. Princes do not own the property they dispose of in times of need. As we have seen, in the beginning, there simply were individual owners who administered their own without consideration for others. But then men, acting on their natural, divinely inspired instinct and persuaded by the reasoning of those among them who could use their reason to better effect, constructed a community. The natural instinct is one which teaches men from their experience as initially solitary acquirers among other solitary acquirers, that the communal life is better for all concerned. And since men also learned from experience that the peace of everyone is sometimes disturbed because of exterior goods, that is, when someone usurps what is another's, or when men, through excessive love for their own things, do not communicate their property to others so that it may be placed at the service of the common welfare, they saw a need to establish a ruler or prince. Individual owners living communally, the people as a multitude of private own- ers, establish a ruler who is then to have the care of such situations. He acts as judge (not owner) and discerns between the just and the unjust. As a punisher of injustice or inju- ries, the ruler is defined as the measurer of the just proportion owed by each individual owner to the common good (chapter 7).

It is important to understand that rulers, once established, do not destroy the private property of individuals or their natural rights to this property. Rather, they organize and direct the private property of individuals so that it serves the common utility, because it is the common utility that is in the care of the ruler who exercises jurisdiction. John thinks that a multitude comprised of private individuals, each seeking their own, will disintegrate unless there is one who has care of the common good and organizes private possessions to secure the good for all (chapter 1). He provides the Thomist analogy when he says that man's body would collapse if there were not some common power *in the body* towards which the common good of all the bodily members intended. A gov- erning organizer is therefore a necessity, since what is an individual's own is not the same as what is common to all. What is an individual's own is not to be destroyed. For men differ as to what is their own, as individuals, whereas what is common to them unites them together. A uniting principle is required to join individuals to their com- mon species. In Thomistic fashion he argues more generally that since different causes have different effects, then necessarily what moves each individual to his own good is different from what moves him to the common good of the many. In other words, private interest cannot be destroyed, but to live well in community, private interest must be subordinated at times to the common interest, and the common interest is in the care of the prince (chapter 1).

John has politicized Aquinas's doctrine of the unicity of substantial form. He says that it is more useful for the rule of a multitude of individuals to be united by one who is potentially more virtuous than for several to rule who are potentially less virtuous, since in one principal ruler, virtue is more united and strong than in many dispersed. Unity and peace is what a ruler intends in the governing of a multitude. John cites Aristotle, who said that the worst of all constitutions is that of the tyrant who seeks his own advantage rather than that of the common good. Just as in every natural governance we see that the whole governance is reduced to a unity of purpose, so too, John notes, in any body composed of a mixture of elements there is one element that dominates. In the heterogeneous human body there is one principal member, the head, and in the whole man, as the soul–body complex, the soul contains all the elements (chapter 1). Individuals remain individuals in a perfect multitude of individuals, where they are united by a governing organizer to serve not only their individual needs, which they will naturally do anyway, but also their common species' needs, the common good. This is a very distinctive understanding of a corporation which understands multitudes as comprised of individuals whose common purpose is what unites them. It is a view that sees public representation of a corporate will only in terms of what *can* be willed individually – the common good. John justifies this perspective by saying that what has validity in private law and concerns the individual, need not have validity in public law, which deals with the common good (chapter 15) and it is public law which serves the 'state', the common good.

This understanding of an organized multitude comprised of individuals is the political extension of Aquinas's discussion[22] of how each person's individuating intelligence, each person's unique understanding, must be retained, even though each man is considered part of the human species with universally shared characteristics. Individual human beings are, for John, actualized as individuals through their existence in a world of things, and the actualization of self is through labouring to acquire possessions. Individual moral responsibility, as such, never gets absorbed completely in and by the public realm. The public realm is uniquely defined as that sphere of decisions which impinge on what each individual understands as concerned with the common good. And what organizes individual possessors in terms of their common purpose, is the prince. The prince is the principal part of the community, united to the body politic, just as the intellect is the principal part of, and united to, the soul–body complex that is man.

What is noteworthy is that according to this view of government, the principal member, the king or prince, cannot operate at all in some autonomous fashion, because the principal member is dependent entirely on the prior individuals for whom he acts as a principled co-ordinator. This is medieval corporation theory founded in constitutional practices. John uses Aristotle, just as he uses Cicero, scripture, citations from Roman and canon law, all in the service of an existing medieval reality. This is made explicit when he extends further his definition of the directive ruler or governor with jurisdiction, whom he has already referred to as judge, discerning between just and unjust, and as a punisher of injustice or injuries, a measurer of the just proportion owed by each to the common good. He argues (chapter 13) that the civil judge judges according to those civil laws which regulate the buying and selling of property in order to ensure that property is put to those proper human uses which would be neglected if everyone continued to hold everything in common. For, he thinks, if things were held unreservedly in common (a Franciscan position) it would not be easy to keep the peace among men. For this reason, private possession of property was 'introduced' by Roman emperors. In natural law, he notes, there is equal freedom and common possession for everyone in everything. Thus, men were originally given the earth in common but they came to differentiate private property through labour. Their rights to particularized property existed prior to the prince, and he was established as a ruler by the people precisely in order to prevent the discomforts of not having an impartial arbiter when their property

22   *De regno* and ST Ia 76.

was usurped by those who would take what was not their own. In Roman law terms, John of Paris's prince is like a municipal civil magistrate with restricted jurisdiction – concerning matters pertaining to the common good – but without *imperium*. Royal powers are those of jurisdictional arbitration in private property disputes where the prince is not an owner but a judge.

Should we think this to be pure 'blue sky' political theory, we need only look at the *Confirmatio Cartarum* of England's King Edward I (1297), where Edward acknowledged that his subjects' goods were their own and he could enjoy a share in them only by 'the common assent of the whole kingdom and for the common benefit of the same kingdom'.[23]

In countering the Franciscan positions, John of Paris has therefore established that the traditional and *de facto* independence of the monarch (from both emperor and pope) and the independence of the property-holding individual, could indeed be vindicated *de iure*. Co-ordinating government is the consequence of the priority of the existence of individual human beings as private owners. The people elect a co-ordinator who exercises jurisdiction for the common good. And the public function of the first kings, which John insists were historically in place before the advent of a true priesthood, was the service of the needs of collective, human, public life which he has already defined as the self-sufficient life preserved by peace and concord (chapter 4).

Limitations on Government

Indeed, John goes on to argue that a king who offends in spiritual matters like faith and marriage falls under ecclesiastical jurisdiction where the pope has the power to admonish, then to excommunicate him, but *only* by acting with the people can he remove him (chapter 13). And when a ruler offends in temporal matters whose cognizance is not ecclesiastical, then the initiative in starting the correcting process is that of the barons and peers of the kingdom. It is the *people* or their representatives, the *maior et sanior pars*, who actually depose a king with the pope acting 'incidentally'. This is the far more specified correcting procedure to be applied to 'states' that Aquinas had only implied when he maintained that a church-educated community, aware of the necessity to scrutinize civil laws against the yardstick of natural reason and natural law, would alone be the legitimate public authority to move against a tyrant, without the church having anything other than an 'incidental' role in such a removal.

The Origin of the Priesthood

How then does John think the priesthood came into being? Historically it emerged after the establishment of the first kings, but what is its institutional justification? Like Aquinas, John argues that since man cannot secure eternal life through purely human acts of virtue, a divine king, that is Christ, leads men to that higher end, rather than a human king who serves the temporal well-being of the community. Political society is a natural

---

23   C. Stephenson and F. Marcham, *Sources of English Constitutional History*, vol. 1 (London, 1972), p. 165.

development, emerging out of individuals uniting instinctively and upon rational persuasion to form a community with elected kings. We have already seen him argue that
the church was instituted to remedy the injury done to God the Father by the common,
original sin of humankind. Christ, as *priest* (and not as king) offered himself as a sacrifice
on the cross to God the Father, and by his death removed original sin, which is the
universal obstacle to man's spiritual salvation. Thereafter, it was necessary to establish
certain remedies through which Christ's general benefit might be applied to man in
some way. Such remedies are the sacraments of the church. In Thomist fashion, John
argues that it was suitable that these sacraments should be of the sense order and thus
meet the demands of the nature of man, since it is by things of sense that man is led to an
understanding of spiritual and intellectual things. Since Christ intended to withdraw his
physical presence from his church, John argues that it was necessary for him to institute
ministers who would administer these sacraments to men. The priesthood is therefore
defined as the *spiritual* powers given by Christ to ministers (note the plural) of his church
for administering the sacraments to the faithful (chapter 2).

The hierarchy in the church is constituted by those who have the power to confer the
priesthood on others in ordination and consecration. Bishops who are not in any way
superior to ordinary priests in so far as consecrating the Host is concerned, are superior
in their supervisory role in that bishops are important and complete in their powers,
since they make other priests, which lower clergy cannot do. Just as in each diocese
there is one bishop who is head of the church of the people, so in the whole church and
Christian people as a whole, there is one supreme head, the Roman pope, successor to
Peter. This head *presides* over the whole, hierarchically arranged (chapter 2). But then
John cites the Bible, Hosea 1:11: 'and the children of Judah shall be gathered together
and *they shall appoint themselves one head* and they shall come up out of the land'. What
function is this collectively appointed, presiding head meant to perform? John says that
with the removal of Christ's physical presence there sometimes occur questions concerning the faith where a diversity of opinions might divide the church's unity. A single
opinion is required to maintain unity and the one who has this unitive role in the church
is Peter and his successor, from Christ's own mouth when he said: 'Feed my sheep'.

The priesthood is to be considered higher in dignity than kingship, but it is historically posterior to natural political communities. However, the less dignified power, the
secular, does *not* stand related to the more dignified, the spiritual, as to its origin and
derivation. The power of neither of these two derives from the other, but rather from
the same superior power, God. The natural order is not done away with, as Aquinas had
explained, but is perfected by a higher and separate order, that of grace. John takes up
the dualist position concerning the Gelasion doctrine and argues that God wishes the
two powers to be distinct in their existence, not only in themselves, but also by the
subjects in which they are found (chapter 10). Kingdoms are ordained towards that
which enables the congregated multitude to live according to virtue, and such a multitude is further ordained to a higher end, which is the enjoyment of God. It is noteworthy that he thinks that the multitude's direction towards this higher end is in the care of
Christ whose vicars and ministers are priests (again, note the plural) rather than the pope.

John is not simply concerned to establish his own Dominican view but to show it to
be very different from that proposed by Franciscans and other hierocrats. He argues in
chapters 6 and 7 that there are those who wish to elevate the pre-eminence of the
priesthood over the royal dignity to the degree where the priesthood is not merely

superior in dignity but even superior in the order of causality. They claim, he says, that
the secular power is contained in the spiritual power and established by it. But John
insists that at the heart of this error which allows his opponents to elevate the pope as
supreme *dominus* over all secular rulers is their misunderstanding of how the church
acquires property. The church is *given* property by laymen. Laymen, however, are not
given property but acquire it through their own individual, natural labour and skill.
Through the civil law of inheritance, sale, etc., they enhance their natural rights to be
owners by acquiring even more than they have directly laboured for. And they can,
through wills and gifts, give what is theirs as superfluities to others.

The Relation of the Church to its Property

Hence, he presents the Dominican view: ecclesiastical property as ecclesiastical is given
by prior, original owners to communities and not to individual persons. No one person
has proprietary right and ownership over ecclesiastical property. An ecclesiastical individual may have right of use, but he has this not as an individual in his own right but
purely as part and member of an ecclesiastical community. It is the duty of the bishop to
allocate just dues to his subordinates, and therefore he dispenses for the common good
of his college or church, but he is not the owner. Bishops are administrators of collectively owned goods. And just as the bishop dispenses in his own cathedral church, so the
pope has the same office, but in a more universal way, regarding the whole church. The
pope is universal steward of all ecclesiastical goods. He is not the owner of these goods,
since the community is mistress and proprietress of all goods universally, and individual
communities and churches have ownership collectively in the property allocated to
them by original lay owners. The pope is instituted to preside as a steward for the good
of the whole church community. If he betrays the community's trust by not acting in
good faith, he must do penance by restoring the property which he has wrongly treated
as his own. The incorrigible betrayal of trust can and must lead to his deposition, to the
forfeiture of his stewardship.

   Central to this argument is John's rejection of the Franciscan understandings of Christ's
royalty and therefore his position as universal owner, *dominus*. Franciscans had argued
that a king's crown, his rights and prerogatives, were dependent on the crown of Christ.
Christ's royalty, expressed in his universal ownership and jurisdiction, was thereafter
represented by his vicar, the pope. But John provides the Dominican understanding of
Christ's royalty when he says that Christ *as God* is lord of all property, but as man he is
not an owner. As man he had no corporeal communication or contact with those who
are in the church. Christ himself as man did not have such power or jurisdiction. 'If it is
argued', says John, 'that Christ as man was king, and here I mean of a temporal kingdom, having direct and immediate authority in temporalities, this is altogether false'
(chapter 8). Christ as man did not have authority or judicial power over temporalities,
but instead paid tribute to Caesar and ordained that it be paid always. No priest may
therefore claim to be Christ's vicar in temporal *dominium* or jurisdiction, for Christ has
not granted to anyone what he did not have himself (chapter 8).

   John goes further and argues that original owners who confer property on the church
do not intend to transfer right and ownership to Christ. As God, he has these already,
and as man, he had no use for either property rights or ownership. Furthermore, during

Christ's human life he never had such ownership voluntarily to give up (as the Franciscans argued); nor did he have jurisdiction, and he certainly did not transfer either to Peter (chapters 8 and 10). Instead, the intention of donors is to give their property to Christ's ministers collectively; ecclesiastics then dispense it according to need within the collective church for the common good.

Deposition Theory

The argument of *On Royal and Papal Power* centres on whether the pope, who is universal steward and not owner of ecclesiastical wealth, has the right to take the property of churches for reasons other than the common good of the church. To John, if the pope acts as a private owner he can be deposed, because he has broken the trust of his stewardship through which he is meant to carry out his office. On the canon law principle that was already established within the church, if it can be shown that any lesser steward, an abbot or bishop, has misused the collective property of monastery or church for private gain rather than for the common good, then he can be removed. So too, by analogy, the pope. And this general theory is put to work in order to provide a solution to the events of 1296–7 when, in his dispute with the two Colonna cardinals, Boniface VIII deposed them and confiscated their property. The specifics need not concern us here. Rather, the theoretical point John seeks to maintain is that were a pope judged delinquent in spiritual matters, for example conferring benefices for payment or in squandering church property, or depriving churchmen and chapters of their rights, or by false profession or teaching in matters touching the faith and morals, then he is to be warned by the cardinals who stand in the place of the whole clergy. Should he prove incorrigible and the cardinals cannot on their own remove this scandal from the church, then the cardinals may have recourse to the secular arm to support the rule of law. John refers specifically to the *emperor*, as member of the church, who at the request of the cardinals who represent the whole church should proceed against the pope to accomplish his deposition (chapter 13). The emperor's own legitimacy, where his rulership is his by law, is as with kings, a consequence of the will of the people (chapter 19).[24] Kings, once legitimate, are heads of their own kingdom and the emperor, if there is one, is monarch and head of the whole world (chapter 18).[25]

John of Paris's remarkable tract, *On Royal and Papal Power*, has been concerned to establish, on the one hand, that lay individuals are owners and administrators of their own property and, on the other, that ecclesiastical corporations are collective owners and administrators of property given to them by pious laymen. In defending individual and collective ownership, John of Paris definitively denies to kings and popes the power of true *dominium*. Instead, government is a stewardship, and as a fiduciary power is exercised for the common good of individual and corporate owners. Should it not carry out its mandate, it is removable on the authority of the people, the congregated, rational, multitude or their representative.[26]

24 See his response to the hierocrat Henry of Cremona.
25 There was no emperor at the time.
26 Locke's arguments in the *Second Treatise of Government* emerged from this medieval political discourse, and yes, his own library contained John of Paris's *On Royal and Papal Power*! See J. Coleman, 'Dominium', pp. 73–100.

4

Marsilius of Padua

Dominicans continued to contribute to political theorizing during the early fourteenth century, drawing heavily on Aristotle but addressing in particular problems that were most disturbing in Italy. Ptolemy of Lucca, a student of Aquinas, sought to complete Aquinas's fragmentary *De regno* and in the process his continuation (*c.* 1305) changed the focus of his additional later chapters to an advocacy of the kind of political rule suited to Italian city-republics.[1] The Dominican Remigio de' Girolami (*d.* 1319) brought Parisian scholasticism to Florence where he composed his *De bono communi* (*On the common good*) and his *De bono pacis* (*On the good of peace*), similarly applying Aristotelian arguments to Italian city-republics. To Dominican arguments were added political tracts written by secular, civic authors, especially focused on disruptions to the traditions of self-governing communes in northern Italy. The disruptions came from two fronts: the papacy and local, feudal *signori* who, in turn, fostered internal factional discord in cities.[2] Hierocratic papalist arguments continued to be produced but they were vociferously and ingeniously pushed into the background.

In the extraordinary tract *The Defender of Peace* (*Defensor pacis*) by Marsilius of Padua, the problem of the papacy's interference in the temporal peace and tranquillity of cities or 'states' was tackled with unparalleled virulence.[3] Marsilius would, like his contemporaries, draw on Aristotle, Cicero and other ancients, but self-consciously argue that the problems of the ancients were nothing like as grave as those experienced in his own times. Aristotle could not have imagined the unusual cause of the discord or intranquillity of civil regimes which, Marsilius notes, have long troubled and still plague his homeland, the northern city-states of the *regnum Italicum*. According to Marsilius, it is the bishops of Rome who over the centuries have increasingly assumed for themselves the universal coercive jurisdiction over the whole world under the all-embracing title 'plenitude of power', and thereby disturbed the peace of civil regimes. Marsilius insists that they have treated most harshly those who have been less able to resist their power, such as communities and individuals among the Italians whose 'state' is divided and wounded in almost all its parts and so can more easily be oppressed. But they have also moved, albeit more

---

1 See Ptolemy of Lucca, *On the Government of Rulers, De Regimine Principum,* trans. J. M. Blythe (Philadelphia, 1997).

2 See chapter 6, below, on factionalism in Italian cities, between the nobles and the people.

3 For bibliography see J. Miethke, 'Literatur über Marsilius von Padua (1958–92)', *Bulletin de philosophie médiévale* 35 (1993), pp. 150–65; and C. Dolcini, *Introduzione a Marsilio da Padova* (Bari, 1995).

mildly, against kings and other rulers whose resistance and coercive power these Roman bishops fear. However, the popes, says Marsilius, are gradually creeping up in their attempt to usurp the temporal jurisdictions of all civil regimes and have openly ascribed to themselves the power to give and transfer governments. Roman bishops have gradually seized one jurisdiction after another so that now they finally say that they have total coercive temporal jurisdiction, even over the emperor as Roman ruler.[4]

Marsilius intended to warn all manner of cities and 'states' of this present and impending danger which was the cause of universal civil discord, and in the process he wrote a treatise, dedicated to the German king and then emperor, Ludwig of Bavaria, on the office of coercive rulership, its origins and limitations. The *Defender of Peace* has been regarded, especially with hindsight, as one of the most magisterial analyses to emerge from the Middle Ages of the nature, origins and purpose of legitimate government. Like all medieval political theorists and especially those of the early fourteenth century who wrote for a specified cause, Marsilius speaks in more generic terms about good 'government' (*regimen*) and bolsters his own arguments with appeals to Aristotle's *Ethics*, *Politics* and *Rhetoric*.[5] But he also makes very specific use of the arts faculty familiarity with Cicero's *De officiis*. Like his contemporaries, and notably Italians who increasingly drew on their ancient Roman past to seek solutions to their present, Marsilius uses ancient authorities eclectically to further his argument. His expressed aim was to discover the causes of legitimate political communities, and to preserve their stability and tranquillity from those forces that would always constitute the greatest dangers to the achievement of man's desire to live in a civil community and establish the common good as the sufficient life of the whole. He will draw on practices of self-governing communes like his Padua and generalize to make his theoretical point about the universal nature of good government. In the process he formulates a doctrine of *raison d'état*. From his eclectic use of a variety of ancient and contemporary sources he constructs his notion of human society, distinguishing as did his contemporaries, two ends of human existence: in the world and beyond. Life in the world is sufficient in itself and the social order permits the realization of this end. As such, the social order is autonomous.[6] Man is naturally a social and political animal and a perfect community in this world is possible so long as tranquillity and peace are safeguarded.

More than any theorist we have yet encountered, Marsilius will defend the ancient myth of the empire as Roman in the sense of its being the director of Christianity, where the *sacrum imperium* is independent of the papacy, and its legitimacy rests in the Roman civil law tradition. This does not mean, however, that he defends the German Empire's universal sovereign jurisdiction over all other communities.[7] His theory

---

4   *Defender of Peace*, 2 vols, trans. A. Gewirth (New York, 1956), text: vol. 2, Discourse I xix. This is the translation used below, with some changes, following the Latin editions, *Defensor Pacis*, ed. C. W. Previté-Orton (Cambridge, 1928) and R. Scholz, *Defensor Pacis* [Monumenta Germaniae Historica, Fontes Iuris Germanici Antiqui, 7] (Hanover, 1932–3).

5   On Marsilius's use of Parisian arts faculty commentaries on Aristotle's *Politics* see C. Flüeler, 'Die Rezeption der "Politica" des Aristoteles an der Pariser Artistenfakultat im 13. und 14. Jarhundert', in Miethke, *Das Publikum politische Theorie*, pp. 127–38.

6   Compare John of Paris, above.

7   For a good brief summary of his purpose see A. Black, *Political Thought in Europe, 1250–1450* (Cambridge, 1992), pp. 58–71, although Black's view (p. 62) that Marsilius's distinction between philosophy and theology may suggest a certain scepticism towards the totality of prevailing religious beliefs, is not accepted here; see below.

supports a plurality of 'states' of which the empire is but one. But combined with his use of Rome's legacy to northern Italy, Marsilius also demonstrates his familiarity with arts faculty methodologies in interpreting texts, namely from Aristotle's *Analytics*, *Topics*, the *Sophistical Refutations* and other logical and rhetorical works. He demonstrates, where he thinks he can, by syllogisms. It is this methodology, central to his argument in the first Discourse of the *Defender of Peace*, which would lead him to establish one of the most distinctive arguments concerning what is self-evident to all men, on the one hand, and on the other, what can be demonstrated logically, and without recourse to authority, about the nature of political community. It is important to place this Discourse within the context of contemporary discourses and to indicate here (and demonstrate below) that for Marsilius, the nature of political community reveals a certain quality that under-pins *all* subsequent, good constitutional arrangements and this quality may thereafter be found in both republics *and* monarchies, in cities and *regna*.

That he argues for the autonomous nature of the political community living the sufficient life in tranquillity has, somewhat anachronistically, been called his secular po-litical theory. It has also been regarded as the first 'lay' political theory. Georges de Lagarde thought of Marsilius as the first theoretician of the lay spirit, defined as 'that ensemble of tendencies which progressively opposed the civil and the spiritual authori-ties in all domains of western European life'.[8] If this leads us to believe that we are about to confront a political theory that has no room either for the church or for the role of religion in civil regimes, we would be much mistaken. It is precisely this opposition and distinction between 'lay' and 'ecclesiastical' which Marsilius refuses to accept and it was the very distinction of spiritual and temporal jurisdictions which Marsilius saw as the fundamental evil of his times. He will try to show that there is no such thing as spiritual jurisdiction because the very meaning of jurisdiction is the capacity to establish laws which coerce the non-compliant, and this capacity may only be legitimately actualized by the corporate will of the citizen body of any city or 'state'. Therefore his solution, as we shall see, is to reverse the papal hierocratic theory of absolute jurisdiction and incor-porate the church into the state. To describe, as he does (I, 5, 1), the perfect community as necessarily divided into functional parts, and to say that the *priestly*, the warrior and the judicial parts are in the *strict* sense parts of the 'state' makes the modern attribution 'secular political theory' in need of careful qualification. We shall see that although he speaks of the good ordering of civil regimes in generic terms, his model of the best citizen body is undoubtedly Christian.

In the process of examining the origin, purpose and structure of civil community and in demonstrating what powers the clergy could not possess, Marsilius will disendow the church, but make it a crucial educational, physically non-coercive, functional part of civil life, replacing the man-made historical institution of the church hierarchy with a corporate gathering of all believers, the whole people in its religious activity. It is they who authoritatively determine doctrinal education and matters of faith. It is they (not the papacy or a self-styled hierarchy of clergy) who excommunicate. But coercion in matters of *faith* cannot be exercised by this corporate gathering of the church, the *univer-sitas fidelium*. We shall have to examine, however, what he means when he says that beliefs in the internal forum of conscience are not the province of civil government

---

8   G. de Lagarde, *La Naissance de l'esprit laïque au déclin du moyen âge,* 5 vols (Louvain and Paris, 1956–70); for an excellent refutation of this view see J. Quillet, *La Philosophie politique de Marsile de Padou* (Paris, 1970).

either. Aquinas said something similar.[9] As we shall see, beliefs, especially if in some way non-conformist, need to remain internal and may not be turned into what he calls transient acts. Once they are externalized in the external forum they are open to judgement, not as beliefs but as acts, preserving or countermanding public tranquillity. And if civil peace in a Christian community is judged to be threatened by those who *act* in ways that do not conform to defined articles of the faith, then civil peace (rather than correct belief) is to be achieved through coercive sanction of the civil law. This kind of argument would be central to debates over religious toleration well into the early-modern and modern periods of European history.[10] We shall examine below the degree of freedom of action this offers to members of a community who hold religious views that do not conform to majority opinion.

What is often meant by calling Marsilius's theory 'secular' is that the civil authority alone is permitted to be an agent with monopoly powers of coercion. Government rests on the ultimate authority of the whole corporation of citizens, the *universitas civium*. The corporation of citizens when gathered together is called the *human legislator* and it is its *explicit* consent to the laws which establishes the laws as coercive and therefore binding. Furthermore, the human legislator elects the executive or regulating part (*pars principans*) of the 'state' and can depose it. The regulating executive part, be it one, few or many, then establishes other 'state' offices. Marsilius's emphasis is on the sovereign will and consent of citizens or their representatives to the laws and to the executive which puts that will into motion. The separate canon law has, for him, no validity and papal decretals are nothing other than oligarchic ordinances, issued without reference to the will and without the consent of the human legislator of any community. Without such consent the church's laws cannot be coercive or binding in the external forum of civil life. But we must realize that religion is brought back in as essential to every civil regime and canon law is replaced by infallible decisions of the people when wearing, as it were, their religious hats. It is important to note that the execution of the decisions of the congregated council of believers, the *universitas fidelium*, is to be carried out by the civil legislator, the corporate gathering of all citizens or their representatives, through civil law. When the same corporate gathering considers purely civil matters, it too is authoritative and constitutes the human legislator which, in effect, has the plenitude of power as the whole people in its law-making capacity.

Marsilius's theory is medieval corporation theory with a vengeance.[11] He has enormous confidence that the human legislator, the corporate gathering of the people, more than any individual wise man or men, can come to know and will the laws which are most conducive to the sufficient life of the collectivity, and that these laws would be conducive to justice as rationally understood by all healthy men, everywhere. The people, as the *universitas civium,* and in their religious capacity as the *congregatio fidelis* or

---

9   See chapter 2 on Aquinas.

10   See H. R. Guggisberg, 'The Secular State of the Reformation Period and the Beginnings of the Debate on Religious Toleration', in J. Coleman, ed., *The Individual in Political Theory and Practice* (Oxford, 1996), pp.79–98: 'The creation of religious pluralism was generally unwelcome in the age of confessionalism. Confessional parity or limited religious freedom were only established as a consequence of external factors, such as economic or political pressures' (p. 98).

11   As Black, *Political Thought*, p. 60 says, to understand medieval corporation theory one has to forget Rousseau and keep in mind medieval notions of representation; also see J. Quillet, *La Philosophie politique*, pp. 11–19 and ch. 3.

universitas fidelium, possesses a kind of sovereignty that is unparalleled in any medieval political theory we have so far confronted. His theory provides some insight into thirteenth- and early fourteenth-century communal practices in Italy, but it is important to recognize that political theory is not merely historical redescription.

Biographical Details

Marsilius dei Mainardini (1275/80–1342/3) was born in Padua and counted as his immediate relatives civil lawyers, judges and notaries who were directly involved in the government of the city commune. His father was the notary of the University of Padua. He was a friend of Padua's civic leader, the pre-humanist Albertino Musato, and clearly was familiar with his city's political affairs. But Marsilius chose to study medicine in Padua, possibly under the distinguished Peter d'Abano, instead of the law. Thereafter, he went to the University of Paris to continue his studies and then to teach natural philosophy in the arts faculty. As the text of the *Defender of Peace* demonstrates, especially in the first Discourse, Marsilius learned the method of Aristotle the logician and the natural philosopher and applied this method to his examination of political problems. At Paris he learned how to produce an observational study of biological entities and to argue dialectically to necessary conclusions. He became the rector of the University of Paris in 1313. He was thereafter promised ecclesiastical preferment by Pope John XXII in 1318, but is known to have engaged in diplomatic missions on behalf of the della Scala family of Verona and the Visconti of Milan, who, as Italian *signori* were pro-imperial. German emperors had appointed local rulers as 'imperial vicars', *podestà,* in Italy, who ruled local subjects with legitimate and *de facto*, near-autonomous authority.[12] Marsilius will affirm that the autonomous nature of their authority derived, in fact, from the traditions of local self-government.

Nothing is known of what specifically caused him to write the *Defender of Peace*, but it was finished in Paris in 1324 and circulated anonymously. When his authorship was revealed in 1326 he fled Paris with his colleague John of Jandun. Both found refuge at the courts of the German King Ludwig of Bavaria, who was in dispute with the papacy over his rights to exercise royal and imperial jurisdiction in Germany and northern Italy.[13] The earlier struggle over the limits of secular jurisdiction in opposition to unlimited papal jurisdiction – between France's Philip IV and Boniface VIII – was continued between Ludwig of Bavaria and John XXII twenty years on. Nor would this be the last conflict between empire and papacy: others would succeed it until and beyond the Great Schism in 1378 when two popes would be elected, and Europe's spiritual allegiance would divide along national lines.

---

12   See chapter 6 below.
13   For a discussion of the relation between Ludwig and the learned 'political theorists' whom he protected see J. Miethke, 'Wirkungen politischer Theorie auf die Praxis der Politik im Römischen Reich des 14. Jahrhunderts. Gelehrte Politikberatung am Hofe Ludwigs des Bayern', in J. Canning and O.-G. Oexle, eds, *Political Thought and the Realities of Power in the Middle Ages/Politisches Denken und die Wirklichkeit der Macht im Mittelalter* (Göttingen, 1998), pp. 173–210. On the audience for fourteenth-century political theory see J. Miethke, 'Das Publikum politischer Theorie im 14. Jahrhundert. Zur Einführung', in Miethke, *Das Publikum,* pp. 1–24. For background see C. Dolcini, *Crisi de poteri e politologia in crisi. Da Sinibaldo Fieschi a Guglielmo d'Ockham* (Bologna, 1988).

At Ludwig's courts, especially in Munich, Marsilius is certain to have met at one time or another the numerous exiled intellectuals, many of whom were Franciscans like the English philosopher and theologian William of Ockham, the Minister General of the Franciscans, Michael of Cesena, and the theologian Ubertino de Casale, all of whose views were under investigation as heretical by the papal *curia*. In 1327 Ludwig moved into the *regnum Italicum*, those provinces of northern Italy which were traditionally subject to the German Empire but were, *de facto*, self-governing, and later arrived in Rome. He was crowned Emperor by the Roman Senate in the name of the Roman people, and he deposed Pope John XXII, denouncing him as a heretic who had usurped civil powers and who publicly taught that the (Franciscan) doctrines of evangelical poverty and the absolute poverty of Christ were heretical. Ludwig replaced John XXII with his own anti-pope, Peter of Corvario, whom he named Nicholas V. But his triumph was short-lived and with increasing papal efforts to remove him from Rome, Ludwig went north, reasserted his deposition of John XXII, and returned to Germany. Marsilius is thought to have been Ludwig's adviser during his Roman campaign. Leading themes extracted from his *Defender of Peace* had been condemned by the papal bull *Licet iuxta doctrinam* (1327), namely that the pope is to submit to the emperor; that the church's temporal goods are to be submitted to imperial jurisdiction; that St Peter is equal to all other apostles; and that the church possesses no coercive jurisdiction.

The *Defender of Peace* is organized into three Discourses, the third of which is a brief summary of conclusions that are more fully demonstrated in the previous two. It is extremely useful for a student to read the brief third Discourse first, in order to grasp the scope and interwoven intentions of both of the preceding Discourses as Marsilius himself saw them. Discourse or Dictio 1 is a discussion of the origins and nature of earthly political authority of such a kind that any rational human would consent to what is presented there, either as self-evidently true or as logically demonstrated from what is self-evident. Discourse or Dictio 2 is much more extensive, and elaborately engages scripture, the church Fathers, Roman and canon law, and various other authorities in order to criticize the claims made by the papacy to exercise temporal jurisdiction; it also provides an alternate, 'congregationalist' or conciliar structure and function of the church. Nederman is correct to argue that we must resist the impression that each of these Discourses is a separate, self-subsistent and internally coherent treatise.[14] Hence, Discourse 1 argues for those arrangements that any rational person would take to be necessary to ensure the stability and unity of the civil community and thereby repulse the discord brought by papal interference; and Discourse 2 reinterprets the role of the church, replacing the erroneous papal monarchy with a conciliar ecclesiology. The key concept that unites both discourses is that of the people, first as a *universitas civium*, and then as a *congregatio fidelis*.

A Reading of Discourse 1

What follows attempts to preserve the salient issues of the first Discourse and the ways in which Marsilius deals with them. Perhaps rightly, numerous secondary commentaries have focused on selected themes in the hopes of explaining the remarkable, even

---

14   C. Nederman, *Community and Consent: the secular political theory of Marsiglio of Padua's Defensor Pacis* (London, 1995), p. 14.

modern, aspects of some of Marsilius's chosen perspectives. But in the analyses of these selected themes, related and often distinctly medieval qualifications get set aside, so that Marsilius is often brought into a modern classroom as though dressed democratically in jeans, or with an early-modern republican aversion to monarchy. But Marsilius's *Defender of Peace* comes out of an experience of communal government in early fourteenth-century northern Italy and the serious use of Roman civil law adapted to the governance of a medieval city like Padua; out of Aristotelian logic and natural philosophy; out of the University of Paris and its corporate organization; and out of the intellectual ferment of the German Emperor Ludwig of Bavaria's courts, inhabited not least by some very threatened Franciscan theologians, forcibly turned into political theorists by the contemporary papacy's policies towards their own Order. To grasp something of what Marsilius means by what he says we must always take these varied contexts into consideration.

Civil regimes, says Marsilius, that can ensure peace and tranquillity, benefit man by providing what is their greatest good, the sufficient life. But since contraries produce contraries, then discord, which is the opposite of tranquillity, produces the worst of fruits in civil regimes. The history of the *regnum Italicum,* that is, the empire of ancient Rome, exemplifies this: when the inhabitants of Italy lived in peace, they experienced the fruits of peace and made such progress as to bring the whole habitable world under their sway. Marsilius establishes a continuity in the history of the Roman Empire with that of northern Italy in his own times. He says that when the *regnum Italicum* as a historical entity experienced discord and internal strife, they were dominated by hateful foreign nations. Today, that part of Italy which is continuous with the ancient empire, the north, is once again battered because of strife and is almost destroyed and could be invaded by anyone. Marsilius cites numerous ancient authorities to support his general observations: Sallust, Cassiodorus, Plato, Cicero. Marsilius notes that Aristotle, in his *Politics* book V, had much to say about why civil strife arises, but there is an additional cause by which the Roman Empire has long been troubled, a cause that Aristotle could not have known: it is the papal greed for secular power.

It is important to recognize that *de facto* self-governing cities in northern Italy are, for Marsilius, threatened by the papacy and not by the feudal *signori* who would figure increasingly in other tracts focusing on the destruction of communal self-government in Italy. Indeed, Marsilius spent much of his life attached to the Visconti and the della Scala, two powerful seignorial families. And he does not argue for a republican kind of liberty which *excises* the idea of the Roman Empire as the ultimate defender and guarantor of communal self-government. As we shall see, his understanding of liberty comes from another tradition of discourse. We shall also see that the preservation of his self-sufficient model of peaceful government depends on the empire and its law as a distant defender of peace, the ancient Roman model of empire which, in the last resort, represents the popular will to civil life and acts against the chief source of discord in his own times: the papacy. The sphere of application of his argument is expressly not northern Italy alone.

Marsilius emphasizes rhetorically that if we recognize the fruits of peace and the unbearable evil of its contrary, then individual brethren, and in even greater degree groups and communities, are obliged to help one another, both from the feeling of heavenly love and from the bond or law of human society. Marsilius is drawing on two traditions here: one, the Christian obligation of charity to neighbours as expressed in the evangelical law of perfect liberty of the gospel; and the other, from the Roman tradition of *ius gentium* or the law of nations, particularized and strengthened in the bonds of one's society. Cicero had explained in his *De officiis* that although the civil law is not always the same as universal law, the universal law should be the same as civil law. Cicero had also explained, and Marsilius now cites, that we were not born for ourselves alone; to part of us our native land lays claim, and to part, our friends. It is our duty to give the question of how to achieve the common utility our diligent attention, and thereby destroy the hidden sophism, the false logic, that argues that the church's power in society is beneficial and honourable. If unchecked, it will bring unbearable harm to *every* city and 'state'. Following the example of Christ, he says that we must strive to teach the truth, whereby the aforesaid pestilence of civil regimes may be warded off from the whole human race and especially from the worshippers of Christ. We must teach the truth which leads to the salvation of civil life and which also is of no little help for eternal salvation. Indeed, it is a sin to know the truth and to have an understanding of the causes of civil strife and not to do something about it (I, 1–5). Hence, Marsilius rhetorically reveals himself as the author of this tract, saying that he is the 'son of Antenor' (the legendary founder of Padua), 'heeding and obeying the admonitions of Christ, the saints and the philosophers, and moved by the spirit of an understanding of these things (if such grace has been given me)'.

Marsilius then explains the method of the three discourses. Discourse I proceeds through logical demonstration, that is, by human intellectual methods based on self-evident principles, by which he means self-evident to all whose rationality is not corrupted by nature (i.e. are ill or mad), by custom or by perverted emotion. This draws on Aristotle's ethics, logic and rhetoric and on the views of what constituted right reason that had already penetrated canon and Roman civil law's understanding of human rationality and responsibility. Bad custom could, for Aristotle as well, lead to perverted emotions, obscuring the rational. 'Evident' and 'self-evident' refer to those truths that all rational humans know without requiring that they be logically proved. This follows the stipulations of propositional logic, the arts faculty discipline which every student would have learned during his early years at university when he studied Aristotle's books on logic and the commentaries of Boethius and Porphyry. Starting with self-evident truths one then logically demonstrates, that is, deduces, certain conclusions. Then, having demonstrated logically, the second Discourse confirms these conclusions by established authorities, which are the testimonies of the eternal truth in scripture and its saintly authoritative interpreters. Marsilius's aim is to reveal the sophisms of the church and the papacy, and to show that their arguments are logically invalid readings of authority and experience. The third Discourse is a summary which infers logically certain, that is, sure conclusions, from previous logical demonstrations, to provide useful lessons for citizens, both rulers and subjects.

Marsilius insists that a ruler is a citizen as much as is his subjects in so far as he, like them, is beneath the law. As we shall see, Marsilius combines Aristotle's views on constitutional monarchy with the civil lawyers' view, going beyond Aquinas's understanding of a virtuous ruler who *voluntarily* is beneath the moral law and is to be judged by the standard of natural law reason. Marsilius says that these conclusions of the third Discourse will be evident from his previous findings. He wishes to unmask the cause of civil strife so that it may be excluded from *all* states or cities, whether they are part of the contemporary Roman Empire or not, in order that rulers and subjects may live more securely in tranquillity. Civil happiness, he says, is the best of the objects of desire possible to man in this world, a view similarly maintained by Aquinas, and in drawing on Aristotle he too notes that civil happiness is the ultimate aim of human acts. That civil happiness is an object of desire, and that prudent reasoning should enable men to attain that desire, is a view shared by Aquinas and Marsilius.

Marsilius goes on to analyse the contraries 'tranquillity and intranquillity' in the city or 'state' (*regnum*). Since we assume that both are dispositions of the city or 'state', then how is the *civitas* and the *regnum* to be defined? *Regnum* or 'state' has many meanings and Marsilius lists them. First, *regnum* can be a quantitative, territorial concept telling us nothing of the kind of constitution that is in place, that is, a *regnum* can be a number of cities or provinces simply under one regime. Second, *regnum* also can signify, qualitatively, a distinct species of temperate polity or regime, which Aristotle calls a 'temperate monarchy', so that a *regnum* can consist in a single city as well as in many cities so long as they are under this specific kind of temperate regime. Third and most familiarly, *regnum* can be a combination of the quantitative, territorial and the qualitative kinds. But Marsilius chooses to use a fourth meaning of *regnum*: a *regnum* is properly applied whenever there can be found in it 'something common to every species of temperate regime, whether a single city or many'. Hence, we are looking for 'something common to every species of temperate regime, whether a single city or many'.

Marsilius has not singled out a special, formal constitution, either monarchy or 'republic', for his approval. He seeks to define a *regnum* in a generic fashion, as simply that which possesses a characteristic that can be shared by a single city or many; indeed, by every kind of temperate regime. As we shall see, sovereign power in any regime that is ruled over by one, few or many, must always be with the people whose will is thus represented by the one, few or many. The people as the sovereign power is 'the common something' that is shared by all *regna* or 'states' capable of being called temperate regimes.

To define tranquillity and its opposite, Marsilius says we need to assume, as with Aristotle, that the *regnum* or 'state' is 'like' an animate nature or animal, composed of naturally proportionate parts ordered to one another, mutually functioning for the life of the whole, and established in accordance with reason and not therefore by chance. The relation of 'state' and its 'parts' to tranquillity is similar to the relation of an animal and its 'parts' to health. Marsilius says that this is a logical inference based on what all men understand about each of these relations; that is, health is thought to be the best disposition of an animal in accord with nature, and likewise, we can draw the analogy and infer that tranquillity is the best disposition of a 'state' that is established in accord with reason. As in an animal studied by doctors, so too in the 'state': a healthy disposition is one where the parts perform their operations perfectly, in an animal by nature, and in the 'state' by reason. Animals operate naturally by instinct; 'states' operate appropriately by reason. Animals do not require conscious efforts to keep their bodily parts functioning healthily; 'states', however, do require conscious, rational efforts to be maintained in functional and harmonious order. If tranquillity is health, both for animals and the *regnum*, then its contrary, intranquillity or strife, is an unhealthy disposition. Following these logical inferences, Marsilius says a good definition consignifies contraries, therefore once we signify what tranquillity is, we have consignified, that is, implicitly and at the same time signified, its opposite. Marsilius is appealing to logical definition and not to empirical evidence. We would use empirical observation in making statements about the animal or natural world, but regarding 'states' we use reason based on the accepted assumption that the 'state' is, as for Aristotle, 'like' an animate nature where the animal is well disposed in accordance with nature and the 'state' is well disposed in accordance with reason (I, 2).

Generically, the perfect community, the *regnum* as the civil community, has an origin and Marsilius believes the various species or kinds of 'state' have progressed naturally and historically from imperfect to more perfect kinds. Species or kinds of 'state' are references to their natures and not to their constitutional orderings. Progress from the less to the more perfect is always the path of nature and its imitator, art. Thus civil communities had small beginnings in diverse regions and times: the first and smallest combination of human beings, from which other combinations emerged, was that of male and female. Procreation led to one household being insufficient for its members' needs and many households, called a village, came to be established. Marsilius calls that collection of households into a village, the first community.

But within the single household, men's actions were regulated by an elder. This was also the case in the first community called the village. He draws on Aristotle's discussion of primitive kingship in *Politics* I, where early kings had power of law over children and wives, but then Marsilius diverges to accommodate a Ciceronian understanding of utility. He says that some villages took a different path. Where the head of a single household could punish or pardon domestic injuries according to his own will, in some communities this was not allowed the head of the community. Rather, in this community, the head had to use not his own will as he might in his household, but rather, he had to regulate matters of justice and benefit by a more general ordinance of reason or quasi-natural law. How did he learn this more general ordinance of reason? This more general reasonable rule of his judgements did not come about through prolonged rational investigation or enquiry but was a common dictate of reason that all men know: it is knowledge of a certain duty that all men know they owe to human society which extends beyond their families. Cicero, whom Marsilius had already cited, is the source of this notion. In *De officiis* Cicero had argued that as men we know that we are not born for ourselves alone; to part of us our native land lays claim and to part, our friends. Men are born for the sake of men and in this we ought to follow the lead of nature and to bring forth common utilities for all. We are not therefore born self-interested and without obligations to others. Hence, Marsilius says that a single ruler of a primitive village community would come to know that he ruled this community by means of an almost instinctive appeal to a common dictate of reason possessed by all men: one is not the head of a first community in order to decide on communal difficulties according to one's whim and pleasure, but rather according to a certain equity owed to human society. In using Cicero, Marsilius is confirming (as did Aquinas) the distinction made clear in Moerbeke's translation of Aristotle's *Politics*, between *politicum*, or *principatus politicus* on the one hand and a *regimen* known as *regale, yconomicum et despoticum* on the other.

Thus, the more perfect of the earliest communities were not ruled arbitrarily, the way early households were ruled. In these early communities there was an implicit appeal to a commonly held rational dictate that equity must be done to all for the sake of the common good. This implicitly known, quasi-natural law becomes evident to us through the experience of living in communities. And as these communities increased in size, men's experience became greater, and more perfect arts and rules and ways of living were discovered. The various parts of communities were also more fully differentiated functionally, regarding the utility of the whole. Nature herself, Marsilius will later say (I, 6) initiated this differentiation among men of different abilities, an initiation which men must rationally complete.

The parallels with Cicero's theory of four *personae* in the *De officiis* seem clear. It is there that Cicero argued that although nature dresses us in a *persona* which is common to all men in that we all have a share in reason, nature also dresses us for a second 'role' which is specifically assigned to individuals and their personal traits and talents. Some men are witty, others serious, others ambitious and earnest, some cunning and crafty. Each person should hold on to what is his so long as it is not vicious. Cicero had maintained that each person should weigh the characteristics that are his own and then *regulate* them according to circumstance, rank and status. Hence, for Marsilius, we are not biologically determined to play a specific role in the 'state', but in recognizing nature's differentiation of talents specific to each, men must then use their reason in the circumstances and carve out an 'office' in and for the common good.[15] Marsilius continues by noting that the rational completion of personal differentiation led, at last, to those things necessary for living and living well being brought to full development by men's reason and experience. The perfect community, the *regnum* or 'state', was established naturally through experience and rational reflection on it, with a differentiation of parts functioning for the common utility.

Marsilius cites Aristotle to confirm that the perfect community, having the full limit of self-sufficiency, came into existence for the sake of survival or living and continues to exist for the sake of living well. By this he means that those who live the civil life (*viventes civiliter*) do not live as beasts and slaves live, but live well, and he explicitly says living well means having the leisure for those liberal functions above the bestial and slavish, in which are exercised the virtues or excellences of the human soul's practical and theoretical reasoning (I, 4, 1). Much is often made in modern commentaries that Marsilius presents a minimalist politics based on what appears to be material self-sufficiency and not on the good life of active virtue among citizens. Thus, he is thought to argue for the life of peace, concord and order and not for the Aristotelian higher political life. But this is extremely misleading, because he says explicitly that civil happiness is the *fruit* of peace or tranquillity and the things which are necessary for living and for living well were brought to full development by men's reason and experience, and there was established the perfect community, called the *regnum*, with the differentiation of its parts (I, 3, 5). This is an argument which will be developed to show that through civic engagement, not simply through a ranked participation in office but through a universal and active consent to laws, and through election of representatives of a communal will, all men who constitute the sovereign 'people' are engaged in the active life, even if some are more actively engaged in advisory and executive functions thereafter, according to rank, than others.

This is not simply an argument for tacit acceptance of any rule so long as material security is maintained. Rather, it is a conflation of Aristotle's living well where there is at least a minimal, universal participation in self-governance, with Cicero's life of active virtue in the public forum. Marsilius has extended the meaning of the 'sufficient life' to include all men's deliberative reasoning about the most fundamental means to the com-

---

15   See volume 1, chapter 5 of *A History of Political Thought* on Cicero and compare with Machiavelli, chapter 6 below.

mon utility: that there must be a universal standard of justice established in the civil regime, and their consent to or dissent from proposed laws that specify that universal standard. The pursuits of justice and philosophy are 'liberal' in the sense that they do not arise strictly from material needs. Furthermore, in extending the meaning of a city or 'state's' 'sufficient life', Marsilius is doing more than adopting Aristotle's utility friendship and applying it to civil regimes. He specifically argues that moral and intellectual virtues must be engaged in an extraordinarily active way to ensure that all the needs of civil life are met, and these do not simply equate with a materially adequate existence. A temperate regime provides the structure which allows for the natural human need, a psychological imperative, to exercise responsible, deliberative choice through assembled communication. Marsilius is still working within the Moerbekeian notion of civil life as *communicatio*. The aim is to attain the fruits, that is, what is beneficial, through the exercise of diverse arts and functions which tranquillity and peace permit to flourish. The differentiation of function is *for* something else, a higher but natural good. This appears to be Marsilius's way of reconciling the Latin translation of Aristotle's *Politics* with Cicero's attempt to align what is useful (*utile*) to what is also right (*honestum*).[16]

Marsilius argues that all men, not deformed or otherwise impeded, naturally desire a sufficient life. This is the first principle he can demonstrate. It is true that this principle, the natural desire for the sufficient life, is freely granted and believed by all without further demonstration. Thus men flee what is harmful to this sufficiency. He cites Cicero's *De officiis* again, but now he wishes to prove it by Aristotelian methods: we believe this, but as a principle it can be demonstrated as well by everyone through sense induction. Marsilius means that anyone who experiences the world with his five senses logically concludes from his experience that the sufficient life is to be sought and its contrary avoided. It is not a conclusion of abstract reason divorced from sense experience and it is a necessary, rather than simply a plausible, conclusion. This is no mere opinion but a logical truth.

Marsilius then goes beyond the principle of the sufficient life and thinks we understand 'living well' to mean two different things. One is earthly living well and the other is eternal and heavenly. Heavenly well-being cannot be proved by logical or rational demonstration and it is not self-evident. Aquinas would not have disagreed with this statement. Since Marsilius's method in this Discourse is only to treat what is either self-evident or logically demonstrable from the self-evident, then he will not concern himself with this heavenly good living at this point. But there is no doubt that he does *believe* in eternal well-being and salvation and he will later argue that it is necessary for all men to believe it. He then asks: how do we come to prove that men can know the necessary means to the good life *on earth*? He says that the ancient philosophers have understood this almost completely through logical demonstration. And from these logical demonstrations they concluded that the attainment of the good life requires the civil community without which the sufficient life cannot be achieved. Aristotle says in the *Politics* that all men are driven towards such an association by a natural impulse. Marsilius comments that we can learn this from sense experience, but he wishes to go further. Once again, he refers to contraries. Man is born of contrary elements because of whose contrary actions and passions some of his substance is continually being destroyed, that is, life is a conflictual

---

16   For a different view see Nederman, *Community and Consent*, p. 53.

process towards bodily death. And he is born bare and unprotected, capable of suffering and destruction. Consequently, he needs arts of different kinds to avoid harms and these can be exercised only by a large number of men in an association. Hence, in such assemblages of men practising different arts, there could arise disputes were they not regulated by a norm of justice. There had to be established in this association a standard of justice and a guardian or maker thereof. The guardian – the judicial system – has to restrain wrongdoers within and outside the association. We have already been told that this general norm of justice is known to us as communal, rational beings to protect the utility of the community. Men therefore were assembled through experience and instinct for the sake of the sufficient life and were able to seek out for themselves what was necessary, the standards of justice, to that sufficiency. This assemblage, thus perfect, self-sufficient, with a guardian who preserves an already known standard of justice that serves the common utility and protects the whole, is called the *regnum* or 'state'. Were Marsilius to end here, then one might think him to have provided an argument for the 'state' as a secular, utility calculation. But he goes further.

Men rationally and naturally recognized that besides the relief provided by the community regarding the necessities of survival in the present life, there is something else which all men, associated in a civil community, need for the status of the future world that is promised them by God's supernatural revelation but which is also useful for the status of the present life. Marsilius defines this need as the worship and honouring of God and the giving of thanks for benefits received here and hoped for in the future life. The *regnum* or 'state', this utilitarian assemblage of men maintaining a standard of justice, therefore designated certain teachers who might direct men in their felt need to worship and honour God. Since religion is, for Marsilius, a self-evident human need, the 'state' recognizes this and designates those who teach men how to worship the divine (I, i, 4).

Indeed, the 'state' is differentiated into functioning parts which serve the whole, and these parts are the agricultural, the artisan, the military, the financial, the priestly and the judicial sections of the community. Three of these, the priestly, the military and the judicial are in the strict sense parts of the 'state' and in civil communities they are usually called the *honorabilitates*, the honourable offices (I, 5, 1). The other parts are such only in the broad sense and the multitude, usually called the *vulgus*, occupy these other offices of the *regnum*. Marsilius claims that the necessity of these parts has been demonstrated from what is self-evident, namely, that the 'state' is a community, established for the sake of living and living well, of the men in it. Living and living well are natural desires of men as their ends. On the one hand, animals and man instinctively desire these ends and we can study the natural causes which lead them to this desire and end through natural biological sciences. But Marsilius is being more than a medical doctor here, and wishes to discuss this question not by means of an examination of natural causes, that is, why and how the lungs take in air to keep us alive, but rather, in terms of the ways in which we achieve our natural ends through art and reason, through conscious effort, to construct an environment that best suits our rational species (I, 5, 3).

He argues that we rationally may conclude that to live well, men's actions must be done in proper proportion, and the modification of our passions and actions is not simply biologically natural, but consciously and rationally achieved. For instance, the natural causes of our actions and passions come about through the contrariety of the elements that compose our bodies. But, he says, other actions or passions are performed by us through appetitive desire and through cognition, that is, not simply through instinctive biological response to external conditions. Some of these considerations are only internal to us; they deal with our dispositional attitudes and intentions which are not externalized in our actions. Some, however, are actions and passions performed by us as a result of our knowledge and conscious choices which do affect others. The latter Marsilius calls *transitive* or *transient acts* and they are crucial to his vision of the scope of legitimate political rule.

Marsilius thinks that any 'state' is primarily concerned with the *consequence* of intentions, that is, it is only capable of being interested in those acts which we perform that affect others. There are certain acts which cannot be proved to be present or absent to someone – these are mental intentions. A *regnum* does not, because it cannot, enquire as to why we act as we do, but rather, it oversees how we act and whether these actions foster or obstruct the conditions for the achievement of the common good, that is, the tranquillity necessary for the collective sufficient life. That part of the *regnum* that deals with transient acts and corrects these to achieve equality or due proportion is the judicial or ruling and deliberative part, and its function is to regulate matters of justice and the common benefit (I, 5).

This is the first time we have come across what is, in effect, the lawyers' view of government against which arts and theology faculty lecturers had, in effect, raged from the thirteenth century onwards. It appears to deny that a public official, governor or his advisers, need be concerned with the moral disposition of citizens. Their concern, in keeping the peace and unity of a civil society, is to observe and evaluate transient acts, the acts that spill out, whatever the intentions behind them, into what was called the *foro externo*, the external or public forum. The judgement of such acts was to be in terms of whether or not peace and tranquillity were disturbed. Political acts are those judged in terms of their contribution to or disruption of public utility.

We recall that Aquinas had already thought it appropriate for one to modify one's moral perspective by judgements of utility. For instance, should an individual rationally consider it appropriate to disobey an irrational law, or collectively, should it be judged appropriate to overthrow an unjust tyrant but, upon consideration, disobedience or the tyrant's overthrow might bring about even more disruption to the city, then disobedience or the tyrant's deserved (by reason) deposition were not to be implemented. But Marsilius establishes that the long-enduring argument over moral intention, which was precisely what allowed the papacy to invade temporal politics *ratione peccati* in the first place, is to be considered from a wholly different perspective.

Does this mean there is no role for conscience, or moral intentions, in his theory? He answers this in an extraordinary way by establishing the *necessity* of the priestly 'part' in communities. He notes that there are those acts which, in not being capable of proof as to their presence or absence (because they are internal to men's minds), cannot therefore be regulated by human law. Aquinas said the same thing. But this does not mean they do not matter to men. These acts, which are mental intentions, he says, nevertheless cannot be concealed from God (I, 5, 11). Moral intention matters enormously to humans who have always been concerned with praising God and hoping to be rewarded with an afterlife, and it matters to every 'state' in that correct mental intentions are another means of ensuring, beyond coercive positive law, that men, if only out of fear, will constrain their passions and keep the peace.

Marsilius tells us that all nations throughout history agreed that it was appropriate to establish a priesthood for the worship and honouring of God. This makes the religious 'part' of the 'state' something like a conclusion of the law of nations, the *ius gentium*. Most laws and religions, not only Christianity, promise that in the future world God will distribute rewards to those who do good and punishment to doers of evil. But besides the fact that such laws have been established throughout history, Marsilius says that we cannot demonstrate and we can only believe the future utility of religious observance. What we *can* demonstrate is that religions have always served a purpose that is *necessary* for the status of the earthly life. Religions ensure the goodness of human acts, both individual and civil, on which depends tranquillity. Religious laws are therefore utilitarian in this world, because besides civil laws, such religious laws induce men out of fear of divine punishment to revere God, flee vices and cultivate virtues. No human legislator can regulate whether men believe in religious laws. But the legislator benefits from men eschewing wrong out of fear of God and from men's piety and virtue, since this additional check on human behaviour halts disputes and injuries in communities. Hence, the utilitarian need for religious law, and the desire of the *regnum* to appoint teachers of these laws and doctrines. His argument, however, does not end here.

Marsilius gives a historical overview of, effectively, pagan Rome's attachment to religious laws as part of the civil regime, but he may well have seen parallels in Aristotle's treatment of the office of priesthood in ancient Greek *poleis* as Aristotle discussed this in his *Politics*. He says that those appointed as 'teachers' were not just anyone, but rather, virtuous and esteemed citizens who had held military, judicial or deliberative office and who had retired from secular affairs. Such men, says Marsilius, through a lifetime of virtuous civil behaviour and contribution to the common good, possessed characters that were removed from the passions. Marsilius does not *believe* that correct teachings about God were taught by gentile laws or religions. He says that only the Catholic Christian faith and not those faiths outside the tradition of what is contained in the Bible, is correct. Only the Mosaic and the evangelic law, that is the Christian law, contain the truth, although 'law' is used more loosely of the religious rules of Mohammed or the Persians or the pagan philosophers (I, 10, 3). But religion in and of itself was rightly seen, even in pagan societies, to have its utilitarian role in the civil *regnum* (I, 5, 14). However, Catholic doctrines – on original sin, on grace – cannot be rationally demonstrated. They are only to be taken as plausible positions. But as such, Marsilius is not arguing that these plausible positions are irrelevant to civil communities and therefore ought not to be taught. And when considering the 'state', it is the rational utility of religious belief that matters. What is implied is that the Christian religion, even more than pagan religions, can be shown to be of greatest utility to temperate civil regimes.[17]

He thinks that we can see the rational utility of religion 'without belief', in that God, in having handed down laws to Moses to remedy Adam's sin, enabled men to be purged of sin or guilt, and God enabled men to be shown how they could escape both physical earthly punishment as well as eternal punishment. But he emphasizes that only thereafter, through God's grace, by the ordainment of God and the passion of Christ, do our works come by a certain congruity to merit eternal happiness. This merit is not through priests and religious hierarchies, but rather, through scriptural revelation and our belief in God. Indeed, Marsilius argues radically that Christ's passion provided grace whereby now men merit the blessed life. Through Christ's passion the grace whereby men merit the blessed life was received not only by those who came after but also by those who had

---

17   His argument should be compared with Machiavelli's *Discourses on Livy*, I, 12: see chapter 6 below.

observed the first commandments and the Mosaic laws![18] As teachers of this law and as ministers of its sacraments, certain men were *chosen* within early Christian communities, called priests, and their office, their duty, was to teach the commands and counsels of the Christian evangelical law as to what must be believed, done and avoided. Marsilius defines Christian priests as those who teach and educate men in those things which, according to the evangelical law, that is, the gospel, it is necessary to believe, do and omit for eternal salvation. Beyond this teaching and advising, they cannot coerce, but it is significant that he holds, especially with contemporary Franciscan theologians, that the evangelical law is the true law of liberty and thus replaces, by perfecting, pagan philosophical and Jewish Old Testament teachings on their own (I, 6, 3–7). Marsilius's understanding of liberty is founded in the Christian liberty of the gospels. It is not the so-called 'secular' 'republican' liberty of later civic humanists who mounted arguments against domination by the tyrannous *signori* or foreign invaders.

Since nature inclines (but does not determine) different members of the human species to different functions regarding the natural end of men, that is, living in community, then nature has endowed different men with characteristics suitable for different offices. The productive or efficient causes of all the offices of the 'state' are therefore the minds and wills of all men through their thoughts and desires, individually and collectively. These collectively constitute the human legislator of any and every *regnum*. The human legislator – the minds and wills of men – is the efficient cause of *all* functional offices of whatever *regnum* they happen to live in and it is clear that after Christ's coming, all human legislators now establish the office of Christian priesthood as a necessary 'part' of the civil community and the office is filled by election. Thus, the corporate human legislator, the people in corporate mode, are prior to and the cause of all the offices of 'state', including those who educate according to the gospel.

Formerly, that is, prior to Christ, but in rare cases, Marsilius notes that the immediate and direct efficient cause of the 'state' and its offices was God without any intermediate human determination (I, 7, 3). But in most cases, the establishment and differentiation of the parts of the 'state' were brought about by the community, the human legislator; that is, the minds and wills of men through their thoughts and desires, individually and collectively. First, the *regnum* as a community is established, then the human legislator establishes a ruling or judicial part, and through this, other parts including the religious part. When the *regnum* is well-tempered, the ruler or rulers who are regulators govern for the common benefit in accordance with the will and consent of the human legislator. Such temperate ruling by judicial parts can be found, says Marsilius, either in monarchies, aristocracies or in polities, as Aristotle says. Their diseased versions, tyrannical monarchy, oligarchy and democracy, subordinate the common good to factional interest. A polity, although in one sense something common to every genus or species of regime of government, means in another sense a certain species of temperate government in which *every citizen* participates in some way in the government, or in the *deliberative* function in turn, according to his rank and ability or condition, for the common benefit and with the will or consent of the citizens (I, 8, 3).

This is a statement about the filling of 'state' offices by rank, status and circumstance,

---

18   This reflects Marsilius's familiarity with contemporary arguments about 'justified' pagans and the development of the notion of Purgatory, where those good men who came before Christ would await their final justification at the end of history.

following the Ciceronian notion of the second 'role' or *persona*. There is a differential participation in 'state' office, but, as we shall see, there is also a universal participation which ignores rank, status and circumstance, and this is the participation by the whole body of citizens in deliberative consent to law. Both kinds of participation, one universal and the other according to rank, is what Marsilius thinks constitutes the sufficient life of the civil community. It reflects medieval communal government and the myriad of consensual practices in craft guilds and cities across medieval Europe, supported by the Ciceronian rhetoric of proportional rank.

Precisely how is the regulative, ruling part of the 'state' established by the human legislator? How does a community determine whether it will be ruled or regulated by one, few or many? Marsilius is aware that if we deal with the past, and he means specifically Israel's past as described in scripture, we cannot demonstrate through logical, rational argument that the divine will established the priestly or any other part of the regime. We hold it to have been the case by simple belief.[19] But there is another method of establishing governments which proceeds immediately from the human mind and perhaps remotely from God as a remote cause. He says that God does not always act immediately, indeed, in most cases, God establishes governments *by means of* human minds to which he has granted the discretionary will for such establishment. How such human minds establish governments, by what kinds of action, can be indicated with human certainty from what is better or worse for the polity. This can be logically demonstrated. There are, first of all, several methods of establishing kingly monarchy, which is, we recall, capable of being one of the temperate polities mentioned. Some are better than others. Either the king or monarch is named by an election of the inhabitants or citizens, or he duly obtains rulership without their election. Following Aristotle's *Politics* V, when a monarchy established by whatever means is true kingship, it is over voluntary subjects and according to law that is made for the common benefit of the subjects. Non-elected kings rule less voluntary subjects than do elected kings. The elected king is superior to the non-elected. Indeed, it is expedient that the ruler elected be the best man in the polity since he must regulate the civil acts of all the rest. Marsilius reminds us that we must not overlook the fact that different multitudes in different times and places are inclined towards different kinds of polity and government, as Aristotle says.[20] Legislators and those who institute government must be aware of this fact. They must know the character of the people; that is, a people must know its own character.[21] But this difference reflects better or worse aspects of men's characters because, just as not every man is inclined towards the best discipline or study, so too a multitude may not perhaps be inclined to accept the best form of government. Marsilius then provides examples from Roman history (I, 9).

But what is clear is that in monarchies, as in other regimes that may be called temperate, all civil human acts are regulated by the ruler according to a standard (*regula*), a law which is and ought to be the 'form' of the ruler. The efficient cause of this standard or law is the same as the efficient cause of the ruler: it is the *human legislator*, the people. The very existence of this standard, be it a statute, custom, or law, we assume as almost self-

---

19   This is the common argument, from at least Augustine onwards, that if you were not there to experience or witness the event, you can only hold plausible beliefs or opinions based on the testimony of others.

20   Compare John of Paris, above.

21   Compare Machiavelli, chapter 6 below.

evident by induction in all perfect communities. This reflects Cicero's *De inventione*, where Cicero had argued that justice is a habit of mind which gives every man his due while preserving the common advantage. Its first principles proceed from nature, then certain rules of conduct became customary by reason of their usefulness; later still, both the principles that proceeded from nature and those that had been approved by custom received the support of religion and the fear of law.[22]

How should we understand what law means? Marsilius gives a range of possible and current interpretations, ranging from how medical doctors or students of the natural sciences would understand it, to law as used by university moral philosophers, to law as understood by theologians, to law as used by civil lawyers. Law is (1) a natural, sensitive inclination towards some action or passion; (2) any productive habit and in general every form existing in the mind, of a producible thing from which, as from an exemplar or measure, there emerge the forms of things made by art; (3) in effect, evangelical discipline, the standard containing admonitions for voluntary human acts according as these are ordered towards glory or punishment in the future world. This third meaning of law is in all religions, says Marsilius, although only Christian law, which is the perfect law of liberty (citing the Gospel Epistle of James, 1:25), contains the truth. Fourth, however, law means, in its most familiar guise (that is, to civil lawyers), the science or doctrine or universal judgement of matters of civil justice and benefit and their opposites. Marsilius, importantly, intends to use only this fourth sense of law and to develop it.

Law may be considered in itself, as a universal judgement of matters of civil justice and benefit, showing what is just or unjust, beneficial or harmful, and hence as (Justinian's) science of right, *iurisprudentia*. Alternatively and more specifically, law can be considered as an observance of coercive command, coercive through punishment or reward in the present world. This is the most proper sense of law. Law, for Marsilius, is a discourse or statement emerging from prudence and political understanding; it is a statement of an ordinance made by political prudence concerning matters of justice and benefit and their opposites, and having coercive force. A coercive command is required for there to be a law. Then he says something that will colour his meaning throughout the first and second discourses. He is aware that sometimes false cognitions of the just and beneficial do become laws. But he holds that this kind of law is still *unjust*. True cognition is required for a perfect law (I, 10, 5). Perfect law is the product of right reason. Marsilius therefore has distinguished between justice as the correct cognition of what is beneficial, and law as coercive command. And he clearly thinks that the perfection of civil regimes comes about when there is a concord between justice as correct cognition, right reason, and law as coercive command. As we shall see, this takes the rationality of the human legislator in matters of the sufficient life to a condition of near infallibility, *not* in terms of particular civil laws which upon reflection are open to change and amelioration, but in terms of foundational, self-evident truths about what is required if utility is to be served by civil regimes. At bottom, no rational human being, even the most humble, would seek anything but the *salus populi*, the survival and well-being of the 'state'. Law, when considered as the standards of civil justice and benefit, is established by human authority, is made civilly enforceable by the consent of the human legislator, and comes in the form of conclusions such as customs, statutes, plebiscites, decretals and all similar rules based on human authority (I, 10, 6).

22 See volume 1, chapter 5 of *A History of Political Thought* on Cicero.

It is necessary to establish law in the polity (I, 11, 1). Without it, civil judgements cannot be made with complete rightness. Through the law these judgements are properly made and preserved from defect so far as is humanly possible. The ruler is directed to make civil judgements in accordance with it. The major premise of this demonstration is almost self-evident, says Marsilius, and is very close to being a foundational, indemonstrable truth. Men simply know that it is necessary to establish a standard of justice in communities. The law is that which lacks all perverted self-interested emotion. And it is prior to any particular man or men. As Cicero had also argued, no single man and perhaps not even all the men of one era could investigate or remember all the civil acts determined in the law. Indeed, what was said about them by the first investigators was insufficient and was only completed by later investigators. Marsilius argues similarly that we see from experience that changes, additions and subtractions in the laws occurred at different times. Since prudence deals with singular things which become known through experience, then what one man may discover by himself is relatively little. Instead, we need collections of the wisdom learned by all those who have achieved some comprehensions of a subject, whatever that subject may be. This shows that men's mutual help and the addition of earlier and later discoveries enable the arts and sciences to be perfected. For this reason all rulers should govern according to law, where law is an accretion of the wisdom and experience of the ages, and not without it. Marsilius is following Cicero's *De inventione* by justifying law as increasingly perfected, *de facto* traditional custom, open to prudential alteration in the circumstances, but resting on a foundational and universally shared and known principle of reason that every man is to be given his due while preserving the common advantage. And rulers are themselves regulated by the laws, both in themselves and in relation to their citizen–subjects. When this is the case, Marsilius observes that rulers suffer less from sedition and destruction of government. Marsilius is keen to adopt the Aristotelian observation that the perfect man happens very rarely and even when he does, he is not equal in virtue to the law as collective wisdom since every soul sometimes has a vicious emotion (I, 11, 5–8). In effect, this is an Aristotelian support for the superiority of Roman civil law as determined, *de facto*, in customs and traditions by the minds and wills of the corporate citizenry, the human legislator.[23]

The efficient cause of specific civil laws is, Marsilius believes, capable of demonstration. It can pertain to *any* citizen to discover the law, taken materially in its sense as the science of civil justice and benefit. In other words, any man can study Justinian's *Corpus iuris civilis*. Marsilius could have chosen to become a student of the civil law rather than a student of medicine. He might then have become a practising lawyer in his native Padua. Such a discovery of the law, he says, can be carried on more appropriately and completed better by those men who are able to have leisure, are older and experienced in practical affairs and who are called 'prudent men', than by mechanics who bend their efforts to acquiring the necessities of life. But when law is taken, as Marsilius wishes it to be, in the fourth sense, then that true knowledge or discovery of the just and beneficial is only a measure of human civil acts when there is given a coercive command as to its observance. This comes about not through having studied civil law in Padua or elsewhere but by participating in communal citizenship and consenting to proposed laws which then establish them as coercive commands.

---

23   This argument bears comparison with Machiavelli's understanding of good law backed by coercive sanction in a community brought back to health. See chapter 6 below.

Hence, in answer to the question 'to whom belongs the authority to make laws which command coercively?' he answers: the human legislator makes law in its fourth sense. That legislator or the primary efficient cause of the law is the people or the whole body of citizens or the weightier part thereof, through its election or will expressed by words in the general assembly of the citizens, commanding or determining publicly that something be done or omitted with regard to human civil acts under temporal pain or punishment (I, 12, 3). By the weightier part (*valentior pars*) Marsilius says he means those whose quantity and quality have been taken into consideration in the community over which the law is made. The aforesaid whole body of citizens, or the weightier part thereof which represents the will of the whole, is the legislator, regardless of whether it makes law directly by itself or entrusts the making of it to some person or persons who may be the ruler(s) or regulators(s) and who are not and cannot be the legislator in the absolute sense, but only in a relative sense for a particular time, that is a limited term of office, and in accord with the primary legislator. Such rulers are elected. And even were there no ceremonies of election, the election would be no less valid were it not performed.[24] By means of the same human legislator as the public authority, there may be additions, subtractions and changes undertaken to the law for the common benefit. By this same public authority, the human legislator, must the laws be promulgated or proclaimed after their enactment so that no citizen or alien who is delinquent in observing them may be excused because of ignorance.

A citizen is defined as he who participates in the civil community in the government or the deliberative or judicial function according to rank (I, 12, 4). Marsilius distinguishes children, slaves, aliens and women from citizens of whatever rank. He demonstrates logically that the absolute, primary human authority to make or establish specific civil laws belongs only to those men from whom alone the best laws can emerge. He is not referring to experts in the law. He says that he means the whole body of citizens or the weightier part thereof which represents that whole body. He thinks this to be close to self-evident. He argues that that at which the *entire* body of the citizens aims intellectually and emotionally is more certainly judged as to its truth, and more diligently noted as to its common utility. A defect in some proposed law can be better noted by the greater number of citizens than by any part thereof. Every whole is greater in mass and in virtue than any part taken separately. This is self-evident. Therefore the common utility of a certain law is better noted by the entire multitude because no one knowingly harms himself. *Anyone* can look to see whether a proposed law leans towards the benefit of one or a few, rather than to the community. Also, the authority to make the law belongs to those men whose making of it will cause the law to be better observed, or indeed, to be observed at all. Only the whole body of citizens are such men. This is almost self-evident, since a law would be useless unless it were observed.[25]

If, indeed, the 'state' is a community of free men, then every citizen must be free and not undergo another's despotism. This freedom is defined by Marsilius according to the perfect law of liberty as expressed in the evangelical law.[26] Marsilius takes this freedom to

---

24   This is the only aspect of consent – to the election of rulers – which could be construed as tacit, as when a hereditary ruler came to power. He is none the less expected to do the will of the primary legislator, the people.
25   See J. M. Blythe, *Ideal Government and the Mixed Constitution in the Middle Ages* (Princeton, NJ, 1992), pp. 193–202.
26   James 1:25;. see below, p. 5, on Ockham.

what some see as threatening extremes. He says that a law made by the hearing or consent of the whole multitude, even though it were less useful, would be readily observed and endured by everyone of the citizens because each would seem to have set the law upon himself (I, 12, 6). Furthermore, the power to cause the laws to be observed belongs only to those men to whom belongs coercive force over the transgressors of the laws. These are the whole body of citizens or the weightier part thereof. Hence, they have the authority to make law.

Is Marsilius proposing a kind of legal positivism where the collected will and consent to civil laws on the part of the whole body of citizens, even if these laws are, in reality, less useful for the common good, still have coercive force and are therefore binding? This could mean that what truly may be in the community's best interest is subordinated to a majoritarian will that is ill-conceived. But Marsilius is not presenting what Rousseau would later describe as 'the will of all', made up of individual, free, self-interested wills which, when summed, produce majority opinion.[27] He is presenting, instead, a notion of free individuals in a multitude of free men whose corporate will about the common good necessarily is the *same* and therefore it can be represented by the weightier part, the *valentior pars*. Marsilius, like many of his contemporaries working with medieval corporation theory, believes there to be certain stable, foundational truths which are self-evident to all citizens, whatever their rank or condition, about the requirements of the common good. It is this standard of judgement which all citizens use to determine whether the specific civil law is worthy of consent or not. As with John of Paris, so too with Marsilius, the common good can only be willed by each individual will, but its content is the same for all citizens.[28]

Marsilius represents a distinct tradition of corporation theory discourse.[29] He believes that a collected group of people, the multitude, can have their objective view on the common advantage represented by the voice of one man or several, that a representative can accurately mirror the collective will of a community, a will that is the product of rationally logical inferences from experience. The faculty of the will for Marsilius, as for Aquinas and other theologians, be they Dominicans, Franciscans or secular clergy, was always seen as a cognitive faculty guided by reason. The will is not simply pure sensual desire but a desire informed by what, for humans, it is reasonable to desire.

It is important to grasp how will is guided by reasoned thinking in this period because, by contrast, in the seventeenth century Hobbes would propose another view. He

27   *Contra* Black, *Political Thought in Europe*, p. 65, Marsilius is *not* identifying the common good as the sum of individual interests.

28   See Ockham (p. 5, below) for the same view. A. Gewirth, *Marsilius of Padua and Medieval Political Philosophy* (New York, 1951), pp. 203–25, argued too strongly for the common good in Marsilius to be a simple amalgam of individual, private goods. M. Wilks, 'Corporation and Representation in the *Defensor Pacis*', *Studia Gratiana* 15 (1972), pp. 251–92, rightly saw that the common interest is susceptible to judgements of right and wrong, so that statutes have a truth value, but Wilks perhaps overemphasized that in the truth value overriding the readiness of any particular person to assent to it leads to the conclusion that consent in Marsilius is essentially passive. Wilks was correct in his observation that Marsilius thought that anyone who dissents from or refuses to recognize the common benefit withdraws himself from his status of citizen. We shall see below (pp. 162–4) what effect this has on religious non-conformists in a 'state' with a 'church'. Instead of a tacit recognition, however, Marsilius seems to follow contemporary civil law, whereby the recognition of the common advantage must issue in active, explicit and voluntary consent, in public, by each and every citizen to this civic purpose. This was also the view of the civilians Bartolus and Baldus.

29   See below, p. 5, on Ockham, who disagreed with aspects of a corporation theory of this kind.

would argue that our train of thought or mental discourse is regulated by desire. Our thinking is a learned means of calculating what we first desire. Hence, Hobbes says that from the sensual impressions made by such things as we desire arises the thought of some means we have seen produce the like of that which we aim at (*Leviathan* I, iii). For Hobbes, then, some appetites and aversions are born with men and others, namely of particular things, are acquired by sense experience. Whatever is the object of any man's appetite or desire is what such a man calls 'good'. For Hobbes, deliberation is simply the last appetite or aversion and it is this that he calls the will. Hobbes explicitly argues that the definition of the will given by the schools and universities of his own times who study Aristotle, Cicero and the scholastic authorities, that it is a *rational appetite*, is *not* good. Will is the last appetite in deliberating, so that reason is a learned means to acquire what is simply desired (*Leviathan* I, vi). Marsilius, however, holds precisely to the scholastic understanding of the Aristotelian and Ciceronian notion of the will in man as a rational appetite. And for this reason, since every whole is greater than its parts, that whole, although made up of parts, has a univocal, rational will to the common advantage. This univocal, objective will is, however, individually expressed by every sane member of the whole.

In this theory, 'delegated' representatives do not legislate as they personally think best or in line with their status or rank; they voice the will of the whole about the common advantage, and to which the whole has consented. This kind of delegation, to be found in Justinian's Roman law, is an efficient means of 'standing in for' the primary human legislator which is constituted by the *whole* multitude when collected together. The notables of weightier rank speak the same will as the *vulgus*. That will is not a summation of the different wills of individual persons but a will that is universally and ahistorically common to rational men in communities. *Honorabilitas* can bring civil office, but their rank does not mean that they express a communal will that is different from the will of those who do not hold office.[30]

Men, we recall, came together naturally to form the civil community in order to attain what was beneficial for the sufficiency of life and to avoid the opposite. Those matters which can affect the collective benefit or harm of all ought to be known and heard by all. This is Marsilius's use of the standard Roman law dictate, *quod omnes tangit*, 'what touches all should be approved by all'. Such matters are the laws. Furthermore, in the laws being rightly made consists a large part of the whole common sufficiency of men. He notes the contrary: under bad laws there arise unbearable slavery, oppression and misery of citizens and the polity is destroyed.

Perhaps his most significant argument about how foundational to all men certain common understandings are concerning the common good, is his use of a passage in Ecclesiastes (I, 15). It says there that the number of fools is infinite. But Marsilius thinks men are not *that* foolish. Since all the citizens know that they must be measured by the law according to due proportion, and no one knowingly harms or wishes injustice to himself, Marsilius argues that it follows that all or most men wish to have law conducing

---

30   See the interesting contrast with modern theories of political representation, where there is seen to be a conflict between real interests and desires, as there is not in Marsilius, in Nederman, *Community and Consent*, pp. 83–94, although I disagree with the supposed intended ambiguity of the notion of the *valentior pars* which Nederman proposes to accommodate the observations of C. Condren, 'Democracy and the *Defensor Pacis*', *Il Pensiero Politico* 8 (1980), pp. 301–16.

to the common benefit of the citizens. The Ciceronian assertion that men naturally know that each ought to be given his due and the common advantage served, underlies his observations. Indeed, Marsilius notes that if some 'part' or office of the 'state' could dissolve by its own authority what had been established by the whole, the 'part' would be greater than the whole or at least equal to it, which is self-evidently absurd (I, 12, 8). Marsilius informs us that those who object to the notion of the whole body of people being the legislator use the passage from Ecclesiastes to argue for the stupidity of common men who they say are vicious, unintelligent and undiscerning.[31] But Marsilius has logically demonstrated that *all* men desire sufficiency of life and seek to avoid the opposite, and that is the reason they form themselves into communities. Since the civil community results from the natural impulse in all men (and is not simply an instinct in the educated), then that part of the community that wishes the association to endure must be the weightier multitude. This goes beyond a majoritarian principle to one of near unanimity. Indeed, says Marsilius, those who do not wish the polity to endure are slaves not citizens. It is impossible for there to be so many persons in the government who do not care to live a civil life that they could even constitute a majority. If this were the case, then nature would have erred. Since the multitude of men (and not simply a majority) wish the 'state' to endure, they also wish that without which the 'state' cannot endure – the law, which is the standard of the just and beneficial, handed down with a command. The vast majority of men in a multitude therefore wishes to have law, and no one teaches them this. They learn this from experience and logical inferences based on experience, as well as from self-evident principles (I, 13, 2–6).

Marsilius has assumed as self-evident what he calls the common conception of the mind that every whole is greater than its parts. Hence, the whole body of citizens must be taken for the same thing and can better discern what must be chosen and what rejected than any part of it taken separately. These he holds to be obvious truths. The whole body of citizens is not, he says, vicious and undiscerning. They may not be educated, but they are sufficiently rational to calculate the means whereby they may achieve their desire to live in tranquillity and hence achieve the sufficient life. Like Aquinas, and similarly using Aristotle's *Politics* III, Marsilius says that all or most of them are of sound mind and reason and have a right desire, that is, a rational will, for the polity and for the things necessary for it to endure, like laws and other statutes or customs. Of course, not every citizen is a discoverer of the law, yet every citizen can judge of what has been discovered and proposed to him by someone else, and thereby discern what must be added, subtracted or changed. Their judgement follows induction from individual experiences to more general rules of behaviour, and therefore Marsilius agrees with Aristotle who observed that many men judge rightly about the quality of a picture, a house, a ship and other works of art, even though they would have been unable to discover or produce them. Marsilius notes that when we speak of the multitude, the wise are included in it (I, 13, 7).

But to Aristotle he has added the long experience of consensual practices of medieval communes, practices justified by corporation theory as developed by canon, and more importantly for him, civil lawyers. If by 'stupid' is simply meant those who are less learned or who do not have the leisure for liberal functions, they nevertheless share in the understanding and judgement of practical matters, although not equally with those who have leisure. And even if it is easier to harmonize the views of the few than of the

---

31   Compare this with the arguments prevalent in the fifteenth century; see chapter 6.

many, it does not mean that such views are superior to those of the many. The few would not discern or desire the common benefit equally as well as would the entire multitude of citizens. The few would consult their own private benefit, and they would be open to oligarchy (I, 13, 5). Even when the multitude cannot discern or discover specific laws as means to an agreed end, even when they cannot discover true and useful measures themselves, Marsilius says they can understand what is proposed and whether something should be added, subtracted, changed or completely rejected. They should be numbered among good men (I, 13, 7). The multitude therefore entrusts to the prudent and experienced, preferably through their election either by the ruler or by the citizen assembly, the investigation, discovery and examination of standards, the future laws or statutes concerning civil justice and benefit. But it is up to the whole people, assembled in a general assembly as the human legislator or the weightier part which represents their will, which is itself an expression of their reason, to consent to laws proposed as furthering the common good, in order that such laws be regarded as legitimate and coercively binding (I, 13, 8). The laws are then to be made public.

It is important not to confuse the machinery of election and think that a ranked society that recognizes men who might constitute 'the weightier part', somehow invalidates the rational will of the whole human legislator as the whole body of citizens. Marsilius understands corporation theory as ensuring that the same will of the whole may be represented by those elected to speak 'the corporate will' and not the will of some 'part'. Indeed, he insists that after the future laws have been discovered and diligently examined by those with experience, leisure and learning, they must be laid before the assembled whole body of citizens for their approval or disapproval. If any citizen thinks that something should be added, subtracted, changed or rejected, he may say so, since by this means the law will be more usefully ordained. These laws, made by the hearing and explicit consent of the entire multitude will be better observed, nor will anyone have any protest to make against them. Such laws will then have been made public.

Thereafter, men of proportional quality will be elected as representing the position and authority of the whole body of the citizens. These are the ruling, judicial/deliberative offices with public authority. They understand the corporate will because they are part of it. This is the reason that it makes no difference to Marsilius that an elected ruler will approve or disapprove in whole or in part the standards which had been investigated and proposed by the legal experts, or else the whole body of citizens or the weightier part will do this by itself. But should the *pars principans*, the ruling element, abuse its authority, then it is the human legislator which retains not only the power of appointment to ruling office, but also the power to correct or even depose the ruler, so that the common advantage may be served (I, 15, 2). Marsilius presents the standard medieval conception of the separation of public office from its potentially unworthy incumbent who may be disciplined or, in the last analysis, removed from office.

Only after the corporate will approves the standards by which the civil community is to be regulated can the laws be recognized as coercive. After publication and proclamation it is they alone among human commands that make transgressors liable to civil guilt and punishment (I, 13, 8). From here, the function of the ruler as guardian of justice plays his or their role, executing justice by judging what concerns the common good according to the laws, and having an army sufficient to execute civil sentences against the rebellious or disobedient by coercive force.

Marsilius has in effect provided the ruler, the *pars principans*, with good laws and good arms, both of which are determined by the human legislator (I, 14, 8). Should a would-be prince find himself confronting a community where these traditions of free men engaged in practices of self-government have been corrupted or destroyed, then it will not be to Marsilius of Padua's *Defender of Peace* that he will need to turn but to Machiavelli's *Prince*.[32]

Towards the end of Discourse 1 (chapter 17) Marsilius makes plain that any city or *regnum* must have only one government whatever the specific constitutional form of a given temperate regime is decided upon. His purpose in establishing the numerical unity of the government or ruler(s) is not simply to show that several governments in a city or 'state' lead to multiple internal jurisdictions which cause factional disorder among citizens. He is arguing in general against the accepted medieval division between the two jurisdictions, that of the church and that of the civil government, over the same men's lives, however such separate jurisdictions came to be actualized in different places across Europe. An example of this principle in Italian cities would be the internal division between pro-papal and pro-imperial factions. He says that the men of one city or province are called one city or 'state' because they wish one government in number. And he alludes to his earlier demonstrations that to no individual of whatever dignity or rank, and to no group, does there belong any rulership or coercive jurisdiction over anyone in this world unless this authority shall have been granted to them immediately by the human legislator, that is, not mediately through some other and (self-proclaimed) external jurisdictional authority such as the papacy or indeed the empire, as a separate governing jurisdiction.

Marsilius here calls the human legislator 'divine' (I, 17, 13). In the final chapter (chapter 19) not only does he recapitulate what has been established in the first Discourse but he establishes a link with what is to come in his second Discourse by providing a scriptural account of Christ and the mission of his apostolic church. He notes that Christ wanted the evangelic law to be written, and so it was written by the first apostles. Through this law men should be able to comprehend the commands and counsels of eternal salvation in the absence of Christ, the apostles and the evangelists (I, 19, 4). Christ ordained the apostles as teachers of this law and as ministers of the sacraments according to it. He describes the nature of the priestly authority that was conferred as a certain character of the soul impressed through God's immediate action, so that they could perform their sacramental and verbal ministry, to celebrate mass, bind and loose men from their sins, and appoint men as their apostolic successors. Another authority, however, was given to priests by *man* in order to avoid scandal after the number of priests had multiplied. This human authorization, through the wills and minds of men, was with regard to directing the proper performance of divine worship in the temple and in the ordering and distribution of temporal things established for the use (not ownership) of ministers (I, 19, 5–6). The reader is being prepared for Marsilius's fuller analysis of the church in Discourse 2 as a necessary, primary part of any temperate regime, established by the human legislator.

Some Observations from Discourse 2

In Discourse or Dictio 2 Marsilius entertains a wide variety of scriptural, historical and legal positions to show that the contemporary church as a man-made historical institu-

32 See below, chapter 6.

tion has misunderstood its own mission and nature. It has deviated from the original intentions of Christ's primitive church. Marsilius treats the by-now familiar passage from Matthew 16 about the keys given to Peter to bind on earth as in heaven, and also Luke 22 on the two swords and John 21 where Christ says to Peter: 'feed my sheep'. But Marsilius wants to counter interpretations that support the view that bishops and priests have coercive jurisdiction and that the pope is the supreme ruler of all in this world (II, 3). By marshalling scripture and its examples of Christ's own actions and words along with the approved church doctors who expounded the evangelic law, he argues that the church as an institution, as a primary 'part' of the 'state', is not capable of exercising any coercive power and should have nothing to do with temporalities. No clergyman can absolve subjects from their oath by which they are bound to their Christian rulers. Not only has coercive judgement not been granted to any bishop by divine law, but it has been explicitly forbidden (II, 5, 8–9). His arguments are heavily influenced by those put forward by radical spiritual Franciscans and their supporters, some of whom were in exile at Ludwig of Bavaria's courts.

Especially in communities of the faithful, all churchmen and laymen are subject to the coercive judgement of secular rulers and judges who govern by the authority of the human legislator. Marsilius reconfigures the church as a congregation of the faithful; clergy, following Christ's counsel, ought to refuse rulership even if it be offered to them by someone having the authority to do so. The church is a voluntary gathering of men who believe in Christ and elect priests as teachers of the evangelical doctrine of scripture (II, 17, 8–9). The chief authority and judge in the church lies not with the pope, his decretals or canon law, but with the general council of believers. This association of the faithful may empower others, in the civil sphere, to act on its behalf (II, 20, 2–4). And the worldwide association of the faithful, the *universitas fidelium*, or a general council representing it, may establish a universal faithful human legislator to act on its behalf in matters of public ecclesiastical law and administration, and by its authority this is the Roman emperor (II, 21–2). We have already mentioned that religious belief, in the forum of conscience, is not open to coercion. We must now try to illuminate whether Marsilius is arguing for a religious toleration that would make one's religious convictions matters indifferent to the 'state'.

Marsilius explicitly says that he does *not* think it inappropriate that heretics or those who are otherwise infidel be coerced, but that the authority for this, if it be lawful to do so, belongs only to the human legislator (II, 5, 7). He argues, furthermore, that since excommunication not only affects the status of the future life of the accused but also has dire consequences for his earthly life, in that the excommunicant is publicly defamed and the company of other persons is forbidden to him, then because he is deprived of civil communion and benefits in this life, excommunication is a judgement that pertains to the whole body of the faithful or a general council which represents their views in that community in which the defendant is to be judged (II, 6, 12). If Marsilius is willing to maintain excommunication then we must clarify for what kind of behaviour it is allowed as a penalty.

Marsilius holds that in the community of the faithful it pertains to no one priest or group to make a judgement having coercive power to expel a person from the company of the community because of a disease of the soul. His crime must be of such a kind that by sure testimony it can be proved to have been committed by someone. And based on the conviction of witnesses, both the learned and the unlearned (II, 10, 7), and where the crime be such as merits excommunication not only from the community of the faithful but with civil consequences, the sentence of excommunication is to be pronounced by the whole body of the faithful or their representative, appointed judge (II, 6, 12). So long as the whole body of the faithful or their appointed representatives consent to the excommunication of a 'contumacious' person, the judgement and its consequences are legitimate. They have verbal authority. It is the civil authority which then exercises the rights of coercive power and executes civil punishment on the person judged worthy of it.

Marsilius is careful to repeat that coercive judgements concern human voluntary acts in accordance with some law or custom. He argues that over our uncontrolled acts, such as our natural instinctive emotions, we do not have complete freedom or control as to whether or not they shall be done. But over controlled acts we do have this power according to the Christian religion, that is, the evangelical perfect law of liberty (II, 8, 3). Of the various acts over which we do have control some are called 'immanent' and others 'transient'. He defines immanent acts as controlled cognitions, emotions, and the corresponding habits made by the human mind in its thinking. Immanent acts do not, he says, cross over into any subject other than the agent himself. This is not to be confused with Mill's later self-regarding acts; Marsilius is speaking of mental intentions which do not issue in external acts of any kind (II, 8, 3).

Transient acts, however, he defines as *all the pursuits of things desired, and the omissions thereof*. He observes two kinds of transient acts. Some transient acts harm no individual, group or community other than the agent. These are similar to Mill's self-regarding acts and include castigation of one's own body. But some transient acts do harm someone other than the agent, and Marsilius includes theft, robbery and bearing false witness. It is these which are judged against the naturally and rationally discovered standard of serving or thwarting the sufficient life *both in this world and in the next*.

Some immanent and transient acts are regulated by standards without any reward or punishment being given to the doer or omitter by someone else through coercive force. In other words, some thoughts and some forms of externalized behaviour are guided by what appear to be principles which are naturally known to humans and simply guide their way of existing in the world as humans. The parallel here is with the Ciceronian notion of the first principles which proceed from nature by which justice is a habit of mind which gives every man his desert while preserving the common advantage. No one need teach men these principles: they arise in them through reflection on social experience. But there are other standards in accordance with which such acts are commanded to be done or omitted with reward or punishment being given to the doers or omitters by someone else through coercive force. The parallel here is with Cicero's notion that after the first principles of nature, certain rules of conduct become customary by reason of their usefulness.[33] Of these standards which are commanded coercively there are some which are concerned only with this present life, and these are human civil laws and customs. But there are other standards which are *commanded coercively* in accordance with which doers are rewarded or punished in and for the status of the future life only. The parallel here is with the notion in Cicero's *De inventione* that after the first principles which proceed from nature, and after the rules of conduct which became customary by reason of their usefulness, there later came the support for the natural principles and those approved by custom from religion and the fear of law. Marsilius says

---

33   See *De inventione* II, liii, 160 and volume 1, chapter 5 of *A History of Political Thought* on Cicero.

that while civil laws are established to secure the sufficient life and deal with voluntary transient acts which may benefit or harm others, he adds that the law of Christ is coercive and distributes punishments or rewards, but these are inflicted in the future world rather than in the present one (II, 4–5). Here he maintains that *both* human and divine coercive laws require an executive moving principle, which commands, regulates and judges human acts in accordance with both these laws and which should coerce transgressors.

Marsilius wants to take away the power to judge from priests and place it in the civil magistrate to whom priests as well as laymen are subject. And he will not allow the objection which holds that injuries by word of mouth, or to property or person and other deeds prohibited by human law, are spiritual actions when they are performed by a priest (II, 8, 8). In this he reveals that injury by word of mouth is a civilly actionable transient act for all citizens. He lists the deeds prohibited by law as adultery, beating, homicide, theft, robbery, insult, libel, treason, fraud and *heresy* (II, 8, 8). To what extent, then, do Marsilius's citizens, living in a civil regime with a necessary part of the 'state' being religious educators, have a freedom of action, where speech is clearly considered a transient act? He has already explained that the council which represents the will of the congregated faithful can judge and consent to someone being excommunicated from their midst on the evidence of witnesses, but that only the civil executive may carry out this coercion through civil law. Is it possible in Marsilius's temperate regime to think heresy and not reveal it in some transient act which then will be witnessed and judged?

Marsilius goes on to argue that the intention in the primitive church was never to command that anyone, even an infidel, let alone a believer, be compelled in this world through pain or punishment to observe the commands of the evangelic law, especially by a priest. The clergy who are ministers of this law cannot therefore judge anyone in this world with coercive sanction nor compel an unwilling person, by any pain or punishment, to observe the commands of divine law, *especially without authorization by the human legislator* (II, 9, 7). Does Marsilius mean that should the human legislator seek to coerce unwilling persons to observe the Christian faith (in a political community where most are believers), as this unwillingness reveals itself in transient acts including speech, it is legitimate? The answer must clearly be yes, where the judgement of the collected faithful finds against someone whose behaviour, even in speech, disturbs the tranquillity of the sufficient life.

He does not think that every community establishes the same standards of human temporal acts which guide men towards their ends in both this and the next life. But ideally, it seems that a perfect civil community would establish civil laws that regulated human acts not only for this life but for the future life as well (II, 9, 12). He notes that the evangelic law was not made to effect, by civil means, the reduction of men's contentious acts to due equality or proportion for the sufficiency of this life. But clearly, civil regimes that also are Christian, incorporate the moral commands of evangelic law as the principles which sustain the regulation of human law. Is this merely a conflation of quasi-natural law and the law of nations with the principles of the evangelic law? Or does the evangelic law contain injunctions that add to and perfect natural and international law? From what Marsilius has already told us in Discourse 1, it appears that he thinks there is a perfection that has occurred through Christ's redemptive incarnation. The divine law adds to and perfects what is naturally known and deduced from living a human life. But divine commandments are written so that humans may understand them in ways that humans naturally understand anything: by reason based on experience. Marsilius seems to be implying what William of Ockham, his fellow exile at the court of Ludwig of Bavaria, was later (1334) to state in his Letter to his Franciscan brethren: that the general truths of scripture describing the customs of men can be verified by anyone's daily experience.[34]

Marsilius's argument is not unlike that of Aquinas, and there appears to be for him as well a notion that civil laws, consented to by a Christian-educated human legislator, will necessarily be penetrated with the taught values of scripture which can be verified daily by men reflecting on experience. This appears to define heretics, infidels and schismatics as simply inappropriately acculturated, irrational disturbers of social peace and tranquillity and, at least in speech if not in other forms of transient acts, they will demonstrate this to witnesses in the community of the faithful. On these grounds, not on their essential beliefs but on what appears to be their insufficiently rationally guided behaviour, they are to be corrected or punished. In the end, Marsilius does not appear to believe that thoughts in the forum of conscience remain there.

Hence, Marsilius argues that if human law were to prohibit heretics or other infidels from dwelling in the region, and such a person were to be found, then he must be corrected in this world as a transgressor of human law. If, however, human law does not prohibit the heretic or other infidel from dwelling among the faithful in the same province, as, he says, heretics and Jews are now permitted to do by human laws even in these times of Christian peoples, rulers and pontiffs, then Marsilius says no one is allowed to judge or coerce them. No one, he says, is punished in this world for sinning against theoretic or practical disciplines precisely as such. No one, in other words, is punished for his thinking. Men are only punished for sinning against a command of human law (II, 10, 3). But he has already argued that perfect societies align true cognition with voluntary behaviour. Furthermore, for Marsilius, there can be sins against the divine law which human law prohibits, and a society of the faithful will increasingly establish human laws that reflect this notion of sin. Then a deviant will be punished in this world as a sinner against human law. Taken to the extreme of a perfectly unified civil regime, where a necessary and primary 'part' of the 'state' is its religious educators who educate the congregation of the faithful, then it is clear that if religious non-conformity is judged unacceptable because irrational, and a law against it received the consent of the citizens for the common utility, then to say, do or teach this non-conformity would be a civil crime. In a 'perfect' civil regime with a primary and necessary religious 'part' or office, it is most unlikely that alternative notions of freedom of action, including speech, would be tolerated. Among those things that all men agree to is that God must be worshipped, parents honoured, children reared by their parents up to a certain age, that no one should be injured, and that injuries must be lawfully repulsed. These depend on human enactments, but Marsilius says they are metaphorically called 'natural' rights because in all regions they are in the same way believed to be lawful and their opposites unlawful (II, 12, 7). Atheists certainly have no place here.[35] Is this as far as Marsilius is willing to go? I think not.

In Discourse 2, chapter 19 Marsilius observes that for eternal salvation it is necessary for us to believe in or to acknowledge as irrevocably true no writings except those

---

34   See below, chapter 5.
35   Compare Locke's writings on toleration.

which are called 'canonic', that is the Bible, or those interpretations or definitions of doubtful meanings of the holy scriptures which have been made by the general council of the faithful or Catholic Christians, especially regarding the articles of the Christian faith. That the holy scriptures must be firmly believed and acknowledged to be true is assumed as self-evident to all Christians, but this can only be proved by the authorities of these scriptures themselves (II, 19, 1–2). Christ would have handed down the law of eternal salvation in vain if he did not reveal to the believers its true meaning, belief in which is necessary for their salvation. Hence, it must be piously held that the decisions of the general councils with regard to doubtful meanings of scripture receive the origin of their truth from the Holy Spirit, *the coercive authority for their observance and acknowledgement from the human legislator*, and their promulgation and teaching through the priests and gospel ministers (II, 19, 3).

Marsilius then maintains that the words of Christ or God are not true *because* they are upheld by the testimony of the Catholic church, but rather, the testimony of the church is true because, and when, it utters the true words of Christ, *because Christ's words are true*. Perhaps it is astonishing to us in the twentieth century, but it was not unusual for Marsilius and for many much later generations, to make the following argument: because in Christ's teaching there can be no falsity – and this is an argument about the truth of right cognition and not one dependent on supernatural revelation – then it is not because the church teaches that 'God is three in one' that it is true, but because the Holy Spirit reveals this as true to the church as the congregation of the faithful.

This is very similar to the view that the Franciscan theologian William of Ockham would maintain concerning the nature of heresy. He would argue that heresy in a particular sense is any and every assertion which contradicts scripture. But in its broad sense, heresy is not only contradictory to the Bible but it is also dissension from chronicles or histories or oral traditions deemed worthy of belief by the church. In his *Dialogus* (I *Dialogus* ii, 5) Ockham spoke of mortal error as including contradictions of Catholic truth which are apparently not evident but which *are* (logically) demonstrable in that they are in conformity with reason.[36] Truth is not had on institutional authority for Ockham any more than for Marsilius, but from scripture or from any other source worthy of trust. What is worthy of trust is determined either by experience or by reason. Pertinacity, the adherence to what one should not, is decided after attempts at persuasion have failed. Ockham explicitly says[37] that if a man who has reason and understanding and has lived among Christians denies a publicly known Catholic assertion like 'Christ was crucified', then he is judged pertinacious. Pertinacity is both an unreadiness to correct errors which are contrary to Catholic truths one is *not* bound to believe explicitly *and* the mere failure to assent to Catholic truths one *is* bound to believe explicitly. As with Ockham, so too with Marsilius, there is a relatively small number of propositions to which a simple and illiterate man need agree, but they include such propositions as 'the Christian faith is true' and 'Christ was crucified'. So long as there is public communication of the Catholic faith and what is required to believe explicitly is available, then a pertinacious heretic is simply one who errs knowingly and by rational human

---

36 'Licet ex forma propositionum solis contentis.'
37 In his tract against Pope John XXII, *Contra Ioannem*; see below, p. 187.

cognition he is obliged to approve the truth. In a civil community with a dominant number of the faithful who authorize teachers of the faith, a sane use of reason is linked to belief in the Christian faith.[38]

Hence, it is not simply atheists who will be found no place in Marsilius's Christian civil regime, but anyone who does not acknowledge the truth of the Bible and in particular Christ's words in the New Testament, words that speak of things that go well beyond Cicero's and Roman civil law's natural law and the law of nations. Right cognition, right reason, for Marsilius, in Christian times, appears to come to this and will penetrate the perspective of the human legislator when it consents to laws that are coercive commands on all.[39]

In the seventeenth century, Hobbes argued only in part against this tradition of thinking which insisted that right reason was a universally shared and developed foundational characteristic of men, a tradition which he tells the reader was still alive and well in his own times, in the schools and universities, as elsewhere.

> When men that think themselves wiser than all others clamour and demand right reason for judge, yet seek no more but that things should be determined by no other men's reason but their own, it is as intolerable in the society of men as it is in play after trump is turned, to use for trump on every occasion that suite whereof they have most in their hand. For they do nothing else that will have every of their passions, as it comes to bear sway in them, to be taken for right reason, and that in their own controversies: bewraying their want of right reason by the claim they lay to it.[40]

Hobbes, living in Protestant England, finds room for something equivalent to Marsilius's congregation of the faithful or its representative council to determine doubtful interpretations of scripture, but he proposes a chief pastor, the civil sovereign, to replace Marsilius's perfect, non-coercive, religious teachers as 'parts' of the state. Hobbes observes the following in the third part of *Leviathan*, 'Of a Christian Commonwealth', which few, nowadays, seem to read: that the chief pastor, who alone can speak the true doctrine, be the civil sovereign (*Leviathan* III, xxxix). Like Marsilius, Hobbes argues that the acts of council of the apostles were not coercive laws but counsels, and therefore the books of the New Testament, though most perfect rules of Christian doctrine, could not be made laws by any other authority than that of *kings or sovereign assemblies* (III, xlii). If one wishes to know what is necessary to salvation, then for Hobbes, it is contained in two virtues, faith in Christ and obedience to laws.

> And the laws of God therefore are none but the laws of nature, whereof the principal is, that we should not violate our faith, that is, a commandment to obey our civil sovereigns which we constituted over us by mutual pact with one another. And this law of God that commandeth obedience to the law civil commandeth by consequence obedience to all the

---

38   See J. Dunbabin, *A Hound of God: Pierre de la Palud and the fourteenth-century church* (Oxford, 1991), which shows other contemporary understandings of heresy as treason or *lèse-majesté*, notably the views of Durand de S. Pourcain and the response of the Dominican Peter de la Palud.

39   For an alternative reading of Marsilius's argument in the *Defender of Peace* as well as in his later *Defensor minor*, see C. J. Nederman, 'Toleration and Community: a medieval communal functionalist argument for religious toleration', *The Journal of Politics* 56 (1994), pp. 901–18.

40   *Leviathan* I, v.

precepts of the Bible, which, as I have proved in the precedent chapter, is the only law, where the civil sovereign hath made it so, and in other places, but counsel.[41]

With the seventeenth-century Hobbes, so too with the fourteenth-century Marsilius: the entity with the legitimate authority to make laws that are coercive can determine that worship of Christ and an acknowledgement of the trinity and his crucifixion be a determinant of inclusion in the civil regime.[42]

Marsilius's image of perfect teachers of the evangelic law makes use of the Spiritual Franciscan image of St Francis, living in imitation of Christ and the primitive church. Hence, he disendows the church and argues directly against the position of the contemporary pope John XXII, who established that the Franciscan doctrine of evangelical poverty was heretical. John XXII had argued that charity, not poverty, was Christ's virtue and that Christ did own the purse from which he bought what was needed for the sustenance of his apostles' lives. According to John XXII, use and ownership could not be separated, especially regarding consumables or in the enjoyment of the utility of goods. But for Marsilius, Christian teachers and preachers are users, not owners, of property and they have no coercive force in this world. He says that those elected by the congregated faithful legislator to be educators are, if scripture is followed, to be perfect men living with a contempt for the world and in the status of poverty. This, says Marsilius, is almost necessary for the man who must urge upon others contempt for the world if he wishes to succeed in his teaching or preaching (II, 11, 3). If Christ had thought it proper for a preacher to hold the status of a ruler in this world he would himself have suffered this status; instead, Marsilius says that Christ fled to the mountain in order to preach the rejection of such status. While the status of external poverty and humility does not befit a ruler, because he should have a status which good subjects will respect and bad ones fear, and through which he will be able to use coercion if necessary upon rebellious transgressors of the laws, for this reason the preacher's office is not suitable for a ruler. A ruler will not be believed if he were to urge upon the people the status of poverty and humility, to turn the other cheek when smitten and to give a cloak to the stealer of one's tunic. But Marsilius thinks that these counsels do appropriately come from preachers and they are meant as more perfect encouragements to modify, with charity, men's behaviour which, in this life, is measured by the civil laws of utility. Here we can observe him entering the debate over property which had long entertained Dominican opponents to the Franciscan position. Discourse 2 chapter 13 is an elaborate defence of supreme poverty and evangelical perfection as theoretically maintained and voluntarily practised by contemporary Franciscans.

Marsilius supports, as did Franciscans, a distinction between *dominium* (ownership) and *usus* (use) (II, 12, 13–24; 13; 14, 2–8). He acknowledges that it is currently more common to use the term *dominium* to mean the principal power to lay claim to something rightfully acquired, in accordance with the civil law right taken to mean a coercive command or prohibition of the human legislator, and to conflate this with the use (usufruct) of the thing. This was the Dominican position which was also sustained in civil law. He also notes that 'possession' does more commonly mean both abstract,

---

41   *Leviathan* III, xliii.

42   We need not enter the debate over whether Hobbes was sceptical about the Christian religion to see that he establishes, as did Marsilius, the legitimacy of a 'state' that can find no reason to tolerate those with alternate views.

incorporeal ownership and the actual corporeal handling of the thing or its use. But in wishing to reject John XXII's interpretation of Christ's ownership and use of simple things against the Franciscan position which insisted that Christ had condescended not to be an owner or possessor of temporal goods in private or in common with the other apostles (II, 13, 37) Marsilius says that he denies that everyone who buys and sells or who can buy or sell some temporal thing is necessarily its owner. Every buyer and seller does not transfer the ownership of a thing or its price, and this is especially not the case of perfect men, his religious teachers and preachers (II, 14, 18) who voluntarily, that is, through their mendicant vows, bind themselves to non-ownership. Franciscans had been permitted to establish 'external persons' who were in charge of selling and buying things for Franciscan use, and Marsilius turns these 'external persons' into his civil authority, the human legislator (II, 14, 8). Marsilius's 'state' clergy only use and do not own the property that is defined and legally established by the civil law (II, 14, 18).[43]

Conclusion

Marsilius defends the empire from the standpoint of an Italian, familiar not only with self-governing communes but also with the quasi-autonomous rule of the *signori* who served as the *podestà* in city-states. It is not to the *imperium germanicum*, rooted more or less in the territory of Germany, that he accords his belief, but to his notion of Roman Empire, to the institution which has all the aspects of a quasi-sacramental tradition and where the Roman people constituted the human legislator. His emperor is no mere German prince but an heir of Roman Caesars to whom the Roman people had transferred its revocable authority to rule. And it is to the restoration of this kind of imperial power founded in the authority of the Roman people that he speaks when he rejects the two competing jurisdictions over civil men's lives. He has transferred the *plena potestas* of the papal hierocrats to the human legislator of temperate regimes, be they cities or *regna*. In the last analysis, the Roman imperial civil law, modified by custom, oversees the conditions of tranquillity and peace. Hence, he looks to the Roman Empire, whose direction of Christianity warranted its being called the *sacrum imperium* in that it guaranteed security and peace *between* self-governing 'states'.[44]

If, as some hold, Marsilius's theory of the human legislator as the popular 'sovereign' was destined to play a major role in shaping the most radical version of early-modern constitutionalism,[45] then are we meant to conclude that thirteenth- and fourteenth-century corporation theory, and notably of the Marsilian variety, is at the origin of the modern state? We have reason to question this. This could only be true if by the so-called modern state we mean Locke's, not Hobbes's, or rather, the Weberian definition of the state, itself a product of the later absolutist tradition, read back into Hobbes. The

---

43   For a further discussion of Marsilius on rights see B. Tierney, *The Idea of Natural Rights: studies on natural rights, natural law and church law 1150–1625* (Atlanta, GA, 1997), esp. ch. 5, pp. 104–30, 110–18, where he argues that Marsilius is even more a voluntarist than Ockham since everything depended on the will to assert or renounce a right.

44   For a good brief overview of current views on the relation of Marsilius's *Defensor pacis* and his other works, the *Defensor minor* and the *De translatione imperii*, see J.Canning, *A History of Medieval Politial Thought 300–1450* (London, 1996), pp. 154–8.

45   Q. Skinner, *Foundations of Modern Political Thought* (Cambridge, 1978), vol. 1, p. 65.

modern liberal theory of popular sovereignty in a secular state is not the same as Marsilius's because the modern liberal state holds with Hobbes and relies precisely on the *rejection* of a universal right reason, known by all citizens, which can determine the *objective* content of the common good. Perhaps the only remnant of right reason in modern state theory concerns the ultimate survival of the state and hence the *necessity* of having public authority. This *is* a continuation of the medieval doctrine of *raison d'état*, but for the medievals it only implied that even unjust acts of a government must be tolerated if the state, the *salus populi*, is to be defended in emergencies. For them, *raison d'état* was not a matter of policy.

Furthermore, medieval corporation theory posits *no* distinction between the state and civil society, whereas the modern state relies on this distinction. We have been told that a recognizably modern concept of the state is one where there is an *apparatus of power* whose existence remains independent of those who may happen to have control of it at any given time.[46] It is said to exist as *regulator* of public affairs, brooking no rival as a source of coercive power within its jurisdiction; hence, this regulator of public affairs is said to be the monopolist of legitimate force.[47] The modern state distinguishes state authority from that of the whole society or community over which its powers are exercised.[48] But medieval corporation theory does *not* take the regulator to be independent, autonomous and over and above the corporation and its collective will. A regulator with this kind of absolute and unbrookable power would be a despot or an absolutist with its own will, precisely what corporation theory rejects. The distinction that *is* drawn in medieval corporation theory is one between generic *regimine* with a single corporate will for the common good that makes the community the source of authority, and the alterable range of executive and institutional means that can achieve this common good, through constitutions set up in contingent circumstances, be they monarchies, or aristocracies, or more populist 'polities'. A 'free constitution' can be actualized through a number of constitutional forms. The apparatus of power, understood as executive and institutional, is not constant and independent; for corporation theory, offices of 'state' are functional and contingent choices depending on tradition and circumstance. They are trustees. There is no 'personalism', an allegiance to a particular person who assumes a particular office, but there is an allegiance to the corporate whole whose will is represented and executed by 'state' officers, and such offices are derivative of a prudential reading of the kind of constitutional arrangements that are deemed best in the circumstances. Hence, the liberty of subjects or citizens, in corporate medieval discourse, is a liberty that can be maintained by a variety of constitutional arrangements or 'apparatuses of power', and constitutions can change.

The one political authority which *is* autonomous and exists independently is the whole corporation itself, but the *regulation* of the public affairs of an independent community is down to a variable set of offices determined by the chosen constitution. What corporation theory normally allows for is an ever-living *regnum* as a legal fiction over and above its constituting authorities, the whole corporation, and which is not identified with any incumbent of an office. But its authority is consonant with, not distinct from,

---

46 Q. Skinner, 'The State', in T. Ball, J. Farr and R. Hanson, eds, *Political Innovation and Conceptual Change* (Cambridge, 1989), p. 102.
47 Skinner, 'The State', p. 107.
48 Ibid., p. 112.

the powers of its citizens or subjects. In assuming that the range of powers a community establishes over itself when its members consent to being subject to government must ultimately be identified with its *own* powers as a community, we have corporation theory's legacy to Locke's notion of the 'state', which some see him to have, thereafter, deconstructed in favour of executive prerogatives. The Weberian definition of the modern state, which can be read back into Hobbes, comes from the absolutist tradition, whether it was derived from later divine right theories or later natural law absolutism, rather than from medieval corporation theory or practice.[49]

If we examine modern notions of political representation we see that they assume public officials to be acting in the interest of the represented, but it is an interest that is not necessarily coincident with the desires of represented constituents. This is a notion that Marsilius's corporation theory thinks impossible.[50] Much needs to happen, historically and theoretically, before we reach Hobbes's state and, thereafter, our own. One of the most important steps taken in this direction, but not for secular reasons, was the rejection of Marsilius's understanding of corporation theory and a corporate will. William of Ockham, his contemporary, would throw the liability for ethical judgement and political decision-making onto the individual, prior to his incorporation into any political grouping.

49   Skinner argues that Locke insists we never deliver up fundamental liberties in establishing a commonwealth but merely depute or delegate a known and indifferent judge to safeguard them more effectively on our own behalf. 'Although this means that we commit ourselves to setting up a complex apparatus of government, it also means that the powers of such a government can never amount to anything more than the joint power of every member of the society.' Skinner thinks that this is why Locke never uses the word 'status' to describe the power of civil government (p. 115). Like corporationists, for Locke the 'state' is a trustee. But see the alternative argument in S. Wolin, *The Presence of the Past* (Baltimore, 1989), pp. 168–71, for whom Locke is a pivotal figure in the expansion of reason of state and the powers of the executive through prerogative – the power to act according to discretion for the public good (extension and expansion, at home and abroad, of rational productivity or 'the right employing of resources', without the prescription of the law and sometimes even against it).

50   See Nederman, *Community and Consent*, pp. 83–8; H. Pitkin, *The Concept of Representation* (Berkeley, 1967).

5

William of Ockham[1]

Marsilius of Padua can be considered a political theorist concerned primarily with legitimate power in civil regimes, who thereafter used many Franciscan theological positions to bolster his notions on the nature of the church. But his contemporary and fellow exile at the court of Ludwig of Bavaria, William of Ockham, dealt with questions of human authority because he was more fundamentally interested in theological truth. As a theologian, he engaged in a logical search for Catholic truths in scripture and was particularly averse to canon lawyers' interventions in doctrinal issues. He abhorred what he took to be the canonist Pope John XXII's ignorance of theology and his misinterpretation of theological texts of scripture, especially in John's insistence on interpreting scriptural references to Christ's and the apostles' *use* of things in legal terms. It has often been observed that Ockham's was a limited familiarity with the literature of canon law, knowing some texts well and not others. But to say that his theological focus on scriptural truths makes him a non-political or anti-political writer is to adopt a twentieth-century view of secular intentions behind political expression.[2]

Ockham's political conclusions derived, as did so many of the writings of his contemporaries, from his religious beliefs, which he happened to think could be shown to be reasonable. It was from the perfect law of liberty of the gospels that Ockham developed his notions of the natural rights of individuals and his subsequent understanding of the origin and limits of all institutions with jurisdiction over men's lives.

The writings of Marsilius and Ockham proved influential from their own times well into the fifteenth and sixteenth centuries; Marsilius's *Defensor pacis* would, in part, be translated into English and reissued under Henry VIII. Ockham's philosophical and political writings would be known and used in the seventeenth century, especially by Huguenot theorists.[3] But as with all theorists used by later generations with altered agendas, both men's ideas would be filtered and crucial parts of them ignored to suit other times, places and perspectives.

---

1   An earlier version of this chapter appeared as 'Ockham's Right Reason and the Genesis of the Political as "Absolutist"', *History of Political Thought* 20 (1999), pp. 35–64; reprinted in J. Coleman, ed., *Scholastics, Enlightenments and Philosophic Radicals: essays in honour of J. H. Burns* (Exeter, 1999).
2   See Canning, *A History of Medieval Political Thought 300–1450* (London, 1996), p. 160 and R. Scholz, *Wilhelm von Ockham als politischer Denker und sein Breviloquium de Principatu Tryannico* (Leipzig, 1944), who also took the view that Ockham was primarily a theologian but did not go so far as to think him anti-political.
3   As Q. Skinner has shown in volume 2 of *Foundations of Modern Political Thought* (Cambridge, 1978).

Biographical Details

It is thought that William of Ockham was born *c.* 1280 in Surrey and died *c.* 1349 in the Black Death which swept across Europe and decimated the European population. He entered the Franciscan Order and then studied in Oxford, teaching in the Franciscan *studia* in London and Northampton. He followed the arts course with his Order and then proceeded to the theology degree in Oxford University. He never became a doctor of theology because his academic career as a logician, philosopher and theologian was cut short *c.* 1323 when the Chancellor of the university had excerpts from his philo-sophical and theological writings sent to the pope, who was then resident in Avignon, for examination and possible censure. Ockham was summoned to defend his philo-sophical positions. He was censured rather than excommunicated and in 1328, the year in which Ludwig of Bavaria was established as Emperor in Rome, Ockham escaped from Avignon with the Minister General of the Franciscans, Michael of Cesena, to Ludwig's court in Munich. He took up the Michaelists' position and argued against the papal claim to plenitude of power in matters temporal and spiritual. From the 1330s, then, Ockham set to writing against the pretensions of the papacy and to defend the Franciscans concerning the absolute poverty of Christ and the apostles by means of his own scriptural hermeneutics. His wider views on politics, none of which were ever presented systematically, would develop thereafter.

Some have argued that the two phases of Ockham's life, first as an Oxford academic philosopher and theologian, and second as a political theorist in exile at the court of Ludwig of Bavaria, produced two radically incommensurable sets of writings which cannot be reconciled. It is believed by some that his politics cannot be deduced from his Oxford logic, philosophy and theology.[4]

Undoubtedly, he began as an academic theologian with strong interests in logic, psy-chology and the philosophy of science, all of which reflected the early fourteenth-cen-tury Oxford University milieu as it came to diverge from that of the University of Paris. There is nothing in these early Oxford writings that show him particularly interested in Franciscan 'political' problems, although his philosophical and theological writings de-veloped from his attempts to refine the perspectives of his distinguished Franciscan pred-ecessor in Oxford, John Duns Scotus. My purpose here, however, is briefly to show that his distinctive logical, ethical and theological positions were fundamental to his later, distinctive political conclusions. The break in his academic career was contingent; he was a Franciscan at Oxford and at Avignon, although it was only in Avignon that he became aware of the nature of the contemporary bias of the papacy against his own order. My aim is to indicate that his theory of knowledge and his method of analysing texts of scripture and history (which relies on this epistemology) were developed at Oxford and endured throughout his life as he responded to changing issues and circum-stances. His commitment to truth before institutional authority simply became increas-ingly focused. It is unfortunate that some historians of political thought who are interested in what can be called Ockham's political theory have found his epistemology and his logic so difficult as to ignore them.

---

4   See for instance G. Leff, *William of Ockham: the metamorphosis of scholastic discourse* (Manchester, 1975), ch. 10, where he also cites the similar views of Boehner and others.

Ockham's Positions on Church and State

His political positions on the relations of secular and spiritual jurisdictions are easy enough to draw in main outline. If we look first at the conclusions to be found in his later, political writings, we can thereafter treat the degree to which they may be derived from positions already maintained in his academic logic, ethics, psychology and theology.

After his experience at Avignon, Ockham began his publicist career by writing about Franciscan poverty and its papal adversaries in his *Opus nonaginta dierum* (*The Work of Ninety Days*). He then moved on to discuss the problem of papal heresy (in the first part of his *Dialogus*) and the rights of the Roman Empire. From 1337 on he wrote the major works from which his political views may be extracted: *Contra Benedictum*, the third part of the *Dialogus*, his *Eight Questions on Papal Power* (*Octo quaestiones de potestate papae*), the *Breviloquium* (*A short discourse on the tyrannical government over things divine and human . . .*) and his *On Imperial and Pontifical Power* (*De imperatorum et pontificum potestate*). I shall be drawing on these and other texts in what follows.

Ockham argued that the function of temporal rulers was to chastise and punish wrong-doers in society and to defend the church from them. All rulers derive their power from 'their people' who voluntarily consent to constitute public authority. To neglect the rights of the community counts as a vice.[5]

The right to use the world was conferred on the whole human race, including infidels, in God's original grant to Adam. But after the Fall the power to acquire property and to institute government derived from God's grant to humans of a power to appropriate and divide temporal things as right reason, in fallen conditions, deemed necessary, expedient and useful.[6] As we shall see, right reason operated differently in the conditions prior to and after the Fall. Although the church has exclusive spiritual power, it is subject to lay rulers with regard to the church's properties. Like Marsilius, Ockham addressed the current problem of there being two distinct, mainly exclusive jurisdictional orders, that of temporal and spiritual power. He, like Marsilius, argued that the two must somehow be unified, but Ockham suggested a different locus of this unity: the individual. He thereby maintained two distinct jurisdictions governing men's lives, whereas Marsilius subsumed the ecclesiastical within the temporal, civil order to achieve unity. Ockham argued that men who comprise societies are themselves both spiritual and temporal beings. Hence, divine law governs them spiritually, and human laws govern them

---

5 I *Dialogus* 6, 8; *Breviloquium* 1, 4; 2, 10; 2, 19; 3, 7–13. The Latin edition of the *Dialogus* is in Melchior Goldast, ed., *Monarchia Sancti Romani Imperii,* vol. 2 (Frankfurt, 1614; repr. Graz, 1960). There is no full English translation. Excerpts from III *Dialogus* are in A. S. McGrade, *A Letter to the Friars Minor and Other Writings* (Cambridge, 1995), pp. 118–298. German translations of excerpts with Latin texts are in J. Miethke, ed. and trans., *Wilhelm von Ockham, Texte zur politischen Theorie* (Stuttgart, 1995) and J. Miethke, ed., German trans. and commentary, *Wilhelm von Ockham, Dialogus, Auszuge zur politischen Theorie* (Darmstadt, 1992). The Latin text of the *Breviloquium* has been edited by Scholz, *Wilhelm von Ockham* and is now translated into English in A. S. McGrade, ed., and J. Kilcullen, trans., *A Short Discourse on Tyrannical Government* (Cambridge, 1992). *Breviloquium* 4 is particularly concerned with issues on legitimate secular government established by the people's will and consent.
6 *Breviloquium* 3, 7; *Opus Nonaginta Dierum* in H. S. Offler, ed., *Guillelmi de Ockham, Opera Politica*, vol. 1 (Manchester, 1940; repr. 1974), chs 1–6 and R. F. Bennett and H. S. Offler, eds, *Opera Politica*, vol. 2 (Manchester, 1963), chs 7–124. Excerpts in English translation in McGrade and Kilcullen, *William of Ockham, A Letter to the Friars Minor*, pp. 19–115; on lordship in the state of innocence, pp. 34ff. and on the origin of property, pp. 59ff.

temporally as citizens. Each individual is subject both to spiritual and temporal rules at the same time.[7]

But humans have rights to construct autonomous systems of law which vary. From God and from nature humans have the right freely to give themselves a head, because they are born free and not subjected to anyone by human law; for this reason every city and every people can establish law for itself.[8]

Ockham's focus is on the nature of men as individuals and he is concerned to show how individual men have certain liberties given them as a consequence of God's creation. We will examine how they come to know of this liberty. No man can ever completely alienate certain naturally possessed liberties, either to the 'state' or to the church. In both the spiritual and the temporal spheres of human life, the individual must be considered first as to his rights, capacities and liberties. From an analysis of the individual, Ockham proceeds to speak of collections of individuals as social groups.[9]

This focus on the individual is a consequence of what is often called Ockham's nominalism.[10] Broadly, two philosophical positions endured in medieval university philosophy departments: realism and nominalism. For instance, Aquinas was a moderate realist. But according to Ockham, realism destroyed the possibility of genuine knowledge because it posited non-singular things outside the mind such as universal natures, and he believed this went against all of Aristotle's logic and philosophy in particular, and against the science of truth and reason in general. Ockham's philosophy of knowledge insisted that all there is in the world are contingent (not necessary) individuals, and human beings then apply names *(nomina)* to such present and existing individuals which they know through a cognitive experience called 'intuitive cognition'. They construct sentences or propositions, either in thought or in conventional language, by which they refer to the individuality of the world. Our knowledge, then, is of (mental or linguistic) propositions whose terms substitute for our experiences.

Ockham's Epistemology

Ockham became identified in the minds of contemporaries with this claim that the proposition itself was the object of knowledge. He came to this view by asking the question that derives from Aristotle's writings on logic: what do our concepts signify and how do we apply concepts to individuals? He affirmed that concepts are the basic components of our thought but they are somehow caused by prior existent things. Our knowledge is,

---

7   See, for instance, *Eight Questions on the Power of the Pope*, Q.III, in McGrade and Kilcullen, *A Letter to the Friars Minor*, pp. 300–33. The full Latin text is in Offler, ed., *Opera Politica,* I, pp. 15–217; *Breviloquium* 3, 7; 4, 8.

8   *Breviloquium* 3, 7–8; 3, 14–15; 4, 8. III *Dialogus* 2, 3 and 5–10. See J. Miethke, 'The Concept of Liberty in William of Ockham', in (no ed.) *Théologie et droit dans la science politique de l'état moderne* (Collection de L'Ecole Française de Rome, 147) (Rome, 1991), pp. 89–100. After the Fall, man was granted the *potestas rectores eligendi iurisdictionem habentes* but its actual forms, including the functionaries of government, depend on man's decision. Ockham separates the decision in favour of an actual form of government from the question of the absolutely best constitution in III *Dialogus* I, 2, 20 and III *Dialogus* I, 4, 23.

9   J. Coleman, 'Guillaume d'Occam et la notion de sujet', in *Archives de philosophie du droit* 34 (1989), pp. 25–32.

10   Less misleadingly, it is a conceptualism: universals (or thoughts) are nothing other than names, that is, naturally significant general concepts (natural signs) which are primary; or secondarily, the conventional signs (terms and propositions in language) corresponding to primary concepts.

therefore, *of* concepts themselves or *of* extra-mental individuals, and the latter must be prior. He interpreted Aristotle as saying that sensory knowledge is what is known first and that intellective cognition presupposes sensitive cognition. For Ockham, all knowledge is the result of cognition of individuals which are particular and contingent. Reversing the trend of earlier scholastics, he asked not how the individual derives from an essence or a universal common nature, but how a world of individuals, which is all that really exists, can ever be known in a non-individual and general manner. He went to great lengths to show that while it is true that the universal character of our knowledge requires universal concepts, universality and commonality are properties only of signs, that is, of linguistic expressions and of acts of thought that may also be expressed in language. Universality and commonality are not properties of things. We shall see that his corporation theory reflects this position. For him the problem of individualism is a logical one, and he was concerned to show how general terms which we use in propositions, be they mental or linguistic, refer to individuals that are signified by them.

Everything that exists in reality is singular and individual. The object of knowledge, then, is the mental, spoken or written propositions and not the substance to which the proposition refers. While it is individual substance which we know, it is only known through terms in propositions.

Ockham believed that humans naturally have an immediate and intuitive knowledge of the existence and presence of individual, contingent objects. Normally, we know singulars that exist outside the mind and in the world *through* cognized sense experience of their present existence; thereafter, we know them intellectually as more universal concepts or mental names. The universal concept or thought is a natural sign in the mind, an act of thinking rather than an intelligible species. When a sign or term is a concept, it is an act of knowing which signifies individuals known. A sign or term may also be conventionally established, as is any particular language, and it corresponds to the natural signs or mental concepts which signify the individual things we are aware of having sensually experienced. Ockham insists on the one hand, that what we know of the world had first to be sensually experienced, but on the other, he insists that no external corporeal substance can be naturally apprehended by us in itself. We only know particular and individual substances which exist *through* mental, spoken or written propositions, comprised of signs or terms which substitute (suppost) for extra-mental things experienced. This is what he meant when he famously said that our knowledge in experience derives from terms which suppost for extra-mental things.

The starting point of any knowledge of contingent facts is intuitive cognition. Only after intuitive cognition can we have other kinds of knowledge: abstractive, individual, universal, contingent, necessary or self-evident. By this he means that in the natural course of living, upon sensing, we have first an immediate awareness or apprehension of terms which substitute for the really existing and present things we have sensed (and which themselves, as individuals, existing and present, are not signs). This immediate awareness comes before a *judgement* of the existence of the thing and before a judgement as to the truth of the thing. We cannot logically demonstrate this intuitive knowing of things, but we simply experience it as a fact of life. We start with a pure apperception of individuals and the linkage of such through propositions whose terms substitute for them. We have, therefore, an intuition of the singular, prior to our having a definition of it. We first know it simply as existing and present. This immediate apprehension is an act of intellect distinct from and prior to judgement. In the present order of things, our intuitive knowledge is always *of* what exists here and now (there is no intuitive knowledge of non-existents) and it is caused by this thing known through its term (*ipsa res nota*).[11]

Imagine yourself to be a student studying the arts course among Franciscans in Oxford and hearing Ockham's lectures on Aristotle's logic. He told his students that logic deals with a system of signs that is used to make true or false statements about things signified by these signs. Logic, therefore, is the means by which we unlock our experiences beyond the mere having of them. Spoken and written language is conventionally established to signify what is naturally signified by acts of thought. Thinking is no less a logic than is speaking or writing. Logic is the means by which we can study the properties of linguistic expressions to the extent that they refer to the logically essential functions of the soul's inner discourse. Conventional language has the capacity to signify natural signs or mental acts which themselves, as terms, are caused by intuitive cognition of individuals experienced. This view on what conventional language is and does has important effects on what he believes the texts of scripture can be taken to mean. We shall see that it is the task of the scriptural exegete to determine the true meaning of past, historical individuals' experiences intuitively known by them.

Ockham is not, however, claiming that the universal knowledge we have as a result of intuitive cognition necessarily mirrors the inner constitution of nature. Rather, he says that we only have confidence in what we can and have experienced. From here, we can only *assume a hypothetical necessity* that knowledge, which deals in universals, actually reflects the causes of our ideas in the physical world of particulars. In this life (*pro statu isto*) we live in a probable world of contingency beyond our immediate intuitive knowledge of things and concepts. Experience of particulars on the one hand, and syllogistic, logical demonstration on the other, give us the same kind of conclusions based on the primacy of the intuitions of singulars and our subsequent generalizations. Our theories about the world can only be about mental acts as signs that are thought to be common to contingent and corruptible things in the world. We rely on probable premises and to some extent fallible evidence to make our way in the world of contingent individuals. Hence, Ockham assumes regularities in nature and the constancy of moral norms. Such regularities are derived from observation and abstraction, founded on the prior intuition of the singulars experienced. This attitude to the certainty of experience and our assumptions about natural and moral regularities will be crucial to what he has to say about how men come to constitute secular governments and their understanding of what the church is.[12]

Therefore, Ockham speaks of our 'knowledge in experience' as deriving from terms (mental or linguistic) which refer to extra-mental things. Something is evident by experience (*nota per experientiam*) when it is established by induction, that is, generalization from singular, contingent propositions that are evident first by intuitive cognition. Something can then be said to be evident by experience when we suppose hypothetically that there is a common course of nature and we carry out a kind of induction based on this

11   J. Coleman, 'The Relation between Ockham's Intuitive Cognition and His Political Science', in (no ed.) *Théologie et droit*, pp. 71–88. For a fuller excellent discussion see M. M. Adams, *William Ockham*, 2 vols (Notre Dame, IN, 1987).

12   Especially for Ockham's logical theory of signification and on intuitive knowledge see P. Boehner, *Collected Articles on Ockham*, ed. E. M. Buytaert (St Bonaventure, NY, 1958). Many of these views are presented in Ockham's *Quodlibeta septem*, ed. J. C. Wey, *Opera Philosophica et Theologica, Opera Theologica* IX (St Bonaventure, NY, 1980).

hypothesis. Ockham argues, in the end, that we are as certain of our experiences as we can be of anything. The importance of this certainty for an understanding of what Ockham means by 'right reason' cannot be overstated.

For Ockham, there are three sources of our knowledge: experience, natural reason and infallible scriptural authority. A process emerges whereby cognitive experience precedes everything, to which is applied natural reasoning, and both together enable us to confirm our belief in the truth of scriptural authority by rationally demonstrating its propositions to be reasonable.[13]

As an excellent logician who wrote commentaries on many of Aristotle's logical writings, Ockham developed not only an epistemology but a related theory about how humans interpret language in ordinary cases as they live life and communicate with others. He then applied this to how humans can interpret the texts of scripture. This would have tremendous consequences for the way he interprets the rightful role of the papacy. He takes away from the papacy and the ecclesiastical hierarchy the sole right to interpret the words of God. He argues that anyone who experiences the world and draws conclusions from that experience, so long as he is sane and literate, can also interpret God's words in scripture. In his political writings, he spends a great deal of time demonstrating how the papacy has misinterpreted scripture illegitimately and illogically to suit its own case. Any human can know God's intention as well as, if not better than, the papacy, and hence scripture tells us, if we read it properly as we should read any text, what kinds of jurisdictional power Christ gave to Peter in the spiritual governance of the world.

Ockham's Dualism Concerning Secular and Spiritual Government: Continuing the Narrative

In his treatment of the theme of imperial and papal power,[14] Ockham argued that individuals have rights of which they may not be deprived. In his *Opus nonaginta dierum*[15] he addressed a papacy which he believed had misinterpreted the breadth and extent of its own powers. And in his *De imperatorem et pontificum potestate* he observed:

> As St Ambrose said, the Christian religion deprives no one of his rights. Wherefore, the pope can deprive no one of his rights for a person has such rights only from God, by nature, or from another man, and by the same reason the pope cannot deprive anyone of his liberty which is given by God and by nature.[16]

Ockham uses the language of liberties and rights, taking both to be concessions by some higher authority, and for him, certain authorities, namely God and Nature, cannot be

---

13   This process of experience, natural reason or logical demonstration, and scriptural authority operate in a similar way in Discourse 2 of Marsilius of Padua's *Defender of Peace*, although Marsilius does not propose that knowledge is only propositional.

14   *De imperatorum et pontificum potestate*, ed. R. Scholz, *Unbekannte kirchenpolitische Streitschriften aus der Zeit Ludwigs des Bayern (1327–54)*, II (Rome, 1914), pp. 453–80; also ed. C. K. Brampton (Oxford, 1927).

15   In Offler, *Opera Politica* I and II, and selections in McGrade and Kilcullen, *William of Ockham, A Letter to the Friars Minor*, pp. 19–115. See the interesting discussion largely focused on the *Opus Nonaginta Dierum* in A. S. Brett, *Liberty, Right and Nature: individual rights in later scholastic thought* (Cambridge, 1997), pp. 50–68.

16   *De imperatorum et pontificum potestate*, ed. C. K. Brampton (Oxford, 1927), pp. 9–10.

gainsaid by men, be they princes or popes. Furthermore, he says that scripture tells us, and St Francis the founder of his Order understood this perfectly, that Christ and his apostles only *used* what was necessary to sustain life. Christ and his apostles did not own things, but simply used the world in order to live. Scripture shows us that men have a *natural right of use* of things in the world, rather than ownership or possession of necessities, a right of use given to them by God. This natural right of use came before all subsequent legal or positive rights of possession which men in communities thereafter established. We have a *natural* right of use but no natural right to private property. Lordship or *dominium* was not granted eternally to men according to right reason: they were granted *usus* not *dominium*. Ownership and possession in societies of men is a result of the Fall. Humans thereafter developed their logical reason to appropriate and divide things in these post-lapsarian conditions. Before the Fall, Adam and Eve had a perfect, non-proprietary power over all things, ruling things with right reason rather than by coercion. Fallen nature, however, requires coercion, and *dominium* has therefore been established for utilitarian purposes and made concrete in positive, civil law. But the ideal of spiritual perfection, before the Fall, is expressed by the natural law in us which lets us know – through our experience and reasoning about what there is to be experienced and known – that we have a God-given right to survive and to use the world for that survival without saying that we own the world or any part of it. Only God has rightful ownership or *dominium* of the world.

Since fallen man, for purposes of utility, established positive civil laws of possession and ownership, it is clear that the body in society that has rightful jurisdiction over properties and property relations must be the temporal ruler. Indeed, after the Fall but before kings, men showed themselves voluntarily to divide up things and to be able to say 'this is mine' *a iure humano*. Possession and ownership are logical conclusions to which men agree as fallen creatures, adding to their natural rights of use the specification of ownership. Because priests and popes are men, their relation to property is under the rules of temporal arrangements.[17]

The scope of papal power is circumscribed by what anyone can read in scripture when one reads the evangelical gospel law: there it is said that Christ conferred on Peter not unlimited plenitude of power over things spiritual and temporal, but, rather, a limited jurisdiction to administer the sacraments, ordain the priestly hierarchy and instruct the faithful. Christ's act in instituting Peter was not arbitrary. It was an intelligible way of providing for the needs of his church. And it is reasonable to conclude that in order for Peter and his successors to rule the church for the common spiritual utility it was expedient that there be one church for all. Ockham accepts papal primacy over the other apostles because scripture tells us that Christ gave Peter power when he said *Tu es Petrus*: 'You are Peter and on this rock I build my church'. The Petrine commission is not mysterious and held on faith; rather, it is based on right reason which in and for this world is an intelligible utility conclusion. But Christ did not give to Peter or his followers jurisdiction over men's material survival in the world. The church, therefore, is not a juristic entity in matters political. God gave men liberty and men know of it through experience, even before the coming of Christ and the establishment of his church, so that man's liberty is an inalienable, individual right possessed also by those non-Chris-

---

17   *Opus Nonaginta Dierum,* chs 26–8, 88 and 93. See the detailed and amusing discussion of this in B. Tierney, *The Idea of Natural Rights,* ch. 6 ('Property, natural right and the state of nature') and ch. 7 ('Ockham: rights and some problems of political thought').

tians before Christ's coming. Men had a natural right freely to arrange their material survival for themselves, prior to the church's institution, and they do this first by knowing from experience that in order to stay alive they have a right of use in things of the world to achieve this. After expulsion from the Garden of Eden, they then determined logically that it is more useful in these new circumstances to set up positive laws which build on the natural rights to survive by using the world, so that distinct property boundaries came to be established. The church is not involved in this. Right reason, that is, men's experiences and their rational capacities to come to more general conclusions about how best to survive on the basis of experience in the contingent conditions of fallen nature, may lead them to establish private property, so that the resultant 'state', which has jurisdiction over property disputes among individual men, is to be conceived as an autonomous and even pre-Christian sphere of activity. Within the temporal or material sphere of survival and utility for the community that is made up of individuals, legitimacy is assured without reference to the church. Legitimacy is assured when the consent of the governed is obtained so that the common good may be pursued. The grounds for political legitimacy are not, then, sacred, since governments are not immediate divine institutions but rational creations of men.

Comparisons with Marsilius

Like Marsilius, Ockham does not glorify 'states'; he legitimates them. He is not approving the moral character of Roman or infidel administrations. He is simply acknowledging their rights to administer justice. He finds biblical texts that show that non-Christians may be recognized as persons with legitimate standing. And Christianity has no role in perfecting their rights to administer justice. Government comes to be constituted in the world as instrumental conclusions to solve conflictual conditions and serve peace. Nor is Ockham's criterion for legitimate government the moral desert of the ruler; rather, legitimate government is a rational choice, voluntarily exercised by men to establish the civil regulation of life by means of coercive sanction. Like Marsilius, he also thinks that rulers are not radically superior to their subjects in virtue or wisdom, and the form of any government will depend on the quality of the citizens: the better they are, the better the regime. Hence Ockham, like Marsilius, allows for constitutional variations which accord with changing circumstances and what is seen by those who constitute the government to be the common utility. He says explicitly that legitimate government is primarily instituted so that it may correct and punish wrongdoers, although it also functions by granting and preserving everyone's rights, enacting necessary and just laws, establishing lower judges and other officials, directing what arts ought to be practised and by whom, and to enjoin acts of virtue.[18] Like Marsilius, he goes beyond Aquinas's teaching that the church can remove unbelievers, at least in their rule over Christians.[19] He does not think that an emperor need be a Christian to be a legitimate emperor, but in the *Dialogus*[20] he crucially adds 'except in so far as every rational adult ought to be a Christian especially if he has been able to be informed of the faith'. As for Marsilius, the best government is that

18 *Octo quaestiones* III, 8 in Offler, *Opera Politica* I, pp.112–13.
19 Aquinas, *Summa Theologiae* IIa IIae, q.10, a.10 resp.
20 III *Dialogus* 2, 1, 14.

which is exercised over free men and a community of free men would not easily allow itself to constitute a government that would reduce it to slavery. Like Marsilius, Ockham also holds that Christian law, through Christ's institution of it as a law of freedom, perfects pagan law and the Old Law, which, by comparison, were laws of servitude. We shall see that like Marsilius, Ockham holds that the gospel law of liberty is the nearest to perfection that fallen men can rationally grasp by right reason, so that, in so far as men see the need for government in this life, the perfect secular government would be one which was constituted in order to secure a rational and therefore Christian understanding of liberty. Christ's advent may not have transformed the basis or nature of legitimate imperial power, but Christians have access to more right reason than non-Christians.

Ockham tries to show that what the Roman church calls its legislated customs cannot be recognized unless they are reasonable, and they are not reasonable if they are against divine law, or good customs, if they are prejudicial to the common welfare or to any person's liberty. It is insufficient for the Roman church to try to legitimate its customs through prescription. The papacy cannot simply say that elected kings and emperors are its subjects because this is not according to divine law and divine law may be known by reading scripture. Nor is the papal claim to superiority over kings and emperors a teaching of the *ius gentium* or the civil law. Nor is it from custom, because custom does not have the force of law unless it is rational. It is not rational if it destroys individual liberty against the will of individuals who have such liberty from God or Nature. In legislating for the faith of Christians, then, the pope cannot deprive them of a liberty so that they possess less liberty than do pagans and infidels. He may only teach God's word, maintain divine worship and ritual, and provide such things as are necessary for Christians in their quest for eternal life. The determination of what is necessary for the Christian quest for salvation must be judged neither by popes nor civil rulers exclusively, but through an interpretation of the gospel text by clergy, lay men and women, whether poor, rich, subjects or rulers. The pope has no power to command, coerce or requisition things that are not *necessary* to this end, otherwise the liberty of the gospel law would be a law of slavery. Ockham does, however, leave a space for papal coercion in cases of utility or necessity, but he distinguishes these occasional possibilities from a claim to a regular exercise of coercive power.[21] He believes that the power of the papacy should be disputed openly and authentic scripture made public in order to reveal its reasonable meaning.

The Exceptional Exercise of Coercive Authority

Like others, Ockham found a place for the exercise of exceptional powers in times of necessity beyond the ordinary jurisdictions of both the papacy and empire. He saw that rightly established institutional order might need correction or even rejection, but he thought such cases would be more extraordinary than did most of his contemporaries. He did not deny the pope's ultimate (*casualiter*) jurisdiction in secular affairs, but the conditions for such interference would have to be so grave a crisis, 'where no layman could or would take adequate action', that only then might the pope act by divine right in temporal matters, *to do whatever right reason dictated to him was necessary*.[22] This, as we

---

21   *De imperatorum et pontificum potestate*, ed. Brampton, pp. 6, 23–7, 34–5; and *Octo quaestiones de potestate papae* I, 8.
22   III *Dialogus* 1, 1, 16.

shall see, is an occurrence which Ockham thinks could virtually never take place because it would mean the failure of all men's reason. It is implausible to think that men can operate in this world without assuming the hypothetical necessity that their thoughts are commonly applicable to the presumed regularities in the world. Instead, he argued that secular politics not only has its own process of self-correction, but that it is independent of ecclesiastical power.

Natural Rights

Michel Villey[23] credited Ockham with the first use of a language of subjective, individual rights. But certain earlier canonists had also noted a sphere of individual, personal, moral autonomy, a psychological power or potential capable of exercise as a right, prior to incorporation into any political entity. And even Marsilius has a subjective meaning for *ius* as a voluntary act, power or habit in conformity with objective law.[24] Ockham, too, defined the individual person as one who has certain powers, spoken of as *ius* or *potestas*, and these were to the use of the world in order to ensure survival. It is what Hobbes in the seventeenth century would call the 'right of nature'. According to Ockham, the later appropriation and division of things which were to be recognized as private property were the consequence of human laws drawn up for the utility of fallen men who desire peace and order. It is the natural right of use of things in the world which cannot be taken away. Nor can men's natural powers or rights to make laws and institute rulers be taken away. Each individual knows he has certain natural powers to make positive laws and constitute government on the basis of his own reasoned reflections on his experience. The natural right to survive and to consent, voluntarily, to create a system of laws, a legitimate positive authority to govern men collectively, is a right men claim for themselves as men who, on the basis of experience, logically judge that their safety and moral autonomy is best preserved in a system of positive law. Hence, the acts of any *regnum* are the summation of the willed acts of morally responsible individuals regarding the common good and public utility. A state's rules are general propositions which are to be understood by each individual to whom they apply, while each individual who is covered by the rules remains autonomous and responsible for his acts.

Corporation Theory

Ockham understands collective opinion to be the summation of every individual's opinion concerning the common good.[25] Unlike Marsilius, he does not believe that a

---

23   *La Formation de la pensée juridique moderne,* 4th edn (Paris, 1975), pp. 199–272.

24   *Defender of Peace* II, 12, 10. He also spoke of *dominium* as 'the actual or habitual will to have the lawfully acquired thing' and no one could acquire *dominium* against his own will: II, 12, 13–16. See Tierney, *The Idea of Natural Rights,* esp. ch. 5 ('The languages of rights').

25   J. Miethke, *Ockhams Weg zur Sozialphilosophie* (Berlin, 1969); A. S. McGrade, *The Political Thought of William of Ockham: personal and institutional principles* (Cambridge, 1974); A. S. McGrade, 'Ockham and the Birth of Individual Rights', in B. Tierney and P. Linehan, eds, *Authority and Power: studies . . . presented to Walter Ullmann* (Cambridge, 1980), pp. 149–66; J. Coleman, *Ancient and Medieval Memories: studies in the reconstruction of the past* (Cambridge, 1992), pp. 528ff.

collection of men into a corporation or general council can take on a separate personality which represents its members. He *has* a theory of corporations but it is not that of contemporary, representative corporation theory as one finds it in canon lawyers or in the writings of Marsilius.[26] Collective opinion can only be a summation of individuals consenting to present, contingent circumstances on the basis of their own experiences and thoughts. His corporationism or conciliarism is of the kind where the whole is *nothing more than* the decisions of its individual parts regarding the common good. Therefore, a general council cannot be infallible (*contra* Marsilius). According to Ockham, any whole is the summation of its individual parts, willing what is for the public good. But his individuals are not isolated atoms. They form a community in the sense of a concrete body of individuals whose unity is achieved by their reasoning to the *same* conclusions about the common utility.

He does not have a theory of 'state' where the public authority, the office of the ruler, is a separate and real sphere of rights of its own under law. He treats the ruler as an individual, and he treats the corporation of individuals, not as a legally created *persona* (*non est persona imaginaria et repraesentata*), but as a unified collection of real, individual persons. Only real, autonomous, rational individuals are capable of renouncing or holding legal rights, and precisely because the jurists maintained that the 'state' is not a real person but, rather, a fictive, created legal entity, Ockham insisted that such a fictive entity cannot perform real acts or possess real rights under law.[27] Its acts are the summation of the willed acts of individual members with reference to the collective good, the public utility, and what is expedient is determined by right reason: what is most objectively rational in given circumstances. The communal or political life is therefore made up of interactions between individual persons of the community, all willing, by right reason, the same common good when they constitute government.

So, too, the universal church is made up of its individual believers, priests, laymen and women, a universal church *in and through time* of individual men who comprise the historical and unbroken witness of the faithful.[28] The universal church is made up of all its individual believers, whatever their status, and the ecclesiastical hierarchy, as a fictive rather than real person, cannot claim to represent it.[29]

For Ockham, individuals' wills cannot be represented and a collective will is not a real thing. An individual cannot alienate his moral autonomy and responsibility to another. Hence, each individual is responsible for alienating property when he lives in a society that has set up private property as a utilitarian determination of the natural law right of use of the world, known by all. Each individual is responsible in the exercise of his rights, his liberties, and in his resistance to those who act against right reason, be they popes or kings. When one says that the church must resist papal heresy, Ockham thinks this can only mean that individual members of the church must resist. The proposition 'the church must resist heresy' can only be interpreted as 'this individual Christian must resist, and that individual Christian must resist, and the other individual Christian must resist'.

---

26   *Tractatus contra Benedictum*, in Offler, *Opera Politica* III, pp. 189–91.
27   Effectively, this means the 'state' cannot make a contract with individual citizens; they alone can contract with one another as real persons with wills in order to constitute government. Compare Hobbes.
28   *Tractatus contra Ioannem* c. xiv, in Offler, *Opera Politica* III, p. 65.
29   Ibid.; *Tractatus contra Benedictum* c. 3 in Offler, *Opera Politica* III, pp. 191, 233–4; I *Dialogus* 5, 25–6.

Ockham's 'Absolutism'

Ockham recognized that the temporal sphere which establishes coercive, positive laws, is imperfect. He thought that men would not have needed the 'state' had Adam and Eve not fallen. Because the temporal sphere is imperfect, he argued that secular sovereignty, once established, could be legitimate even when 'absolutist', in that there need not be regular participation of the people in government, nor need there be institutions to restrain the power of kings. But this did not mean that 'the people' could *confer* absolute power on a ruler, because 'the people', not being a real, but rather, a fictive collective entity under human law, cannot and therefore did not historically ever possess such absolute power over individual members who comprised 'the people'. Hence, the people could not alienate a power that they did not actually possess. Furthermore, except in matters judged necessary for the community, no minority in a community can be deprived of their individual rights by a majority.[30] But the constituting of a government, as in Marsilius, requires and achieves a unanimous consent by all rational individuals. Once established, the circumstances dictate whether or not the governor acts according to the positive laws. While he is not above natural equity, he is above human positive laws, especially where he acts for the needs of the common good and the public safety, and in this sense government can be absolutist.[31] Ockham departs from Marsilius in not arguing for a continuous and explicit consent of a human legislator, the people, to the specific powers and laws of government. Their consent is to constituting government which would establish laws in conformity with right reason in the circumstances. Had men not fallen they would not conclude this to be a need and each would rule himself by reason in perfect conditions.[32]

How did Ockham Come to Hold These Views?

So far, I have presented Ockham's various positions on the respective roles of church and 'state' in the lives of individuals. But he is something of an original, certainly if judged against his contemporaries, in his distinctive way of arriving at and justifying these conclusions. In the *Dialogus*, Ockham notes that men know from experience that they are inclined to conflict and to seeking their own interests and not what belongs to the common good. They also know that however much it is beneficial in difficult cases for the truth to be sought by many, it is *useful* that one should have power over all the other advisers seeking the truth.[33] This utility conclusion (he will later call it a supposition), that some unified government be set up over men, is one that has been agreed to unanimously by all. It is a conclusion, given the present and contingent circumstances of

---

30 III *Dialogus* 2, 2, 27. 'Item, imperator non habet maiorem potestatem in temporalibus, quam habuit populus, cum imperator habeat potestatem suam a populo, ut allegatum est supra, quia populus plus iurisdictionis aut potestatis non potuit transferre in imperatorem, quam habuit. . . . Ergo si populus praecipit aliquid alicui de populo, quod non est de necessitate faciendum, non tenetur illud facere, nisi velit, restat igitur, quod imperator non habet talem potestatis plenitudinem.' Cited with comments in B. Tierney, 'Ockham: rights and some problems of political thought', in Tierney, *The Idea of Natural Rights*, p. 184, n. 44.

31 III *Dialogus* 2, 1, 16.

32 Compare Hobbes.

33 III *Dialogus* 2, 1, 13.

this life, that is based on those prior self-evident principles of morality or what follows from them, which are called natural laws.

In III *Dialogus* 2, 1, 15, Ockham speaks of three kinds of natural laws: (1) self-evident first principles of morality which are indubitable; (2) inferences from these which are similarly indubitable; and (3) further inferences from the inferences. Ockham says that there are natural laws of the second kind which are drawn plainly and without great consideration as certain inferences from the first principles of natural law that are known even by the less learned. Even if we have never before thought of them, such natural laws occur to us immediately when we are obliged to do or omit something in accordance with them, *unless* we will to proceed to act or to omit such act without any deliberation and rule of reason. Presumably, not to deliberate by reason is a mark of insanity. Anyone can immediately and without great study know these second kinds of natural laws. There is no excuse for ignorance of the first and second kinds of natural laws. Then there are other natural laws that are inferred from the inferences from the first principles which a few experts, with great attention and study, arrive at 'through many intermediate propositions', but their expert opinions may conflict. Ignorance of this third kind of natural law is generally excusable. An emperor should apply himself to acquire a knowledge of the third kind of natural law, clearly because his own prudent judgement will allow him to make decisions on what is, in the circumstances, excusable or not. The other first and second kinds of natural laws, the first principles and inferences from them, he need not study because they will easily occur to him when necessary.

Later in the text, Ockham treats the problem of whether the Romans have the right to elect the pope by divine law, extending 'divine law' to mean all natural law. Can all natural law be called divine law? He distinguishes three ways in which natural law is understood in his own times, gathering these understandings from his interpretations of a variety of canon law and historical texts. His own discussion is extremely condensed.[34] The three modes or kinds are, first, natural law in conformity with natural reason that never fails, and he gives the examples: 'do not commit adultery' and 'do not lie'. He later makes it clear that it also includes the notion that each man is by nature free, but what he means by free is in effect an inalienable, moral, internal freedom as a rational deliberator with a will to do or not to do what is rational. These must be universally true and foundationally self-evident principles (*per se nota*) to men and such principles are immutable. They are necessary principles and are not based on responses to contingency.

Second, natural law is also taken to mean what is to be observed by those who use natural equity alone and without any custom and human legislation, that is, what for Ockham would be a necessary conclusion known through experience (*per experientiam*) everywhere before the establishment of governments, but after expulsion from the Garden of Eden. Natural equity seems to be a power of reasoning which serves as a rational readjustment for human weaknesses and men's experiences of them. In the state of nature as originally established before the Fall, the conclusions from that perfect experience would *not* have required that men draw natural equity conclusions about what is

---

34   III *Dialogus* 2, 3, 6. My reading of this text differs from that provided by McGrade, *The Political Thought of William of Ockham*, pp. 177–85. I have used the corrected Latin text in H. S. Offler, 'The Three Modes of Natural Law in Ockham: a revision of the text', *Franciscan Studies* 37 (1977), pp. 207–18. Also see the interpretation of Tierney in 'Ockham: rights and some problems of political thought', in Tierney, *The Idea of Natural Rights*, pp. 177–82.

owed to each, because in the original state of nature all things would have been common, neither commonly or individually *possessed*. Before the Fall there would have been no need to consider what each is owed. Men would have been living according to natural reason or divine law. Their pre-Fall natural reason would have been consonant with divine law. And if, *after* the Fall, all men lived according to reason suited to *these* conditions, then the conclusion they would have drawn was that all things should have been common and nothing *owned* (in common or individually). This would have been a natural equity conclusion to suit contingencies, inferred from immutable first principles, and where no government was required. But since it was not the case that after the Fall all men lived according to natural equity reason, ownership (both as common property and as individual property) was introduced (by men) because of wickedness. Fallen men do not therefore have a choice between living without property or setting up property divisions. No one can live simply according to natural equity reasoning after the Fall, and hence appropriation and division in some way or other is a rational human conclusion, their way of fulfilling natural equity, here and now. This does not mean it is necessary that appropriation and division had to be entirely private; but it does mean that the world was divided up – as men's common *possession* – from which private property could thereafter have been a further conclusion in the circumstances.

While there were Franciscans – like the thirteenth-century archbishop Pecham – who seemed to think that natural equity alone would suffice to regulate men's affairs if men, with all their limitations, lived as reasonably as they could, Ockham does not seem to hold this view. Ockham may have defended a life without property, but it is its *voluntary* rejection through, for instance, the Franciscans' vow of poverty, which he defends and not some natural equity state prior to the human law of nations and civil law. Since the church lives where property has been established (both property that is owned in common and individually), those who wish to imitate the natural equity state have to reject all forms of ownership voluntarily. Of course, no one can go back to the original, pre-lapsarian original state of nature, not even the Franciscans.

Now, in the fallen world, where governments and civil laws have been established, the second mode of natural law or natural equity includes the *capacity* licitly or rationally to appropriate things and even to be made slaves. Ockham says we find this in the human law of nations (*ius gentium*) as well as in civil law.[35] The way humans now use (the second mode of) natural law when they speak of the law of nations, indicates to Ockham that there are things which men judge permissible to enact as further utility conclusions in the circumstances. Men's reason in these circumstances demonstrates that the law of nations – by which common possession of all things and the one liberty of all is established – is changeable, since it is judged permissible to enact the contrary, that is, to enslave some men and appropriate property from what was commonly possessed. In our present state, reason dictates that all things are common property until they are appropriated with the consent of men, and the yoke of servitude may be imposed on men who are by nature free. Ockham is speaking of the facts of the matter: men have been running their own affairs by deductive reasoning from their experiences since they

---

35 Ockham speaks of Pope Gregory the Great as testifying to some free men being placed under the yoke of slavery by the law of nations, who are then *made* free in the nature in which they were born. Gregory believed that all men were born free but through a mysterious dispensation some men were set over others, and only through Christ could such men be made free, while retaining their differential rank in society.

were expelled from the Garden of Eden, possessing the world in one way or another.

A third kind of natural law is inferred by fallen men's evident reasoning from the law of nations or another law and we can call this 'natural law on supposition'. This third law seems to correspond to Ockham's earlier discussion of the kind of inference from necessary inferences from first principles, an ignorance of which may be judged excusable by a ruler. Natural law in this sense can include returning something deposited or money lent and the repelling of violence with force. This third kind of natural law would not have existed in the state of nature as originally established, and it would not have existed among those who, living according to reason, were content with natural equity alone, since there would not have been anything deposited or lent and no one would have inflicted force on another. Natural law on supposition depends on our *supposing* that things and money have been appropriated according to the law of nations or human law. If we suppose this, then by evident reasoning, where these are prevalent understandings in the world, we conclude that a thing deposited and money lent should be returned. There is, then, a conditional natural law which derives from human rational responses to contingent circumstances.

Ockham says something unusual about this third natural law on supposition. He notes that we gather its meaning by evident reasoning from the *ius gentium* or another human law, 'unless the contrary is enacted with the consent of those concerned'. When natural law is held in the third way, it proceeds from a prior supposition about what is natural and fair and thereafter makes particular judgements according to this supposition, unless the contrary to this supposition is established by some human law. Humans start from propositions as accepted social premises from which they reason to conclusions. The contrary may be enacted by reasonable cause where what one has come to accept by supposing it to be universally true is discovered to be otherwise. The only way in which this could occur, for Ockham, would be if the conditions in which evident reasoning came to its conclusions were altered. As we shall see, one of the ways this could occur would be to establish the truth of living of those humans who had experienced Christ's words and deeds, and to confirm this truth daily in a society that held this way of living to be the truth.

If, however, it is *supposed* that someone is to be set over certain persons as a ruler, rector or prelate, it will then be inferred by evident reason that, unless the contrary is decided on by the person or persons concerned, those whom he is to be set over have the right to elect him, so that no one should be given to them against their will. Since what affects all should be dealt with by all (*quod omnes tangit*), then those whom it concerns make themselves laws and it belongs to them to elect a head. Government is based on a supposition in this world that rulership needs to be constituted. It always belongs to those whom someone is to be set over to elect the one to be set over them, unless the contrary is decided on by the persons concerned. It can even be supposed that in electing rulers, they each resign their right and transfer it to another whose decision each is bound to accept.[36] But we shall see that there are certain rights which can never be alienated or transferred and such rights are not conditional, *ex suppositione*. All of this discussion is ultimately in aid of interpreting scripture and whether Christ, the superior to the Romans, ever deprived the Romans of the right to elect their bishop. Ockham extends it to temporal rulers.[37]

Once individual members of the community have consented voluntarily to create a legitimate positive authority, Ockham argues that public authority may only be re-

---

36   Compare Hobbes.
37   For an alternative reading see Tierney, *The Idea of Natural Rights*, esp. pp.175–84.

tracted in very extreme circumstances, as when a ruler commits egregious sins or crimes.[38] The ruler is an individual with rights of his own. He cannot ignore certain inalienable rights of the individuals who are ruled, although he can override rights conceded by men, for instance to property, but only in cases of necessity. In the *Dialogus* Ockham presents the opinion that the emperor and the king in his kingdom are not tied by the laws, and are not obliged of necessity to judge according to the laws in the way inferior judges are obliged to do. The ruler needs experience and judgement more than he needs a knowledge of civil laws.[39] It seems that his experience and judgement are brought into play in the sphere of what Ockham has called the third kind of natural law or natural law on supposition. Once constituted, the ruler can alter the suppositional premises from which his subjects draw their conclusions from evident reasoning.[40] In the *Breviloquium* he maintained that the Roman emperor's power came to him from God as a remote cause but immediately from the people who elected him. This power was not absolute in the sense that it could not remove the rights and liberties granted to men by God and nature. Common utility required that rulers respect the natural rights of their subjects, but this common utility could prevail over their private rights in cases of necessity.

This being the case, the imperial power was not easily revocable. Ockham appears to have thought that most rulers throughout history had organized society sufficiently in a rational and utilitarian manner so that whatever crimes they may have committed were of lesser consequence to the collective well-being than would have been their removal. He said: 'We ought to delight more in the life of a people than in the punishment of one bad person. If, therefore, the scandal of deposing such a king threatens to overthrow the people . . . such severity should be abandoned'.[41] Ockham is therefore willing, because he thinks most men are willing, to grant legitimate power to a sovereign, secular govern-ment even when, thereafter, the government may deprive certain individuals of powers or wrongfully interfere against the civil laws with men's property, or involve men in wars where they had not been consulted. Once established by human law, which is itself established by individuals consenting to specific proposed ordinances to rule their indi-vidual and collective behaviour, Ockham says that the 'state' as absolute sovereign must be accepted by those over whom it exercises its powers. There is no social contract of the kind between citizens and regulating ruler, and hence government is not a revocable grant of the people, except in the most extreme circumstances. In effect, he has no resistance theory to already-constituted government, although that government may not remove the natural rights of men given them by God and nature. Furthermore, temporal public authority, created by rational, morally responsible individuals, is independent of any ecclesiastical sanction, whatever its constitution, be it infidel or Christian.

Right Reason

All men, according to Ockham, come to know of their rights, liberties and powers simply by experiencing the world in which they live and drawing conclusions as how

---

38   *Breviloquium* 4, 13.
39   III *Dialogus* 2, 1, 15.
40   Compare Hobbes.
41   *Octo quaestiones* 7.7 in Offler, *Opera Politica* I, p. 180.

best to secure their needs in these fallen conditions. In his *Opus nonaginta dierum* Ockham says that he is following St Augustine by distinguishing between right or *ius* as *ius fori* (right according to public law) on the one hand, and as *ius poli* (right according to heavenly or divine law) on the other. *Ius fori* is the kind of right that is recognized from contracts or human ordinances and established customs or divine explanations of these (presumably such as 'render unto Caesar that which is his'). The superior authority here in determining violations of the *ius fori* is civil. But *ius poli* is a knowledge of natural equity and it is consonant with right reason. This knowledge comes before a knowledge of human and divine positive laws.

Ockham explains that right reason may be construed either as purely by nature (foundational moral principles which are known indubitably and immutably), or it can be understood as what right reason accepts as following from nature (the necessary inferences from moral first principles) which to Christians is divinely revealed. Hence, the *ius poli* is natural law (of the first and second kinds discussed above, but supplemented by scripture and therefore by natural law on supposition). He says it can also be called divine law because much of the divine law is consonant with what right reason accepts, but as it is revealed to men these reasonable conclusions could not be discovered entirely naturally.[42] Humans now cannot think with the reason that was consonant with Adam's reason prior to the Fall. Ockham notes that this further perfection of right reason's conclusions by the divine law cannot be (logically) demonstrated by purely natural reasoning, just as it cannot be sufficiently proved by human deductive logic that the preaching of scripture is true, useful and necessary, although it is all of these. This notion of right reason, and its further perfection by divine revelation in Christian scripture, rationally understood, bears comparison with Marsilius of Padua's use of the term.[43]

We can observe the context in which right reason operates by looking at his *Dialogus*, where Ockham presents a general, theological discussion of heresy. His focus is on papal heresy, but his more general understanding of heresy is the more interesting for political theory. He argues, as did Marsilius, that the fact that the church determines or defines an assertion does not constitute the truth value of that assertion. Rather, the church *approves rightly* one of five kinds of truth. The list is revealing. (1) Truth is what is expressed in scripture or inferred from it by necessary reasoning. (2) Truth is what is handed down to us from the apostles through oral teachings or in the writings of the faithful, but is neither found in scripture nor deduced from it. (3) Truth is what is discovered in chronicles or histories deemed worthy of trust. (4) Truth is what can be concluded from the truth of the first and second kind alone or from one or other of the combined truths of the third kind. (5) Apart from the truth that he has already revealed to the apostles, truth is what God has revealed or inspired in others, or will reveal or inspire.[44]

Truth is not established by institutional authority but from scripture or other sources worthy of trust. And sources that are worthy of trust are determined by individual men's experience and reason. The truth value of sources emerges from the evaluation of human right reason, so that for Ockham truth is defined cognitively before it receives the

42   *Opus nonaginta dierum* c.65, pp. 573–6.
43   For a somewhat different interpretation of the meaning of Ockham's *ius fori* and *ius poli* see Tierney, *The Idea of Natural Rights*, pp.126–30.
44   I *Dialogus* 2, 16. For a discussion of Ockham on heresy see McGrade, *The Political Thought of William of Ockham*, pp. 51ff., citing especially I *Dialogus* 4, 14–21.

assent of any institution. Heresy, then, is a problem of human understanding. Ockham therefore treats the process of heretical correction in cognitive terms rather than as an exercise of institutional power. Not only does he provide a general prescription for examining authoritative pronouncements of all kinds, but he also wishes chiefly to maintain that there can be no *arbitrary* coercion of an individual's will. Right reason is what provides the cognitive certainty and it is available to each and all. And here we note that right reason always operates in social contexts with their respective, prevalent knowledge.

If one is living in a Catholic community, what is prevalently known to every Catholic, no matter how humble or uneducated, determines, for Ockham, the minimal level of knowledge of the Catholic truth that everyone is bound to believe explicitly. If an illiterate layman denies a scriptural truth, then Ockham believes he ought not to be immediately judged heretical before he has been examined and then taught.[45] Although a person's persistence in error in his own mind cannot be known, Ockham lists numerous ways in which someone might reasonably be judged pertinacious on the basis of his words and deeds. We are reminded of Marsilius's distinction between immanent and transitive or transient acts and the requirement that they be witnessed. Ockham asserts that if a man who has reason and understanding and has lived among Christians denies a publicly known Catholic assertion, then he contradicts prevalent knowledge and is judged pertinacious. He must be clearly shown that his assertion is against Catholic truth and if he persists in his error, then he is to be corrected.

How might this be done? Ockham gives an example of showing someone one of the gospels or some church historical text in order to demonstrate that his own assertions are contrary to them. One can be corrected non-coercively by friends, but Ockham thinks that someone whose errors are clearly pointed out to him is bound to give them up at once, no matter who has corrected him. Each individual is, for Ockham, morally responsible for grasping the truth.[46] Ockham is relatively tolerant towards the uneducated but is intolerant of those who hold higher ecclesiastical offices because their amount of theological knowledge should be commensurate with their status. He thinks that experts in scripture are obliged by their expertise to give clear reasons for the truth to which all individual and less expert Christians also bear witness. But every Christian has cognitive access to that truth, if not to the reasons for it.

Ockham did not believe that Catholic truths explicitly or implicitly asserted in scripture were the only truths to be believed, however. Intuitive cognition sufficiently guarantees our certain knowledge of contingent truths. Institutional coercive power, then, only adds a kind of authenticity to an assertion when the latter is already true as well as Catholic. For Ockham, truth is superior to and opposed to mere coercive power. What if an individual is actually correct and all the others, experts and ordinary men and women, still hold him to be wrong? Ockham thought this was a (remote) possibility and said that the only thing left was for him to appeal to God and not fear being cut off by an unjust judgement from the society of men.[47] The Student in the *Dialogus* marvels at what appears to be the Master's suggestion that one man, no matter what his office, ought to prefer his own imaginings to all the learned and wise men gathered together. Ockham

45 I *Dialogus* 4, 6 and 10; *Tractatus contra Ioannem*, c. vi, in Offler, *Opera Politica* III, p. 47.
46 I *Dialogus* 4, 6 and 21; *Tractatus contra Ioannem*, c. 13–15, in Offler, *Opera Politica* III, pp. 60–74.
47 I *Dialogus* 4, 20.

responds, famously, by saying it is not his own imaginings but his own conscience to which he should listen.[48] Every Christian, no matter what his or her status, has a moral duty to defend the truth, and be ready for correction if it is available. But he thinks that the testimony of many men is more likely to be true than the testimony of one.[49]

There seems little doubt that Ockham believed, but could not demonstrate, that Christian communities, having scripture, had available to them a more complete truth than had other communities with their truths that were not supplemented by scripture. With the addition of the Christian description of the words and deeds of Christ, a new orientation and a new motive to act in charity would be added to natural principles of morality. He implies that Christians would be more ready to apply the principles of right reason in the circumstances in which they found themselves, although it is not clear that this was because of an additional stimulus to rational action beyond the impulse to reason itself.[50] Indeed, Ockham seems to be holding to the extraordinary (and modern) position that we know the world as we experience it, and if we experience it in a particular community, here Catholic, then that is our truth of experience. There is a cognitive commonality of individuals and their certitude depends on their experience, which in Christian communities confirms, from their daily life, the truths of scripture. For this reason he was able to say in his *Letter to the Friars Minor* that he was better able to understand the customs of men (in general) from the holy rules of scripture which describe men's customs – and which can be verified daily by experience.[51]

Scriptural Hermeneutics

Ockham seems not to have regarded the scriptural text as describing a particular event that was to be held on faith, but rather as something actually experienced by humans, although in the past. He is unusually clear among medieval thinkers that scriptural events happened at another, long-distant time and place. He raised the kind of question about the past as 'over and done with' that we normally associate (wrongly) with Renaissance and (rightly) with modern attitudes to the past as distinct from the present. Ockham tackled the question: how does someone in the present come to grasp the meaning of the intentions or mental acts of past agents? He used his logic to defend the necessary truth of propositions concerning *facts* in the past, such as 'Christ was crucified'. He argued that we know the past through propositions about it and intellectually we know the past (which is our own) as past. But a present interpreter of scripture is meant to determine the true meaning behind the different terminology of past authors, as a true meaning of individual past experiences. To determine whether a proposition about the past – but stated now (e.g. Christ *was* crucified) – is true or false, he examined whether a present-tense proposition as stated in the past (Christ *is* crucified) was then true or false.[52]

---

48   I *Dialogus* 2, 29.
49   I *Dialogus* 7, 15.
50   I cannot find any text that supports a notion of grace added to nature for this to occur, so that one comes to love God for his own sake, and therefore I disagree here with McGrade, *The Political Thought of William of Ockham*, p. 204.
51   'Nam sanctarum regulas scripturarum mores hominum describentes, dum quotidie per experientiam verificari conspicio, magis intelligo.' Offler, *Opera Politica* III, p. 17.
52   See T. Shogimen, 'Ockham's Vision of the Primitive Church', in R. N. Swanson, ed., *Studies in Church History 33: the church retrospective* (Woodbridge, 1997), pp. 163–75.

Anyone sane and literate can do this because the knowledge anyone acquires by logical demonstration provides the same kind of knowledge, in terms of its conclusions, as does experiential knowledge. Because Ockham's epistemology affirms that we are as certain about our present as we are about our past, then someone else who experienced what he did in that past was similarly certain about it. When we consider what they wrote about their experiences we must conclude that something real and true must have happened to individual men in the past. The disciples of the apostles, and of course St Peter, must have possessed a true understanding of Christ's words.[53] A textual expression of those experiences, scripture, understood by us abstractively, that is, independent of time, place and claims to existence of its referents, must be based on 'that someone's' past intuitive cognition of the reality and existence of his experience. Christians, with scripture, have a fuller access to the past's truths than do others who may only use natural reasoning without the oral and written witnesses to Christ's words and deeds.[54]

Ockham's Ethics

Among the common truths of experience are those that men by nature logically conclude about the need for the establishment of general rules, applicable to all. Thereafter, specific positive laws are calculations in contingent circumstances, a defined set of specific rules that are judged to be required in *these* circumstances, given prevalent suppositions, so that when necessary, fallen men may be coerced when they do not act according to their natural knowledge of what is morally right. Since Ockham argued that it is only by intuitive cognition of our own acts that we are aware of ourselves as intelligent beings, it is therefore only through intuitive cognition that we are aware of ourselves as voluntary agents, free to choose between alternatives. We possess as individuals a *libertas*, a freedom, and we know of it only by experience. This individual liberty may be defined as ' that power whereby I can do diverse things indifferently and contingently such that I can cause or not cause the same effect, when all conditions other than this power are the same'.[55]

Just as we cannot prove that we experience individuals intuitively by demonstrative reason – we can only experience this as a fact – so, too, we cannot prove the will is free by demonstrative reason 'because every reason proving this assumes something equally unknown as its conclusion, or less known'. A man simply experiences the fact that however much his reason dictates some action, his will can will or not will this act. Hence, human liberty, which we know from our intuitive knowledge of existents, we

---

53   III *Dialogus* 1, 4, 13.

54   For a fuller analysis of Ockham's theory of knowledge and language see Coleman, *Ancient and Medieval Memories*, pp.500–37. Brian Tierney rejected Ockham's reasonableness in his biblical hermeneutics by saying 'in Ockham's polemical works right reason meant simply his own reason', which recalls Hobbes's own rejection of this kind of argument in *Leviathan* I c.5. See B. Tierney, *The Origins of Papal Infallibility, 1150–1350*, 2nd edn (Leiden, 1988), p. 230. For a very useful discussion of the primacy of biblical exegesis for Ockham in all of his polemical works see Shogimen, 'Ockham's Vision', pp. 163–75 and his as yet unpublished Ph.D. dissertation, University of Sheffield, 1998: 'William of Ockham and Spiritual Authority: a study of his polemics'.

55   *Quodlibet* I, q. 16, p. 87 in J. C. Wey, ed., *Quodlibeta septem* in *Guillelmi de Ockham Opera Theologica*, ix (St Bonaventure, NY, 1980). Ockham's view is that liberty is not a special quality which man may or may not have; rather, it is identical with man's spontaneous will. See his remarks in his theological work, the 'Ordinatio' on the *Sentences*, book II *Sent.* d. 10, q. 2, in G. I. Etzkorn, ed., *Guillelmi de Ockham Opera Theologica*, III (St Bonaventure, NY, 1977), p. 344.

know evidently as a true term in a proposition, generalized through an extension by induction to all other individuals of the same nature. If we know of our own liberty, we equally come to acknowledge it in others. Together, we then negotiate our collective lives in a variety of different ways, setting up different, legitimate authorities and laws which suit the contingent circumstances.

Ockham thinks of this liberty as the basis of our human dignity and the font of moral goodness and personal responsibility. He holds that this liberty is more central to morality than is the power of reasoning, which only occurs after the simple intuitive apprehension of the term and thereafter, what it signifies, even though reasoning is involved in willing or not willing. Our liberty to will, one way or another, is the basis of our human dignity because man is a free agent; therefore, in being responsible for his acts, he can be judged worthy or not.[56] Following Aristotle's distinction between moral and intellectual virtues in the *Nicomachean Ethics*, Ockham argued that a man is praised for what he wills rather than for what he understands. His cognitive acts are natural, but his power to perform or not, his power to act on what he knows, is what is to be judged. Hence, Ockham's emphasis on rationally guided choice is central to what has come to be called his voluntarism. But like Marsilius (and unlike Hobbes), Ockham is a rational voluntarist. He is not sceptical about human knowing but about our willing what we know. Right reason is an integral requirement of virtue and hence agents must intend to aim at what is most objectively rational. Virtuous acts are those that conform to the principles of right reason, and as we have seen, right reason is concerned with self-evident principles of conduct and the logical inferences that follow from them in contingent circumstances. It is this individual liberty to conform one's will (or not) to right reason which Ockham then invokes when he speaks of the Christian law of liberty by which men know of their rights of use in the world.

In his *Letter to the Friars Minor* he analysed Pope John XXII's official pronouncements against the Franciscans and says he finds heretical, stupid, ridiculous, fantastic and defamatory statements against orthodox faith, against good custom, against natural reason, against experiences that are certain, and against fraternal charity. Judging especially against good custom, natural reasons and the certitude of experiences, he concludes that questions of faith are to be decided not only by a general council or by prelates but also by the Christian faithful laity and this includes women. All are witnesses to scriptural truth.

Although we cannot logically demonstrate the truth of such articles of faith as 'God is three and one', Ockham thinks that we can define morality in its large sense as 'human acts subject absolutely to the will'. This larger morality is, for him, a demonstrative science because its conclusions are deduced from principles that are either foundationally self-evident to all humans (*per se nota*) or are evident as a consequence of their experience (*nota per experientiam*). It is here, deductions from experience, that we feel the force of his insistence that individual experiences in communities with scripture will lead to behaviour that is guided by naturally known as well as scriptural truths which are prevalent knowledge (suppositions) in the community. Hence, he says that a moral science that is a non-positive science is that which directs human acts without any superior precepts. The precepts of this non-positive moral science are known by all men in themselves (*per se nota*, foundationally and without demonstration) or known through experience (*nota per experientiam*). This, he says, is how any man can determine what is

---

56   *Quodlibet* III, q. 19, in Wey, *Opera Theologica*, ix, pp. 275–6.

honest. Non-positive morality is known most certainly by any and every human experiencer of the world who lives in a community with its prevalent knowledge.

But then there is a moral science called 'positive' or the science of the lawyers (*scientia iuristarum*). It is not a demonstrative science because juristic rules are founded on human positive laws which are not propositions that are evidently known, but rather, are the products of expediency, calculated in contingent circumstances. Ockham believes in the necessity of positive law in fallen society, but he will not allow the lawyers and their canon or civil laws the foundational, ethical stability of a higher morality which owes them nothing, but to which they owe everything.[57]

Ockham had entered the ranks of all those arts and theology lecturers who insisted that ethical and political science required the moral foundations that could only be learned through the philosophy of the arts course and not through the study of positive law.

Conclusion

Ockham did not argue for the kind of subjective, individual rights or capacities which would lead each discrete individual to his own *and different* interpretation of moral rectitude. Central to his claims for psychological capacities on the part of humans as members of the same species is the insistence that thinking, no less than speaking, proceeds according to a logic of thought which, at some abstract level above distinctive and historically specific cultural habits, is rationally the same for all human minds that operate in the social with its prevalent knowledge. Above historical cultures is an impartial, logical and critical capacity to evaluate the difference between right and wrong, good and bad habits, a right reasoning that is achieved more completely in Christian societies which have available to them the truths of scripture added to naturally known and otherwise experienced truths. Like all Christian medieval thinkers, he is insisting on 'right reason' of a spiritually supplemented but rationally understood kind, against which customs and laws of any time and place should be judged. In the world as we experience it to be, and where we rely on a hypothetical necessity that how it normally is, *is* how it is, and where we presume, but cannot prove, that this is how God ordained it to be, humans simply do rely on right reason. Their right reason shows them what God must have intended because his intentions in words and deeds were communicated to

---

57   *Quodlibet* II, q. 3, in Wey, *Opera Theologica*, ix, pp. 117–18, 120–2; *Quodlibet* II, q. 14, pp. 176–8. *Dialogus 2* opens with the question of to whom does the determination of Catholic truths and consequently the judgement of heresies belong, the theologians or the canon lawyers. Ockham's answer is the theologians. He refutes the lawyers' argument that their competence arose from their science having been established by the church whose authority was greater than that of the gospels, following Augustine's statement (*Contra Faustum Manichaeum* 25.1, 5, 6) that he would not believe in the gospel except on the authority of the church . Ockham refutes this (1) by interpreting 'the church' as the sum of all believers in the past and present, arguing that the authority of this invisible and universal church, to which Augustine also belonged, *was* greater than that of the gospel; but that (2) canon law owed its origin not to the authority of this enduring, universal church but to that of the popes, a lesser authority. Theology, therefore, is the *scientia superior*. Canon law derives its principles from theology. And there is no law which cannot, if necessary, be corrected by theologians. Lawyers are held to be *non intelligentes, praesumptuosos, temerarios, fallaces, deceptores, cavillatores et ignaros in cordibus suis valde despiciunt*. Ockham accuses them of autonomous legal positivism, over-stepping their competence, arrogating to themselves rights concerning what is to be believed, the relation of law and truth, law and morals. This attack was continued in, for instance, the sermons of the Chancellor of the University of Paris in the fifteenth century, Jean Gerson, 'Liber de vita spirituali animae', *Oeuvres complètes*, vol. 3, ed. P. Glorieux (Paris, 1962), pp. 113–202.

contemporary witnesses who passed on these intentions in scripture and other oral and written texts.

Ockham is describing a normative situation in which God's will is not ordinarily considered by men to be inscrutable or arbitrary. He thinks that we can discover from the ways in which we live and come to know what we know, in this life, *pro statu isto*, that we have been given the capacities which confirm us in a certain confidence that God had actually intended to ensure that our right reason reflects his plan for humans. This did not ignore God's absolute power to do what he willed and to intervene extraordinarily in the 'normal' run of affairs, but that absolute will *is* inscrutable to men and they cannot presume to have access to it as a guiding set of rules and principles by which fallen nature is to live. Ockham distanced the divine power in all its might and possibility from the normal workings of the world and he thought that men had been granted capacities, right reason, by which they could cope with the instability of contingencies. In this, he left the fallen world to man's making. Some would later speak of Ockham's God as a *deus absconditus*, a God that, after his brief appearance, had left the world to human ways of determining it.[58] But while right reason is our guide, our essential characterization is, for Ockham, our liberty to will to follow right reason. He, like others of his time, was speaking of a range of psychological capacities which, when exercised, led to peculiarly human ways of thinking, behaving and evaluating. His ethics requires rationality in public acts.

Nowhere do we find a discussion of the unique and solitary person with his views and values, reconfigured as sensual preferences, uniquely pitted against the different views and values of his neighbour. No doubt he existed, but it was not this isolated self, this 'man' of sense experience, that could claim human rights and expect others to be obliged to recognize them. It was, rather, on the basis of what humans shared as humans, right reason and will, as social, rational, voluntary moral agents that individuals could claim they had rights accorded to each member of the species by God and nature, and thereby constitute governments which acknowledged and even extended these rights. Since legitimate political power can only be exercised over free individuals, Ockham affirmed that any authority which attempted to deny what is, in effect, their psychological liberty by requiring behaviour that was contrary to scripture or reason was illegitimate. His focus on the supremacy of the individual Christian conscience followed from his interpretation of the New Testament. And it was this method and this focus, on the bedrock of scripture and the individual's reason and will, which would shake the foundations of later medieval theology until and beyond the Protestant Reformation.[59]

---

58   On the distinction between God's *potentia ordinata* and God's *potentia absoluta* in Ockham and later nominalist theologians see H. Oberman, *The Harvest of Medieval Theology: Gabriel Biel and late medieval nominalism* (Cambridge, MA, 1963); W. J. Courtenay, *Capacity and Volition: a history of the distinction of absolute and ordained power (Quodlibet 8)* (Bergamo, 1990); E. Randi, *Il sovrano e l'orologiaio, due immagini di Dio nel dibattito sulla 'potentia absoluta' fra XIII e XIV secolo* (Florence, 1986).

59   See J. Miethke, 'Marsilius und Ockham. Publikum und Leser ihrer politischen Schriften im späteren Mittelalter', *Medioevo* 6 (1980), pp. 543–67; W. J. Courtenay, 'The Reception of Ockham's Thought in Fourteenth-century England', in A. Hudson and M. Wilks, eds, *From Ockham to Wyclif* (Oxford, 1987), pp.89–108. See the various contributions in A. Maierù, ed., *English Logic in Italy in the Fourteenth and Fifteenth Centuries* (Naples, 1982). On earlier conciliarists adopting Ockham's view of the church as a collection of individuals and notably the influence of Ockham on Pierre d'Ailly see W. J. Courtenay, 'Covenant and Causality in Pierre d'Ailly', *Speculum* 46 (1971), pp. 94–119; W. J. Courtenay, 'Nominalism and Late Medieval Religion', in C. Trinkaus, ed., *The Pursuit of Holiness in*

The Late Medieval Fortunes of Corporation Theories in the Church's 'Conciliar Theory'

During much of the fourteenth century starting in 1305, the papacy had been resident in Avignon. With its return to Rome and then the disputed papal election of 1378, that protracted period known as the Great Schism in the Western church began (1378–1418). It was to be a period punctuated by repeated attempts to end it. These events ensured the rise to even greater prominence of that kind of ecclesiological constitutionalism known as 'conciliar theory' with which we have already become familiar, for instance, in John of Paris's arguments that a general council, representing the Christian people, could depose a pope. Thereafter, the bishop of Mende, William Durant, had proposed that church councils should be regularly called every ten years, that all church legislation should only take place in such a council, and that the papal budget should be under conciliar control. Durant's ideas proved to be ahead of their time and were rejected.[60] We have also seen how Marsilius of Padua had applied his model of the sovereign human legislator to spiritual concerns of the general council, the *congregatio fidelis*. Thereafter, from the 1380s onwards, numerous learned men, lay and ecclesiastical, sought to resolve the constitutional crisis in the church by means of a general council which had the authority to appoint a true pope. In response to conciliarist beliefs, the Councils of Pisa (1409), Constance (1414–18) and Basel (1431–49) were assembled to put an end to the scandal of two and, for a brief moment, three competing popes by endorsing the view that a general council alone was the proper court of judgement between the rival claimants.[61]

At the heart of conciliarist theory was the belief that the pope was not an absolute ruler but a constitutional monarch, by which was meant that his authority was ministerial and delegated to him for the good of the church; and that final authority in the church, at least regarding especially critical cases, lay with the whole body of the faithful, or their representatives, gathered together in a general council. The principle of Christian unity, then, lay not in a rigorous subordination of all church members to a single papal head, but rather in the corporate association of those members. This community of the faithful was, furthermore, capable of exercising its corporate authority in a general council even in the absence of its head, the pope. Theorists insisted that the church as a whole has a right to rid itself of an incorrigible head to prevent its own destruction, a

Late Medieval and Renaissance Religion (Leiden, 1974), pp. 26–59. On Ockham's later influence in general, see F. Oakley, *Omnipotence, Covenant and Order: an excursion in the history of ideas from Abelard to Leibniz* (Ithaca, NY, 1984) esp. chs 2 and 3; F. Oakley, 'Medieval Theories of Natural Law: William of Ockham and the significance of the voluntarist tradition', *Natural Law Forum* 6 (1961); Oakley, 'Natural Law, the *corpus mysticum* and consent'; Oakley, *The Political Thought of Pierre d'Ailly*; H. Oberman, ed., *Forerunners of the Reformation: the shape of late medieval thought* (New York, 1966) and H. Oberman, *The Harvest of Medieval Theology*; S. Ozment, *The Age of Reform, 1250–1550: an intellectual and religious history of late medieval and Reformation Europe* (New Haven, CN, 1980).

60   Guilielmus Durandus, *Tractatus maior c.* 1308; see C. Fasolt, *Council and Hierarchy: the political thought of William Durant the Younger* (Cambridge, 1991).

61   For documents in translation see C. M. D. Crowder, *Unity, Heresy and Reform, 1378–1460: the conciliar response to the Great Schism* (London, 1977). Generally, see A. Black, 'The Conciliar Movement', in *CHMPT* (1988), pp. 573–87; A. Black, *Council and Commune: the conciliar movement* (London, 1979); B. Tierney, *Foundations of the Conciliar Theory* (Cambridge, 1955).

right not merely based on church custom and canon law, but on an inalienable right of all free communities, more or less explicitly grounded in the dictates of natural law. Such a right pertains to all those over whom any authority, either secular or ecclesiastical, is placed, that is, the right to elect their ruler.[62] The inalienable right to collective self-preservation was recognized as exercised through consent to authority. In other words, the survival of the 'state', the *salus populi*, is a universally acknowledged, explicit reason justifying the necessity for consent to authoritative jurisdiction, that is, government. Debates ensued about the degree to which this consent was tacit or explicit, and over the technical means by which a collective will might be represented.

The decrees of the Council of Constance were meant to ensure that councils would play a leading role in church government, some understanding the decrees as asserting actual supremacy of councils over popes. The Council of Basel then reissued the decrees of Constance but went further and took over the machinery of church government, setting up its own courts, raising taxes, passing decrees on clerical conduct. Where membership of the Council of Constance had been determined in terms of rank and office, Basel was more egalitarian, deciding its own membership, and, what was even more radical, voting by numerical majorities irrespective of ecclesiastical rank. Lower-ranking clergy had the same voting power as bishops and representatives of princes, each participating as an individual.[63] Secular princes began to see the implications of conciliarism for their own regimes and the supporters of conciliar sovereignty in the church began to thin.[64] By the late 1440s most secular rulers were aligning with the papacy rather than with the conciliarists. Black has noted that Basel had been 'the most far-reaching attempt by any representative assembly to establish a regime that was recognizably non-monarchical and parliamentarian'.[65]

In general, conciliar corporation theory gave the church as a whole, from Christ, its authority and power which it delegated to the pope. Legitimate power lay with the congregation of the faithful; as a corporation the church was represented by a general council, and the executive government of the church was to be exercised by the weightier part of those present. For some, this was taken to mean the cardinals and the pope working together to legislate for the *status ecclesiae*. Their authority and power, a *plenitudo potestatis*, was shared but ultimately derived from the representative congregation as a whole. Some argued that in representing the whole church, the decisions of this general council could not err. For others, especially at Basel, it was the congregation of the faithful which exercised *plenitudo potestatis* not only over all Christians but also over the pope, who was no more than an executive minister, not unlike a rector of a university.[66]

Note, however, that conciliar supremacy was *not* a statement about the preferred, particular form of constitution of the church. At the beginning of the fifteenth century

---

62   Pierre d'Ailly, *Tractatus de ecclesiastica potestate*, in J. Gerson, *Opera omnia*, ed. E. Dupin, vol. 2 (Antwerp, 1706), p. 935B; compare Ockham, above.

63   J. Coleman, 'The Interrelationship between Church and State During the Conciliar Period: theory and practice', in J.-P. Genet and B. Vincent, eds, *Etat et église dans la genèse de l'état moderne* (Madrid, 1986), pp. 41–54.

64   J. W. Stieber, *Pope Eugenius IV, the Council of Basel and the Secular and Ecclesiastical Authorities in the Empire* (Leiden, 1978).

65   Black, *Political Thought in Europe*, p. 171.

66   Compare Marsilius, above; Black, *Political Thought in Europe*, p. 171; A. Black, *Monarchy and Community: political ideas in the later conciliar controversy, 1430–50* (Cambridge, 1970); Black, *Council and Commune*; see also Canning, *A History*, pp. 176–84, especially on Zabarella, pp. 179–8; B. Tierney, *Foundations*.

one argument was made that the best constitution for the church is a 'mixed' one where the papal monarch would be tempered with aristocratic and democratic elements.[67] We note that the papacy is considered a monarchy but is constitutionally tempered through a mixture. This theory argued that the tempering mixture meant a brake on absolute papal monarchy whereby the *plenitudo potestatis* was shared by the pope and the cardinals as representatives of the church. It was said that the cardinals had the right to assist the pope as his principal counsellors and co-operators in the government of the universal church. This position makes the mixed constitution of papal monarchy more akin to an oligarchy, the tempered mixture referring to a combination of the exercise of governing power by pope and cardinals along with the calling of frequent general councils. The populist or 'democratic' element, the 'frequent general councils', is seen as exercising its tempering effect in a less than regular way.

Others, however, happened to think that the best constitutional form for the church was a *politia regalis,* a monarchy, that was not to be described as 'mixed' or even 'political' because on this view of monarchy the fullness of power lies with the ruler and not with the community. The church constitution as established by Christ, 'the best of legislators', could not change, whereas it was accepted that the secular polity could alter its constitution from being a monarchy into an aristocracy or a 'timocracy'/democracy.[68] These arguments in favour of one constitutional form or another in church or state were not, however, arguments about absolute sovereignty. Absolute sovereignty could, in principle, be located in a collective body as well as in an individual ruler. Especially with regard to a secular polity, it was usually held that the constitutional form was a matter of prudence and tradition, even of immemorial custom tempered by contingencies, a view that we have already seen made explicit notably by Marsilius and Ockham. We shall see this tradition of discussion re-emerge in a new key in Machiavelli's *Prince* and his *Discourses*. The *salus populi*, achieved through good government, can be realized *either* in a monarchy *or* in a republic, and the preference for one constitutional form over another will depend on a people's character and tradition.

The parallels between ecclesiastical conciliarism and the practice of contemporary medieval parliamentary representation have often been noted. The king, as head, was understood to rule in co-operation with other members, and being identified with the common good of his people he was seen as obliged to attend to their interests. Parliaments had come into being largely during the thirteenth and fourteenth centuries and their most common justification among the learned, especially in the law, was the Roman law dictum *quod omnes tangit*, 'what touches all should be approved by all'. Matters concerning all members of a kingdom should, therefore, be decided on only with their approval, that is, through parliaments. While there is a relative paucity of theorizing

---

67 Pierre d'Ailly, *Tractatus de ecclesiastica potestate,* in Gerson, *Opera omnia,* p. 933.

68 For the views of Jacques Almain and John Major in the sixteenth century that authority in the church is corporate with the pope wielding ministerial power on behalf of the universal church, and therefore in the last instance is subordinate to the community the pope exists to serve (and he is deposable by the council representing the church if he becomes tyrannical), see F. Oakley, 'Almain and Major', *American Historical Review* no. 42, p. 683; J. H. Burns, *Lordship, Kingship and Empire: the idea of monarchy 1400–1525* (Oxford, 1992), p. 127. Some argued that the church, when assembled in a general council, was a mystical body but not a body politic; the latter being capable of error, might deceive or be deceived, whereas this could not be true of the former, the church. See J. H. Burns, 'Conciliarism, Papalism, and Power, 1511–1518', in D. Wood, ed., *The Church and Sovereignty* (Oxford, 1991), pp. 409–28; on Almain, pp. 420–4.

about 'state' parliaments,[69] there is a much larger body of theoretical texts dealing explicitly with representation and the constitutional role of councils in the church even before the late fourteenth- and early fifteenth-century conciliarists. Indeed, the various techniques of representation, along with the idea of assemblies as the legitimate arena for collective decisions in 'states', owed a great deal to the church, its canon law provisions and its ecclesiastical theorists. Canon law, for instance, provided for situations in which disputed elections should be decided by the greater and wiser, the *maior et sanior pars,* or a corporation that was constituted by the great and wise and representing the will of the larger corporate whole. Just as parliaments came to be seen as corporate bodies, so too the church had been thus configured. Parliaments on the one hand, or general church councils on the other, were seen as standing in place of the whole. Popes used councils as kings used parliaments, to publicize, elicit consent to, or effect new measures of government and finance. The conciliar movement among ecclesiastics of the early fifteenth century can therefore be seen as having marked the climax of medieval parliamentary representation. But the failure of this conciliarism by mid century likewise marked the decline in representative assemblies generally.[70] We shall have to keep this in mind when we come to discuss the conditions which Machiavelli experienced and described, not only in his native Florence at the end of the fifteenth and beginning of the sixteenth century, but notably in monarchical France and republican Venice.

The conciliar *movement* was, in the end, defeated at Basel. Elements of its *theory* would, however, be revived during the sixteenth and seventeenth centuries across Europe, and interpreted to be of use outside the church in secular political theorizing and practice. Indeed, by the mid sixteenth century, as John Ponet (1516?–56)was to observe,

> at one clappe, in the conseil holden at Constance . . . were three popes popped out of their places. . . . If it be lawful for the body of the churche to depose and punishe a Pope . . . how muche the more by the like argumentes, reasones, and authoritie, maie Emperours, Kings, princes and other governours, abusing their office, be deposed and removed out of their places and offices, bi the body or state of the Realme or commonwealthe.[71]

Much research has gone into determining the nature of persisting conciliarism from the fourteenth to the sixteenth centuries and the degree to which its different formulations by a multitude of thinkers modified its meaning and scope.[72] For our purposes, it is noteworthy that many who contributed to conciliar debates in the various councils, either as pro-papal or pro-conciliar proponents, were themselves representatives of the Renaissance humanist movement we shall discuss in the next chapter. Many a Renais-

---

69   Although see the work of J.-P. Genet, 'Un Corpus de textes politiques – les textes parlementaires Anglais 1376–1410', *Cahiers de la méditerrannée,* 'Histoire et Informatique' (1996), pp.123–48, which indicates that parliamentary sermons have been insufficiently analysed to extract a theory of government.

70   Black, *Political Thought in Europe,* pp. 162–6, 169–85.

71   *A Short Treatise of Politicke Power* (Strassbourg, 1556), pp. 103–5, cited in Oakley, 'Almain and Major', p. 685.

72   Tierney, *Foundations;* F. Oakley, 'Natural Law, the *corpus mysticum* and Consent in Conciliar Thought from John of Paris to Matthias Ugonis', *Speculum* 56, 4 (1981), pp. 786–810; Oakley, 'Almain and Major: conciliar theory on the eve of the Reformation', *American Historical Review* 70 (1965), pp. 673–90; F. Oakley, *The Political Thought of Pierre d'Ailly: the voluntarist tradition* (New Haven, CN, 1964); F. Oakley, *Natural Law, Conciliarism and Consent in the Later Middle Ages* (London, 1984); J. H. Burns, 'Conciliarism', in D. Wood, ed., *The Church and Sovereignty,* pp. 409–28.

sance humanist no less than many a university scholastic, at different times in their careers, wrote works that favoured *both* positions, the same author composing a 'mirror for princes' on the one hand, and then, on the other, a hymn to collective or republican government.[73] This in itself raises some interesting questions of what kind of government, supported by what kind of principles, a particular author actually or personally adhered to. Is a theorist who composes a tract in favour of princes, and then writes in favour of republics, no more than an ideological opportunist? As we shall see, this is a dilemma for readers of Machiavelli's works, because he wrote one in favour of monarchy (*The Prince*) and another in favour of republics (*The Discourses*).

We will be better prepared to understand what each of Machiavelli's texts is if we keep in mind that there was already established a conciliarist discourse which drew on what Black has rightly described as a range of languages used by European intellectuals: the languages of canon and Roman law, of the university arts course – (Ciceronian and Aristotelian) moral and political practical philosophy – of theology, of humanist diplomatic oratory.[74] Burns has also drawn attention to the fact that in the fifteenth-century debates on monarchical government more generally, many still used the scholastic mode, drawing on elements of the scriptural and patristic language of the theologians, the Aristotelian language of the philosophers and the technical language of civilian and canonist jurisprudence.[75] Furthermore, some authors favouring papal monarchy none the less included elements of conciliarism in their conception of monarchy. This means that there is no simple way to match philosophical or theological positions, or even scholastic and humanist modes of argument, with predictable political or ecclesiological conclusions. Humanists, most notably, did *not* all favour republics, and often those who did, described a republic that was remarkably similar to some forms of monarchy or oligarchy. The point is that both scholastic and humanist modes of argument, in style and content, and often deployed by the *same* author, contributed to discussions of critical issues relating to government in church and state. And what they had to say in their tracts in favour of either position cannot be understood as a direct and unproblematic debate *between* monarchies and republics, monarchies versus republics.

Our necessarily very brief concern here has been to establish that conciliarism was increasingly seen as having political implications which threatened a particular vision of 'absolute' monarchy in church and state and this would be a matter for intense discussion well into the sixteenth and seventeenth centuries. The perceived populist pretensions of conciliarism came to be regarded as the very 'destruction of commonwealths'. Indeed, the conciliar theory that stipulated the community as a whole to be the foundation of derived public authority, was rightly seen as applying not only to monarchy but to any other constitution. By the end of the fifteenth century, conciliarist ideas still continued to contribute to political discourses precisely at a time when European monarchies began to emerge as consolidated 'national' states with more concentrated power in the prince than had existed either in practice or in much theory during the Middle Ages. Conciliarism continued as a contemporary discourse that remained lively until and

---

73   Burns, *Lordship, Kingship and Empire*, p. 126: 'Individuals and groups are less securely categorized than the positions they may at one time or another choose to adopt'.
74   Black, *Political Thought in Europe*, p. 176. See the more specific discussion in A. Black, 'Political Languages in Later Medieval Europe', in Wood, *The Church and Sovereignty*, pp. 313–28.
75   Burns, *Lordship, Kingship and Empire*, p. 7.

at the time when Machiavelli wrote his *Prince* and *Discourses*. The language of conciliarist corporation theory would match the intensification of interest in recovering the language and practices of republican Rome, notably in Renaissance Italy. Conciliarist arguments made many of the same points that civic republican arguments made.

After Basel, a generation of papal monarchists advanced the theory of monarchy as necessarily the best, indeed, as the only form of government for *any* state. More importantly, during the first decade of the sixteenth century they came to reject a parallel between civil and ecclesiastical authority and favoured an exclusive 'divine right' view of the papal monarchy.[76] Increasingly powerful secular monarchs and their publicists listened and found it useful to emulate this vision: they revived the early medieval notion of theocratic monarchy, and supported it with elements of the theories of papal monarchy, in order to establish the basis for the early-modern European development of 'absolute' monarchy, kingship by divine right. An imperialist ideology was revived so that kings claimed to be emperors in their own realms, expressly arguing against any notion of monarchy as constitutionally limited. Legitimate sovereign power and its exercise was to have nothing to do with subjects' consent to it. Monarchical systems came to dominate the European landscape for the next two centuries, and even as the seventeenth gave way to the eighteenth century, royalist doctrines commanded more support and were of greater practical significance than short-lived republican visions and experiments.[77] Theories of divine right monarchy would serve as foundational to monarchy as conceived under the *ancien régime* and, from a nineteenth-century liberal or radical point of view, would still appear to be a problem and a threat.[78]

The problem for us is to determine whether the early sixteenth-century Machiavelli, especially in his *Prince* but also in his *Discourses on Livy,* is looking forward to this notion of constitutionally *un*limited monarchy, or whether, like his humanist colleagues from whom he differed in other ways, he is harking back to older traditions of liberty and a self-governing free people.

---

76   Ibid., p. 142.

77   Ibid., p. 147. On Continental communes acting as partners with absolute monarchs in violating the constitution, laws and royal oaths of the realm to the mutual benefit of monarch and commune see H. Nader, 'The More Communes, the Greater the King: hidden communes in absolutist theory', in P. Blickle, ed., *Theorien kommunaler Ordnung in Europa* (Munich, 1996), pp.215–23.

78   J. H. Burns, 'Absolutism: the history of an idea', *The Creighton Trust Lecture*, University of London, 1986, pp. 1–30. Burns reminds us that the concept of absolute power, well known in the Middle Ages as *potestas absoluta*, is not the same thing as 'absolutism', the earliest appearance in English dating from 1830. As in the Middle Ages, so too for Locke in the *Second Treatise*, II, xiv, para.163 and II, xciv: the principle governing the right use of absolute power or, what he calls prerogative, is the precept *salus populi suprema lex esto*, and for Locke as for conciliarists, such power is in the hands of the prince 'by allowance of the community', the legislature being placed in collective bodies of men, call them senate, parliament, etc. See Burns p. 15, n. 39 and p. 30. For an important debate on the importance of medieval conciliarism to medieval and early-modern constitutionalism see F. Oakley, 'Nederman, Gerson, Conciliar Theory and Constitutionalism: *sed contra*', *History of Political Thought* 16 (1995), pp. 1–19, and the response by C. Nederman, 'Constitutionalism – Medieval and Modern: against neo-Figgisite orthodoxy (again)', *History of Political Thought* 17 (1996), pp. 179–94, both with extensive citations to relevant literature.

6

The Italian Renaissance and Machiavelli's Political Theory

'O Mantovano, io son Sordello
Della tua terra.' E l'un l'altro abbracciava.

'O Mantuan, I am Sordello
From your own town.' And they embraced.

Dante, *Purgatorio* vi, 70ff.

The great urban flowering that had occurred throughout Europe from the eleventh century onwards brought cities into being which were more or less 'autonomous' political entities, in east-central France (Champagne), Flanders, southern Germany, the Rhineland, the Baltic region, and in north and central Italy. The towns themselves did not suddenly appear by a sort of spontaneous generation. During this period certain established towns became centres of long-distant trade, injecting enterprise and wealth into the countryside. They had become part of a more widespread change: the growth in population and wealth which in turn stimulated urban growth and the goods and services which towns provided. Urban communes became the centres of an intense development of mercantile, manufacturing and commercial activities. However, the growth and expansion of cities did not usually bring them full emancipation from the larger territorial bodies – principalities and duchies, kingdoms and the Empire – in which they were embedded. Indeed, the independence of most urban centres from the feudal restrictions prevailing in the agricultural hinterland came at a price: that of a more or less dependent relationship on increasingly centralized territorial nation-states.[1]

The Italian City-states Compared with Other European Cities

Generally, medieval European cities have been considered islands in a sea of feudality. On closer scrutiny, this happens not to have been the case, especially for emergent urban

---

1   See S. Reynolds, *Kingdoms and Communities in Western Europe 900–1300* (Oxford, 1984), ch. 6; J. K. Hyde, *Society and Politics in Medieval Italy: the evolution of the civil life 1000–1350* (London, 1973), ch. 4; and the interesting discussion in M. Mann, 'The European Dynamic, II: the rise of coordinating states, 1155–1477', in *The Sources of Social Power*, vol. 1 (Cambridge, 1986), pp. 416–49.

centres of trade and production during the twelfth and thirteenth centuries, like Troyes and Provins in east-central France, or in the textile-producing regions of Flanders, centred on Bruges and Ghent. Towns in Northern Europe were often the seats of local feudal lords' government and the line between feudal lords, 'industrialists' and financiers was less sharp than is often supposed. Certain northern textile towns obtained charters of self-governance which none the less allowed the local feudal lord to hold a monopoly over mills, property and other economic ventures. Hence, where urban charters of self-governance by an elected council undoubtedly existed, geographical and political conditions necessarily modified their independence in practice.

Only in north and central Italy did autonomous political entities, the geographically compact city-states, emerge *comparatively* free of continuous restrictions imposed by an otherwise engaged German empire, the Holy Roman Empire, of which they were a part. Their formative phase occurred during the eleventh and twelfth centuries and their self-proclaimed autonomy sometimes came without endorsement by a higher power, or else they received imperial privileges to confirm customary rights over markets and local jurisdictions. When, during the twelfth and thirteenth centuries, German emperors (Frederick Barbarossa and Frederick II) attempted to restore imperial authority, Italian communes had already established a tradition of independent self-governance that proved, for the moment, irreversible. Emperors increasingly recognized the office of *podestà*, a citizen from another commune and therefore a 'foreigner', as a single executive administrator of a commune, a rector, the head of the judiciary and therefore not a sovereign ruler. He was appointed with a limited term of office to each city in order to oversee its affairs and minimize internal factionalism. He took an oath to give justice according to the city's own laws.[2] Cities from the Alps to the border of the Norman kingdom of Naples and Sicily (where a monarchy prevented the growth of fully independent municipalities) established for themselves, on the basis of customary practices, their independent, *de facto* autonomy in matters of self-governance.

The majority of Europe's cities achieved recognition out of a more or less conscious effort on the part of kings and princes to seek alliances with new and financially useful urban corporations as clients, thereby enabling them to check, or at least balance, the resistance of individual feudal lords who insisted on their old liberties to maintain private local economies and their own courts.[3] During the later Middle Ages there was throughout Europe a proliferation of new cities with royal charters. Not so in Italy. There, the number of cities between the thirteenth and fifteenth centuries remained limited and stable.

From the classical period it had been a characteristic of much of the Mediterranean area that a large proportion of the population settled in towns rather than in scattered villages. Medieval Italian communes were able to draw upon aspects of their inheritance of the imperial Roman administration which had merged civil and ecclesiastical government, so that cities were, early on, also the seats of ecclesiastical dioceses: this enabled them to dominate vast territories beyond their walls. Furthermore, Italian cities were

---

2   Compare Marsilius's 'regulator' or *pars principans* above; by the fourteenth century the *podestà* was a profession for administrators with a legal training, some moving from city to city, and some families building up a tradition of producing such administrators.

3   S. F. C. Milsom, *Historical Foundations of the Common Law*, 2nd edn (London, 1981) saw the replacement of local law by centralized, national law as an unintended, juristic accident in England.

not simply islands of merchants and commercial interests within a feudal, agricultural landscape, but rather, were amalgamations of landed feudal *and* mercantile interests. Holders of seignorial rights in the countryside played a large part in the very establishment and consolidation of the Italian urban communes. Collective loyalties were likely to have been fostered by the continued existence in many Italian *civitates* of a core of lawyers and notaries who saw themselves to be guardians and repositories of civic traditions and pre-existing local, customary law. There are, however, parallels to be drawn with other Northern European commercial cities.

It has often been pointed out that Italian communes were mixed societies of noblemen, shopkeepers, artisans, notaries and peasants in which it was common to combine professions, say, that of a notary with a craft, or a landowner with both agricultural and commercial activities. Noble descent was not seen as incompatible with trade, and lawyers and judges came from the very same families as the most prominent nobles whose ancestors had ranked among the feudal aristocracy. Notaries and judges belonged to the same corporate guild, although the rank of a notary was normally lower than that of the judge and it indicated he was rarely of noble descent. A successful notary, however, could elevate his own family in the social scale. The ability to read and write, as well as a knowledge of aspects of Roman and customary law, proved crucial for personal advancement across Europe, as we have seen. But notaries became a distinctive feature of Italian communes. Notaries recorded in writing all commercial and politico-legal transactions, and being involved in this amount of paperwork enabled them to be involved in government. It is the presence, early on, of large numbers of these literate laymen which is believed to have distinguished Italian city life from the life in other European cities. Indeed, Waley asked how the members of this inflated profession were all able to make a living, so many were there, and he suggested that, as with so many other occupations, notarial skills were compatible with trade, medicine and a variety of crafts.[4]

During the second half of the eleventh century Italian cities began to gain their civic independence at the expense both of imperial and episcopal authority, a result of their experience of that wider European debate between church and state which we have already discussed. By the twelfth century, Italy was organized into a pattern of city-states, each with its jurisdictional extensions over vast tracts of outlying territory which provided the resources of men and finance that were necessary for the policy objectives of the commercially minded communes. Judges and notaries occupied a disproportionate share of the city's offices, attended council meetings to vote and give counsel, and they recorded speech after speech given by lawyers and notaries at these meetings. The conciliar body of the commune, the assembly of its citizens, was a kind of parliament called the *arengo*. Most communes would see this *arengo* evolve into a large council. But important decisions and the arguments which preceded them took place not in the assembly but in smaller, often 'secret' councils. And numerous ad hoc committees (*balìe*) were set up to give advice on specific issues concerning military or financial crises, drawing on 'experts' whose powers were normally extra-constitutional. The image of the city-state as a unified body, with the city's *magistrates* its head and the countryside its limbs, is the peculiarly Italian version of the organic metaphor that was sustained elsewhere in Europe, where the king was head, and the functional estates the various limbs. Lawyers observed that cities, which as a matter of custom and observation, 'do not

4   D. Waley, *The Italian City-Republics*, 2nd edn (London, 1978), p. 13.

recognize a superior' must, for the purposes of public law, be considered independent, self-governing bodies with sovereign power. In Italy, the city as a corporate entity *was* the prince well before the fourteenth-century civil lawyer Bartolus used the phrase *civitas sibi princeps*, the city is its own prince.[5]

The importance of learning how to address the city's councils was recognized early on in the number of grammar and rhetoric teachers in each city, whose salaries were paid by the commune and who provided model speeches for their students to imitate. By the thirteenth century, municipal schools were established in many communes to teach Latin grammar and more advanced legal courses for notaries and lawyers. Teachers wrote manuals which gave instructions on how to take summarizing notes of speeches delivered.[6] These teachers specialized in and developed the genre of oratorical public address for one-off public occasions. While the literacy rate, by the end of the thirteenth century, appears to have been unusually high, it is not clear what kind of literacy this was for most men: pragmatic and commercially minded or more scholarly and literary? In other words, how many 'literate' men could actually compose the public speeches they undoubtedly heard in one public forum or another? The impression one gets is of members of thirteenth-century Italian communes experiencing a great deal of oral speechifying rather than engaging in reading alone and in reflective mode.

But this must be balanced by the fact that school education remained in the hands of ecclesiastical bodies, and the educational tone right into and throughout the fourteenth and fifteenth centuries was set by these religious schools and the texts they taught from and commented upon. And whatever the local conditions and traditions in Italian communes, or in the hierarchical organization of the institutional church, it must always be recalled that Christian teaching itself, and everywhere, emphasized a universalistic, egalitarian, decentralized and civilizing *community* which, in the face of worldly rank was, in the sight of God, made up of equals in a community of the faithful if not the saved. God, after all, transcended all worldly social structure and salvation was open to all in the Christian community. The threat to all was excommunication from this community, since outside the church community there was to be no salvation. The community of the Italian commune was, therefore, a resultant combination of local historical experiences and customs on the one hand, and the more universally shared internalized convictions of religious preaching, on the other. Christian social ethics concerning interpersonal and familial relations (what sociologists call normative pacification, which substitutes for coercive pacification used elsewhere) happily matched what was said in ancient Roman moralizing texts from which everyone in such schools learned to read. Church schools may have provided the required, rudimentary literacy for success in the social and economic world, but the rationale for their own institution was founded in the need to communicate Christian ideas and cultural practices about community, and literacy served these ends in Italy as elsewhere in Europe.

Such schools were then supplemented either by private individuals who taught more vocational courses in basic law and commercial arithmetic for those seeking jobs as notaries or in a business. Giovanni Villani (*d.* 1348) described the situation in early fourteenth-century Florence, where eight to ten thousand male children received elementary education, around one thousand received a commercial education, and around

---

5   See A. Black, 'The Juristic Origins of Social Contract Theory', *History of Political Thought*, 14 (1993), pp. 57–76.
6   Brunetto Latini, *Li Livres dou trésor*, III, 2.

six hundred went on to receive further education in Latin and logic in ecclesiastical schools.[7] Although it has often been observed that minute accuracy was not one of Villani's strong points, not least because he reports events which he was too young to have experienced himself, in his dealing with his own times and with events immediately connected with Florence he is held to be a trustworthy witness. Villani is particularly revealing about how, by 1282, the *de facto* trade-guild organization of the city of Florence was made into its *de jure* constitution with the formal recognition of the Priors of the crafts guilds as the supreme magistrates of the city. Thereafter, they struggled to bring the military aristocracy, the magnates, within the control of the laws and constitution of the Florentine commercial community. It is this story of the Florentine people against the nobles which is taken as paradigmatic of Italian communal history in its golden age of 'republican', constitutional government.[8]

Citizens of Italian cities not only had the right to govern outlying territories but were granted other jurisdictional and economic privileges (*privilegium civilitatis*) which were not shared by the inhabitants of the countryside (*contado*). This allowed them to exploit the wealth of rural areas in a reciprocal but imbalanced relationship which contributed to a transformation of agrarian economies. As these cities took great innovative strides in developing mercantile, manufacturing and financial activities they linked themselves commercially with Northern Europe, Byzantium, the Mediterranean, North Africa and beyond. Their triumph emerged out of their maritime commerce and the banking and credit arrangements they developed to service it.[9]

The Unconventional Aims of this Chapter

It is important to have some idea of the nature of Italian communal wealth and its development for us to grasp the degree to which Italian cities, as part of a more general European historical urban phenomenon, shared in the developments and experiences cities had elsewhere. We must also treat the relationship between this wealth and citizenship in the city-state or commune in order to clarify what engagement in communal self-rule meant in practice. This will enable us to evaluate the degree to which the political theory that was generated from within Italian city-states took on its own – and different – purpose and function. We shall be able to determine the ways in which municipal schools and private teachers moulded and modified public education to serve the needs of these enterprising city-states and their active citizens. We shall observe how and why what is called 'civic humanism' emerged in these cities. We shall also see that this 'humanism' did not represent the sum total of contemporary thought and learning, even about politics.

---

7   Giovanni Villani, *Nuova Cronica*, ed. G. Porta (Parma, 1991) lib. xi.

8   But see Villani's description of the subsequent 1301 coup, where the wealth, happiness and glory of Florence led to ingratitude and corruption, and the victory of the gentlemen–warrior Blacks over the *nouveaux riches* Whites: *Cronica*, ix, 38–9.

9   For overviews see P. Jones, 'La storia economica. Dalla caduta dell'impero romano al secolo XIV', in R. Romano and C. Vivanti, eds, *Storia d'Italia*, vol. 2 (Turin, 1974), pp. 1,469–1,810; Waley, *The Italian City-Republics*; R. Lopez, *The Commercial Revolution of the Middle Ages, 950–1350* (Cambridge, 1976); C. Cipolla, *Before the Industrial Revolution: European society and economy, 1000–1700* (London, 1976); T. Dean and C. Wickham, eds, *City and Countryside in Late Medieval and Renaissance Italy: essays presented to Philip Jones* (London, 1990); P. Jones, *The Italian City-state* (Oxford, 1997).

Some understanding of Italian communal wealth, its relationship to citizenship and to eligibility for public office, will also enable us to come to a view as to the novelty inherent in that concomitant cultural 'movement' which is called the Italian Renaissance. We have already treated the so-called twelfth-century renaissance (chapter 1), but this earlier 'movement' is named by analogy with the 'real' Renaissance, that of the Italian fifteenth and sixteenth centuries. We shall attempt to assess the effect of this cultural 'movement' on both the form and substance of Renaissance political discourse. The Italian Renaissance is usually thought to have been fully realized during the fifteenth century and its legacy informs Machiavelli's writings. The 'newness' of Renaissance perspectives, especially on matters ethical and political, however, has for centuries been a much contested issue among scholars. The intellectual border between what may be considered medieval and what distinctively Renaissance in Italian political theorizing from the thirteenth to the sixteenth centuries has been a terrain of enduring skirmishes. During much of the past one hundred years of historical scholarship and interpretation, however, the main voice heard has been the one that has an unacknowledged stake in Renaissance 'newness'. In part, this is because the Italian Renaissance has come to represent a set of characteristics to later Europeans whose cultures had developed out of experiences of the sixteenth-century Protestant Reformation and the Catholic church's response in the Counter-Reformation. And the confessional divide fed into alternative developments, in theory and practice, of increasingly centralized 'state' government. Later political theorists appealed to a kind of 'secular' instrumental rationality that was meant to be divorced from unproven and unprovable religious and metaphysical – and therefore, ethical – doctrine held on faith or by cultural imposition. The originating 'fathers' of the use of this kind of modern reason were then located in the so-called 'secular humanist' Italian Renaissance, and Machiavelli was hailed as their chief exponent. To most political scientists today, Machiavelli is 'one of us', the kind of realist about political strategy whose own cultural formation is an irrelevance, except in the untested belief that if he came out of the Renaissance, then the Renaissance must have shared our modern values.[10]

To the historians and political theorists of the Italian Renaissance has also been attributed an early historicism in order to underpin their purported relativism.[11] From the Renaissance interest in mounting rhetorical debates between ancients and moderns (which is what they called themselves, meaning 'contemporaries'), the conclusion has been drawn that they held to a notion of truth as mutable and relativistic, a cultural 'construct'. Much of what is now written about the Italian Renaissance therefore harbours

---

10   For an interpretation of Machiavelli's situation as the modern situation see H. C. Mansfield, *Machiavelli's Virtue* (Chicago, 1996); see the critical review by J. G. A. Pocock in *History of Political Thought* 19 (1998), pp. 661–4. A historically more nuanced position is provided by P. Burke, *Tradition and Innovation in Renaissance Italy: a sociological approach* (London, 1974), pp. 245–7, who argues that it is possible to distinguish traditional from modern views as we move from the Middle Ages to the Renaissance of the fifteenth and sixteenth centuries, by highlighting axes of bias which he thinks relevant to Renaissance thought: tendencies towards the natural (versus the supernatural), achievement (versus birth), letters (versus arms), thrift (versus splendour), the active (versus the contemplative), virtue (versus fortune), reason (versus faith), man's dignity (versus his misery). In contrast, on the continuities between the Middle Ages and the Renaissance see J. Coleman, *Ancient and Medieval Memories* (Cambridge, 1992), ch. 23.

11   See especially D. R. Kelley, *The Foundations of Modern Historical Scholarship: language, law and history in the French Renaissance* (New York, 1970) and D. R. Kelley, 'The theory of history', in C. Schmitt, Q. Skinner, E. Kessler and J. Kraye, eds, *The Cambridge History of Renaissance Philosophy* (Cambridge, 1988), pp. 746–62.

an unacknowledged perspective based on the later emergence of early-modern and modern 'liberal' and 'absolute' state models. Consequently, the Italian Renaissance is not only treated teleologically as a step in the direction of 'us', but Renaissance sentiments about personal and collective identity are said to be no different from our own. They are the first 'modern' men – historicizing relativists when they write history, and secular, instrumental rationalists when they write about politics.[12]

Our aim here, however, is to look at the Renaissance as it emerges out of medieval Europe and to set aside, in so far as this is possible, the question of what Renaissance political discourse was later taken to mean by people in different circumstances and with correspondingly different hopes. We shall see that especially during the fifteenth century, the ideal-type republic was intimately linked with civic liberty, and that this appeal to liberty occurred, curiously, at a time when many Italian republics either had already fallen to despots or were unstable, that is, their liberty was virtually nil. We shall have to examine what this idealized liberty entailed for Renaissance thinkers and the degree to which it has its roots in an older discourse on liberty.

We shall also have to examine whether civic liberty is associated only with a particular constitutional form, a republic, which is thought to have eliminated, for them, the possibility of a monarchy serving public liberty. The reason why it is important to clarify what they meant by republican liberty is that today 'republican liberty' has come to be applied too loosely and certainly unhistorically. Not only is it taken to mean the removal of interference or coercion (negative liberty), but it is also sometimes taken to mean the conditions in which a man's security and possessions are at his *own* disposal, free from the dominion or claims of any ruler, however benign. These understandings of republican liberty reveal a long-held assumption that liberty is positively connected to the European miracle of economic growth. But this loose, even libertarian use of the concept of liberty hides more than it reveals. The institutionalized distribution of political liberty has been assumed to parallel the economic growth within societies in general. The strong ideological commitment of modern liberal economists to the view that the absence of political coercion is fundamental to ensuring economic growth, however, is not borne out by a history with which we have already become somewhat familiar: ancient slavery and feudal serfdom proved economically rational and efficient, and this should at least imply that those societies based on unfree labour would have seen themselves as no better off economically had all their members been free. Furthermore, the connection between past political liberties and high rates of economic growth is not only unproven but, in some contexts, civic liberties may have been the very cause of economic decline: Renaissance Italy is a test case for this. As we shall see, the history of Italian cities from the thirteenth to the end of the fifteenth centuries actually subverts the direct causal link between urban political liberty and economic freedom, some of the

---

12   For an overview of such views and a bibliography dealing with those who believe political historiography was invented in the Renaissance, see S. Bagge, 'Medieval and Renaissance Historiography: break or continuity?', *The European Legacy* 2 (1997), pp. 1,336–71. Also see Burke, *Tradition and Innovation*, who says (p. 37): 'I started this book with a fairly clear picture of the pattern of achievement in the arts at this time. They flourished; they were the origins of the modern; and they exemplified certain major trends, notably realism, secularization, and individualism. All these certainties tended to dissolve as the book proceeded. If they can be saved, it is only at the price of marked reformulations.' But the reformulations provided are less marked than is implied. Also see P. Burke, *The Renaissance Sense of the Past* (London, 1969).

most economically successful cities having been governed by despotic *signori*. More generally, the constitution of a political regime, be it republican or monarchical, does not explain the relation between political liberty and economic success in Europe's or Renaissance Italy's history. Indeed, were we to take the story further and beyond the scope of this book, we would find that the history of the comparative success of liberal or absolutist states of the early-modern and modern era is a history of the greater or lesser success of centralizing administrative, fiscal and military efficiencies and not a history of civic liberty versus its absence.

Despite their rhetoric of civic liberty, we shall see that many humanists tolerated despots as no medieval political theorist writing about the 'state' had done, including those medievals who wrote in favour of constitutional monarchies. Many of the same humanist supporters of despots, redefined as Platonist philosopher–kings, went on to write other tracts where they praised civic liberty, by which they meant 'the rule of law'. Its opposite was absolute, irrational will above all law. Therefore, many advocated mixed or limited government. This could be a monarchy of the sort Aquinas and his continuator Ptolemy of Lucca called a *regimen politicum* (as opposed to what was called a *regimen regale* or, as Ptolemy has it, a *regimen despoticum*) where the monarch's powers were executive, established by, and doing the will of, the sovereign legislature, but with whose will the monarch or prince was meant to be in accord. A mixed or limited government could also be called an aristocratic rather than a more popular republic. In some cases all that was required was an infrequent call for popular assent to proposed law with little or no role for popular deliberation or legal emendation. Behind even this view which restricted the active engagement of the wider 'people' lay the belief that the conditions of a man's security and possessions could never be conceived as uniquely at his own disposal because government, whatever its institutional form, was meant to serve the common good, a collective good, which defined the very charge laid on governing office, however constitutionally formulated. Hence, one's own liberty was incapable of being unhinged from communal liberty. Monarchy subject to the law was a widely held ideal of government both north and south of the Alps and Italian communes ruled by a *podestà* were attempts to put this ideal into practice.[13] It is an ideal that travelled well into the fifteenth century in altered economic and political circumstances.

We shall see the older and earlier arguments resurfacing, arguments that were structured by Ciceronian and Aristotelian texts, by Roman law and history, and by the indigenous communal practices which evolved 'prudentially' to suit contingent circumstances. It is with regard to their prudential reading of contingent circumstances from the thirteenth to fifteenth centuries that we shall observe the equation of liberty and participatory citizenship to have been narrowed from an earlier view that all citizens of whatever status, as 'political animals', should take turns in ruling and being ruled, to a notion that collective politics is about finding the right leaders to govern the led. This would be as true for their conceptions of monarchy as for republics, both of which were seen to serve economic growth *and* civic liberty. But the political was never simply collapsed into the economic.

In the process, our aim is to become more aware of the distorting tendency in much modern historical analysis of the Italian Renaissance which separates off unduly the

---

13   Hyde, *Society and Politics*, pp. 103–4.

experiences and modes of discourse of inhabitants of Italian city-states from their urban contemporaries across the Alps. We *can* observe an undoubted shift in genres of private and public writing and styles of address to political or politicized audiences in Italy. The bigger issue, however, is whether new styles altered substance and if so, in what ways.

Lastly, the intellectual ferment of the Italian Renaissance is often represented as almost uniquely focused on throwing off the shackles of intolerable institutionalism, especially of the scholastic, university and ecclesiastical kind. We shall have to determine the degree to which this is true. Those who think it true have a tendency to speak teleologically of Italian Renaissance 'modernity' in contrast with the medieval world. The 'bourgeois' Italian commune, thereby, becomes the harbinger of that much later liberal state, where religion is private and a matter of political indifference, where feudalism and the patrimonial *familia* are discarded, and where economic individualism funds liberty and civic rights of the kind that are only preserved in republican constitutions, never in monarchies. What follows is an attempt to preserve us from such anachronisms.

Communal Discourses and Citizenship

There is now no doubt that the political *structures* which evolved in Italian communes to foster their new economic activities and independence owed little to ancient or late imperial Rome. Instead, they were indigenous solutions to medieval problems, accretions of customs and dilutions of classic Roman law, each city establishing its own rules as the consequences of its traditions, interests and circumstances. Without written constitutions, communes operated under local customs, laws, regulations or statutes that established the functions and duties of magistrates and the composition of councils that were different from those of their neighbours. Into the sixteenth century the idea persisted that each city-state was unique and hence there was resistance to adopting 'foreign' forms of government. This produced characteristic civic outlooks and local patriotisms that were, perhaps, unrivalled anywhere else in Europe. Men thought of themselves as Paduans, Florentines, Genoese or Venetians rather than Italians. The destiny of one's town was seen as the work of its citizens whose individual and collective welfare were the outcomes of their own endeavours, both economic and political. The respective mechanisms of different cities' governance had emerged through trial and error, momentary leaders rising to power as manipulators of temporary factions and, most notably, grouping around pro-papal or pro-imperial positions. The city-states of northern and central Italy were geographically located in a place of extraordinary political pressures. Marsilius of Padua has already given us some insight into their circumstances.

During the twelfth and thirteenth centuries internal turmoil was endemic to these cities, but if one reads the contemporary Italian writers on politics, notably the *dictatores*, one finds very little reference to the special problems of the city-state,[14] other than the observation that in every town there is a division and enmity between the two parties of

---

14   For instance, 'the problem of incorporating new territories and new populations into its existing structure, of involving really large numbers of people in its political life . . . its relative military weakness and hence, its tendency to become the victim of conquest'. See J. R. Strayer, *On the Medieval Origins of the Modern State* (Princeton, NJ, 1970), p. 11; and Hyde, *Society and Politics*, pp. 104ff.

citizens, the magnates and the people.[15] Instead, one finds a *theory* of communal govern-ance which is meant to minimize this factionalism, through concord, drawing on Ro-man moralists and Aristotle, when he became available, to insist that citizens are meant to rule and be ruled in turn, under one law. Many of these manuals were addressed to the office of the *podestà*, giving administrative and military advice along with assistance in speech-making, such as the *Oculus pastoralis,* John of Viterbo's *Liber de regimine civitatum* and Brunetto Latini's *Li Livres dou Trésor.* The genre in which these manuals was written is similar to that of the 'mirrors for princes' written elsewhere in Europe and which were also often addressed to city officials as well as kings. Where Italians addressed the *podestà* and referred to *seignors* or *sires*, for instance, the English adapted the same message but altered the official titles to *soverain, governour* or *meire* (mayor). If we wish to know more about the 'nitty-gritty' *practice* of city governance, in Italy or elsewhere, we must read the writings of local historians and chroniclers, and especially for Italy, dig in the aston-ishingly rich communal archives, rather than these moralizing 'political theorists' of the commune.[16]

Their restricted debt to their inheritance of ancient Rome and especially to Justinian's *Corpus* was perhaps most sharply expressed in the explicit concerns of thirteenth-century lawyers and local political 'theorists', in Italy the *dictatores* who taught public oratory, to seek technical definitions of citizenship, which are, for the most part, absent from Jus-tinian's collections. Jurists defined the city and validated it simultaneously.[17] And teach-ers of oratory like the thirteenth-century notary Brunetto Latini who had himself studied in Paris, returned to Florence to observe: 'The city is a gathering of people formed to live justly. Thus they are not called citizens of the same commune because they were accepted together inside the same walls, but rather, citizens are those who have agreed to live under one law'.[18] But if Latini intended his work for an exclusively Florentine 'republican' audience, his early fourteenth-century readers in England, a monarchy rather than a republic, thought his views applicable to their own situation too. Excerpts from

15   See the account of the late thirteenth- and early fourteenth-century historian Dino Compagni, *Cronica,* ed. G. Luzzato (Turin, 1968) and English translation by D. E. Bornstein: Dino Compagni, *Chronicle of Florence* (Philadel-phia, 1986), for whom internal strife, notably between the Guelfs/Ghibellines, Whites/Blacks and nobles and *popolo* is accepted as the (lamentable) norm in Florence.

16   See for instance N. Rubinstein, *The Palazzo Vecchio 1298–1532: government, architecture and imagery in the civic palace of the Florentine republic* (Oxford, 1995); G. Cadoni, ed., *Provvisioni Concernenti L'Ordinamento della Repubblica Fiorentina, 1494–1512,* vol. 1 (Rome, 1994).

17   Justinian's prohibition on interpretation actually led, during the Middle Ages and Renaissance, to jurists claim-ing authority in matters of language and meaning, taking the place of the authorities to which they were meant to be subservient. For an excellent study of the very great extent to which Renaissance lawyers relied not only on their medieval predecessors but were continuators of the scholastic arts faculty studies of grammar, logic and forensic rhetoric, based on the core texts of Aristotle, see I. Maclean, *Interpretation and Meaning in the Renaissance: the case of law* (Cambridge, 1992).

18   *Li livres du trésor,* III, 72–3. Note the parallel with Aristotle's statement at *Politics* III, iii/(i), 1276a25–1276b15 that a *polis* is not regarded as a unity because it has walls but, rather, the state is a kind of association or partnership of citizens in a constitution, that is, obeying the same law. Latini explicitly mentions Aristotle's *Nicomachean Ethics* as the source of his account of politics as the science of prudence, but refers to Cicero's view that cities assemble men to live under one law. Similarly, in arguing that ruling a city requires the ability to speak in a way that benefits a community of free and equal citizens, for without language there can be no justice, no friendship and no humane community (III, 1), Latini sought to harmonize Cicero with Aristotle's views on language and the political commu-nity in *Politics* I.

his tract were copied into the *Liber customarum* of London, the administrative heart of the English monarchy.

Latini is typical of all the *dictatores* in that he speaks in this work of how all lordship and dignity come from God and that to ensure the good ordering of this world, God wills that governments of towns should be sustained by justice, reverence and love. Justice belongs to the governor and is so firmly enclosed in his heart that he shall do right to everyone. Citizens must have reverence, for that is the one thing in the world which secures the merits of faith and endures all sacrifices. Love must belong to both ruler and ruled; the ruler must love his 'subjects' with a true heart and pure faith, watching night and day for the common welfare of the whole city and all the people. In turn the 'subjects' or citizens must love their ruler with true heart and honest intent; giving him counsel and aid to sustain his office. The mayor (in London) or the magistrate (in Florence) is the head of the citizens, and everyone desires to have a sound head, for if it were unsound, all the limbs would be sick. The people must, above all, study how to have such a governor as will lead them to a good end, according to right reason and justice. They must choose him not by lot or chance, but by full provision of wise and careful counsel.[19] We have heard this message before.

Nor was it communal Italians alone who were called citizens, even by Italians themselves. The distinguished fourteenth-century civil jurist Bartolus of Sassoferrato spoke of the kings of France and England as Roman citizens, *cives Romani*, and all people who obey holy mother church *sunt de populo Romano!*[20] This reminds us to remain aware, despite local, historical peculiarities, of the underpinning Christian discourse of community, no matter how attenuated or legalized its momentary formulation.

The extraordinary concern to seek definitions, of the good ruler or magistrate, or of citizenship, was characteristic of medieval schools in general, and of law faculties and practising lawyers in particular. Learned men thought and operated within corporatist or conciliar paradigms that suited a European society with numerous collective and consensual practices. And the mobility of town populations was assumed almost everywhere, a fact that gave rise to concerns about citizen rights and, even more, obligations. In Italy in particular, there were compulsory transfers of population to strategically fortified places or when a city destroyed one fortified area and decreed that they were no longer to be inhabited. Furthermore, with numerous merchants involved in long-distance trade and finance, and with immigrants from the surrounding countryside arriving, cities by the middle of the twelfth century were engaged in 'making citizens', nominating men to a kind of nobility in order to create a larger class of men who would owe the commune military service.

The civilian Bartolus, in the fourteenth century, observed that the acknowledgement of citizenship is a convention of civil law, based on the *ius gentium* rather than on natural law; citizenship is a convention of the law of the *civitas*.[21] No contemporary juristically

---

19 *Munimenta Gildhallae Londoniensis*, vol. 2, ed. H. T. Riley (London, 1859–62), pp. 16–24; see S. Reynolds, 'Medieval Urban History and the History of Political Thought', *Urban History Yearbook, Leicester* (1982), pp. 14–23 from which this summary of Latini, slightly modified, comes. Brunetto Latini, *Li livres dou trésor*, ed. P. Chabaille (Paris, 1863), pp. 575–620, with the London text referring to Latini at pp. 575–81, 611–14, 608–11.

20 Bartolus, *Corpus Iuris Civilis* ad D. 49.15.24 para. Hostes.

21 'Est . . . constitutio iuris civilis que facit aliquem civem propter originem vel propter dignitatem vel propter adoptionem . . . immo est dicendum quod omnes sunt cives civiliter'; text edited in J. Kirschner, 'Civitas sibi faciat civem' in *Speculum* 48 (1973), pp. 694–713.

minded Englishmen would have disagreed; the common law and custom which were established in England as opposed to the Roman law, also saw urban citizenship as a convention of town law and custom based on the *ius gentium* which sustained all contracts.[22] Furthermore, contractual relationships between kings and subjects were widespread: in German-speaking lands, the emperor and other princes entered into contractual agreements with subjects, including cities; this was especially the case in the mercantile–industrial areas of the Netherlands. Bartolus noted that in practical terms, a foreign merchant who was made a citizen of a city-state by law would be considered as much a *civis verus*, a true citizen, as would a native inhabitant. The convention of the civil law acknowledged his free acceptance of the public authority of the government and this, says Bartolus, transforms the individual into a public person with liberties recognized before the law, a law to which he had himself freely assented and by which he was then bound by civic obligations. The picture is one of an *already* creative, voluntary agent, capable of engaging in contractual obligations and being recognized as such by the law of the *civitas*.[23]

For Baldus de Ubaldis, somewhat later in the fourteenth century, political agency is a product of incorporation into a *civitas or regnum*. The *civitas* is only one such constitutional manifestation of man's political nature. Membership of the *populus* imbues the social individual with active political characteristics which he would lack were he not so incorporated. The political, civil man, as a member of the citizen body, is thereafter a particular kind of perfected social man. His citizen status is an acknowledgement of his capacities as well as a grant of liberty to engage as an active political agent in the community, of whatever kind.[24]

These, however, are the considered statements of intellectual jurists. Waley has observed that most Italian city codes paid little attention to the nature of citizenship and its modes of acquisition, and that there was not a large element in the population knocking angrily at the door for admission to the privileges of citizenship.[25] And Hyde has noted that as the Italian communes grew, they did not build up a citizen body with uniform rights. The population was instead divided into numerous legal and social categories.[26] The bigger issue, in fact, concerned eligibility for civic office, and citizenship was often conferred on those who had already performed civic duties or even on non-citizen residents, as in Padua. Some towns, on the other hand, granted a form of citizenship which carried no right to hold public office. Elsewhere, as in Parma, the General Council was made up of 'old and true citizens who perform and undertake the burdens and services of the commune', implying that the citizen was a property-holder or was to become one, or else, as in Pisa, one had to prove that one had been born there or that one's father had been. Citizenship could often be sold to pay off debts to mercenaries.

22 See Ockham, above.

23 See Bartolus, *Tractatus de regimine civitatis*, ed. D. Quaglione in *Il Pensiero Politico* 9 (1976), pp. 70–93. See the discussion of membership of the city–community: political man and citizenship, with reference to Bartolus and Baldus, in J. Canning, *The Political Thought of Baldus de Ubaldis* (Cambridge, 1987), ch. 4, esp. pp. 170–6. For an interesting discussion see P. Riesenberg, *Citizenship in the Western Tradition* (Chapel Hill, NC, 1992), esp. chs 4 and 5.

24 H. Walther, 'Die Legitimität der Herrschaftsordnung bei Bartolus von Sassoferrato und Baldus de Ubaldis', in E. Mock and G. Wieland, eds, *Rechts und Sozialphilosophie des Mittelalters* (Frankfurt, 1991), pp. 115–39; Canning, *The Political Thought of Baldus de Ubaldis*.

25 Waley, *The Italian City-Republics*, p. 51.

26 Hyde, *Society and Politics*, p. 107.

The attitude of communes to citizenship, therefore, varied with time and place, and this varied picture was repeated elsewhere in Europe.[27]

However, an understanding of the *status civitatis,* whatever the local conditions for its acquisition, emerges from an observation of the contractual genesis of the commune itself. This was the case throughout Europe, and not only in communal Italy, where oaths were taken by individuals or groups of people.[28] It is not the passive membership of the Roman *urbs* but the active adherence to the communal contract which designated the act of acquiring citizenship, everywhere. This was not unique to Italian cities.[29] City statutes in general imposed various obligations in the form of oaths (such as obedience to city officials, the prohibition against menacing the goods, peace and honour of the city, military service and the purchase and care of real property). Retrospectively viewed, only those recognized as full citizens, that is, those who were *in practice* party to the contract, had the right to participate in its political life and to hold office in the commune, thereby taking an active role in assemblies and approving laws, swearing in magistrates, electing others or being elected to city office. It is particularly clear in Italian communal statutes, but again, not unique to Italy, that the citizen with *optimo iure* status had the right to enjoy benefits, deriving from that communal solidarity, such as those which protected his goods and person.[30] Italian jurists, by the fourteenth century, came to speak of the various *de facto* means of acquiring and losing citizenship, and they distinguished between native citizenship – granted by being the son of a citizen or by having been born within the territory of the commune – and naturalized citizenship – a grant by the commune to a 'foreigner' and made on the petition of individuals or entire groups of people. By then, the granting of citizenship was becoming one of the commune's most solemn acts.

It is important that we discover just who these citizens were, especially when we consider Florence. At the start of the thirteenth century Florence had perhaps 50,000 inhabitants and nearly 100,000 at the century's close. We are speaking here of the city itself and not of the inhabitants of its outlying territories. What percentage were citizens?

---

27   For further examples see Reynolds, *Kingdoms and Communities in Western Europe*; S. Reynolds, *Introduction to the History of English Medieval Towns* (Oxford, 1977).

28   See G. Dilcher, 'The City Comunity as an Instance in the European Process of Individualization', in J. Coleman, ed., *The Individual in Political Theory and Practice* (Oxford, 1996), pp. 281–301, esp. with regard to Prussia; S. Reynolds, 'The History of the Idea of Incorporation or Legal Personality: a case of fallacious teleology', in *Ideas and Solidarities of the Medieval Laity: England and Western Europe* (Aldershot, 1995) item VI, pp. 1–20.

29   On the parallel and simultaneous argument of feudal contractualism and the juristic arguments in mercantile Italian city-states, see A. Black, 'The Juristic Origins of Social Contract Theory': 'It is not improbable that concern for civic independence was one reason why the contractual argument was of such interest to Italians' (p. 63). Black is right to argue for a dualism, feudal contractualism and the jurists' *ius gentium* origin of communes. Where, in Italian cities, a partnership or *societas* in the sense of a joint commercial venture was envisaged, this specific type of collectivity was characterized as having been created as a legal entity upon the mutual agreement of its members, adapting Roman law, *Digest* 17.2.5 and 19, where partnerships are drawn up by contract. The analogy between the *civitas* and *societas* was then drawn, as by the early sixteenth century M. Salamonio, *Orationes ad priores Florentinos,* in the *De principatu* (1512–14) (Black's citation, p. 70). For an excellent overview see A. Black, 'The Commune in Political Theory in the Late Middle Ages', in P. Blickle, ed., *Theorie kommunaler Ordnung in Europa* (Munich, 1996), pp. 99–112, who none the less argues that Italians alone produced anything approaching a communal ideology before the Reformation (p. 109).

30   E. Cortese, 'Cittadinanza (Diritto Intermedio)', in *Enciclopedia del Diritto,* VII (Milan, 1960), pp. 137–8. Also see G. Dilcher, in J. Coleman, ed., *The Individual in Political Theory and Practice,* esp. pp. 293–300 with references for Northern Europe.

And how many were actively involved in the city's governance or indeed eligible to be active? The distinction between citizenship on the one hand, and eligibility to civic office on the other, as pointed out above, is important. In general, at the end of the thirteenth century the greater councils of some communes ran to a thousand members and there is evidence that a high proportion of citizens acted as councillors, the minutes of these meetings revealing an impressive number of active participants. The question to which we shall return is: who, during the thirteenth, fourteenth, fifteenth and then, early sixteenth centuries, constituted the governing class in Florence? This will enable us to clarify just what republican self-rule was taken to mean, over three centuries and especially in Florence, Machiavelli's city.

Urban Commerce

If we look briefly at how Italian communes more generally shared in the urban experiences found elsewhere in Europe, we see that during the thirteenth century until the first decades of the fourteenth, there were three European 'nodes' of long-distance, international trade that formed a single circuit of exchange: east-central France where there were the fairs of Champagne; the textile-producing regions of Flanders, especially the towns of Bruges and Ghent; and the international trading ports of the Italian peninsula, notably Genoa and Venice. The Counts of Champagne, who during the twelfth and thirteenth centuries had established independent monopolies over fairs and merchants, setting up local systems of justice, taxation, enforced contracts and fines, were to lose out when, in 1285, their independent feudal territories came under the jurisdiction of the king of France. With the Champagne region absorbed by France, the French monarchy placed restrictions on Italian merchants' access to these fairs. The fairs were then shifted to Lyons which was half-way between Italy and Flanders. Italians, in port cities, and in Lombard and Tuscan towns, were thereafter motivated to find new sea routes to Bruges to collect Flemish woollens which would be processed in Florence into luxury cloth. Genoa and Venice, deadly rivals over these sea lanes, built galleys with all manner of navigational improvements, which were sailed in convoy and protected by 'state' warships. In exchange, Italians brought spices and silks from North Africa and the Middle East or through Muslim intermediaries from the Far East. Italians, engaged in this non-local trade, derived their prosperity from establishing connections with Constantinople, the Middle East and North Africa, putting Europe into contact with trade from the central Asian caravan circuit and, via Baghdad, southward through the Persian Gulf to the Indian Ocean.[31]

During the thirteenth century many Italian citizens were involved in one way or another in this long-distance trade and finance and were often away on business.[32] Indeed, during the twelfth and thirteenth centuries, merchants were often itinerant, but already during the thirteenth century the organization of Italian businesses began to change.

---

31   R. Lopez, *The Commercial Revolution*; Hyde, *Society and Politics in Medieval Italy*, pp. 158–64.

32   Waley, *The Italian City-Republics*, p. 18, provides an amusing, if unsubstantiated, remark that St Francis of Assisi, the founder of the Franciscan Order of mendicants, was called 'Francis' by his merchant father who was away in France at the fairs at the time of his birth in 1182. For a detailed overview see R. de Roover, *Money, Banking and Credit in Medieval Bruges: Italian merchant bankers, Lombards and money changers, a study in the origins of banking* (Cambridge, MA, 1948).

And increasingly during the fourteenth century, instead of travelling, the head partners of what were almost always family firms (the *fraterna* or its variant, *commenda/colleganza*) began to stay at home while salaried factors ran their branch offices abroad. Through developing new techniques of book-keeping they were able to amass large amounts of capital and could switch investments rapidly. Italian merchant bankers as 'branch managers' became permanently installed in resident colonies abroad, organized themselves into 'nations' or colonies composed of merchants of the same home city, and they secured official recognition of their incorporation, with commercial privileges, from the local authorities. With variations in complexity of the types of trade partnership extending beyond the family, there was a growing need for records and agreements to be notarized. In addition, once Italian merchants began to stay at home, a more complex instrument was required than the earlier contract: this was the bill of exchange, which was a document in which buyers and sellers agreed that payment would be made in a place that was different from the one in which the goods were to be delivered, and usually in the home currency of the seller. The methods of doing international business by correspondence with local factors, where foreign trade was now carried out by keeping accounts of bills of exchange, that is, where the mobility was that of capital rather than of merchants, became a virtual Italian monopoly well into the sixteenth century. An international trade in money and credit became as important as commerce in goods, and Italian merchant bankers monopolized the international exchange of money and credit.[33]

The Venetian Way

In each commune there was a special but different relationship between private entrepreneurial or venture 'capitalism' and the communal government that existed to defend and assist it. Venice, for example, with its municipal facility for shipbuilding, the Arsenal, replaced individual entrepreneurs with what some call virtual 'state capitalism' alongside sub-components of individual enterprise. The Arsenal built galleys to be commanded by a state-appointed captain who sailed within a convoy organized by the state. Furthermore, Venice does not seem to have imported its elite from the agricultural hinterlands but, rather, developed it indigenously. Therefore, it suffered less from inter-family feuds than most other Italian city-states whose nobilities derived from the landowning class and who perpetuated old feudal battles in the new arenas of urban business and competition for government office.[34] All communes required military commitments of both citizens and countryside dwellers, the 'citizen army', usually supplemented by mercenaries, of which we shall hear much from Machiavelli. In Venice, the fate of the nobles and the populace alike depended on the success of the commune's sea trade and the military prowess to sustain it. The crews of the merchant marine and the navy were the same people.[35] And the sheer volume of the recorded transactions suggests that in port

33   J. L. Abu-Lughod, *Before European Hegemony: the world system, AD 1250–1350* (Oxford, 1989), esp. pp. 91–4; also for extensive bibliography linking the Italian commercial world with Northern Europe, the Middle East, the Arab world, Asia and beyond.
34   F. C. Lane and R. Mueller, *Money and Banking in Medieval and Renaissance Venice*, vol. 1 (Baltimore, 1985); B. Kedar, *Merchants in Crisis: Genoese and Venetian men of affairs and the fourteenth-century depression* (New Haven, CN, 1976).
35   F. C. Lane, *Venice, a Maritime Republic* (Baltimore, 1973).

cities like Venice, business investment was not restricted to a small group of extremely wealthy investors but, rather, permeated the city's entire thirteenth-century economy.

The Venetian constitution was described as 'mixed' by the early fourteenth-century Dominican Henry of Rimini, whose writings retained their influence beyond his own times. But by the time Henry was writing (*c.* 1308) the anti-magnate legislation that many cities had passed to restrict the power of a hereditary nobility had failed. Henry praised the Venetian constitution by reference to Venice's stability which he thought came from public officials being *elected* by nobles and guildsmen (*honorabilitates*) acting together. The possibility of Florence adopting this Venetian form of government would become a matter of much debate in mid- to late fifteenth-century practical politics, the difference between Venice and Florence being in the manner in which offices where filled: by lot in Florence and by election within a restricted, privileged group in Venice. It is noteworthy that Henry makes no reference to the wider *popolo*, and speaks of the head magistrate, the Doge, as the monarchical element in this republican 'mixed' constitution. Henry's preference is for a Venetian 'mixed' constitution that is aristocratic, the best of the simple constitutional forms, but he admits that if the constitution were absolutely the best, it should be a monarchy.

By the end of the fourteenth century and at the beginning of the fifteenth, humanists would further develop the myth of Venice. Pier Paolo Vergerio the Elder left a fragmentary *De Republica Veneta* but he also composed a treatise *On Monarchy* addressed to the noble Carrara family. In the latter he argued that peace can only be secured under hereditary *signori*. Like many theorists he was engaging in the rhetorical argument *in utramque partem*, arguing from both sides of a case in respectively different tracts. But when he spoke of the Venetian republic he praised it as a mixture, comprised of an aristocracy with a Doge elected for life. Machiavelli was to be perhaps the only early sixteenth-century Florentine political thinker who was not an admirer of Venice, although he recognized that among contemporary republics Venice stood out. Vergerio had observed that in Venice the power of the Great Council and the whole city actually resided in the Council of 100 called the Senate, while the people had no power. Machiavelli, as we shall see, thought this unsuitable for Florence's more popular republic. But Venice, which remained a republic when most other cities had been taken over by despots, is a good example of how a republican constitution survived by responding to changing economic and political situations: the governing class was narrowed into a mixture of monarchical and aristocratic elements, and hence the popular element in the mixture became a tradition that had died. We shall need to recall this Venetian solution when we treat more fully of the fifteenth-century Florentine republic, in practice and in rhetoric.

Perhaps the most characteristic practice of the Venetian and Florentine communes' 'state' activity was their reliance on loans, voluntary or forced: a funded state debt paid by citizens. By the beginning of the thirteenth century, citizens voluntarily leant money to the commune in return for 'shares of stocks' which paid regular, if variable, interest. These shares were redeemable when the commune's funds were plentiful. By the end of the century both Florence and Venice developed a system of forced loans to finance their respective merchant–military campaigns. This institution of public debt, either voluntary or levied according to percentage of family wealth, shaped the specific relationship between the city government and its merchant wealth. In general, the city-state was seen as an outlet for profitable investment. One would expect that merchants were eager to participate in, that is, control, 'state' decision-making, especially if government was run as a corporation of merchant proto-capitalists.[36]

Undoubtedly Italian geography played its role in the formation of a few large dominions ruled by urban communes whose government structures expanded and adapted to their increasing mercantile wealth. Both Florence and Venice established commercial agreements abroad and mercantile and financial independence at home. Both cities saw the transformation of an older communal government into government by a ruling class, in effect an oligarchy, comprised of a mercantile patriciate, sustained by an organization of various craft guilds. But by the mid-fourteenth century, the public debt of Italian city-states grew to be enormous. Furthermore, in Florence, several of the most important banking houses ran into bankruptcy. European monarchs, dependent on Italian bankers, defaulted on loans. Economic instability and political factionalism across Italy by mid-century would lead a number of the city-states to abandon, if they had not already done so, the communal rule by a merchant patriciate in favour of more dictatorial rule by a single strong man, the 'prince'. Florence attempted to resist this, in one way or another, during the fifteenth century. Venice succeeded in resisting this in its own way rather longer.

Perceived Benefits of Citizen Status

Was the merchant or banker, once established at home, someone who saw it to be in his and his family's interest that he or his sons engage actively in the governance of the commune? Did it make a difference if this sedentary merchant was *nouveau riche* or whether he came from an old and noble family? How much of the answer is primarily a matter of individual families' economic self-interest? If definitions of citizenship were sought and found, across Europe, and especially in Italy, so too would definitions of nobility be sought and found across Europe, and especially in Italy, within the context of changing communal requirements, both economic and political. We must beware of collapsing the political into the economic. If we did so collapse the two we would be deaf to the peculiar and distinguishing characteristics of Renaissance political theory.

In Italy, the acquisition of citizen status was undoubtedly part of a complex strategy of individuals and families to achieve the material benefits of social status, benefits to their business life, protections in banking and commercial operations at home and abroad.[37] But this was supplemented by the acquisition of an identity that merged with their city's collective honour, wealth and power. Citizen status allowed one to be involved in approving at least, and administering at most, the commune's laws, whose jurisdiction over waterways, roads, markets, manufacturing, agriculture and taxes extended over the entire district. Did the juridical liberty envisaged as a property of citizenship mean anything to any family that was economically weak? Who, more precisely, cared, and for what reasons, about the establishment and maintenance of the city-state and the concomitant citizen obligations which many modern historians and political theorists often idealize in a contemporary, democratic–republican discourse of conscious, chosen,

---

36   Abu–Lughod, *Before European Hegemony*, pp. 114–15.
37   P. Riesenberg, 'Citizenship at Law in Late Medieval Italy', *Viator* 5 (1974), pp. 333–46; and more extensively, Riesenberg, *Citizenship in the Western Tradition*, ch. 4.

public engagement and collective obligation? Beneath this modern praise often lies the presumption of an individualist, liberal economy as motor. But can we apply modern strategies in so undifferentiated and determinist a manner to enable us to say that Italians, in the golden age of thirteenth-century self-rule, and thereafter during the fourteenth-century merchant patriciates, were driven primarily on the waves of self-interested economic expansion to assert their own forms of law-bounded community in order to serve private utility? This reduces to: liberal economy is always the necessary precursor of individual and communal freedom.

To consider the reasons for the putative attractiveness of citizen status in Italian communes takes us some way towards revealing aspects of a much larger question: the reasons on the part of any interest group for actively willing the creation of the city-state itself with a constitution capable of guaranteeing, through its institutions and laws, a collective autonomy beyond any one individual citizen's own lifetime. If one accepts, as I do, Michael Mann's explanation of the emergence of the (full blown and later) European national state, not as dependent on conscious human action (favoured by ideological and class explanations), but rather as an unintended consequence of human action, the state as 'interstitial emergence', then does the emergence of the earlier, politically autonomous republic in Italian cities share a similar genesis in unintentionality?[38]

When we come to discuss the transformation of the legacy of medieval ethical and political discourse in civic humanism, we shall see that economy was itself transformed by this ethical frame. This ethical frame prevented the adoption of a modern liberal notion of liberty as an individual freedom to pursue, unimpeded, whatever ends one may choose for oneself, so that the 'state' becomes a prudential means to private ends. The consequence is that the roots of liberalism will have to be sought elsewhere than in the Italian Renaissance and its various theorists' reflections on the relation between man and 'state'. We shall see that the humanist is tied far more to customs, traditions, indeed, to a mind set, shaped by a somewhat fictional ancient world filtered through Christian medieval perspectives, than he is a forerunner of that modern 'state' and the subject's obligations to it, to be found in Hobbes in the seventeenth century. In short, we shall indirectly be explaining why Machiavelli was not on his way to 'intending' what Hobbes later said.

Community, *Civitas*, Ranked Citizenship and Local Patriotisms

So far, I have attempted to set Italian urban experiences within a wider urban phenomenon across Europe. The collective and communal sentiment of this urban world, however, did not evolve suddenly as some strange form of civic bonding, unrelated and

---

38   Mann, *Sources of Social Power*, vol. 1, p. 436, in speaking of later European developments beyond the scope of this book, notes: 'The only interest group that consciously willed the development of the national state was the state elite itself, the monarch and his creatures, who were puny and pressured by inflation. The rest – the merchants, younger sons, clerics, and eventually almost all social groups – found themselves embracing national forms of organization as a by-product of their goals and the available means of reaching them. The national state was an example of the unintended consequences of human action, of "interstitial emergence". Every time the social struggles of these groups were occasioned by tax grievances, they were pushed farther into a national mould. The political struggles of the merchants above all, but of the landed nobility and the clergy too, focused more and more at the level of the territorial state.' It is important to underline that group goals were not uniquely economic.

opposed to earlier social networks. Nor was it unique to Italy. It emerged out of and sustained a range of assumptions regarding authority, power and loyalty that were typical of Christian discourse and its integration into a feudal society with its patrimonial system. The collective sentiment of *communitas* first developed out of kinship networks of the family and was later transferred to the concept of the *civitas*. Genealogies of kin were actively created and manipulated through dynastic marriages and unexpected social elevations of families with land or other forms of wealth and power. Both manifestations of collective sentiment, in family and city, bore some relation to a more extensive sense of social identity in the Christian community.[39] There was not an opposition between loyalty to the city and loyalty to the feudal overlord but, rather, a shift in the object of allegiance which none the less followed the same hierarchical patterning, just as it did when men joined other corporate structures, in the church or university, for instance.[40] Among the sustained characteristics was a notion of rank or status among citizens so that good government was said to be achieved when the common good is served 'secundum statum suum', that is, when honours and financial rewards are divided up according to one's status, 'quando honores et munera equaliter dividuntur secundum debitos gradus'.[41] Cicero's sentiments on differential due expressed in his *De inventione* and *De officiis* could be, and were, accommodated to the aristocratic and feudal structures which remained in commercial Italy. Aristotle's arguments in favour of merit and retrospectively judged commitment to the common good on the part of active citizens, as expressed in his *Ethics* and *Politics*, were likewise accommodated to the aristocratic and feudal structures which remained in commercial Italy. Both ancient authors were similarly adapted elsewhere. In Italy, not only was there a categorization of citizens into *maiores* and *minores* but numerous finer distinctions were drawn, largely in terms of wealth, sometimes of birth, which encompassed the non-noble people (*popolani*), rich and poor, 'new men' (*gente nuova*) who had recently come to play a more prominent role in city politics, the older nobles, and the newly arrived. Across Europe, in communities of all kinds, there was, likewise, a general acceptance of social inequality and hierarchy, and a determination to draw finer distinctions between rank and status. But, as in Italian communes, this was to be balanced by an expectation that law and right custom should enable different groups and orders to live in harmony.

Quaglioni has observed that individual nobility and honour in Italian cities came to be measured against those of the *civitas* to which one belonged. It was considered that there was more power and status in being a citizen of a noble and honourable city than in being a citizen of only a mediocre city, as the civilian Bartolus observed.[42] The

39   See Mann, *The Sources of Social Power*, vol.1, esp. pp. 380–1 for an amusing hypothetical, sociological reconstruction of collective identities, *c.* 1150, the researcher being armed with questionnaires, tape recorders and the necessary skills in archaic local languages: 'The main conclusion is unmistakable. The most powerful and extensive sense of social identity was Christian, although this was both a unifying transcendent identity and an identity divided by the overlapping barriers of class and literacy', and cross-cutting these divisions were commitments to local and more national obligations.

40   J. Verger, 'The Contribution of Medieval Universities to the Birth of Individualism and Individual Thought', in J. Coleman, ed., *The Individual in Political Theory and Practice* (Oxford, 1996), pp. 59–77, on the university experience releasing students from former constraints and alliances.

41   Bartolus, *Tractatus de regimine civitatis*, ed, D. Quaglioni, *Politica e diritto nel Trecento Italiano* (Florence, 1983), I, 24–5, 31–2, p. 150.

42   D. Quaglioni, 'The Legal Definition of Citizenship in the Late Middle Ages', in A. Molho, K. Raaflaub and J.

citizens of specific Italian cities also expressed crude patriotic views about either the French or the Germans, partly determined by whether their city had a history of being pro-papal or pro-imperial. These attitudes were not encouraged uniquely in Italy however.

In England, a similar patriotic rhetoric explained that there was more power and status to be had from being an Englishman, subject to the laws and customs of England and her king, than from being a Frenchman, whose national characteristics were said to be effeminate, and whose people were subject to a fraudulent and illegitimate king![43] Sporadic and continuous warfare across Europe spawned propaganda everywhere about the fecklessness, lack of courage, and illegitimacy of other governments and peoples in comparison with one's own traditions, real or imagined. From at least the fourteenth century on, local patriotisms across Europe and not only in Italy, came to be connected with an increasing interest in the cult of classical antiquity, encouraging writers to dig through their recent and medieval pasts to reveal that their country or city too had been part of Rome's outreach. Fourteenth-century popes, resident in Avignon, collected impressive libraries of classical Latin writings and encouraged authors to 'invent' classicizing commentaries on the Bible or to comment on Livy's history of Rome. The Germans, for their part, emphasized the Roman historian Tacitus's acknowledgement of their ancestors' valour and the French focused on Caesar's commentaries which referred to the sterling character of the Gauls. The fourteenth-century English bishop of Durham, Richard de Bury, argued that one could not understand the church Fathers or the Bible if one did not have access to the classical poets. All sorts of peoples across Europe saw themselves as descendants of Brutus or from Troy. Increasing antipathies between cities and nations continued well into the sixteenth century, helping to define Europeans more clearly to themselves, often based on developed prejudices, fictitious or 'historical', about others.[44]

But in Italy there was a special appropriation of classical Rome, its republican history and an attempted revival of its language, curiously at the same time that the vernaculars across Europe, and not only in Italy, were beginning to win the argument as the means of general communication. Machiavelli's *The Prince* was written in Italian and not in humanist Latin. Even works first written in Latin were rapidly translated into vernaculars, leaving Latin as the medium of international exchange in matters of scholarly concern by the sixteenth century. The Italian appropriation of ancient Roman history, however, led them to see other European nations as 'barbarians', and in the process they conveniently forgot that, say, the Lombards had a similar 'barbarian' origin prior to being absorbed into the Roman Empire. A major aspect of the local patriotisms of Italian communes, especially in Florence, would be a notably refined construction of their continuous history from ancient Rome to their present, missing out several hundred years of their more recent, medieval past, while at the same time seeing few distinctions between ancient, pagan virtues and those praised as Christian.

Emlen, eds, *City-states in Classical Antiquity and Medieval Italy* (Ann Arbor, 1991), pp. 155–67; J. Kirschner, '"Civitas sibi faciat civem": Bartolus of Sassoferrato's doctrine on the making of a citizen', *Speculum* 48 (1973), pp. 694–713; J. Kirschner, 'Paolo di Castro on "cives ex privilegio": a controversy over the legal qualifications for public office in early fifteenth century Florence', in A. Molho and J. A. Tedeschi, eds, *Renaissance Studies in Honor of Hans Baron* (Florence, 1971), pp. 227–46.

43 See J. Coleman, *Medieval Readers and Writers, 1350–1400* (London, 1981), pp. 71–8.

44 J. Hale, *The Civilization of Europe in the Renaissance* (New York, 1994), pp. 29 and 51; see also J. Coleman, *Ancient and Medieval Memories*, ch. 23, pp. 538–99.

Indeed, at the end of the fourteenth century, the early humanist Petrarch wrote a letter to the Roman historian Livy[45] where he says he wishes either that he had been born in Livy's age or Livy in Petrarch's. He has no problems imagining himself maintaining his own values and ideals were he transported back to Livy's age or that Livy, if transferred to the fourteenth century, would have the slightest problem understanding Petrarch's lay Christian sermonizing. Petrarch would praise man's moral autonomy and show it to be a concern shared by the pagans Cicero and Seneca as well as by Christians, for what else, he thought, is the concern for the individual in the Christian doctrine of grace and justification? Similarly, in Florence, the ancient republic of Rome, which Italians uncovered further by ransacking monastic libraries, was not to be taken as Florence's model. Rather, ancient Rome was to be used as Florence's fortuitous historical justification. The Roman past would not be taken to be a blueprint on which to base Florence's future, but, when correctly interpreted and used, as Bruni and others believed, it was to be understood as a reaffirmation of her present success. To the Renaissance historians of Italian communes, history taught prudence, by which was meant that history is useful for justifying one's own affairs. We shall see how Italian Renaissance rhetorical history engages a distinctive sense of the past *as present* and what the consequence is for Renaissance political theorizing of the kind in which Machiavelli engaged in his *Prince* and *Discourses on Livy*.

The Involvement of Citizens in Late Thirteenth-century Communal Government

By the mid-thirteenth century it was claimed that the Italian cities 'live by the laws they make themselves'. Communes engaged an extraordinary zeal in constitutional fine-tuning and legislation, reorganizing city statutes, and arranging collective finance, in part to secure revenue to pay for official salaries, but even more to cover the cost of numerous wars – with one another. Neighbouring cities having become neighbouring powers, a city's neighbour rapidly became its enemy, so that rival civic patriotisms were consciously nurtured and actively engaged, externally, in the conduct of wars and diplomacy. In fact, one of the signs of increasingly intense civic patriotism was the growth in a laudatory genre of literature praising the writer's own commune in overblown and idealistic terms. Here, everyone is a lover of justice and his city is the most noble, with a *populus* that is wise, good, free and wealthy. The period of the later thirteenth and early fourteenth century is the 'golden age' of city panegyrics, when civic patriotism was said to ensure the failure of external tyrants.

Internally, Italian city-states also set the conditions of sale, fixed prices and rates of interest, and decided maximum wages for certain categories of labourers. Since expenditure was met from taxation and loans, hearth taxes, property taxes, tolls, customs duties, and taxes on commercial transactions were continuously revised (and usually increased). Great expense was incurred on beautifying each city, building new cathedrals as well as public 'palaces' and civic spaces.[46] Each commune's concern for official, 'state' art, that is,

---

45 *Epistolae Familiares*, xxiv, 8.
46 See details for Florence in N. Rubinstein, *The Palazzo Vecchio*, ch. 1.

its visual 'propaganda', was mirrored by similar concerns of other patrons including craft guilds, notable families and the church. That so much of this official art still survives today is almost a miracle and it allows a visitor to Italian cities to experience, in concrete form, the collective, communal ideology which survives elsewhere more often in dusty libraries.

Communal outreach also extended to church properties where, as in the rest of Europe, they argued over the limits of the two jurisdictions and the degree to which the church could maintain fiscal exemptions when the 'city-state' was threatened. The relationships between communes and local clergy were complex. Communes, like territorial nation-states elsewhere, had weak claims to interfere in the appointment of ecclesiastical office and many bishops came from a city's more prominent families. The local records provide us with a microcosmic picture of intermittent judicial warfare with clerical authorities of the kind that Marsilius of Padua magnified into a general disease of papal interference through-out Italy and extending Europe-wide. Cities were motivated to extend their own authority at the expense of older seignorial ties, at the expense of the empire, at the expense of local ecclesiastical powers, and at the expense of the papacy. The imperial presence, by the end of the thirteenth century, however, became less of a threat than the machinations of local magnates, ecclesiastical grandees and foreign expansionist powers.

The Communal Ideal and the Menace of Factions

In fact, despite the dream of communal concord, and the hoped-for unity of public civic sentiment, so eloquently expressed in urban panegyrics, seething beneath the surface was an internal enmity between nobles or magnates and 'the people' in each and every commune. The common good was menaced by factions. The magnates were sometimes landed aristocrats, some but not all of ancient feudal descent, and were themselves often involved in commerce so that they lived partly in the commune but also had rural estates. Over the years, it became increasingly difficult to define the magnate in legal terms, some becoming members of the *popolo*, but by common repute were called *potentes*, the men with power, nobles. The reference was to an individual's family from which he derived his reputed standing. Nobles constituted a corporation within the commune, with extended feudal components, and within this corporation were rivalries and long-enduring family vendettas. Noble families built defensive towers in communes 'for do-ing harm to their enemies' and the magnate relied on his extended *familia* to provide his private, military retinue. Communes recognized the dangers of these retinues as rivals to their own control in the city. Nobles were perceived as a law unto themselves or, at least, as concerned to flout the laws of the commune through their maintenance of forms of feudal power, privilege and vassalage. Most modern historians focus on a his-tory of the thirteenth-century communes struggling against these magnates and achiev-ing some remarkable successes if only for a relatively brief period. But to read the chronicles of this period which chart extra-communal events, one sees another perspective: that which focuses on the histories of regional, rival magnate families (the Visconti, the Da Romanos, the Estensi, etc.), with the history of the communes, which they dominated, as something of a side-issue in their pursuit of seignorial power.[47]

---

47   See for instance the chronicle of Ezzelino and Alberico da Romano by Gerardo Maurisio, in Gerardi Maurisii, *Cronica dominorum Ecelini et Alberici fratrum de Romano*, ed. G. Soranzo, *Rerum Italicarum Scriptores*, viii, 4 (1913–14).

In opposition to these magnates was 'the people', led by prominent and successful guildsmen, who were merchants, wealthy craftsmen and educated professionals such as lawyers and notaries. 'Mechanics and plebs', agricultural labourers, men without property, 'need not apply' if only because it was feared that they were servants of the magnates. The people, *popolani*, also constituted a corporation comprising distinctions between the better and more powerful, and the poorer. It is the success of the guild-structured *popolani* during the early to middle thirteenth century in achieving for themselves a constitutional role in the governance of the commune, especially against the magnates, that is seen as a distinctive moment in the creation of Italian, republican, constitutional government.[48]

Let us not get overly excited about this. Their success did not last. It may have been because economic and social mobility led too many into becoming magnates themselves, or because 'the people' divided themselves into internal factions driven by envy and more local and conflictual loyalties. Italian city-republics, despite the idealizing and inspiring rhetoric of the *dictatores*, were, on the ground, precarious, and they suffered spectacularly in the catastrophes of the mid-fourteenth century, notably during the Black Death which affected the whole of Europe. But even well before the economic disasters of mid-century, all but a very few (although important) Italian communes had settled for the rule of *signori*. Conciliar or corporatist government, regulated by law, had been abandoned in favour of unity and efficiency which it was thought could be found in the personal and familial regimes of despots. Although the republican communes did not provide stable regimes, what they had provided was a complex and active corporate, civic mentality, tied not simply to revived historical myths of a Roman past, but to personal and familial social and economic success and an impulsion to collective self-governance, not only to sustain and extend that success but to include in the meaning of 'success' an engagement in rule-making and the corporate expression of consent. The past of the ancients, perceived as *their* Roman–Italian past, was grist to their ideological mill. But when communal factionalism seemed unending and without resolution, even before the moment when it became clear, mid-fourteenth century, that something was seriously wrong with the economy, communes that had not already accepted the *signori* also sought an answer in the rule of a strong man. The early decades of the fourteenth century may already be regarded as the end of an era. There were ambitious men readily available who sought to govern by their own will rather than by the commune's laws. All over Italy they gradually came to power in one way or another. The offices of *podestà* or of Captain of the People served as the two-fold routes to power of the despotic *signori*. From offices with limited tenure came an office, sometimes for life.

The success of the *signori* is a history of the triumph of tyrannies, sometimes modified by remnants of communal, republican institutions, over full-blown communal, republican rule. It is not the triumph of constitutional monarchy over constitutional republics. It begins in parts of Italy as early as in the mid thirteenth century, often sustained by imperial legitimization, continues into the fourteenth and, by the fifteenth century, it is rampant.[49] When fifteenth-century humanists recalled the rise of the *signorie* in north and central Italy during the thirteenth century, they recalled the then contemporary

---

48   For the complicated story of the rise of the *popolo* in different cities and their leaders, see Hyde, *Society and Politics in Medieval Italy*, pp. 108–18; P. Jones, *The Italian City-state* (Oxford, 1997).

49   See Hyde, *Society and Politics in Medieval Italy*, chs 5 and 7 for the story into the fourteenth century.

perception of the fundamental antithesis between despotic rule and rule that was characterized by the *libertas populi*, where the people lived in liberty (*popoli che vivono in libertà*).

In the fifteenth century they replaced the earlier term for commonwealth as found in
Moerbeke's translation of Aristotle's *Politics*, the *politeia*, with the term *respublica*. And the
difference they highlighted between a republican and a despotic regime was the contrast
between absolute and arbitrary exercise of government, on the one hand, and the exercise of government limited by law and popular will, on the other.[50] The contrast was, of
course, the one with which we have already become familiar from medieval political
theory tracts. The communes with governments limited by law and popular will which
survived into the fifteenth century were rare and, as we shall see, the most famous ones,
Florence and Venice, came to be, in their respective ways, either extended or narrow
oligarchies or, if viewed with favour, extended or narrow aristocracies. The political
class in either case by the fifteenth century was considerably narrower than the one
which participated in self-government for brief periods during the thirteenth- and early
fourteenth-century golden age.

The Evolution of the Florentine Governing Class

If we turn back to the Florence of the thirteenth century, we discover that from the
origins of the Priors in 1282 until the 1340s, the high offices in Florentine city government were dominated by a narrow but shifting oligarchy, and this maintained a kind of
continuity with the character of the communal government under the regime of the so-
called *popolo* of the late thirteenth century. But the attitude to holding office in general
was one which was inclusive at the end of the thirteenth century, and it appears to have
emerged from a corporate expectation that 'what touches all should be agreed to by all';
hence, membership in guilds entailed the right to hold office and be represented. The
object of elections was not to give individuals the right to express their private opinions
but to represent the whole community. From the acclamations in open assemblies to the
co-options of councils, the methods of voting were designed to express the will of the
community as a corporate whole in conformity with law and custom. It was the Florentine
guild community, by the end of the thirteenth century, which had imposed its own
definition of republican government on the institutions of electoral politics. But this was
to be defeated by an oppositional oligarchy at the end of the fourteenth century. Najemy
has traced the century-long conflict between what he calls the corporate approach to
political organization of the guild community, and the consensus-based approach developed by the oligarchy. He has observed a fundamental clash between proponents of
corporatism and of consensus revealed in the two competing conceptions of communal
society and politics. In the process, he has traced the changes in the perceived scope of
governmental authority and the size and composition of the class of citizens allowed to
exercise this authority.[51]

There has been an immense amount of research into the relative degrees of governmental openness to new men throughout the fourteenth century. It has been discovered

---

50 N. Rubinstein, 'Machiavelli and the Florentine Republican Experience', in G. Bock, Q. Skinner, M. Viroli,
eds, *Machiavelli and Republicanism* (Cambridge, 1990), pp. 3–16.
51 J. Najemy, *Corporatism and Consensus in Florentine Electoral Politics, 1280–1400* (Chapel Hill, NC, 1982).

that during the 1330s Florence lived under the narrowest government it had experienced since the end of the previous century. Up to the 1340s, after which they experienced serious financial and commercial troubles, Florentine merchants had ensured the city's exceptional commercial expansion, often at the expense of themselves engaging in political office. The high offices of the Florentine commune tended to rotate among the members of a restricted circle of families especially associated with the textile guilds along with some bankers and judges. Later on and especially during the fifteenth century, they could not so easily choose not to get involved. Wealthy Florentines would come to see government office of some kind or other as a possible, indeed, necessary career for their sons. By this time they had worked out, in theory and practice, a vision of communal government and its 'aristocratic' ruling group, and this was the vision to be reflected in the political theory of civic humanists.

If the thirteenth-century corporatist image was one based on guild principles, a republic based on a federation of equal and autonomous corporations, where members were equals, where there was collective rule of the full membership, a delegated quality of ascending executive authority, and a theory of consent recognizing the right of either direct participation or representation of each of the constituent parts of the corporation, by the fifteenth century the image was different.[52] By then, the great merchants and bankers, the landed and entrepreneurial interests of the oligarchy, rejected the idea of corporate guild equality. Instead, a hierarchy of guilds was confirmed, with the lawyers, international merchants and bankers comprising an elite. The oligarchs of the great international trading and banking families, despite their guild affiliations, saw themselves as a class apart that was united by business, patronage and family ties.

Through a series of fourteenth-century reforms in election procedures for the Priors, which took a middle road between oligarchic elitism and popular corporatism, the popular fear of the monopolizing of high office by very small coteries of powerful families was balanced by controls, maintained by scrutiny committees, on the size and composition of the political class in general. Guild nominations to high office were kept at numerically modest and politically safe levels and gradually there was a break with the tradition between guild membership and the right to elective office. This altered view of political eligibility, in no longer being a function of membership in a corporation, removed the constraints against upper-class families who were not continuously engaged in commerce.[53] From an expectation that office holding was on offer to citizens on an equal basis emerged the later civic humanist principle that at least the *hope* of office was denied to none, even if it could not be promised to all.[54]

The intermittent swings to a government that was open to more 'new men' throughout the fourteenth century had led to what is seen as a quantum leap in the admission of many more citizens to eligibility to election to office by 1382. This was the consequence of worsening internal factionalism, of having fought a disastrous and costly war against the papacy (1375–8) and then an uprising of woolworkers, known as the revolt of the Ciompi.[55] As in other European centres of production and commerce, cities in Italy also

52   Ibid., p. 9.
53   Ibid., pp. 174–5, 178–9.
54   Ibid., p. 182.
55   For details see ibid., pp. 167–262; G. Brucker, 'The Ciompi Revolution', in Rubinstein, *Florentine Studies*, pp. 314–56.

became increasingly 'class' polarized, with a patriciate at one end and labourers at the other.[56] A short-lived popular regime was established between 1378–82, which few wanted to recall thereafter. Only in the wake of the Ciompi did the Florentine government seem committed to broadening its political and social base, but it did this by co-opting into government as many 'middle-class and presumably conservative citizens' as possible.[57] If the lower classes were not considered fit for positions in government, the citizens who were eligible for office holding of some kind appear, by 1427, to have numbered around 10,000 men out of a population of 37,000.[58] Those eligible to high office, however, were much more limited in number. It was the members of families such as the Albizzi, the Uzzano, the Strozzi and the Ridolfi who had gained favoured political status after the restoration of the patrician government in 1382, and who would determine communal policy during the 1420s.

It was this later fourteenth- and early fifteenth-century constitutional structure of offices and eligibility to them, and not the government of the thirteenth century, which later Florentine generations seem to have regarded as the most significant manifestation of republican government yet experienced in Florence before the end of the century, and they either praised it or blamed it. Machiavelli blamed it, saying several times that Florentine government had never been what could truly be called a republic. In his *Discursus florentinarum rerum post mortem iunioris L. Medices* (c. 1519/20) and in his earlier *Discourses on Livy* he noted that the regime or *stato* in Florence since 1393, when it came under the influence of the Albizzi leadership, was a 'repubblica governata da ottimati' (a republic governed by optimates), effectively, an oligarchy, which lasted until 1434 when it was replaced by the Medici regime. His most severe criticism was that the regime excluded the *popolo*, 'who never played their part'.[59]

Nicolai Rubinstein has studied in detail the actual Florentine experience of government during the fifteenth century, treating the period before 1434, then the changes when the Medici magnates came to power, and after their expulsion in 1494.[60] He concluded that if what is meant by the Florentine republican experience is based on *eligibility to office,* then its range, despite all the gradations of that eligibility, was remarkably wide. But if we define the republican experience in terms of *actual participation in decision-making*, the picture is very different.[61]

Although there were about three thousand-odd posts to be filled each year, including minor administrative offices in the city and its territory, and membership in the legisla-

---

56   Compare studies on Flemish cities in the thirteenth and fourteenth centuries: W. Blockmans, 'Vers une societié urbanisée', in R. Doehaerd, ed., *Histoire de Flandre* (Brussels, 1983); D. Nicholas, *Town and Countryside: Social, Economic and Political Tensions in Fourteenth-Century Flanders* (Bruges, 1971); D. Nicholas, *The Van Arteveldes of Ghent* (Ithaca, NY, 1988).

57   D. Herlihy, 'The Rulers of Florence 1282–1530', in Molho, Raaflaub and Emlen, *City-states in Classical Antiquity*, pp. 197–221.

58   D. Herlihy and C. Klapisch-Zuber, *Les Toscans et leurs familles* (Paris, 1978), pp. 348, 375.

59   Cited in Rubinstein, 'Machiavelli and Florentine Republican Experience', p. 3.

60   Ibid., pp. 3–16; N. Rubinstein, *The Government of Florence under the Medici (1434–94)* (Oxford, 1966); N. Rubinstein, 'Oligarchy and Democracy in Fifteenth-century Florence', in S. Bertelli, N. Rubinstein and C. H. Smyth, eds, *Florence and Venice: comparisons and relations* (Florence, 1979), pp. 99–112; N. Rubinstein, 'Florentine Constitutionalism and Medici Ascendancy in the Fifteenth Century', in N. Rubinstein, ed., *Florentine Studies: Politics and Society in Renaissance Florence* (London, 1968), pp. 442–62.

61   Rubinstein, 'Machiavelli and the Florentine Republican Experience', p. 10.

tive councils – the Council of the People (over 300) and the Council of Two Hundred (established in 1411 without whose assent no military action could be undertaken, and with special responsibilities and powers) – the executive branch of government was occupied by a small, elite section of eligible citizens. 'The overriding experience the average Florentine citizen had of his republic must have been the power, and indeed the majesty, of the Signoria',[62] an executive which after 1382 was comprised of nine chief magistrates, comprising eight Priors and one standard-bearer (Gonfalonier) of justice. These had immeasurable power with authority to initiate legislation and with a right to intervene in criminal jurisdiction when public interest was thought to demand it. The Signoria deliberated jointly with two colleges comprising sixteen Gonfalonieri and twelve Buonuomini. They held these offices for short terms. But citizens would extend their notion of the governing body of their republic to other important magistracies: there was also the Otto di Guardia (eight), charged with 'state' security and they had extensive police powers. Then there was the Dieci di Balia (ten), who in times of war were in charge of military and diplomatic operations. Finally, there were the Ufficiali del Monte, who administered the funded debt and became the central financial magistracy of the commune.[63]

From the early fourteenth century, election to public office had been based on periodical vettings for eligibility, 'scrutinies', to office. Names of eligible citizens were then placed in separate pouches for different offices. Citizens who had been nominated did not know whether they had been made eligible until their names were withdrawn from the pouches. The secrecy of the electoral system was paralleled by the secrecy of the workings of the executive and legislative branches of government. But if the election process itself was secret, scrutinies were open to influence by citizens from prominent families canvassing members of the scrutiny commissions to nominate them. The periodical scrutinies were carried out by specifically convened commissions consisting of the Signoria, its two colleges, *ex officio* members and eighty additional members elected by the Signoria and Colleges. Hence, the executive played a key role in determining the very composition of scrutiny commissions. And the Signoria made regular use of extra-constitutional advisory committees, the composition of these meetings, *pratiche*, being determined by the choice of the Signoria. The choice was based on the convention of summoning eminent citizens, and here the aristocratic element of the republic, in practice, was most clear. The citizens, regularly summoned to these consultative meetings and whose advice was seldom ignored by the Signoria, represented the elite of the *reggimento*. In the early fifteenth century, there were about seventy such men.[64]

Florence was divided into sixteen districts each of which had an assembly presided over by the above-mentioned Gonfalonieri, who represented their districts in electoral scrutinies by nominating residents for eligibility to office. It was presumed that the sixteen Gonfaloniers, themselves members of the ancient military companies, were well-acquainted with the citizens of their districts. They helped the Commune distribute the tax burden that was allocated to their district. Meeting in the principle parish church they elected committees of residents to function as syndics for tax assessments. This gives

62   Ibid., p. 5.
63   Rubinstein, 'Machiavelli and the Florentine Republican Experience', p. 5; A. Molho, *Florentine Public Finances in the Early Renaissance, 1400–1433* (Cambridge, MA, 1971).
64   G. Brucker, *The Civic World of Early Renaissance Florence* (Princeton, NJ, 1977), p. 264.

us a view of the modicum of civic participation at the local level. But Rubinstein observes that even here, over a period of forty-six years studied, two thirds of the citizens who attended seem to have belonged to only ten to fifteen patrician families who ruled the city, and who also, therefore, provided leadership in the local world of these districts.[65]

And the role of the legislative councils, especially the Council of the People (300 members)? After matters were considered by the Signoria and voted on by them, resolutions were presented to the Council of the People for their assent. If the proposal was approved, it would (from 1411 and briefly thereafter for a few decades) be put before the Council of the Two Hundred, and if approved by them as well, it would be put into effect as law. To the Council of the People had been granted the concession of a veto. Although popular consent remained the legitimating principle of government, there was none of the earlier notion of representatives of equal and autonomous corporations, each with a will of its own, to establish the expression of consent. Instead, a notion of a unitary and general popular will was advanced, a will belonging to the whole people and capable of being expressed only through a general convocation. They were to be convened and to hear the proposals, expressing a unified consent as a single sovereign entity.[66] This is what was meant by the checks on executive authority and its dependence, *in the last resort*, on the will of the people as voiced in their legislative councils.

Comparisons are often made between these popular assemblies and the 'human legislator' of Marsilius of Padua's *Defender of Peace* whose explicit assent is required for law to be established. But there is no reference, as there is in Marsilius, to the reflective and disputative possibilities of individual citizens contributing to and modifying laws proposed to them by experts. Hence, the comparison with Marsilius's theory (and even possibly with later thirteenth- and early fourteenth-century Paduan practice) looks excessively optimistic. In fifteenth-century practice, these popular assemblies were summoned only on rare occasions to approve constitutional reforms or to grant full powers to specially elected councils (the 'experts' or *balìe*) for them to decide on such reforms. The parallel that seems more obvious is with what happened to ecclesiastical conciliarism by the mid-fifteenth century: a rejection of Constance and a failure of conciliarism at Basel, marking the decline of representative assemblies generally. Marsilius's position, in contrast, defended the ideal of free Lombard communes, like Padua, with its *consiglio maggiore* of a thousand members, before they were taken over by the ideology of the *signorie*.[67]

The fifteenth-century ladder of public office, then, began perhaps with a man's election to the consulate of one of the guilds – although he now need not have been a guild member to be eligible for public office – then communal offices, and finally the plateau of top offices in the government and administration: the Signoria and its Colleges, magistracies such as the Dieci di Balia, the Otto di Guardia and the Ufficiali del Monte. By 1429 a new magistracy (Conservatori di legge) had been created whose function was to exclude unqualified citizens from office-holding and the prosecution of those who abused

---

65   Rubinstein, 'Machiavelli and the Florentine Republican Experience', p. 11; D. V. Kent and F. W. Kent, *Neighbours and Neighbourhoods in Renaissance Florence: the district of the Red Lion in the fifteenth century* (New York, 1982), pp. 17–19, 77–8.
66   Najemy, *Corporatism,* p. 268.
67   See chapter 4, above, on Marsilius.

their public positions. By now, the ambition for office, especially on the part of those seeking the top positions, was riven with factionalism and the idealized 'aristocratic' republican regime of the early fifteenth century was replaced by the regime of Cosimo de' Medici after 1434.

From the beginning of the fifteenth century, the top citizens were the *reggimento*, and comprised a constellation of a remarkably small number of families. Despite the influx of new men at the end of the fourteenth century, 'the traditional oligarchy did well for itself',[68] proving itself durable and capable of recovery. In 1411 the *reggimento* comprised just over one thousand citizens; by 1433 this had risen to two thousand. The prevalence of certain families with proliferating branches who were made eligible to the highest offices is a key feature of these figures.[69] But after 1434 there were increasingly long intervals between scrutinies and the most powerful offices were more and more frequently filled by election in Medici councils and, in the case of the Signoria, through controls of the the the electoral procedures. The Signoria came to be elected by a select group charged with recruiting supporters of the Medici regime. Political participation was being determined from within the Medici inner circle.

The relation between citizenship and eligibility to office is most starkly revealed in statistics for the middle of the fifteenth century. When the citizen body had reached its largest recorded size in 1454–64 it appears that new families comprised only 15 per cent of all those represented (36 out of 244 families). By the mid-fifteenth century those who were 'viewed' for office were drawn chiefly from the proliferating branches of the same older houses. The legislative Councils of the People and of the Commune had come to be replaced with Medicean *balìe* and, from 1459, by a new Council of One Hundred. Even the *pratiche*, the traditional aristocratic advisory meetings, were virtually abolished and replaced by informal meetings in the Medici's palace. Participation in government at all levels underwent profound changes under the various Medici who 'ruled' the Florentine republic from 1434 until 1494, when they were thrown out. Temporarily.

Machiavelli thought the Medici regime from 1434 on inclined more to a *principatus* than to a *republica*. But if we ask whether the constitutional progress of the fifteenth century saw the replacement of the Florentine aristocratic republic of the early part of the century with a despotic prince, during what was, after all, sixty years of Medici dominance, most contemporary scholars answer 'no'. This is because, despite the increasing criticisms of various Medici regimes, most notably that of Piero de' Medici in 1465–6, the criticisms issuing from a loosely structured patriciate now forced to seek Medicean patronage, the 'republican experience' to be had in Florence throughout the century is thought to have had much in common with that which prevailed at the beginning of the century. There was still the elitist concentration of effective participation in decision-making in relatively small groups of citizens, and there was still a kind of social mobility to be had within the regime's structure of office. But as Machiavelli observed, the people, *il popolo*, did not play their part. Machiavelli favoured a *governo largo*, a republic with a role for the *popolo*. We shall examine below what he meant by this.

In 1494, with the Medici removed, a Great Council of over three thousand members was established in Florence. There was a great deal of enthusiasm. It was to exercise an

---

68   Najemy, *Corporatism,* p. 298.
69   Rubinstein, 'Machiavelli and the Florentine Republican Experience', p. 9.

unprecedented control over the executive Signoria and this Great Council provided the framework for Machiavelli's own republican experience. But admission to the Great Council was restricted to those citizens whose forebears, over the previous three genera- tions, had been made eligible to government under the Medici! As Rubinstein has observed,[70] its members became a virtually closed class that monopolized office-holding as well as legislation. Is this what Machiavelli favoured?

Who Wanted to Play an Active Role in Fifteenth-century Florentine Government?

How willing were Florentines to pay taxes and support the ever-mounting public debt? The answer depended on the city's commercial expansion. State expenditure and rev- enues grew enormously after the troubled 1340s and into the fifteenth century. Florence engaged in frequent and costly wars, expanding her sway over large parts of the territory of Tuscany. She acquired Arezzo (1384), Pisa (1406), Cortona (1411) and Leghorn (1421) through conquest. Preparation for or engagement in the state of war would be a constant element in Florentine territorial enlargement. Wars were fought with Milan (1423–8) and Lucca (1429–33). Between 1423 and 1433 Florence underwent a pro- longed fiscal crisis that affected the city's constitutional and institutional framework. The lack of funds, and the inability of the Florentine government to devise acceptable modes of raising them, led to the creation of governmental agencies which acted without much regard to established procedures. The authority to assess forced loans gradually passed into the hands of special plenipotentiary commissions (*balìe*), periodically appointed, and undermining the traditional authority of the legislature. The Medici bank wielded enor- mous economic power in these conditions, advancing loans to the commune and ex- tracting large amounts of interest on them. Cosimo de' Medici had advanced huge sums to Florence and reminded Florentines of his generosity.[71] The government, therefore, controlled patronage and wielded powers of taxation that could destroy the wealth of families. Its desperate fiscal needs prompted the government to open its offices to all who could pay, and those who paid high taxes got a trade-off: access to paid public offices. The very highest offices, however, did not carry salaries.[72]

A direct connection has been demonstrated between the institution of the public debt, with its forced contributions, and an increasing investment in works of art among the greater families in the fifteenth century. When wealth was assessed for tax purposes, items of household furnishings and domestic consumption were excluded. Private wealth in the form of paintings, wall-hangings, objets d'art was sheltered.[73] Wealthy Florentines found it to be in their interest to defend their property and family against the demands of the government by obtaining public office which could influence those who assessed taxes. City legislators liked to speak of their activities as renewing or extending the achieve-

---

70   In Bock, Skinner and Viroli, *Machiavelli and Republicanism*, p. 15.
71   R. de Roover, *The Rise and Decline of the Medici Bank* (Cambridge, MA, 1963); R. Goldthwaite, *Private Wealth in Renaissance Florence* (Princeton, NJ, 1969); Molho, *Florentine Public Finances*, pp. 183–92.
72   Herlihy, 'The Rulers of Florence', pp. 212–13.
73   D. Herlihy, 'Family and Property in Renaissance Florence', in H. Miskimin, D. Herlihy and A. Udovitch, eds, *The Medieval City* (New Haven, CN, 1977), pp. 3–24.

ments of the Romans and their law. But we shall see that the rhetoric of didactic civic humanism of the fifteenth century, in speaking of Florentines learning how to live civilly, as had the Romans, was meant to educate these kinds of men with these interests and in these turbulent fiscal circumstances, to the active life of political engagement in public governance. They were remarkably successful in 'inventing' a civic discourse which could be adopted by the most apparently self-interested among wealthy Florentines, and in so doing, ensured that a language of republican, rather than despotic values, was maintained until the end of the century. Thereafter, arguments surfaced that republicanism of whatever kind always bred instability and civil war and the only answer to this was a principate.

It seems important to emphasize that the general thirst for participation in politics, from the early fifteenth century onwards, was especially, but not exclusively, that of the upper class. The view appears to have developed that leaders are successful and durable when there are many people willing to be led. A change in the political climate of this sort required an alternative to the older thirteenth-century ideal where the corporate ethos of members of guilds *expecting* to take turns in ruling and being ruled was replaced with a more static notion of leaders and led: an aristocratic republic. People had to believe that it was only the latter picture which purchased security, an end to endemic factionalism, and a kind of liberty, understood as political opportunity offered in equal measure but achieved only by 'those who merit it'.[74]

Not only is true nobility now defined as something earned rather than inherited, but it is also a fairly unique achievement, and not capable of being accorded to all citizens. Civic humanism coincided with and fostered an ethic of civic nobility among wealthy Florentines who saw themselves as a class apart with a distinctive set of values. This view was being repeated in the circles of the ruling classes elsewhere in Europe. In fifteenth-century Burgundy, the Valois dukes, notably Philip the Good and Charles the Bold, placed great emphasis on *la chose publique* and on the virtue of justice, on true nobility meaning civic contribution to the common good. They used Cicero as well as French translations of Italian humanists' Latin editions of ancient philosophers to formulate their views. They adapted the humanist Poggio Bracciolini's argument that true nobility lay not in inherited titles, wealth or riches but in one's own developed virtues, and is best achieved and exercised in cities among other citizens, and not in the solitude of country estates, where the only company one has are wild beasts and on occasion, haggling farmers![75] The contrast was being drawn between a meritocratic, civic nobility expected of a ruling elite and the nobility of the *signori*, 'ennobled' either by wealth or inheritance but not by deed.

And so we find the expression of this very fifteenth-century sentiment in the writings of Leonardo Bruni (c. 1369–1444), a man who had studied law, rhetoric and Greek, became a secretary at the papal *curia* and then took up the position of Chancellor of the Florentine republic in 1427. He remained in office until his death in 1444 after the Medici ascendency had been well established. Bruni, a man who knew his Aristotle, as we shall see, clearly saw Cicero to have proffered the message which could better be adapted to Bruni's experience of the Florentine commune of the fifteenth century. He wrote:

---

74   See N. Rubinstein, 'Florentina Libertas', *Rinascimento*, 2nd ser. 26 (1986), pp. 3–26.
75   Poggio Bracciolini (1380–1459), from his *On Nobility*, as cited in A. Vanderjagt, *'Qui sa vertu anoblist': the concepts of 'noblesse' and 'chose publique' in Burgundian political thought* (Groningen, 1981), p. 34, n. 16; see pp. 45–74.

> Equal liberty exists for all . . . ; the hope of winning public honours and ascending to office is the same for all, so long as they possess industry and natural gifts and lead a serious-minded and respected way of life [*modo ingenium et vivendi ratio quaedam probata et gravis*]; for our city requires virtue and probity in its citizens. Whoever has such qualifications is thought to be of sufficiently noble birth to govern the republic. . . . This is the true liberty, this the equality of a city: not to fear violence or injury from anyone and to enjoy equality among citizens before the law and in the undertaking of public office [*paritatem esse iuris inter se civibus, paritatem rei publicae adeundae*].[76]

In echoing Cicero, Bruni's equality is of a proportionate kind, in line with one's status, itself revealed by one's personal industry and the natural gifts that are not universally distributed.

Humanism and Humanist Conceptions of Florentine Republicanism

Leonardo Bruni translated many Greek texts, which he appears to have been the first to read, into clear Latin, intelligible to Latin readers who were not professional academics. He also composed a 'life' of Aristotle, dedicated to cardinal Albergati, and a 'life' of Cicero.[77] He is historically situated at the beginning of an extraordinary expression of interest in acquiring not only Latin, but Greek texts of antiquity. Already during the fourteenth century there had been a great flurry of activity to recover works of classical latinity, notably in ecclesiastical circles but also among educated laymen. But by the fifteenth century, ancient Greek texts began to pour into Italy at an unprecedented rate due to the efforts of Italian scholars, returning to Italy from Greek journeys prior to the Turkish invasion of Constantinople in 1453. It was the Latin translations of these Greek texts which remained the chief medium of ancient philosophy well into the sixteenth century.

Bruni translated Aristotle's *Ethics* (1416–17) and his *Politics* (1438) because he was determined to replace what he took to be the barbarism of Moerbeke's medieval Latin 'word for word' rendering with a style that conformed to standard Ciceronian Latin. Bruni believed that Aristotle had been an eloquent writer whose rhetorical skills had been obscured by medieval translations, a view he inherited from Petrarch and from statements found in Cicero about Aristotle's eloquence in his lost early dialogues.[78] But it is noteworthy that Bruni's translations were nowhere as popular as Moerbeke's continued to be. And when from 1470 the invention of printing was able to make books cheaper for all and increased the circulation of new and old ideas alike, printers helped to increase the weight of the ancient and medieval tradition when they printed both Aristotle and Aquinas in more accessible, convenient and accurate editions than literate people had ever previously enjoyed.

But if we ask how they understood ancient and medieval texts, Bruni is an interesting

---

76   L. Bruni, *Oratio Funebris* for Nanni Strozzi (1428), in H. Baron, *The Crisis of the Early Italian Renaissance* (Princeton, NJ, 1966), translation p. 419 (modified above) and text p. 556.

77   E. Fryde, 'The First Humanistic Life of Aristotle: the 'vita Aristotelis' of Leonardo Bruni', in P. Denley and C. Elam, eds, *Florence and Italy: Renaissance Studies in Honour of Nicolai Rubinstein* (London, 1988), pp. 285–96.

78   L. Bruni, *Dialogi ad Petrum Histrum* in E. Garin, ed., *Prosatori latini del Quattrocento*, La letteratura italiana, Storia e testi, 13 (Milan–Naples, 1952), pp. 56–8.

witness. His account of earlier Florentine history follows Villani's and he undertakes no independent research, although he rearranges Villani's narrative to suit his own interests, with the effect that great and noble men had always to remind the people of their condition and obligations to the republic and the common good.[79] In his translations, where he substituted *societas civilis* for Moerbeke's translation of *communitas* and *communicatio politica*, Bruni provided a distinctive, fifteenth-century Florentine civic understanding that replaced the more organicist vision of political groupings in Aristotle, an organicist vision that had suited thirteenth-century Florentine politics but not the politics of fifteenth-century Florence. Aristotle's communitarian notion was to be found in Aquinas, whom fifteenth-century laymen continued to read, not only because Aquinas relied on the Moerbeke text but because he attributed rational self-governance, a rational will, to all men of whatever social status. Bruni replaced Moerbeke's attempt simply to translate the ancient Greek 'Hellenism' with his preferred vision of Livy's and Cicero's Rome, so that the communitarian became an associative dimension more applicable to his Florence.[80] The rational will, once a presumed characteristic of all men, had become a rare characteristic of natural governors.

Marsilius, we recall, had argued the corporatist view, 'that most citizens are neither vicious nor undiscerning most of the time; all or most of them are of sound mind and reason and have a right desire for the polity and for the things necessary for it to endure, like laws and other statutes or customs; for although not every citizen nor the greater number of them be discoverers of the laws, yet every citizen can judge of what has been discovered and proposed by someone else and can discern what must be added, subtracted or changed.[81] On the contrary, the humanist literature that emerges in the fifteenth century often insists that most of humankind neglects to cultivate virtue, which is no more than right reason, and therefore they must look to those who are more noble, that is, with more intelligence and virtue than others.[82] Those who considered themselves up to this task had to learn how to cultivate all factions but join none. In believing that there was a pervasive tendency for men to do evil rather than good, such men thought it essential to be educated to moral virtue and the active life in order to counter the evil machinations of the majority.[83] This is but one example of a generally pervasive tendency among humanists to stand against seeking continuities with their own immediate pasts or with other parts of Europe, a continuity that was taken for granted by men like Marsilius whose theory of government was explicitly meant to apply to all parts of Europe and all constitutions so long as they were 'temperate'. The humanists, in contrast, used the metaphor of rebirth and Renaissance to express their desire to draw selectively from the past in order to justify a civic life that they held to be distinctive in Florence and capable of being lived by a self-selecting minority.

79   Bruni, *Historiarum Florentini populi libri xii*, ed. E. Santini (Città di Castello, 1934), vol. 19: 3 of *Rerum Italicarum Scritores*.

80   D. Colas, *La Glaive et le fléau, généalogie du fanatisme et de la société civile* (Paris, 1992), pp. 34–7. For other views concerning Bruni as a historian see D. Wilcox, *The Development of Florentine Humanist Historiography in the Fifteenth Century* (Cambridge, MA, 1969) and M. Phillips, 'Representation and Argument in Florentine Historiography', *Storia della storiografia* 10 (1986), pp. 48–63.

81   Marsilius, *Defender of Peace*, I, xiii, 3.

82   E.g. Poggio Bracciolini, *On the Misery of the Human Condition* (1455) Book 1, translated by M. Davies in J. Kraye, ed., *Cambridge Translations of Renaissance Philosophical Texts,* vol. 1 (Cambridge, 1997), pp. 22–3.

83   Giovanni Rucellai, *Il Zabaldone* (1464), written for his sons, ed. A. Perosa (London, 1960), pp. 85ff.

Bruni was aware that Cicero and other ancient Romans had used the term *studia humanitatis* to refer to a kind of education that was centred on authoritative texts in Greek and Latin teaching grammar, rhetoric, poetry, history and moral philosophy for a purpose: to serve the active life of public engagement. Although he was committed to the merits of the active over the contemplative life, he also found room to praise the qualities of the contemplative life by interpreting book 10 of Aristotle's *Ethics* in this light. But when he wrote about the Florentine constitution, and when he translated ancient classical texts, historical and philosophical, he was concerned to transmit the values and political affairs of his own times and what he took to be like values of ages past, reformulated in a language, order and structure that would suit his own contemporary audience, in order to provide lessons about how to sustain his republican ideal. This was dependent on the activity of an exclusive group of creative citizens and he sought to motivate them. Bruni warned Florentine humanist historians that the history of antiquity had already been written, so the task that remained for 'moderns' could only be the provision of summaries and the addition of explanatory notes. No attempt by Bruni or any other humanist was made to discover whether ancient historians were correct. Rather, their record, selectively presented to a present, fifteenth-century audience, was meant to inspire a select group of men to similar deeds of civic virtue and honour.[84] History, past and present, provided examples of good living and virtue in all times, and if imitated in the present, the successes of the past would likewise be repeated. Study the lives of great men. The *studia humanitatis* had this in mind for its students.

The *studia humanitatis*, for Renaissance educators, self-consciously excluded the study of logic or the *quadrivium* of the university's liberal arts course. While the old liberal arts, along with theology, jurisprudence, medicine and the philosophical disciplines including natural philosophy and metaphysics, continued to be studied at late medieval and Renaissance universities in Italy and elsewhere, those who styled themselves humanists came to dominate Italian secondary schools. By the fifteenth century their constituencies were students with an upper-class consciousness, one of whom was Machiavelli. In Florence, classical learning had become the preserve of an aristocracy.[85] But humanism's earlier origins as 'pre-humanism' were outside the universities in the experience of lawyers and notaries involved in the public affairs of thirteenth- and fourteenth-century communes. Their students needed a knowledge of Latin rhetoric and the elements of law. They needed courses to teach them how to write correctly, compose what looked like private but actually were public letters, and make speeches. The bulk of written business in Italian city-states was in the hands of chancery notaries. They rejected what they thought were pedantic, pedagogic conventions of scholastic discourse and thereby provided themselves with a sense of their separate identity in a world that increasingly boasted literate and professional men who were not clergy.[86] However, the humanist

84   Bruni 'explained that he never translated the "Republic" of Plato because there were things in it that displeased him and which departed deplorably from the "customs of our society"'. Fryde, 'The First Humanist Life', p. 289.
85   R. Black, 'Florence', in R. Porter and M. Teich, eds, *The Renaissance in National Context* (Cambridge, 1992), esp. pp. 35–7.
86   In general, see P. O. Kristeller, 'Humanism', in Schmitt, Skinner, Kessler and Kraye, *Cambridge History of Renaissance Philosophy*, pp. 113–38; P. O. Kristeller, *Studies in Renaissance Thought and Letters*, 2 vols (Rome, 1956–85); P. O. Kristeller, *Renaissance Thought and its Sources*, ed. M. Mooney (New York, 1979); P. O. Kristeller, *Medieval Aspects of Renaissance Learning: three essays*, ed. and trans. M. P. Mahoney (Durham, NC, 1974); and the important studies of J. Monfasani, *Language and Learning in Renaissance Italy: selected articles* (Aldershot, 1994), who

movement advanced to become a coherent programme for educating society's leaders only when there was a sufficient unity among an elite in that society whose vision of government separated them off from the rest. This was to occur during the fifteenth century, when humanism advanced as 'civic humanism' by way of state chanceries (Milan and Florence) and at princely courts (Mantua and Ferrara). The chanceries and princely courts were the sites of propaganda, the places where official histories were written, panegyrics composed, and the life of patrician commitment to worldly honours and fame through public life, exalted. Humanists in these circumstances were pens for hire. And so they wrote in praise of princes *and* republics. In either case, their audience was a governing elite.

To thrive in this world, the humanists provided an educational programme based on oratorical techniques, grammatical and philological analysis of ancient Latin texts, and they recovered even more of the writings from classical antiquity than had previously been achieved by earlier scholars. From 1390 to 1420 a range of Latin philosophy, including works little known to the Middle Ages, like Lucretius' *De rerum natura* and a complete edition of Quintilian's *Institutio oratoria* (discovered by Bracciolini when he attended the Council of Constance in 1417), along with much material that *was* familiar to the Middle Ages, like the philosophical works of Cicero, was gathered into coherent collections by avid book hunters. More of Cicero's letters were uncovered in monastic libraries. Cicero's *De oratore*, the *Orator* and the *Brutus* were found. In the *De oratore* (I.15.66–9) Cicero made it especially clear that the orator's province is ethics, which is the moral science of human nature. And in Quintilian's *Institutio* (XII.2.6–20) this Roman pedagogue agreed that orators must concern themselves with the actual practice and experience of life, which includes psychology and ethics. We have heard this one before. So had they, and Aristotle's *Ethics* and *Politics* became for them the focus of much of their rhetorical endeavours.[87]

At the same time Cicero's philosophical works (*De officiis, Tusculanae disputationes, De inventione,* the 'dream of Scipio' from the *De re publica* VI, the *De natura deorum,* etc.) continued to play exactly the role that had often fallen to them in the monastic and cathedral schools of the Middle Ages. They remained texts for language teaching and informative compendia. It has been noted that Leonardo Bruni undertook to write a 'life' of Cicero as well as of Aristotle, in addition to retranslating the latter's major ethical and political works. Others found new sources of Plato's major dialogues (*Republic, Theaetetus, Symposium*) which had remained unknown during the Middle Ages. But Plato never achieved the overwhelming diffusion of either Cicero or Aristotle. And even when, by the later fifteenth century (1469 and printed in 1484) his works would come out in Marsilius Ficino's Latin translations with commentaries, the Renaissance Plato remained mixed with neoplatonisms from Plotinus, Lactantius, St Augustine and

---

emphasizes that we must look at medieval rhetoric to understand Renaissance rhetoric, many humanist rhetorical manuals *rejecting* the structure of classical rhetoric, returning instead to a medieval understanding of the purpose and content of this art, but providing a new direction for the use and value of rhetoric as opposed to dialectic. Despite having recovered the full classical heritage in rhetoric, quattrocento Italy produced little innovation except in letter writing, where the Latin classical tradition had little to offer by way of instruction. On medieval rhetoric and the early *dictatores* see J. J. Murphy, ed., *Medieval Eloquence* (Berkeley, 1978).

87   R. Sabbadini, *Le Scoperte dei codici latini e greci ne' secoli XIV e XV*, 2 vols (Florence, 1905–14, reprinted Florence, 1967).

other church Fathers, as well as from the ancient hermetic tradition,[88] and hence was never read 'pure'. But then, of course, neither Cicero nor Aristotle was read 'pure', but each was instead taken to be confirming a range of positions already penetrated by customary practices and Christian principles, and most, like Bruni, believed that Plato and Aristotle did not differ on essentials.

Most of the humanists' effort, then, was expended in providing retranslations of works – most of which were already known – into more classical Latin and providing commentaries on these. There is no doubt that their burst of interest in amassing the remnants of the ancient world had a profound effect on the proliferation of new genres and alternative discourses in which to frame social and political ideals. Notable here was the oration and, even more so, epistolary literature: state and private letters. Furthermore, they mastered the Roman Latin language, some mastering ancient Greek, more seriously than anyone since ancient times. But as Grafton has observed, following the important work of Charles Schmitt, after all this translation and rewriting effort, 'whether the ordinary arts graduate of 1600 knew Aristotle better than he would have in 1300 or 1450 remains to be established'. Grafton also observed that 'the Cicero of the Renaissance had a fuller biography, a purer text and a clearer historical visage than the medieval one; but he was not wholly the *Cicero novus* that Bruni and others claimed to present'.[89] What did emerge in the process of all their labours was an extraordinary sensitivity towards the historical development of language. As never before, they were able, through philological analysis of texts, to establish what they held to be an accumulation of barbarisms across the centuries which deviated from the authentic classical latinity they sought to revive and imitate. They became aware that language has a history, that the conventional ways of speaking (*modi loquendi*) change over time.[90]

But what they did *not* discover was a notion of the past as over and done with, where values are unique to the historical conditions in which they flourish and hence are inimitable in other times and places. Had they held to this view it would have entailed the kind of historicizing perspective which would have led them to view their ancient Roman mentors as hopelessly irretrievable for their own contemporary use. Instead, they spoke with their ancient forebears, wrote letters to them, read them in the evenings as friends to be relied on when their contemporaries could not be,[91] and insisted they shared the same values, indeed, that they 'lived through them'.[92] In focusing especially on the works of Roman moralists and historians, and privileging *spoken* oratory following ancient Roman models, humanists felt themselves to be engaged in liberating men from the barbarity of the medieval scholastic *viri obscuri* (obscure men). With the orator as a cultural hero, the humanists claimed to represent a distinctive intellectual position – in which intellectual activity must have practical results – to challenge the pre-eminence

---

88   See D. P. Walker, *The Ancient Theology: studies in Christian Platonism from the fifteenth to the eighteenth century* (London, 1972).

89   A. Grafton, 'The Availability of Ancient Works', in Schmitt, Skinner, Kessler and Kraye, *Cambridge History of Renaissance Philosophy*, pp. 767–91. This volume has contributions of very varying quality, Grafton's being one of the most useful analyses. See C. Schmitt, *Aristotle in the Renaissance* (Cambridge, MA, 1983).

90   See Coleman, *Ancient and Medieval Memories,* for the medieval scholastic precursors of this insight; also see I. Maclean, *Interpretation and Meaning*.

91   See Machiavelli's letter to Vettori, in D. Wootton, ed. and trans., *N. Machiavelli: selected political writiungs* (Indianapolis, 1994), p. 3.

92   There is no space to demonstrate this here. See Coleman, *Ancient and Medieval Memories*, esp. pp. 538–99.

of scholastics and their presumed encasement in speculation, the *vita contemplativa* (the contemplative life). In particular, they attacked the kind of sophisticated and, in their view, sophistical logic that had been advanced especially in Oxford University by Italian university followers of William of Ockham, who returned home to Italy to make their ways.[93] But here, they were pushing at an open door.

We have seen that the science of politics had already been linked to plausibility and contingency among medieval Aristotelians who referred to Aristotle's rhetorical (as opposed to dialectical) proofs and the role of prudential practical reasoning in the conduct of governing a city. We have seen that in the medieval university arts course rhetoric and poetics had explicitly become attached to the practical moral sciences, ethics and politics, concerned as they were with particular choices to act in one way or another in contingent situations. Practical moral philosophy and its tools, poetry for persuasion of the individual to virtuous action, and rhetoric for persuasion in the public sphere of the common good, were already detached from dialectic argument about what is necessary. The Renaissance humanists saw themselves to be in a position to grasp further the importance of language, seeing rhetoric as the vital accomplishment of the active life. In writing works on man and his social relations with others, whether as a ruler over subordinates or at a court among equals, they praised eloquence as a means of moral education. What Aristotle had to say in *Politics* book 1 about the extraordinary nature of human speech and the dependence of any political community on moral communication about the good and bad, the useful and the harmful for man, was allied to Cicero's praise of the orator, the expert persuader to moral agency. And with all the humanists' patriotic references to Cicero and his (their) Rome, they were happy to have him married to the Greek Aristotle in order to justify the Florentine system of government. The rhetoric of an ideal mixed constitution could satisfy the conditions either for Aristotle's law-governed and therefore limited monarchy as well as Cicero's aristocratic republic. Just as humanists spoke with ancient friends, Greeks and Romans, so they reconciled different traditions, mixing Aristotle, Horace, Seneca, Cicero and others to justify their own positions.

Humanists were not professors of philosophy, although during the fifteenth century some obtained chairs of rhetoric, Greek, logic and moral philosophy in the arts faculties of Italian universities. When they taught rhetoric they drew on the ancient philosophers for their definition of the virtues and vices. Humanists absorbed wholesale the perspectives on ethics to be found in the works of Cicero, Quintilian, Seneca and Aristotle, themselves contributing little to ethical theory or its terminology. Instead, humanists claimed to provide a practical application of ethics in their instruction in rhetoric and poetry. Which ethical perspective did they reveal? we ask. Some adopted a Stoic perspective, others an Aristotelian, others an Epicurian, and still others a kind of Platonism as understood through Cicero's writings on the different ancient philosophical schools and from the 'dream of Scipio', often merged with its Christian variant in the writings of St Augustine.[94]

93   E. Garin, 'La cultura fiorentina nella second meta del 300 e i "barbari britanni" ', in *L'età nuova: Ricerche di Storia della Cultura dal XII al XVI secolo* (Naples, 1969), pp. 141–66. Burke, *Tradition and Innovation*, p. 40, observed: 'Contemporaries cannot be trusted to describe their own achievements accurately. They said that they were imitating the ancients and breaking with their own past. In practice, they borrowed from both traditions and followed neither . . . the new was added to the old rather than substituted for it'.

94   There is now a good display, in translation, of the range of perspectives in Kraye, *Cambridge Translations of Renaissance Philosophical Texts*, vol. 1: Moral Philosophy, vol. 2: Political Philosophy.

Humanists explicitly stated that they were more interested in grammar, rhetoric, poetry, history and ethics, economics and politics, all of which were meant to be of use in pursuing the active life in the contemporary civic world. Indeed, they wanted what they understood of university logic to be reformed and allied to rhetoric so that it suited practical persuasion rather than scientific demonstration. We have already seen that this is precisely the route that had been opened at the end of the thirteenth century when Aristotle's *Rhetoric* had been translated, and then its precepts used by Giles of Rome in his effort to persuade France's King Philip to become an orator as well as a ruler. The humanists took this much further. In 1407 we find the humanist Gasparino Barzizza, a professor at Padua, lecturing annually on that old medieval text, the pseudo-Ciceronian *Rhetorica ad herennium*, on Cicero's *De oratore and* on Aristotle's *Rhetoric,* and training future humanist specialists in rhetoric (Vittorino da Feltre, Filelfo and George of Trebizond) to see it as a key tool in the study of the Latin language's history, its genres and literary forms, but most importantly, for ruling a republic. Their aim was to revive the standards and values of classical antiquity, and, in teaching these to their students, they would be preparing them with a new oratorical literacy, and through this, a set of values, that would be suitable for their future civil and ecclesiastical careers. The belief was that reason, moral virtues and social order all depended on the right use of language, and hence eloquence was to be pursued for its political utility. Rhetorical skill was to be used to persuade fellow citizens by means of words so that they perform actions that are advantageous to the 'state', and refrain from those that are damaging.

Civic humanists preached the classical virtues but which actions did they judge advantageous to the 'state'? It is here that we see that rhetoric is a skill applied prudentially to whatever 'state' one happens to live in, not least because 'stato' usually meant 'regime', the government, a generic term which included a variety of constitutional forms. One speaks in one way to those ruled by despotic *signori* and another to those ruled by republican institutions. It is to this humanist reliance on the ruler's rhetorical skill, shaped to whatever constitutional conditions pertain, that Machiavelli will add something even more necessary: military force, when persuasion no longer secures motivation to action. We shall see that all successful governments, be they monarchies or republics, rest on 'good laws and good arms', but for Machiavelli, and especially for his new prince, good laws must be predicated on good arms, since order and harmony are not inherent in some providential plan but are coercively imposed on things and men by rulers. And when men have forgotten their traditions of self-rule their only civil salvation is good order by princely imposition. Hence, the prince must study warfare. Like Scaevola who repudiates Crassus' praise of oratory in Cicero's *De oratore* I, Machiavelli objects that orators do not found and preserve cities. He holds, instead, with Aristotle's *Politics* book 5, where Aristotle speaks of the causes of changes from one constitution to another, and specifically from democracy to tyranny, noting that oratory is insufficient to seize power.[95]

But we must not think that Machiavelli cuts himself adrift from the uses of oratory. It is beyond doubt that he believed as did most humanists that rhetoric was more useful to the sons of the Italian elite than scholastic dialectical logic and philosophy, which spoke in terms of what men might be rather than what they were in given circumstances.

---

95   Aristotle observes in *Politics* V, v, 1305a7f that 'Today with the spread of skill in oratory the able speakers become popular leaders but owing to their ignorance of warfare they do not attempt to seize power except in a few insignificant instances.'

Indeed, it was precisely at the end of the fifteenth century, when Machiavelli was active in the Florentine chancery, that debates arose among humanists as to what rhetoric's purpose was. Some, following Quintilian, argued that its purpose was to speak well (*bene dicere*), whereas those who followed Cicero, whom they allied with Aristotle, argued that rhetoric's purpose was persuasion (*persuasio*) as part of the science of politics. In short, the debate was between rhetoric as power versus rhetoric as cultivated entertainment.[96] According to Machiavelli, while the prince's main objective should be to acquire skill in warfare, he also needs to develop arguments from probabilities and thereby learn how to persuade. And he must study history because history teaches that appearances, on which plausibilities rest, matter most to men. The prince's prudence must control speech and appearances. He must aim to be judged honourable and universally be praised for apparent results. He must know the character of the people he conquers and rules and shape his *persona* accordingly. History is itself oratorical persuasion: it will not teach a successful leader of men how to acquire conventional virtues but it will teach him something much more important: how to acquire the *reputation* for possessing them.

Civic humanists, however, insisted that the ends of the 'stato' depended uniquely on the ability of men of affairs to persuade others into or out of a proposed course of action. Persuasion is the key here. And their interest in history was a part of this project in persuasion. They expressed their own values under the guise of historical narrative. Hence, their choice of historical subject matter was Rome, above all, and classical Greece. Thereafter, the history of one's own city brought up to date with the most recent and contemporary events enabled an orator to provide a commentary on his own times. The study of Roman history as revealed in the writings of Livy, Sallust, Caesar and Plutarch was, for them, a study in selective relevance, in the lessons to be learned from the past to be used in their own practical politics and government. Bruni made this plain in his *De studiis et literis* (*c.* 1405) when he said: 'The careful study of the past enlarges our foresight in contemporary affairs and affords *to citizens and to monarchs* lessons of incitement or warning in the ordering of public policy. From history we also draw our store of examples of moral precepts'.[97]

Hence, the study of rhetoric enabled one not only to speak with polished expression but also provided the means of achieving persuasive arguments deemed plausible by various audiences. The study of ethics engaged one with the principles of morality. And the study of history offered specific examples of virtue and vice and provided the outlines of a science of politics. For Bruni and for other humanists, Rome was the light that was to be rekindled by erecting a bridge between antiquity and the Italian city-state, passing over the medieval 'dark ages'. Lauro Martines has put it exceedingly well:

> In the life of Greek and Roman cities, they found their own cities; in orators and literati, they found themselves; in public men – rulers, statesmen, orators, professional soldiers – they found their friends, acquaintances, patrons and again themselves. In eloquence . . . they found an ideal which could be turned into a recipe for cultivated men of the world, a

---

96   See J. Monfasani, 'Episodes of Anti-Quintilianism in the Italian Renaissance: quarrels on the orator as a *vir bonus* and rhetoric as the *scientia bene dicendi* ', in J. Monfasani, *Language and Learning in Renaissance Italy*, pp. 119–38.
97   For a discussion of how this differs from our contemporary understanding of 'history' and its uses see J. Coleman, 'The Uses of the Past (14th–16th Centuries): the invention of a collective history and its implications for cultural participation', in A. Rigney and D. Fokkema, eds, *Cultural Participation: trends since the Middle Ages* (Amsterdam, 1993), pp. 21–37.

recipe for ruling classes. And in celebrity – fame, glory, honors – the humanists singled out the highest earthly prize to which they themselves aspired, a prize conferred only in signorial and oligarchical cities, in the forms of embassies, university chairs, high office, tax immunities, and literary commissions.[98]

In being committed to oligarchical republicanism, Florentine humanists of the fifteenth century praised the virtues, the life and the politics of Cicero's republican Rome and they traced the origins of Florence back to the Roman republican period. Civic humanism, in being an educational programme for the ruling classes, revitalized an 'objective' Roman history that was filtered through the blur of their own self-images. Humanism made explicit what a medieval university education had held implicitly: that societies are destined to live their intellectual lives, their histories, through ideology not fact. This is one of the major lessons Machiavelli learned from his own humanist education, and passed on.

Fifteenth-century Florentine Ideology

Bruni wrote three tracts on the Florentine constitution: an early panegyric *Laudatio Florentinae urbis* (1403);[99] an analysis ten years later in the form of a Letter to the Emperor, Sigismund, King of the Romans;[100] and lastly a treatise, written in Greek, *On the Florentine Polity* (*c.* 1439)[101]. In the early *Laudatio,* which is heavily influenced by Roman authors, he describes a mixed republican constitution with a more inclusive mixture than that found in Venice. He uses the Roman law argument that what touches all should be approved by all (*quod omnes tangit*) to indicate that Florentine liberty flourishes when what concerns the people is decided by their will. But he also compared the authority of the Signoria, although collectively exercised, to royal authority, with the sovereign attributes of political decision-making, a legislative monopoly, and full judicial capacities.[102]

The second and third texts show a distinctively enhanced Aristotelian classification of constitutions as applied to Florence, although the last, Greek text describes the constitution no longer as *popularis* (as he had described it in his Letter to the Emperor) but rather as an aristocratic mixed constitution. This may reflect Bruni's better information, since he wrote it after having been for many years Florentine Chancellor. In his earlier Letter to the Emperor he had spoken of the greatest noble families being excluded from government (to prevent the oppression of one class by another and the rise of a single

---

98   L. Martines, *Power and Imagination: city-states in Renaissance Italy* (Harmondsworth, 1983), p. 269. This is still, by far, the best general discussion of the relation between the ideals of the Italian Renaissance and city-state government.

99   Discussed by H. Baron in *Humanistic and Political Literature in Florence and Venice at the Beginning of the Quattrocento* (Cambridge, MA, 1955); Baron, *The Crisis of the Early Italian Renaissance* and in H. Baron, ed., *From Petrarch to Leonardo Bruni* (Chicago, 1968).

100   Edited in Baron, *Humanistic and Political Literature,* pp. 181–4.

101   Edited in A. Moulakis, ed., 'Leonardo Bruni's Constitution of Florence', *Rinascimento,* 2nd ser., 26 (1986), pp. 141–90.

102   '. . . supremus magistratus, qui quandam vim regie potestatis habere videbatur . . . rei publice consulunt, iura sanciunt, equitatem decernunt.' *Laudatio florentine urbis,* in Baron, *From Petrarch,* p. 259.

despot), so that what remains is an Aristotelian 'mean', created by the laws which ensure an equality of hope among citizens in attaining public office. Supreme authority is vested not in one man (hence, preventing tyranny) but in a magistracy of nine, the Signoria, with limited office and various limitations on its exercise of power. But in his last Greek tract, he no longer mentions safeguards against autocratic power. Here an aristocracy prevails over democratic elements in the mixture. And what he takes to be the democratic elements are short terms of office of the highest magistracies and their appointment by lot which, indeed, he criticizes elsewhere. The aristocratic elements consist in the fact that new laws had first to be approved by a small body of citizens before being presented to the larger councils, and that these latter councils had no right either to initiate or to amend legislation. Again, there is an exclusion of the greatest Florentine families from government but there is also an exclusion of men of the lowest social rank, all to achieve a city with a 'middle condition', while the dominant tendency is towards the aristocratic.

What stands out in all of these analyses are certain basic principles which Bruni thought fundamental to understanding the Florentine system of government: *ius* and *libertas*. The executive Signoria possessed almost regal authority but was limited by various means; in the last resort, it depended on the will of the people as 'voiced' in the legislative councils of People and Commune. Furthermore, citizens had liberty under the law and an equality which implied among other things equal opportunity to rise to high office. Bruni describes a balance between patricians and people which is tilted towards the patricians. But Rubinstein has observed that Bruni omits an important aspect of the Florentine concept of equality, namely fiscal equality, and he also omits what others came to regard as the basic principle of freedom of speech in the councils.[103] Furthermore, Bruni's claim that there existed in Florence a basic equality in attaining high public office can hardly be taken at its face value, especially by the time he wrote his last tract in Greek. Indeed, the equal opportunity to rise to high office was an ideal that was hardly on offer throughout the fifteenth century, since the weighted appointment of scrutiny committees ensured the preferential treatment for an inner elite. And once the Medici were in position, high public office was a gift of their patronage. We may well question the extent to which Bruni's accounts of the Florentine constitution describe existing political conditions rather than political ideals, no matter how he modified these three accounts in the face of the increasing clamp-down of the nascent Medici regime.[104]

But once we recognize this civic humanism as ideology, a normative discourse rather than historical description, we can observe something that is more interesting about it. An aristocratic elite seems to have accepted a republican language with its normative notions of consent and representation as the foundation of legitimate republican government, of the supremacy of law, of the delegated quality of formal power, and this is what survives in the chancery language of Bruni. Fictions to be sure, but it has been argued that they affected the political *style* of the elite. The normative language of civic humanism actually limited, by modifying, their exercise of power. Doubtless the inner elite manipulated, behind the scenes, the institutions of government and society but they had to do so by co-opting the ideals of an aristocratic republican ideology. As Najemy has

---

103   On the limits of free speech in Florence, especially at the time when Bruni wrote his *Dialogi* (1401), see D. Marsh, *The Quattrocento Dialogue: classical tradition and humanist innovation* (Cambridge, MA, 1980), pp. 31–2.
104   See Rubinstein, 'Florentine Constitutionalism', pp. 452–5.

observed, when the oligarchy began to use notions of popular sovereignty to legitimate their own authority, the *popolo* lost control of its political language; but also the elite were now forced to speak, behave and govern in ways that modified their own governing style. Had they been left to get on with it and simultaneously establish their own language, Florence would have been, in rhetoric and practice, on its way to an absolutism more oppressive than the older feudal and less efficient forms of government. The elite, however, ran the show by using the language of the *popolo*, and during the Medici ascendancy in mid-century it was they who challenged Medicean appointments and controls with calls for freedom of speech in the *pratiche* and for a return to political liberty through elections to the Signoria by lot.[105] It was the educated civic humanists who provided this elite with this normative language, not least by reminding them that Florentine constitutionalism had its roots in communal political traditions 'remembered' in a distinctive and selective way. As a consequence, the *ottomati* in fact became the most conspicuous defenders of a republican constitution against the Medici ascendancy and against despotism.[106]

What they meant, however, was a republic along the lines of Ciceronian ideals rather than the Roman republic of the past or of the more recent Florentine 'golden age'. As Najemy has observed, the civic humanists enhanced the oligarchy's legitimacy by removing any memory that the elite had ever been other than the civic-minded aristocracy it now claimed (and wanted) to be, likewise removing any notion that the *popolo* or the guilds had grabbed a kicking and screaming elite into a new sense of itself. Forgetting certain things made the emerging oligarchy seem even more inevitably anointed in its power and responsibilities.[107]

No historian of this period would today dispute the inappropriateness of any notion of participatory democracy in Florence's republic (or elsewhere), a position that was once a nineteenth-century idealization but is still maintained in oversimplified histories of Western civilization or 'cultural histories' which begin with the Renaissance. During the last decade of the fifteenth century when the Medici were replaced by a Great Council and the regime would be considered a *popularis administratio*, reference was not being made to a participatory democracy where all citizens of whatever social rank were thought eligible to take turns in rule. Reference was being made to some three thousand or so citizens, members of whose families had already held the highest offices during the Medicean period. A *republica populare* or a *governo populare* is not a participatory democracy. There would be an ongoing debate concerning the broadening or narrowing of Florentine citizenship into the early decades of the sixteenth century, a debate between a *governo stretto* or a *governo largo*. But both referred to what was, in effect, a narrower or wider 'oligarchy'. What is interesting, however, about the fifteenth- and early sixteenth-century Florentine political scene, beyond the undoubted elite of great families who functioned as a ruling class, is the degree to which a certain kind of humanist ideology could make for a certain social mobility and the establishment of a penumbra of civic nobility in the Florentine chancery around 'inherited' nobility. Behind the institutions of government was a discursive frame that was penetrated by a republican ethical per-

105   See Rubinstein, 'Constitutionalism and Medici Ascendancy', pp. 457–9.
106   See J. Najemy, 'The Dialogue of Power in Florentine Politics', in Molho, Raaflaub and Emlen, *City-states in Classical Antiquity*, pp. 269–88.
107   Ibid., p. 287.

spective in which educated men, the powerful and those seeking power, wished to share.

Niccolò Machiavelli

Machiavelli (1469–1527) descended from a Florentine family which had risen to major public office during the fourteenth century, but he was not among those who was a member of the Great Council or could hope to be elected to the civic magistracies. His father was a lawyer of little note. Like other descendants of ancient families, he was neither among the aristocratic group nor was he included in the *popolo*.[108] But he received an education which placed him among the Florentine social elite.

A private classical education had become a status symbol in Florence at the time when Machiavelli, *c.* 1480, attended the grammar school of Paolo da Ronciglione. We have already seen that to study grammar was to study Latin from numerous set texts, not least those of various Roman historians whose 'message' was harmonized with the substance gleaned from the authors on the humanists' lists of readings on ethics and rhetoric. Patrician families engaged teachers to educate their children as a sign of the family's wealth, exclusive social position, ancient lineage, public office and marriage alliances. Without such a private tutor a satisfactory Latin, that is, 'grammar', education had become difficult to attain, grammar having suffered such a decline for most of the Florentine population that only 2 per cent of boys were in grammar school, and Machiavelli was among them.[109] Unlike lesser cities in Tuscany under Florentine domination, Florence also failed to establish a first-class university, and the one it had was subject to inconsistent funding.

Some argued that Florentine citizens had always devoted themselves first and foremost to commerce, with the result that the study of the liberal arts had been less highly regarded than elsewhere; hence, learned men and students were not accorded respect.[110] Indeed, Machiavelli's correspondence is filled with his condescending railings against the middle ranks of office holders elected to major executive office for short terms and who apparently did not have the ability to read Latin. And he would complain famously in the introduction to his republican *Discourses on Livy*, that while jurists and medical doctors used the wisdom of the ancients to guide their present judgements, contemporary princes, and even more so republics, were unprepared to have recourse to ancient examples, the implication being that those who ruled Florence either could not read the Latin texts or were insufficiently trained in making use of them for the purpose of governing. Florence, unlike elsewhere, had developed a two-tiered education system, where the upper social classes received a classical training from a private tutor, and the masses received a commercial and practical education. Both aligned civic glory with wealth, and *grandezza* with liberty, as the aim of the city.

---

108   E. F. Guarini, 'Machiavelli and the Crisis of the Italian Republics', in Bock, Skinner and Viroli, *Machiavelli and Republicanism*, pp. 17–40. On his life see P. Villari, *The Life and Times of Niccolò Machiavelli*, 2 vols, 4th edn, trans. L. Villari (New York, 1969); R. Ridolfi, *The Life of Niccolo Machiavelli*, trans. C. Grayson (London, 1963); S. de Grazia, *Machiavell in Hell* (Princeton, NJ, 1989). For a survey of Machiavelli's main works see Q. Skinner, *Machiavelli*, revd edn (Oxford, 1985).

109   R. Black, 'Florence', pp. 34–6.

110   R. Black, 'Higher Education in Florentine Tuscany: new documents from the second half of the fifteenth century', in Denley and Elam, *Florence and Italy*, pp. 209–22, citing Otto Niccolini, pp. 209–10.

But the mass of such men would be sceptical of government by *ottimati* and prefer a *governo largo* – a more broadly based republic with legislative authority in the popular councils. The social elite, on the other hand, would favour the arrangements of a Venice with its kind of mixed constitution to produce a *governo stretto* – emphasizing its royal and aristocratic elements. The primary issue for Florentines was which kind of constitutional form, an aristocratic republic or one with a Great Council, best prevents tyranny. And this question was part of an older and larger discussion with which we are already familiar: it distinguished not between monarchies and republics, but between any good constitution whatever, so long as it was *a legibus restricta* and serving the common good, and a *regimen dispoticum* which did not.[111] Given the character of Florentines it was asked: what kind of government would best suit this kind of people as a whole?

Machiavelli, after what looks to us like a surprisingly non-partisan public career administering, rather than making, public policy, would spend years in enforced retirement reflecting on precisely this issue, for he had come to know the Florentines, their characters and their ambitions, exceedingly well. He had also read enough ancient Roman history to insist that it should be used, indeed its successes imitated, rather than simply admired. To organize a republic or rule a kingdom requires a knowledge of the character of the people to be ruled and a sufficient knowledge of history so that its lessons might be applied to contemporary problems concerning the governance of men and the maintenance of states, be they princedoms or republics. In his dedicatory preface to *The Prince* he says that his dearest possession is his knowledge of the actions of great men, which he has acquired in two ways: through long experience of contemporary events and learnt at the cost of personal privation and danger, and through a constant reading of antiquity. Just as those who draw maps station themselves on the plains to consider the mountains, and then take up a position on high ground in order to get a good view of the plains below, so it is necessary for a prince to know the nature of the people and to be of the people to know the nature of princes. He would recognize in his republican treatise, the *Discourses on Livy*, that a *vivere politico* could be had either in a republic or in a monarchy, *o per via di repubblica o di regno*.[112] The traditions, circumstances and character of a people would determine the nature of that *vivere politico*.

Machiavelli may have followed his grammar education with university lectures on the humanities during the 1480s, but these could only enhance what would become his career from 1498–1512 as a chancery humanist with skills in appropriate epistolary style and orthography. In being a member of the educated Florentine social elite, he had friends among the patrician notables, and as such had been trained as a humanist to prepare written documents, especially writing letters to foreign individuals and states, to diplomats, Florentine officials serving in subject territories, and to private citizens abroad as second chancellor and secretary to the Dieci. He took the minutes of the *pratiche* and supervised the recruitment of troops in the countryside. Indeed, his main domestic project was a reorganization of the Florentine militia.[113] His duties took him outside the city,

---

111   We must remember that even for Aquinas there was a distinction between monarchy as a *regimen politicum* and a kind of despotism which was called a *regimen regale*. This distinction was taken further by Ptolemy of Lucca who continued Aquinas's unfinished *De regno / De regimine principum* (IV.8) where Ptolemy said: 'includendo in despotico etiam regale'.

112   *Disc.* I, 25.

113   Much later he would publish his *Arte della guerra* (The Art of War, 1521).

travelling in the countryside to recruit soldiers or negotiating abroad. Like other chancery officials he never wrote his dispatches to Florentine office holders and magistrates in Latin.

By the end of his career he would have a wealth of experiences. Like other 'civil service' humanists he undertook missions as a negotiator and diplomat, within Florentine territories, elsewhere in Italy, to the papal court in Rome under Pope Alexander VI and Pope Julius II, and to the former's ambitious son Cesare Borgia, abroad to the king of France and to the Holy Roman Emperor. But as a public servant without full political rights he was excluded from any decision-making power. His were executive functions and he could exert some influence as an adviser or 'expert'. It appears that he was regarded as thinking too highly of his own abilities as an adviser, for his chancery colleagues complained that on missions he wrote too infrequently and when he did so, he did not merely report back but included his own conclusions and interpretations. He proved himself to be by far the most active among the chancery secretaries during his period of employment from 1498–1512, but like other chancery officials who wanted to keep their jobs despite changes in regimes, he has been described as a political fence-sitter. He also made enemies because he allowed himself to be seen as too independent and arrogant.[114]

When, in 1512, Spanish troops attacked Florentine territory, the republican regime dissolved and the Medici returned to power, Machiavelli would be dismissed from office. In 1513 he was accused of a role in an anti-Medici conspiracy. He was tried, tortured and imprisoned, and upon his release he retired to his farm seven miles outside of Florence and composed a draft of the text we call *The Prince*.[115]

Machiavelli's experience of the Florentine republic in its various reformulations had begun during the 1480s at the time when Lorenzo de' Medici 'the Magnificent' was in position,[116] and ended with the return in 1512 of another Medici, Giuliano, who was in turn replaced by his nephew, the younger Lorenzo in 1515. *The Prince* was originally dedicated to Giuliano and re-dedicated to Lorenzo in 1515. It was aimed at a Medici with princely ambitions. By this time Italy had been subject to a succession of foreign invasions and Machiavelli would include as his final chapter of *The Prince* an exhortation that such a man free Italy from the stench of foreign domination. Machiavelli would still be alive in 1527 when Rome was sacked by the forces of Charles V, King of Spain and Holy Roman Emperor, and Florence revolted against the Medici, establishing a new republic. But by then he was viewed as a Medici collaborator, and he died shortly thereafter, in poverty.

The first Lorenzo, 'the Magnificent', had in 1480 set up a new and virtually permanent Council of 70, chosen by nomination and co-optation from among his supporters,

---

114 R. Black, 'Machiavelli, Servant of the Florentine Republic', and J. Najemy, 'The Controversy Surrounding Machiavelli's Service to the Republic', both in Bock, Skinner and Viroli, *Machiavelli and Republicanism*, pp. 71–99, 101–17.

115 There is no really definitive text of *The Prince*, which was published in 1532, five years after Machiavelli's death. In the manuscripts it is entitled *De principatibus*, 'of principalities', and written in Italian with titles to chapters in Latin. Nancy Struever has argued that it was precisely the failure of Machiavelli's public career that made possible his private theoretical innovations. See N. S. Struever, *Theory as Practice: ethical inquiry in the Renaissance* (Chicago, 1992), p. 146.

116 N. Rubinstein, 'Lorenzo's Image in Europe', in M. Mallett and N. Mann, eds, *Lorenzo the Magnificent, culture and politics* (London, 1996), pp. 297–312.

to control the executive affairs of the Florentine republic. It legitimated itself by relying on the formal authority of the Signoria and legislation was now concentrated in this council, a kind of Senate, virtually marginalizing the older statutory councils. There had been an unprecedented degree, even by Florentine standards, of political manipulation and clientage under the fifteenth-century Medici. Humanists wrote not only in praise of increasingly oligarchic government, praising Venice and assigning no role to the body of the people, but they also penned pro-monarchical tracts which were largely Platonic in character, praising the despotism of the wise.[117] With the death of Lorenzo the Magnificent in 1492 his son Piero was brought in, but when in 1494 Charles VIII of France invaded Italy and took Florence, Piero was judged to have given away the people's security. Florentines revolted and Piero was exiled. The republican constitution was first restored, notionally in the form which had prevailed before 1434 and three weeks later the Great Council, the *consiglio maggiore,* was established, but as we have already noted, eligibility was granted only to those who came from families whose members had held high office under the three previous generations. Eligibility was based on a quasi-hereditary principle and for the first time in their history Florentines were defining and fixing the social basis of their present and future governors, the *reggimento.* In short, there remained an underlying continuity of government after the Medici, a continuity between the Medicean *reggimento* and that of the *governo popolare.*[118]

Bitter factionalism within the ruling elite ensued from 1494–8, during which Florence saw the guiding influence on politics of the Medici replaced by a Dominican friar, Girolamo Savonarola.[119] It is too infrequently mentioned in general histories of the Renaissance that religion and rhetoric interacted in preaching; indeed, that religious preaching remained the most universal form of contemporary oratory and was often influenced by humanist theory and practice. As a friar who not only lacked political rights as a foreigner but whose religious status prevented him from direct participation in government, Savonarola was a powerful preacher who condemned the Medici as tyrants dominating a free republic. He came to play an exceptional role in Florentine republican politics when the government invited him to advise the citizens on constitutional reform. In 1494 he preached:

> You are frightened by no one now, but when you had a head or tyrant, you know that the law of the tyrant is his will . . . that's how the tyrant is. . . . in future no more tyrants can arise in our city because having been given the Great Council and holding firm to it, be certain of this, there will be no more heads in Florence.[120]

Instead, he argued in true Dominican fashion that since neither God nor Christ were heads of state, then it must be 'the people' who were lord of Florence: 'government is in the hands of the people which is the true and legitimate Lord of our city', not the Signoria but the Great Council as sovereign legislator.[121] The Great Council, com-

---

117   See Q. Skinner, 'Political Philosophy', in Schmitt, Skinner, Kessler and Kraye, *The Cambridge History of Renaissance Philosophy,* pp. 389–452.

118   See H. C. Butters, *Governors and Government in Early Sixteenth-century Florence, 1502–1519* (Oxford, 1985); A. Brown, *The Medici in Florence: the exercise and language of power* (Florence, 1992).

119   D. Weinstein, *Savonarola and Florence: prophecy and patriotism in the Renaissance* (Princeton, NJ, 1970).

120   Cited especially from his *Prediche sopra i Salmi,* ed. V. Romano (Rome, 1969), vol. 2 in A. Brown, 'Savonarola, Machiavelli and Moses', in Denley and Elam, *Florence and Italy,* pp. 57–72.

121   Ibid., p. 59.

prising some three and a half thousand citizens who themselves, their parents or grand-parents, had held one of the three major offices of state, were to be advised by Savonarola. He spoke of himself as a new Moses, a prophet, legislator and disciplinary leader of his people. This was Savonarola's popular republicanism, preaching popular participation in discussion and voting to Florentines in the Great Council as the people of Israel.

There is much that is reminiscent of Marsilius of Padua's 'human legislator' in Savonarola's 1496 homily on the importance of popular participation in free discussion and voting. He told his popular supporters to allow the leading citizens to have their say but

> if you don't like it, go up yourself then . . . [and] do as those fine fellows do and say: the reasons given are good but it seems to me there are other reasons to consider – and then give your reasons forcefully, and at the end say: So it seems to me, with due respect to opinions better than mine – and in this way you will find the truth and what is best for you. Don't believe all they say, however. . . . Votes count more than fine words.[122]

Oligarchs, of course, could accept that aspect of the Marsilian vision (but not for Marsilian reasons) where small bodies of expert citizens had the leisure and learning to discuss and formulate legislation, so that policy was made by few and approved by the many. But they could not accept that the Great Council was comprised of anything other than the ignorant, holding that the people are not good judges of men's qualities and should not be able to elect to important offices, since they are more swayed by opinion than by reason.

Savonarola does not seem to have demurred from this sceptical view of the people's right reason either. Hence, he modifies the Marsilian vision of the natural rationality of the 'human legislator' in the Great Council. His language is penetrated by a prophetic quasi-royal imperative that can also be found in contemporary discourse on mixed constitutions, not least based on the Venetian model of an aristocratic republic with its doge. Savonarola first favoured the Venetian model but then changed to favour a *governo populare*. He thought the character of the Florentine people did not suit them for monarchy, although his early preaching indicates that princely government, superficially along the lines presented by Thomas Aquinas, was his ideal. And so, like the Medici before him, who used the language of the Platonic philosopher–king to justify their arbitrary power, Savonarola appropriated for himself the regal role in the mixed government. It was through him as judge and prophet, as their Moses, that Florentines in their Great Council were, in effect, counselled by God. Like Moses, Savonarola was believed to talk with God. Led by its prophet–king, Savonarola saw this as a true republican regime, a *vivere civile*, a *vero vivere libero et civile*.

Machiavelli heard Savonarola's sermons, not only those delivered in February 1498 where Savonarola warned that Florentine factionalism, that is, the corruption of pursuing particular interests, was encouraging a tyrant in their midst to rise up. Machiavelli summarized the sermons for the Florentine ambassador in Rome, saying that Savonarola kept digressing and changing with the times, telling the people lies to suit them.[123] He

---

122   Cited in ibid., p. 61.
123   *Lettere*, 9, March 1498, ed. F. Gaeta (Milan, 1961), pp. 32–3.

had read the Bible 'judiciously'. Machiavelli would later observe in his *Discourses* III, 30 that this was a necessary but insufficient ploy. In 1498 Savonarola's regime ended and Savonarola was tried and executed, having been excommunicated by church authorities for his criticism of Catholic corruption. A new Signoria was thereafter elected and the chancery was purged of its political activists. A new staff was brought in, all of whom came from outside the arena of Florentine politics, were foreigners or Florentines beneath the patrician class. Machiavelli was one of them. During the next fourteen years he worked for the republic. In 1502 the republican constitution was again modified so that the leading political office, the *Gonfaloniere di giustizia* became a post for life, *Gonfaloniere a vita*, similar to the doge in Venice. Piero Soderini was elected to this position, but he refused to accept the addition of a Senate of aristocrats curtailing his powers. It was Soderini's regime that collapsed largely through aristocratic hostility in 1512, Machiavelli having served him well and reaching a position of diplomatic importance that was unusual for his social rank. While there is no evidence that Machiavelli played any role as Soderini's political agent, and there is evidence that he manoeuvred among the various political factions, it is known that he expressed intense hatred for the aristocrats who destroyed Soderini's government.[124]

Just before he entered the Florentine chancery, then, Machiavelli had heard Savonarola preach, like Moses, of the importance of arms for success, but he was aware that unlike Moses, Savonarola was an unarmed preacher who lost control of his followers after they ceased to believe him. He observed that Moses got his laws adopted by murdering men opposed to him, and Savonarola said it was necessary to murder the sons of Brutus – *but he never did it*. Machiavelli came to the view that oratory, whether from behind the pulpit or as taught by humanist handbooks on persuasive rhetoric, was necessary but not sufficient either to motivate men to action or to maintain them in that motivation. If one is concerned to reorganize a corrupt city of self-interested factions so that it can live a *vivere civile*, then the difficulties of maintaining a regime, the 'stato', or creating one anew – its constitutional form as a republic or monarchy being irrelevant so long as rule is by law and not by the will either of one man or a faction – will be virtually insurmountable if oratory is your only means to that end. If free government, a free 'stato' is defined as one ruled by law, then it is imperative to discover how this is established and how maintained. Machiavelli was on his way to formulating his theory of political success based, in part, on the lessons of violence and the need for arms. As Skinner has amply demonstrated, Machiavelli challenges his own humanist heritage in denouncing the humanists' failure to emphasize the significance of sheer power in political life. They misunderstood the scope of necessity. Not only is it not enough to devote oneself either to ancient or Christian virtue. The maintenance of successful government also depends on an unflinching willingness to supplement the arts of persuasion with the employment of effective military force.[125]

Machiavelli's political theory would eventually surface in his *Prince* (1513) and *Discourses on Livy* (1513–19). These works in particular (and Machiavelli wrote others,

---

124   Black, 'Machiavelli, Servant of the Florentine Republic', pp. 71–99. Black cites the important work by R. Pesman Cooper: 'Pier Soderini: aspiring prince or civic leader?' *Studies in Medieval and Renaissance History*, n.s. 1 (1978); 'The Florentine Ruling Group under the 'governo populare' 1494–1512', *Studies in Medieval and Renaissance History*, n.s. 7 (1985); and 'Machiavelli, Pier Soderini and *Il Principe*', in C. Condren and R. Pesman Cooper, eds, *Altro Polo: A Volume of Italian Renaissance Studies* (Sydney, 1982), pp. 119–44.
125   Q. Skinner, *Foundations of Modern Political Thought*, vol. 1 (Cambridge, 1978), pp. 128ff.

including plays, poems and his *Florentine Histories*)[126] provide two perspectives on government or 'stato', princely and republican. Most analysts have observed that there are fundamental differences between these two works, Skinner arguing in particular that *The Prince* is organized around the basic value of security, and the *Discourses* around the value of liberty.[127] Like other humanists, Machiavelli argued *in utramque partem*, writing a tract in the tradition of the mirrors for princes, and one on republics, both works taking up the agendas revealed in contemporary writing on monarchies and republics by civic humanists. But in shifting humanist priorities, both works display a belief that history, one's own, that of successful leaders of men in the past, and of whole peoples like the Romans, can teach us, if we read it correctly, that success is not had through persuasion or even good laws, in the first instance, but rather comes through the prudential deployment of force responding to necessity.[128]

As Cicero had said: *historia magistra vitae*, history is the teacher of life. History is used by Machiavelli as a source of examples. But what it teaches is not quite what Cicero said it taught. For Machiavelli it teaches that successful men who have followed the conventional virtues when *possible*, have always used force when *necessary*. They then took care to give the appearance of having been conventionally virtuous. The aim of a prince, then, is to be judged honourable and be universally praised. Especially if he is not, in fact, a conventionally virtuous man, he should be so prudent as to know how to escape the evil reputation attached to those vices which could lose him his state. His prudence deals with treating the unintended consequences of necessity, *fortuna*, opportunistically. Princely *virtù*, in Machiavelli's interpretation, cannot always be consonant with Christian or civic humanist virtues, although he does not preach abandoning conventional moral norms in general. Princely *virtù* becomes whatever range of qualities the prince may find it necessary to acquire in order to maintain his regime and achieve great things. And the collective *virtù* of the citizen body in a republic serves the same ends, to maintain the republic so that it survives forever and achieves great things. But how princes and republics respectively achieve these ends, how they govern, are different: a prince through institutions which eliminate conflict and a republic through institutions which maintain conflict.

Machiavelli's Political Morality

Before we look more closely at *The Prince*[129] and compare and contrast it with views expressed in his *Discourses*,[130] we must observe that in neither of these tracts is there

---

126 English trans. L. F. Banfield and H. C. Mansfield, *Florentine Histories by N. Machiavelli* (Princeton, NJ, 1988); for a recent evaluation of Machiavelli as an historian see A.-M. Cabrini, *Per una valutazione delle 'Istorie Fiorentine' del Machiavelli: note sulle fonti del Secondo Libro* (Florence, 1985).
127 Skinner, *Foundations*, p. 158.
128 *The Prince* ch. 14.
129 The standard Italian edition is in N. Machiavelli, *Tutte le opere*, ed. M. Martelli (Florence, 1971); also, S. Bertelli, ed., *Il Principe e Discorsi* (Milan, 1960). Some easily available editions in translation: Machiavelli, *The Prince*, ed. Q. Skinner, trans. R. Price (Cambridge, 1988); *The Prince and Other Political Writings*, trans. and ed. S. J. Milner (London, 1995); *Machiavelli, Selected Political Writings: 'The Prince', selections from the 'Discourses', Letter to Vettori*, ed. and trans. D. Wootton (Indianapolis, 1994); *The Chief Works and Others*, ed. and trans. A. Gilbert, 3 vols (Durham, NC, 1965); *The Prince and the Discourses*, intro. M. Lerner, trans. L. Ricci, revd E. R. P. Vincent (New York, 1950). See also the collection of reprinted important articles edited by J. Dunn and I. Harris, *Machiavelli* 2 vols (Cheltenham, 1997).
130 Machiavelli, *The Discourses*, ed. B. Crick, trans. L. J. Walker (Harmondsworth, 1970).

counsel to call what is evil, good, or the vicious, virtuous. Neither tract is sceptical of the moral domain. In neither tract is there a redescription of injustice as justice. The underlying political morality of both works is the same. Machiavelli, when speaking of Agathocles who rose from a lowly position as the son of a potter to become king, tells how he called the people and Senate together and killed the senators and the rich. Machiavelli observes that it cannot be called *virtù* to kill one's fellow citizens, betray one's friends, be without faith, without pity and without religion; by these methods one may indeed gain power but not glory. The barbarous cruelty of Agathocles does not permit his being named among the most famous men and we cannot attribute to fortune or *virtù* that which he achieved without either (*The Prince*, ch. 8). True princely *virtù* will have to include capacities other than the unrestrained and continuous use of force. Machiavelli advocates 'an economy of violence',[131] but only in the sense of being economical with violence by analogy with our modern understandings of politicians being 'economical with the truth'. Therefore, Skinner is, I think, correct in arguing that 'the difference between Machiavelli and his contemporaries cannot adequately be characterized as a difference between a moral view of politics and a view of politics as divorced from morality. The essential contrast is rather between two different moralities, 'two rival and incompatible accounts of what ought ultimately to be done'.[132]

What Machiavelli teaches is an understanding that 'evil', 'good', 'vicious', 'virtuous', 'justice' and 'injustice' are always determined by circumstances. Rhetoricians, and especially those who took Aristotle's *Rhetoric* to heart, understood this well. Skinner has an interesting discussion on rhetorical redescription, paradiastolic speech,[133] and he analyses Machiavelli as a master of redescription. My own view is that Machiavelli is making the Aristotelian rhetorical point that virtues and vices exist but what they mean to any agent depends on the circumstances in which acts are performed and characters are then subsequently judged. Virtues are not judged such by theoretical reason but rather by practical reason, prudence. Prudence deals with the unintended consequences of necessity, opportunistically. In both works there is a sustained observation that past successful leaders and peoples could never have been successful in maintaining appearances had virtue and vice not been understood by all men as determined by circumstances. Modes of behaviour are always to be tempered to the quality of the times.

Nor is this a statement about moral relativism; rather, it is the classical, *rhetorical* understanding of prudent choice, in particular and contingent circumstances, that a prudent man, or people, determine what is the right thing to do, at the right time, in these circumstances now, and to the right person(s). In the *Discourses*, Machiavelli advises a republic:

> when the safety of one's country wholly depends on the decision to be taken, no attention should be paid either to justice or to injustice, to kindness or cruelty, or to its being praiseworthy or ignominious. [Note that this does not insist that justice or injustice, kindness and cruelty, are epiphenomena, mere words or imaginings.] On the contrary, every other consideration being set aside, that alternative should be wholeheartedly adopted which will save the life and preserve the freedom of one's country.

131   S. Wolin, *Politics and Vision* (Boston, 1960), pp. 220–4.
132   Skinner, *Foundations*, p. 135; also see I. Berlin, 'The Originality of Machiavelli', in *Against the Current*, ed. H. Hardy (London, 1979), pp. 25–79.
133   See Q. Skinner, *Reason and Rhetoric in the Philosophy of Hobbes* (Cambridge, 1996), pp. 170–2.

This recalls Cicero's appeal to the *salus populi*, an argument which *we* have come to call *raison d'état*, reason of state. It is a view that was well established in medieval legal discourse about the prior rights of the collectivity, the 'stato', to survive. Once the prior rights were affirmed, discusions of the *means* by which survival was to be achieved developed through discourses we recognize as constitutional. From antiquity one learns that to preserve Rome's newly recovered liberty the sons of Brutus had to be killed; in contemporary times, Machiavelli thought Soderini should have taken extra-legal action to secure his hold on power and crush Medici supporters.[134] A prince 'today' needs to know *how* to maintain his 'stato' no less than does a republic.[135]

This is precisely what ancient and humanist rhetoric teaches: plausibility in the circumstances. The rhetorical virtue of decorum teaches appropriateness and it is merged with the ethical virtue of doing what is right, that is, useful in these circumstances, for you. Cicero's discussion of the second of his four *personae* in his *De officiis* made this plain. It is here that oratory is crucial in preserving semblant reputations, praising and blaming through the filter of what appears plausible to ordinary men in the circumstances, this being ideology rather than fact. The Machiavellian innovation was the observation that while men may live their intellectual lives through ideology rather than fact, they do not live their collective lives by ideology alone.

The Prince is the product of an epistolary dialogue which Machiavelli had sustained with his former diplomatic colleague under Soderini, Francesco Vettori. Although eventually dedicated to Lorenzo de' Medici it is not certain whether it was ever sent to him, but Machiavelli's aim was to regain employment of some kind. He would spend the next years of his 'retirement' writing, while frequenting the discussions of republican patricians in the gardens of Cosimo Rucellai, to whom he dedicated his *Discourses on Livy*. Because *The Prince* is in the genre of the mirror for princes, and the *Discourses* is an idealization of republics with an expanded role for the people, it has often been asked whether the intentions of the 'real' Machiavelli can be discerned: was he in favour of princely or republican government? We must remain ignorant of his own intentions, but what these two tracts reveal is an *argument* in favour of the health of men in civil regimes and the establishment and maintenance of liberty. His argument favours both monarchy and republic, but not in all circumstances or for all peoples.

In both *The Prince* and the *Discourses* he stresses that in conditions of advanced political corruption, where factionalism is rife, the best laws are of no avail unless they are administered by a man of such supreme power that he may cause the laws to be obeyed *until* the mass has been restored to a healthy condition.[136] It is difficult or impossible to maintain liberty in a republic that has become corrupt or to establish it there anew, so that if liberty is to be introduced and maintained, then it will be necessary to reduce the state to a monarchical, rather than a republican form of government; for men whose turbulence could not be controlled by the simple force of law can be controlled in a measure only by an almost regal power. To attempt to restore men to good conduct by another means would be virtually impossible.[137] It will always be necessary in both a

---

134 *Disc.* III, 3.
135 S. Wolin, *The Presence of the Past* (Baltimore, 1989), pp. 164–5 is correct in arguing that this is not intended for princes to violate the law or disregard conventions. Addressed to the citizen it reminds him to beware of a republic that relies on extraordinary measures as policy, dispensing with constitutional methods.
136 *Disc.* I, 17.
137 *Disc.* I, 18.

republic and a principality to rely on the strong rule of a single man to restore the *virtù* of the 'stato'. In the *Discourses* he makes it clear that this healthy condition is one in which men practise their liberties, singly and collectively, to serve the common good, the 'stato', and he appears to express a personal preference for this kind of life of political liberty in a constitutional republic. Appearances, as Machiavelli will teach us, can be deceptive. What he does make clear is that the welfare of a republic *or* monarchy does not consist in having a prince who governs it wisely during his lifetime but in having one who will give it such laws that it will maintain itself even after his death.[138] Machiavelli is speaking in terms of constitutional rule, rule by law rather than will, that is constrained by the goal of the common good in perpetuity. And *successful* rulers, of monarchies or republics, are the ones who have always recognized claims for personal and collective liberty and political autonomy, which law-governed regimes, and not tyrannies, have always acknowledged and secured. No matter how forceful a Machiavellian prince with princely *virtù* may be, once established he is not a tyrant who rules by unguided whim alone.[139]

The Prince falls within the category of 'mirrors for princes', accepting the categories and concepts which contemporary political theorists of his generation used to express their views.[140] But it is also a critique of the advice proffered in these works. Machiavelli's *Prince* is justly seen as a rejection of the content of other civic humanists' essays of like kind, such as the writings of Petrarch, Patrizi, Bracciolini and Pontano, all of whom were writing for hereditary *signori* of well-established ruling dynasties. They addressed themselves to a ruler and spoke of his duties, the idealized personal virtues he must acquire and his education in virtuous living and paternalist government for the common good.[141] But Machiavelli's *Prince* is not simply a parody of civic humanist tracts turned on their head. If we come at this tract from what we already know about political theorizing and discourses in classical antiquity and during the Middle Ages, Machiavelli's *Prince* reveals itself as an extraordinary and eclectic, magpie selection of insights from Aristotle, Cicero, Roman historians, and civic humanist dialogues on princes and republics, all turned to address the seminal questions of how the 'stato' comes into being and how it is maintained. Machiavelli shows himself to be especially concerned to illuminate the varied nature of principalities in general, in the past and present (the tract was originally called *de principatibus*) and, in particular, to address a *new* prince.[142]

138 *Disc.* I, 11.
139 See J. Coleman, 'Structural Realities of Power: the theory and practice of monarchies and republics in relation to personal and collective liberty', in M. Gosman, A. Vanderjagt and J. Veenstra, eds, *The Propagation of Power in the Medieval West* (Groningen, 1997), pp. 207–30.
140 See A. Gilbert, *Machiavelli's 'Prince' and its Forerunners: the Prince as a typical book de Regimine Principum* (Durham, NC, 1938); also C. J. Nederman, 'The Mirror Crack'd: The *Speculum Principum* as political and social criticism in the late Middle Ages', *The European Legacy* 3 (1998), pp. 18–38, including a useful and up-to-date bibliography.
141 See Skinner, *Foundations* 1, pp. 129ff.
142 There has been some discussion of whether Machiavelli intended *The Prince* for the Medici since they were not new, but newly restored to power in 1513, Wootton arguing that Medici problems were not the problems that Machiavelli was addressing. Instead, he was attempting to procure a job in Rome to direct papal foreign policy, the Medici pope being assumed to wish to ensure the Medici family, and Giuliano de' Medici in particular, acquired a hereditary state elsewhere in Italy. See Wootton's introduction to *Machiavelli, Selected Political Writings*, pp. xvii–xviii.

Founding and Maintaining the 'Stato'

Machiavelli begins in chapter 1 by asserting that all 'states' and dominions which hold or have held sway over mankind are either republics or monarchies. He distinguishes between monarchies as (a) hereditary or (b) of recent foundation. Monarchies of recent or new foundation rule over a people who either (1) have been previously accustomed to the rule of another prince, and hence, having no tradition of self-rule, the new prince simply grafts them on to his own possessions, or (2) have themselves constituted free states, that is, been accustomed to self-rule. In this case, they must be (a) annexed by force of arms of the new prince or else they have fallen to the prince (b) by good fortune or (c) through his special ability. Free states, that is those with a tradition of self-rule and a tradition of their own liberties, must be conquered by force, fortune or a prince's special ability. It is the latter, the prince's special ability, which Machiavelli will call princely *virtù*. Just as Aristotle had drawn the distinction between making and doing and the different but related skills required for each,[143] so Machiavelli says that there is a difference between establishing a princedom by force, fortune or *virtù*, and governing or maintaining it. The overriding concern for a new ruler is to maintain his rule, *mantenere lo stato*. If the main foundations of every 'stato' are 'good laws and good arms', then, according to Machiavelli (chapter 12), where there are good arms, good laws inevitably follow. And the good arms must be one's own army and never hired mercenaries.

In chapter 2 he notes that he has spoken elsewhere about republics, presumably in an early draft of his *Discourses* dealing with how republics can be governed and maintained, so that in *The Prince* he will deal only with monarchies, hereditary or new, with an emphasis on the latter. When it is possible, a new prince should leave intact the language, customs and institutions of a people. Certain pre-existent structures do not disturb his own security, but these must be structures put in place by previous princes to whose institutions and laws the people have become accustomed. Otherwise, a new prince will need both good fortune and great industry to retain his acquisition of dominions with different customs, laws and languages. Machiavelli will have much to say about the processes of habituation, what we would call 'acculturation'. All new principalities, however, suffer from what Machiavelli thinks of as *natural* problems, *natural* and *normal* constraints. These are the consequence of human nature being what it is on the one hand, and necessity being what it is on the other: that men are *always* ready to change rulers when they believe they can better their condition, and that new rulers are *always* forced to injure new subjects, both through their troops and other injuries that are involved in conquest. We are being alerted to enduring themes throughout this tract: the fixity of aspects of human nature and the fixity of the force of necessity.

But however acquired – by force, fortune or *virtù* (and in chapter 7 he will reduce these to two: fortune and *virtù*) – Machiavelli (chapter 5) insists that there is *no* sure method of holding or maintaining cities or dominions that, prior to being occupied, lived under their own laws, that is, were free and self-governing, *except by despoiling them*. Whoever becomes the ruler of a free city and does not destroy it can be expected to be destroyed by it, for it can always find a motive for rebellion in the name of liberty and of its ancient customs, which are forgotten neither by lapse of time nor by benefits

143   See chapter 1, on Aristotle's *Rhetoric* and *NE*6.

received. Hence, a new dominion, especially if it is used to its own liberties, must be conquered by force and to maintain it you must despoil it, using your own army and your own ability (*virtù*) (chapter 6).

Machiavelli makes it clear that once conquered and despoiled, a once-free city is in a similar position to those cities that were used to being ruled by a prince and thereby had never developed or had forgotten their ancient customs or liberties of free self-govern-ance. To maintain *lo stato*, all memory of customary self-governance must be wiped out, and this is an achievement of forceful imposition rather than rhetorical persuasion. Once this situation has been accomplished, the character of *this kind* of despoiled or traditionless people will ask nothing but not to be oppressed. It is a traditionless people that will remain content so long as the new prince does not rob men of their property or take their women and honour. It has often been noted that a prince requires a passive people. But this is not some natural characteristic of social man, for Machiavelli, but an 'achieve-ment' of a certain experience which is a response to necessary events they have been forced to endure. We are being forewarned that Machiavelli has a view on the way an individual's and a people's *character* is open to manipulation, while men's *nature* is fixed. We must remain alive to the distinction between character formation and man's nature.

The Fixity of Man's Nature

Man's nature is fixed for the species and is universally shared. Men's characters, how-ever, are the consequence of habits built up by experience. For Machiavelli and all ancient, medieval and Renaissance thinkers, man's nature does not change over time: hence, ancient, medieval and Renaissance men share the same natures. In all societies throughout history men can be observed to have demonstrated through their actions the same kind of nature, a nature that is specific to humans. Hence, there is one truth for mankind no matter in what period of history or in what culture they have lived.

It is to this fixed model of human nature that modern political scientists find them-selves attracted, thinking it to be evidence of Machiavelli's 'modern' approach to man from which he and they can induce the universal 'laws of politics'. But this is not a modern position. Rather, it is a very ancient view of the distinction between human nature on the one hand, and *ēthos* or character on the other. Some of the universally shared characteristics which Machiavelli attributes to human nature as such may be listed as follows: men change their masters voluntarily, believing they can better themselves (chapter 3); men walk almost always in paths trodden by others, proceeding in their actions by imitation (chapter 6); men are incredulous, not truly believing in anything new until they have had an actual experience of it (chapter 6); men commit injuries either through fear or through hate (chapter 7); it is the nature of men to be as much bound by the benefits that they confer as by those they receive (chapter 10); for it may be said of men in general that they are ungrateful, voluble dissemblers, anxious to avoid danger and covetous of gain (chapter 17); love is held by a chain of obligations which, men being selfish, is broken whenever it serves their purposes; fear is maintained by a dread of punishment which never fails (chapter 17); men forget more easily the death of their father than the loss of their patrimony (chapter 17); men love at their own free will but fear at the will of the prince (or anyone else who has sufficient force at his disposal) (chapter 17); men are bad and would not observe their faith with you (chapter 18); men are so simple and so ready to obey necessities that one who deceives will always find those who allow themselves to be deceived (chapter 18); men in general judge more by the eyes than by the hands, that is, men see appearances but do not feel what things are (chapter 18); the common people are always taken by appearances and the occurrence of events, and the world consists only of the common people (chapter 18); there are three 'breeds' of human brains: one which understands things by itself, another which learns what others understand, and a third which understands neither by itself nor by others: the first is excellent, the second also excellent but the third is useless (chapter 22); men are much more taken by present than by past things and when they find themselves well off in the present they enjoy it and seek nothing more (chapter 24); a common fault of men is not to reckon on storms in fair weather (chapter 24); all men aim at glory and wealth but proceed in different ways to achieve their aims (chapter 25).

In short, men are by nature primarily self-interested and what they take to be their interest is material wealth and glory (reputation, the esteem of others).[144] The desire to acquire possessions is a very natural and ordinary thing (chapter 6). All their actions are aimed at self-betterment as they perceive it. This is an Aristotelian observation as Aristotle explained it not only in his *Rhetoric* but also when he spoke about less than ideal constitutions, democracies and oligarchies, in *Politics* IV.[145] Like Aristotle, Machiavelli does not picture man's self-interest as characteristic of an atomistic isolate, calculating utility maximization prior to his social embeddedness. Rather, he describes humans as inclined by their *nature* to live in societies. Machiavelli has learned this not only from the ancients but from his own experiences in Florence. Hence, he emphasizes even more than does Aristotle that the conditions of society are such that men are fearful of threats to perceived self-interest. His picture of society is conflictual, along the lines of magnates versus the people, where Aristotle had emphasized the prime division of the state into the poor and the rich so that in such cases there seem to be two constitutions, 'democracy' and 'oligarchy', where the interests of the poor are 'freedom' (that is, from oppression) and those of the rich are 'wealth'.[146]

Indeed, Machiavelli acknowledged, as did Savonarola, the notion that Florentine politics was and always had been a contest or dialogue for power between an elite of *grandi* or *nobili* and a *popolo* of men engaged in commerce. Society is natural and it consists of natural enmities between the people and nobles, caused by the desire of the latter to command and the former not to obey (chapter 9). These natural enmities continue to exist in civil principalities and in civil republics. In both there is more danger from the *nobili* than from the people. The naturalness of society with its natural enmities remained in all his writings an organizing principle for the interpretation of politics in city states: the enmities are the cause of all the ills, but he would read Roman history to show that in ancient Rome the contest had beneficial results, whereas in Florence the struggle between *nobili* and *popolo* had perhaps less happy consequences, yet it was decisive for the city and its noble families.[147] Given the natural enmities in society, 'all the qualities

---

144 Modern negative connotations of selfishness were not developed in the sixteenth century. See R. Price, 'Self-love, "Egoism" and *ambizione* in Machiavelli's Thought', *History of Political Thought* 9 (1988), pp. 237–61.

145 See chapter 1 above and vol. 1, *A History of Political Thought* chapter 4.

146 E.g. *Politics* IV, 1291b9 and 1294a11.

147 See Machiavelli's *Istorie Fiorentine* 2.12, and 3.1 on the natural humours in cities between nobles and people and the necessity that these be maintained but balanced, with reference to the difference between Rome and Florence.

that are reputed good cannot all be possessed or observed, human conditions not per-mitting it' (chapter 15). As a consequence, men are not grateful or faithful to others unless necessity forces them to be: self-interest in these conditions leads them to look for ways to avoid danger and covet gain. They commit injuries in these conditions through either fear or hatred. They deceive and are deceived.

The heart of the matter is that human nature demonstrates that it has a particular way of coming to know what it takes to be in its self-interest: men judge only by appearances; that is, they know about the world first by having sensed it, and they judge what they see and think about what they have judged. Even the best of brains which understands things by itself begins with sense experience and proceeds to judge by appearances. Men do not believe anything unless they have first experienced it, and their experience is founded on perception. Knowledge can be only of what has first been perceived. Men's senses do not grasp what things really are but only what they appear to be. And they proceed in their lives by imitating what they see. What they see and then imitate is the action of others. They cannot know another man's intentions; they can only judge a man by his actions, which may or may not reflect what he is thinking. The knowledge men acquire is the consequence of what appears to their senses to be the case: events and actions. This is why men are more taken by the present than by the past. They see the present. If one writes down what one has seen and if one reads the writings of others who have recorded what they have seen in their present, then human nature will be shown to be constant over time. The constancy consists in the apparent 'fact' that men have always judged what they take to be their self-interest and how to act to achieve it on the basis of the perception of appearances. This psychological theory of motivation behind action is Machiavelli's understanding of the ancient, indeed, Aristotelian rhetorical theory of mo-tivation integrated with Cicero's observations on character formation and skewed to answer questions relevant to Machiavelli's own times. Self-interest, being known through appearances, is a plausibility in contingent circumstances. And the numerous historical examples, contemporary and ancient, which Machiavelli provides in *The Prince*, are merely further demonstrations that history preserves reputations of great men, their *personae,* what they appeared to do and be, but not what they really were.

Character Formation

The stability of human nature, however, is distinguished from character. Individually and collectively as cultures, men *develop* their universally shared human natures so that they come to have the discrete characters they have, such characters being the conse-quence of their individual and collective experiences. These experiences are not random and unconscious events which happen *to* men. It is true that men cannot control contin-gencies, that is, the times and circumstances they are born in, no matter how prudent they may be. Machiavelli says that 'time brings with it all things and may produce indifferently either good or evil' (chapter 3). But experiences are the psyche's responses *to* the world of times and circumstances, and experiences have effects on men's charac-ters. Men are agents and their experiences are their willed responses to contingent events, so that from these willed responses characteristic habits of behaviour become fixed. Hence, he notes that the character of different peoples varies (chapter 6).

Indeed, the characters of individual men also vary: some men proceed cautiously and others impetuously on their way to what they perceive to be their self-interest (chapter 25).[148] Character is the result of habits established over and above a foundational, shared human nature. It is these willed responses that constitute their experiences and, taken together over many years, are built up as inclinations or dispositions to respond to certain conditions in characteristic ways. Men become habitually fixed in their ways. Hence, it is their acts which, when considered by others, demonstrate to observers the *kinds* of characters they possess, and from observation of character, which is an observation of appearances, one can predict with a certain degree of probability how such a habituated person will respond to future contingencies, when, of course, the circumstances appear to be similar to those to which he responded in the past. A new prince who confronts a free people is obliged for his own security to take some drastic steps to reformulate their character, turning them initially into passive subjects rather than active citizens and thereafter allowing them to develop different characters by habituating them through good laws to proceed cautiously towards their perceived self-interest.

Machiavelli, therefore, describes two constraints on the randomness or 'freedom' of human behaviour. One is human nature itself, which is fixed for the species and shows that men always make judgements on the basis of appearances. The other is the relative 'fixity' of habituated character, dispositions that are dependent on experiences. A man learns how to proceed in life through imitation and by developing habits based on the experiences he has had. His experiences in a monarchy produce one kind of character and those in a republic produce another kind of character. And the more experiences, as willed responses to contingencies, past or present, the more 'experienced' or prudent he becomes in recognizing similarities in conditions and acting accordingly to produce like results. An experienced man is a better 'crisis manager' and what he retains is a memory of past experiences and the means to possible solutions.

Men with experiences of 'liberty' have characters that make them less amenable to princely government. Should a new prince come to rule such men with enduring memories of their own free, self-governing experiences, he had better 'despoil' them of such collective imaginings and, preferably through the short, sharp shock, make them think that each is unsafe, alone, without a tradition of collective practices to ensure safety, and dependent on him. Once this is achieved, his job is to ensure that his subjects are stabilized and made secure. He strengthens their habits of loyalty and dependence on him by devising ways in which they will remain dependent on him in times of necessity. Indeed, he builds up a citizen militia and he assumes personal command and captains his troops himself. Hence, a new prince habituates his people by new laws and thereby creates their characters *a novo* to suit his 'stato', the new collective realm of their experience.

It is important to realize that Aristotle thought it was virtually impossible, or at least extremely difficult, to rehabituate mature men, but Cicero thought it eminently achievable for ordinary men who, unlike Hercules who sprang from the seed of Jupiter, were not inwardly unified moral personalities. Instead, the successful ordinary man plays roles which enable him to appear virtuous, and in Machiavelli's version, he has his natural impulses regulated by law and necessary force to perform duties deemed appropriate to his position and circumstances in the princely 'stato'. Machiavelli notes that the prince will then appear to have been long established and will quickly become

---

148 See *A History of Political Thought*, vol. 1, above, chapter 5, on Cicero's four *personae* theory in the *De officiis*.

more safe and secure in his government than if he had been ruling his state for a long time (chapter 24).

However, an experienced man is not infallible. There are no absolutely safe policies. Machiavelli believes it is better to consider the probable results of certain policies because the nature of things is such that one never tries to avoid one difficulty without running into another (chapter 21). Prudence consists in being able to know the nature of particular difficulties and taking the least harmful as good. Prudence is practical reasoning in the midst of particular and contingent circumstances, determining specific means to an end. It never achieves absolute certainty; its scope is plausibility in the circumstances. Rhetorical theory, even Aristotle's, does not ask one to evaluate the ethical status of the end towards which prudence determines the specific means. The end is culturally given, a social premise, learnt from experiences and judged as apparently 'good' or at least as less harmful in the circumstances. Human life proceeds on the basis of the probable, spurred on as it is by judgements founded on appearance.

But Machiavelli insists that no matter how many experiences a man may have, no matter how experienced or prudent he is, he will never be able to respond freely to the near infinite contingencies of time and circumstances, for 'time brings with it all things and may produce indifferently either good or evil'. A prince needs to know that man remains absolutely fixed in nature and more or less fixed in character, 'either because he cannot deviate from that to which nature inclines him, or else, because having always prospered by walking in one path, he cannot persuade himself to leave it' (chapter 25). No man can change his human nature or have that human nature changed by another. And persuasion is not usually sufficient to change his character. But necessity can force a change in character and this necessity is a coercive imposition from outside his self. Practical reasoning cannot choose whether or not to respond to what is necessary. Practical reasoning only operates in the sphere where one's choices can make a difference. The prince as a prudent, practical reasoner has a sphere of operation where he can opportunistically mould the unintended consequences of necessity, fortune, to his advantage. He cannot change men's nature but he can affect their character. Hence, a new prince must be an orator, working on the soul's passions, affecting men's emotions, but he must also be prepared to affect the emotions by replacing language with the sword. He must rehabituate a people that has no tradition of self-governing habits, where habits are emotional responses 'guided' by practical reasoning, his prudence. Nothing brings a man greater honour than founding a new principality, bringing new laws and new institutions. This is the classical legislator who treats a traditionless people as children, persuading and forcing in turn until their characters have been reformulated to suit his 'stato'.

If a man *could* change both his nature and character to suit *all* times and *all* circumstances, he would not only not be as he has appeared to be throughout history, but his *fortuna* would never change, contrary to what his history appears to show (chapter 25). Man's life is not *determined*, by God or providence or biological necessity, but his life is *constrained* because of the kind of being he is.

The 'Fit' Between Character and the Times

Some men's characters, however, show themselves to be more ready than others to meet the needs of the times, largely through preparing themselves by foreseeing a *range of possibilities* and changes in conditions with which they are likely to be faced. Machiavelli is re-presenting the advice Cicero offered in his *De officiis* to men with certain natural talents and given status to regulate and reshape their own *personae* to suit the circumstances.[149] But Cicero's optimism concerning the possibilities of re-presentations of self is given a more pessimistic turn by Machiavelli. Human nature, being what it is, prevents a man from doing this for all times and all circumstances. As a consequence, great men have been those who have had the kinds of characters that happen to suit most of the contingencies of the time in which they happened to have lived. Moses was one such man whose character suited the times. Cesare Borgia, however, whom Machiavelli describes as an example to be imitated by all who by fortune and with the arms of others have risen to power, was a man of great courage and high ambitions and who, consequently, could not have acted otherwise than he did. Although he is to be praised, Machiavelli notes that he can be accused of having created Julius II as pope, and this was a bad choice, for not being able to choose his own pope he could still prevent any one individual being made pope and he ought never to have permitted any of those cardinals to be raised to the papacy whom he had injured or who, when pope, would stand in fear of him. Cesare erred in his choice and this was the cause of his ultimate ruin (chapter 7). But are we also to understand that his bad choice was 'in character' and that therefore his character was not suited to the times? Indeed, was Lorenzo de' Medici a man whose character suited his? *Only* when this is the case, when one's character suits the times, does Machiavelli remind us that 'God will not do everything in order not to deprive us of free will and the portion of the glory that falls to our lot' (chapter 26). This is a terrible irony; our free will is not as free as some have thought, but it is freer than what most men in Machiavelli's own times seemed to have believed.[150]

Fortune

The more traditional 'mirrors for princes' spoke of the forces that opposed the heroic prince despite his plans, notably the capricious force of fortune which can do irreparable harm even to the most prudent man. But fortune can also permit a man to achieve great things. In his *De officiis* Cicero had also spoken of the accidental determinants of a man's public identity which is imposed by some chance or circumstance. This he referred to as a man's third *persona*: 'Kingdoms, military powers, nobility, political honours, wealth and influence, as well as the opposite of these, are in the gift of chance and governed by circumstances'.[151] Likewise, Machiavelli speaks of his hero Cesare Borgia, who acquired his 'stato' through good fortune (he was after all Alexander VI's son), but even he could not rely on fortune's support to maintain it. And just as Cicero closed his account of the four *personae* by adding that 'in assuming a role that we want ourselves is something that proceeds from our own will', for we assume a fourth *persona* for ourselves by our own

---

149   See M. Colish, 'Cicero's *De Officiis* and Machiavelli's *Prince*', *Sixteenth Century Journal* 9 (1978), pp. 81–94, for what Colish sees as the satirical relationship between *The Prince* and classical humanism.

150   For a more extensive analysis linking Machiavelli's position with medieval and Renaissance philosophical and theological positions, see J. Coleman, 'Machiavelli's *via moderna*: medieval and Renaissance attitudes to history', in M. Coyle, ed., *Niccolò Machiavelli's The Prince: new interdisciplinary essays* (Manchester, 1995), pp. 40–64.

151   *De officiis* I, 115.

decision, likewise Machiavelli tells us that Cesare, the Duke Valentino, found the opportunity to appoint Remiro de Orco, who exercised the necessary hated and harsh authority in his lands, but Cesare wished to show the people that Remiro's cruelty was not his own. He had him cut in half and placed in the public square at Cesena, this, for Machiavelli, being a lesson in how to exploit cruelties well. For 'well committed' but undoubted cruelties are those useful to securing one's self and which are then rapidly exchanged for measures useful to your subjects (chapter 7). Indeed, he says that a prince must live with his subjects in such a way that no accident of good or evil fortune can deflect him from his course, for necessity, arising in adverse times, you are not in time with severity and the good that you do does not profit, as it is judged to be forced upon you, and you will derive no benefit from it. A successful prince must therefore be sufficiently experienced so that he is prepared to seize opportunities that require that he does what is necessary before adverse times come upon him (chapter 9).

Machiavelli makes it clear, however, that experience is a necessary but insufficient ingredient of success. To recognize what is necessary before adverse times come is a characteristic of prudence, a practical reasoning based on experience of men and things, which enables him to recognize troubles in his 'stato' as, or before, they arise. Machiavelli acknowledges that it is given to few to be thus (chapter 13). Given by whom? By nature: certain men show themselves to have certain natural talents and, as Cicero had observed in the *De officiis*, they differ not only in bodily strength but even more so in mental powers.[152] Beyond our common human nature there are countless dissimilarities of 'nature' and conduct, and Cicero had insisted that each person should hold on to what is peculiar to himself. The prince must therefore weigh the characteristics, his emotional peculiarities and tendencies that are his own, his *ingegno*, and regulate them. Even here, he may not achieve success, for his character may not suit the times. As Machiavelli was to say in his later *Florentine Histories*:[153] 'I believe that as nature has made each man an individual face, so she has made him an individual *ingegno* and an individual *fantasia*. From this results that each man conducts himself according to his *ingegno* and imagination'. Similarly, in the *Florentine Histories* Machiavelli presented a portrait of Lorenzo the Magnificent, famous for its ambiguity and describing the two opposing *personae* of his character.[154]

Machiavelli is aware that many believe that fortune and God rule worldly events to such an extent that a man's own prudence cannot change things. They are resigned to the view that things are ruled by chance. But Machiavelli seeks to show how human free will may not altogether be extinguished and proposes as plausible the view that the goddess fortune is the arbiter of half the things we do, but the other half is within our own control (chapter 25). Fifty per cent, if one thinks about it, is not so extensive a scope for personal autonomy unless one lives in a pre-modern world of inherited rank and status and is accustomed to a social environment that judges 'personal' achievement according to such unchosen status and unwilled circumstance which, accordingly, dictate relevant expectations and duties. Furthermore, freedom of choice is at best freedom

152   See the interesting discussion in A. Parel, *The Machiavellian Cosmos* (New Haven, CN, 1992) on the different humours – choleric, sanguine, melancholic, phlegmatic – which define one's temperament and which prompt the *spirito* (the sensitive soul which is *not* the intellective soul) to act in the ways it does.

153   Edited by Martelli, *Tutte le opere*, p. 1,083 and cited in Parel, *The Machiavellian Cosmos*, p. 89.

154   VIII, 36 in Martelli, *Tutte le opere*, p. 844.

to act within one's 'humoural' structure. In times of upheaval, of rapid changes in government and invasion from foreign states, Machiavelli sees why some would argue that fortune rules all. But his alternative 50 per cent proposal is not one that would delight modern believers in an ideology of the self-made man. Rather, a prince is less a unique individual than he is an office, a type, a *persona*. His *virtù* is role-specific. Within these constraints of status and circumstance he must rely on his own *virtù* if he is to maintain his 'stato'. His *virtù* must be exercised prudently, given his status and his natural *ingegno*, in response to the opportunities that result from the unintended consequences of necessity.

Perhaps the most important distinction a prince must be able to make is between what is necessary and what are the opportunities that flow from it as unintended consequences. It is possible to understand Machiavelli's argument as the standard one that necessity is outside of anyone's deliberation, but that his innovation is in proposing that one overcomes necessity not by fighting it, but by imitating it, creating *artificial* or political necessities. But Machiavelli makes it clear that this happy capacity to distinguish what is necessary from the opportunities that flow from its unintended consequences is not completely within anyone's control, for he says that a prince is happy whose mode of procedure accords with the needs of the times; similarly, he is unfortunate whose mode of procedure is opposed to the times. Men proceed in different ways towards glory and wealth, one with circumspection and another impetuously, one by violence another by cunning or patience. It is the nature of the times which does or does not conform to their method of procedure, so that it is the times and the circumstances which are the primary constraints on whether or not success is had by a man's mode of procedure! No man is ever found so prudent as to be able to adapt himself to all times and all circumstances. Hence, the fortunes of states follow the qualities of their times.

Of course, it is advantageous to 'tame' fortune and make her serve you, but Machiavelli believes that those who have been less beholden to fortune have maintained themselves best, having been princes who have come to power through their own merits, like Moses, Cyrus, Romulus and Theseus. This is a rhetorical insight. For instance, in his *Rhetoric*, Aristotle had made clear that rhetoric is defined as dealing with specific circumstances, particular individuals and their circumstances. Here he had discussed the objective of an epideictic orator, one who is engaged in praising and blaming, revealing the honourable and shameful. He observed that since praise is based on actions and to act in accordance with deliberate purpose is characteristic of a worthy person, an orator should try to show the person about whom he is speaking acting in accordance with deliberate purpose. It is useful for his subject to seem to have so acted often. Thus, the orator should take coincidences and chance happenings as due to deliberate purpose.[155] He further advises that an orator ought to come up with propositions; for instance, that one ought not to think highly of things gained by chance but of things gained through one's own efforts. As praise, this takes the form: 'He did not think highly of what came by chance but of what he gained by his own efforts'.[156]

But Machiavelli takes this further and says that while an examination of the lives and deeds of Moses, Cyrus, Romulus and Theseus will show that they owed nothing to fortune, it will also show that opportunity gave them matter to be shaped into whatever

155   *Rhetoric* I, 9, 32.
156   I, 9, 36.

form they thought fit. Without that opportunity, their own powers, their *virtù*, would have been wasted, just as without their own powers, their *virtù*, the opportunity would have come in vain. Just as it was necessary that Moses find the people of Israel slaves in Egypt, so that they were disposed to follow him in order to escape, so it was necessary that Romulus be unable to remain in 'Alba' and be exposed at birth, in order to become king of Rome and founder of that nation. If Machiavelli's historical examples had neither existed nor had been written about, he would have invented them to make this point.

The Impetuous Prince Who Must Learn How Not to Have Fixed Dispositions

Machiavelli's *fortuna* is equated to the sum of forces (some hostile, others neutral, some helpful, but always changing) lying beyond one's abilities, a prince's *virtù*. Good luck ought not, then, to be relied on and both bad luck and the changes in fortune from good to bad cannot be overcome by remaining steadfast in adverse circumstances. At first glance, this looks like Cicero's recipe for success as well: be prepared to re-present your 'self' in the circumstances. But Machiavelli rejects Cicero's injunction that one consistently pursue what is honourable. While he accepts that each person should hold on to what is his own set of talents, he omits Cicero's insistence that this be done 'so long as it is not vicious'. For Machiavelli it is dangerous to remain steadfast, a paragon of Christian *or* classical virtues.[157] Like young men who are less cautious and more ardent, who are, as Aristotle had said, dominated by their emotions and therefore considered by Aristotle to be unsuited to benefit from his lectures on ethical and political theory, a prince is only able to dominate fortune and thereby take control of that half of his life whose direction *is* open to his own control, by conceiving of fortune as a woman, coercively shaping her to his own will. Continuing the metaphor of the goddess *Fortuna* as a woman, Machiavelli advises that it is better to be impetuous than cautious, for fortune, as a woman, lets herself be overcome by youthful force and boldness. But can one choose to be an impetuous rather than a cautious man? No. But if impetuous, one must learn other skills. Machiavelli advises that if a ruler wishes to maintain his 'stato' and achieve the goals of honour, glory and fame, he must be prepared to go beyond the cultivation of the conventional range of Christian and moral virtues; indeed, he must forgo ethical and political habituation and, in his own case alone, actively prevent the acquisition of settled dispositions. He should not maintain a steadfastness but rather a prudential restlessness and impetuosity.[158]

Aristotle's *phronimos* is here totally rejected. While Machiavelli accepts that a people's character has to be worked on through rehabituation to a prince's laws, he proposes that the prince himself is a person who can somehow forgo this habituation into stable dispositions. Aristotle had said in *Nicomachean Ethics* X, 9, 1179a33 f:

> Some thinkers hold that it is by nature that people become good, others that it is by habit, and others that it is by instruction. The bounty of nature is clearly beyond our control; it is bestowed by some divine dispensation upon those who are truly fortunate. It is a regretta-

---

157   See Skinner, *Foundations* 1, pp. 126–8 on the humanist endorsement of Christian and 'cardinal' virtues.
158   N. Struever, *Theory as Practice,* p. 150, puts it thus: 'the prince is construed as an isolate, deprived of the character, the identity, which is the product of specific communal discourse . . . an isolate entangled but not involved with other protagonists, functioning against . . . a jumble of historical scenes'.

ble fact that discussion and instruction are not effective in all cases; just as a piece of land has to be prepared beforehand if it is to nourish the seed, so the mind of the pupil has to be prepared in its habits if it is to enjoy and dislike the right things; because the man who lives in accordance with his feelings would not listen to an argument to dissuade him, or understand it if he did. And when a man is in that state, how is it possible to persuade him out of it? In general, feeling seems to yield not to argument but only to force. Therefore we must have a character to work on that has some affinity to virtue. . . . For this reason upbringing and occupations should be regulated by law because they will cease to be irksome when they have become habitual. But presumably it is not enough to have received the right upbringing and supervision in youth; they must keep on observing their regimen and accustoming themselves to it even after they are grown up; so we shall need laws to regulate these activities too, and indeed, generally to cover the whole of life; for most people are readier to submit to compulsion and punishment than to argument and fine ideals. . . . [Hence] one must first have been brought up in the right way and trained in the right habits, and must thereafter spend one's life in reputable occupations, doing no wrong either with or against one's will: then this can be achieved by living under the guidance of some intelligence or right system that has effective force. Now the orders that a father gives have no forceful or compulsive power, nor indeed have those of any individual in general, *unless he is a king or somebody of that sort*; but law, being the pronouncement of a kind of practical wisdom or intelligence does have the power of compulsion.

Aristotle insists on habituation under the guidance of some intelligence or right system (of law) that has effective force and he observes that in the majority of states matters of this kind have been completely neglected. Machiavelli responds by providing a successful prince who has succeeded in shaping the character of a people precisely through his law, backed by effective force. Leo Strauss once argued that Machiavelli's political teaching was a kind of decayed Aristotelianism.[159] Perhaps it is better to say that it is a truncated Aristotelianism that finds more inspiration in Aristotle's rhetorical teaching on psychological motivation than it does in his ethical teaching in the *Nicomachean Ethics*. But is Machiavelli's prince meant to be above the laws and therefore not habituated as are his people? Is Machiavelli providing a description of a despot who rules by a will that is unguided except by whim and impetuosity alone? Is he describing the tyrant and despot of ancient and medieval political discourse? Or is Machiavelli's prince a man whose responsibilities to the 'stato', to himself and his status, require that he be otherly habituated, but habituated none the less? Machiavelli's argument is that the successful prince need not necessarily have all the reputedly good qualities but he must be skilled enough to appear to have them and hence be prepared to become a great liar and deceiver. According to Machiavelli this is no natural talent but must be learnt, just as oratorical skills must be learnt. Natural impetuosity is insufficient. Although most men remain fixed in their habituated ways, Machiavelli's prince, an impetuous type, must hone that impetuosity in a direction. Such a man must learn how *not* to be conventionally virtuous and to make use of this *or not* as the circumstances require. Indeed, the prince must be 'otherly' habituated and Machiavelli makes this clear in chapter 18. Although it is laudable to keep one's faith and live with integrity, experience of our times shows princes to have done great things who have had little regard for good faith, having been skilful in confusing men.

---

159 L. Strauss, *What is Political Philosophy? and other studies* (Glencoe, IL, 1959), p. 47.

Learn to Imitate Foxes and Lions

Machiavelli famously proposes that a prince must learn how to imitate both the lion and the fox, learning how to recognize traps as does the fox and to frighten away wolves as does the lion. A prince must learn the skills of both beasts as well as employing the human means of regulating the environment by law. Using laws is appropriate for men, and using force is appropriate to animals.[160] Laws, however, are often ineffective and one needs to have recourse to force and animal cunning as well. Ancient writers speak of how rulers, like Achilles, were entrusted to Chiron the centaur, to be raised by him, Chiron being half-man and half-beast. A ruler needs to learn how to use both natures, and that one without the other is ineffective. A prudent ruler then, ought not to keep faith when by so doing it would be against his interest and when the reasons which made him bind himself no longer exist. Here one should imitate the fox's cunning but conceal it, men being so dominated by immediate necessities that a skilful deceiver always finds people who will allow themselves to be deceived. Plausible reasons can always be found as to why a prince failed to keep his promises. It is well to seem to be merciful, trustworthy, humane, upright and devout, *and also be so,* but a prince must have a mind so disposed that when it is necessary to be otherwise he is able to change. He must have a mind disposed to adapt itself according to the wind and as the variations of fortune dictate, not deviating from what is good if possible, but being able to do evil if constrained. A prince should therefore seem to be merciful, trustworthy, full of integrity, humanity and religiously devout; he must especially appear to be pious, for men judge more by the eyes than by the hands, all see what a prince appears to be, few feel what he is, and those few will not dare oppose themselves to the many when the opinion of the majority of the common people is sustained by the majesty of the political community and regime.

It is here that we have wrongly become accustomed to the translation that 'the end justifies the means'. Rather, Machiavelli (chapter 18) says that in *all* human actions and especially actions of princes, where there is no appeal to higher judgement, one looks to the result.[161] Humans, in always judging particular actions in the circumstances and men's characters by appearances, have no access to an agent's intentions or higher reasons: they show themselves to be consequentialists. The end does not *justify* the means; they have no access to the means which may have been many and various, and only see the end, judging it against what appears to be their self-interest.[162]

A prince should avoid being hated by the people, but if he cannot be both loved and feared, it is safer to be feared if one must make the choice (chapter 17). None the less,

---

160   Compare Cicero *De officiis*, I, ii, 34 where he speaks of two ways of gaining ends: persuasion, proper to men, and force, proper to beasts. He speaks of the force of the lion and the deceitful fraud of the fox, saying that both are to be avoided by men.

161   'e nelle azioni di tutti li uomini e massime de' principi, dove non e iudizio da reclamare, si quarda al fine.'

162   Likewise Aristotle, when discussing expediency and probability, also says that the decisions and acts in a life of action do not relate to the end result in the way that a chain of reasoning leads to a philosophical conclusion. Although the end result could not have been achieved without the previous acts, other courses of action might have been taken to produce the same result and the end result of actions does not reflect or embody the process by which it was achieved. In his *Poetics* he says that this kind of action is historical rather than poetic or philosophical, and it is historians or writers on rhetoric who tell about civic actions, philosophers and poets do not. *Poetics* 1451b.

Machiavelli stresses that the best fortress is to be found in the love of the people, for fortresses will not save you if you are hated by them (chapter 20). Avoid being hated and despised, largely by not attacking the property and honour of the people, for the generality of men will then live contented (chapter 19). Well-ordered regimes and wise princes have always studied diligently not to drive the nobles to desperation and to satisfy the people and keep them contented. Hence, the skills needed to cultivate appearances, a *reputation* for being great and excellent, are the skills that will encourage a people's love.

Again, the reason for all this is that no one ever judges anyone's intentions or intrinsic qualities, this not being open to men, but rather, judgement is always of appearances. And this advice, to develop the art of dissimulation and concealment, is not a simple message but one founded on a 'higher' plausible truth about human psychology, known to rhetoricians: that praise and blame attach not to essential, internal qualities but rather to external performances in the circumstances. These are not illusions but they are appearances. It is for this reason that the gulf between how one should live and how one does live is so wide. In discussing 'of the things for which men, and especially princes, are praised or blamed' (chapter 15) Machiavelli argues for a real truth of things (*verità effetuale della cosa*) as opposed to what men have imagined ([*non*] *che alla immaginazione di essa*). He acknowledges that many have written on this and they have imagined republics and principalities which have never been seen or known to exist in reality. But how we live is so far removed from how we ought to live that he who abandons what is done for what ought to be done, will rather learn to bring about his own ruin than his preservation.

This is Machiavelli's way of getting the contemporary church, with its theological intrusion into men's inner intentions and its presumed monopoly of the moral domain, out of politics. He is well aware that in ecclesiastical principalities which were acquired by *virtù* or fortune but are maintained without either, there are ancient religious customs which keep subjects enthralled, such principalities being upheld by higher causes (not least, the fear of God) which the human mind cannot attain to. He abstains from speaking about them (chapter 11). He thought, however, that what the contemporary church taught had actually deprived Italy of religion. Had the Christian religion from the beginning been maintained according to the principles of its founder, then Christian 'states' and republics would have been much more united and happy than they are.[163] To Machiavelli, the Christian religion is now corrupt, and the court of the church of Rome has destroyed all piety and religion in Italy. Not only had the current church presided over the replacement of ancient religious customs with a humility that prevented Italians from securing their civic well-being.[164] The church as a temporal power, in not having been powerful enough to master all Italy, nor having permitted any other power to do so, has been the cause of Italy not having been united under one head, thereby becoming prey to powerful barbarians. Machiavelli undoubtedly believed that where religion

---

163 *Disc.* I, 12.

164 *Disc.* II, 2; *Disc.* III, 1: 'The new orders (of St Francis and St Dominic) [returned Christianity to first principles and] were so severe and powerful that they became the means of saving religion from being destroyed by the licentiousness of the prelates and heads of the church. . . . By means of confessions and preachings they then obtained so much influence with the people that they were able to make them understand that it was wicked to speak ill of wicked rulers, that it was proper to render them obedience and to leave to God the punishment of their errors. Thus wicked rulers [prelates?] do as much evil as they please because they do not fear a punishment they neither see nor believe.'

exists an appeal by rulers to divine authority gives rise to good laws, and good laws bring good fortune and from good fortune results happy success in all enterprises.[165] But where men do not fear God, a country will come to ruin unless it be sustained by the fear of the prince which may temporarily supply the want of religion. Savonarola had been successful in persuading even civilized Florentines that he conversed with God. Machiavelli thinks Savonarola's success was the consequence of how he appeared to Florentines: living a pure life, and choosing with skill the subjects of his discourses.[166] But when appearances and persuasion fail to maintain men in their faith then recourse must be had to force in order to maintain them in that faith. States that cannot rely on their unity being maintained by ancient religious customs and the fear of God had better discover ways and means of establishing political customs which will similarly provide security and contentment.[167]

We have already seen this to have been an established tradition of discourse on the autonomy of the political which Machiavelli entered rather than created. Although it has often been observed that Machiavelli returns to a pagan morality of the ancients, his is a new version of that morality adapting selected old virtues to new times. He was neither alone nor unique in this. In previous chapters we were able to chart the development of a language of two jurisdictions over men's lives with the consequent establishment of a self-justifying and autonomous domain of politics, which recognizes the importance of religious belief and, at times, maintains it as a function of the state. John of Paris, Marsilius of Padua and William of Ockham each in their own way contributed their different views on this. Like Marsilius in Discourse I of his *Defender of Peace*, Machiavelli in *The Prince* puts forth the view that while on purely logical grounds it may not in the circumstances be prudent for a prince to be a Christian, it is prudent in the circumstances to persuade others that he is. Each of these 'medieval' theorists agreed that men structure and order their collective well-being, *de facto* by otherwise unauthorized practices, then by custom and laws. So did Machiavelli.

We are also being presented with Machiavelli's way of continuing that tradition of discourse which affirmed that the science of politics, dealing as it does with the particular and contingent, is linked to rhetorical plausibility rather than to dialectical certainty. A prince concerned to maintain his 'stato' – and here his aim will coincide with that of his subjects, because it is *natural* for men to be social and to structure their relations by rules – must learn what orators already know: that men judge by appearances and apparent results, and never have access to agents' intentions. Hence, morality is *never* divorced from politics: moral evaluations are intrinsic to the political, they are judgements of appearances, of acts which are plausibly believed to reflect your character. Orators praise and blame on the basis of these judgements of appearances, and if one does what is necessary in the circumstances to maintain the 'stato', one will be judged to have a character that has achieved great things, to have achieved honour, glory and fame. This

---

165   *Disc.* I, 50: 'In Germany alone do we see that probity and religion still exist largely among the people, in consequence of which many republics exist there in the full enjoyment of liberty, observing laws in such manner that no one from within or without could venture upon an attempt to master them.'

166   *Disc.* I, 11.

167   For a range of views on Machiavelli's attitude to Christianity and religion see, for instance, M. Hulliung, *Citizen Machiavelli* (Princeton, NJ, 1983); V. B. Sullivan, *Machiavelli's Three Romes: religion, human liberty and politics reformed* (De Kalb, IL, 1996); H. C. Mansfield, *Machiavelli's Virtue*.

is especially the case for princes who are placed at a greater height and distance, and are *reputed* for certain qualities which bring them praise or blame.

Machiavelli says that everyone, presumably including himself, will admit that it would be highly praiseworthy in a prince actually to possess all the qualities that are reputed good, but as they cannot all be possessed *or observed,* human conditions not permitting it,[168] it is necessary that he should be prudent enough to avoid the scandal of those vices which would lose him the state. A prince should not mind incurring the scandal of those vices without which it would be difficult to save the state. Certain forms of behaviour are regarded as vices, judged by appearances. But if one considers well, it will be found that some things which seem virtues would, if followed, lead to one's ruin and others which appear vices would result in one's greater security and well-being (chapter 15). The real skill is in judging which apparent vices and virtues really *are* vices and virtues in the circumstances. And the problem is that a prince will not know if he 'got it right' until after he has made his move! Some men, however, through more experience and prudence, are better able to assess the range of possibilities and see an opportunity. But their characters need to match the times.[169] Was Machiavelli thinking of the peculiar character of Lorenzo the Magnificent whose role in the government of Florence, pre-1494, had come to be reassessed after the fall of the republican regime in 1512? He would describe this Lorenzo as possessing 'due persone diverse, quasi con impossibile coniunzione congiunte'.[170]

We have seen that there were sufficient civic humanists who believed that the mass of men were irrational and evil, but reserved for an elite of self-nominating governors the rare attributes of rationality and conventional virtues, if, at any rate, they absorbed the education that civic humanists wished to provide. Machiavelli, however, expresses no illusions about a 'rational and virtuous' *nobili.* His message about 'so many men not being good' so that one who makes a profession of goodness in everything must come to grief in their midst', was not, in his Florentine milieu, a uniquely negative thing to say.[171] If men were good, then Machiavelli acknowledges his advice would not be satisfactory, but as they are *tristi,* treacherous, then his is the only advice worth listening to. He simply generalized from global appearances and thereby included *nobili* in that great universal class of mankind which, he observed, and thought everyone else had observed, were not capable of sustaining goodness in the circumstances of natural, social enmities. Natural social enmities are themselves the consequence of what Machiavelli has to say about what men can know, the limits of human knowledge. The heavens are not open to human scrutiny and the world of action is not open to a knowledge of intentions or higher truths. Some see this as a kind of atheism. But a reading of the vast literature on

---

168 Note: human conditions, natural societies with natural enmities between rich and poor, and not human nature divorced from the social; that is, this is not a comment on 'original sin'.

169 A course in what today comes under the rubric of modern political science (descriptive or analytical, comparative government, rational choice theory) or a degree in management cannot help. Courses in history, psychology and the means to rhetorical persuasion might. Machiavelli's discussion concerns the right as opposed to the wrong *normative* political teachings in the circumstances.

170 *Florentine Histories* VIII, 36 in Martelli, *Tutte le opere,* p. 844. See N. Rubinstein, 'Lorenzo's Image in Europe', p. 299 where he cites Machiavelli: 'Sua prudenza e fortuna fu da' principi . . . stimata'. Also see his extraordinary portrait of Cosimo di Medici (*d.* 1464), whose life ended with private and political disappointments: *Florentine Histories* VII, 5–6.

171 Skinner, *Foundations* 1, p. 137 argues for a more unique deeply pessimistic view of human nature.

the relation of *fortuna*, divine providence, the scope of human free will and divine fore-knowledge, written during the fourteenth and fifteenth centuries, would demonstrate the extraordinary extent to which these subjects were on the Christian agenda, dealt with by scholastics and humanists alike. Much was made of the *Consolation of Philosophy* by the late Roman–Christian Boethius in which such dilemmas were extensively treated. Some solved the problem of human liberty by appealing to a psychological determinism. Others argued that philosophy and theology could not be reconciled and that religion did not need the protection of philosophy. Here, in an undoubtedly religious society, was the range of debates on necessity and fortune, a knowledge of future contingents and the possibility, or otherwise, of man's penetration of providence and the divine will. Any student who wishes to read one particularly original example of this genre can turn to Lorenzo Valla's *Dialogue on Free Will*.[172] Valla wrote in his concluding exhortation that 'we stand by faith and not by the probability of reason'. In matters of civil science, Machiavelli argued that the probability of reason was sufficient.

Of course, if all one reads is his *Prince*, knowing nothing about the late fifteenth- and early sixteenth-century Florentine milieu in which it emerged and for which it was meant to provide solutions, knowing nothing about the traditions of humanist discourses and the patrons who were meant to receive their tracts, knowing nothing about the various medieval and early Renaissance discourses concerning motivation to civic action, one may be shocked by Machiavelli's 'pessimism' or 'realism' about human greed, self-interest and the apparent human inability to sustain moral obligations when confronted by foreign invasions, one constitutional reform after another, and a factionalism especially among a rapacious ruling elite. But there is no political theorist whom we have read, especially from the Middle Ages, who would have said anything different about corrupt societies where the common good is daily seen to be destroyed. It is a moot point whether their societies were as dysfunctional as Machiavelli seemed to think Florence was. But *The Prince* was written for a dysfunctional society and suggested ways in which a people could be brought back to health, that is, to acting for the common good, the 'stato' as a law-governed and secure whole. In this it was innovatory as political theory because every other theorist whom we have discussed wrote about collective, consensual customs and laws which worked.

Machiavelli's 'Popular' Government: His Views of the *Popolo*

Did Machiavelli trust the people? In both *The Prince* and the *Discourses* he praises popular judgement, but his confidence is always in those who can manipulate that judgement for the good of the 'stato'. A multitude without a head is useless.[173] He notes that those who have been present at any deliberative assemblies of men will have observed how erroneous their opinions often are; and in fact, unless they are directed by superior men, they are apt to be contrary to all reason.[174] The strength of the people comes from their being led and thereby united, and states, be they monarchies or republics, need skilled rheto-

---

172   L. Valla, *Dialogue on Free Will*, trans. and intro. C. E. Trinkaus Jr, in E. Cassirer, P. O. Kristeller and J. H Randall Jr, eds, *The Renaissance Philosophy of Man* (Chicago, 1948), pp. 147–82.
173   *Disc.* I, 44.
174   *Disc.* II, 22.

ricians who can persuade men into seeing what is right in the circumstances and for the *salus populi*.[175] To elevate popular judgement is to elevate the skill of the leaders in manipulating that judgement. We shall see that the people's skill is limited to maintaining the state, not founding it, and to judging good proposals, not inventing them. The people's skill is the skill of a good audience judging.[176] Machiavelli observes that people form their judgement of the men to be appointed to public offices, being guided in their choice either by what is said of a man by the public voice and fame, even if by his open acts he appears different, or by the preconceptions or opinions which they may have formed of him themselves. They are impressed by a man's family or the company he keeps, or by his extraordinary action. They judge by appearances and common opinions. And they can be deceived by all. Machiavelli thought that such a good audience had to be created; in well-organized republics, in order not to appoint inefficient persons to the highest offices, every citizen should be encouraged to publish in the assemblies the defects of anyone named for public office.[177] This should give us some insight into what Machiavelli meant when, for a republic, he favoured a *governo largo* and what he meant when he complained that the people had never played their role in Florentine republican history.

Machiavelli means by 'liberty' independence from external, barbaric, foreign aggression and tyranny. He also means the habitual capacities that accrue to a people having been accustomed to self-government.[178] Using Roman examples, he says that ancient history shows how difficult it is for a people that has been accustomed to live under the government of a prince to preserve its liberty, if by some accident it has recovered it. He makes it clear that such a prince is a tyrant (and not a constitutional monarch). Liberty is a condition that is contrasted with corruption. When liberty is preserved he says that the good prevails over the bad. A 'state' is defined as having a free government when it bestows honours and rewards according to certain honest and fixed rules, so that those who obtain such honours and rewards do not consider themselves under obligations to any one, believing that they were entitled to them by their merits. Free government then, is government under law, with *ordini*, constitutional provisions and institutional arrangements that ensure stability. Free government benefits the mass of people, enabling them to enjoy their own property without any apprehensions; neither have they anything to fear for the honour of their wives, daughters or themselves. It is clear that Machiavelli's prince in *The Prince* was advised to provide precisely this: free government under a monarchy.

---

175   *Disc.* I, 58.

176   E. Garver, 'After Virtù: rhetoric, prudence and moral pluralism in Machiavelli', *History of Political Thought* 17 (1996), pp. 195–223. In his *Florentine Histories* Machiavelli observes that the nobles are necessary for military success, the people for respecting law, thereby emphasizing *relationship*s between citizens and leaders. See J. Najemy, '*Arti and ordini* in Machiavelli's *Istorie Fiorentine*', in S. Bertelli and G. Ramakus, eds, *Essays Presented to Myron P. Gilmore* (Florence, 1978), pp. 161–87.

177   *Disc.* III, 34; but see *Disc.* I, 25.

178   *Disc.* I, 16. My understanding of liberty in the *Discourses* differs from that in Skinner, *Foundations* 1, pp. 158–9. Skinner thinks that Machiavelli's general attitude in the *Discourses* towards any form of monarchical government is one of marked hostility. My view is that he makes a clear distinction between constitutional monarchies where there is rule by law and settled institutions, and rule by corrupt tyrants who constitute no more than rule by a faction of one. For a range of different approaches see H. C. Mansfield, *Machiavelli's New Modes and Orders: a study of the Discourses on Livy* (Ithaca, NY, 1979); Mansfield, *Machiavelli's Virtue*; M. Hulliung, *Citizen Machiavelli*; M. Viroli, *Machiavelli* (Oxford, 1998).

In *Discourses* I, chapter 16, Machiavelli speaks of a prince who wishes the good will of an initially hostile people. He advises that such a prince–tyrant should discover what people really desire and it is two things: to revenge themselves on those who have enslaved them, and to recover their liberty. The prince can satisfy the first desire because, as Machiavelli makes clear, those who enslaved the people were the noble and rich, and a prince can follow the example of the tyrant Clearchus and massacre the nobility to the great satisfaction of the people who desired revenge. But about the other popular desire, the recovery of their liberty, he will discover two things. He will find that a small part of the people wish to be free for the purpose of commanding, while all the others – who constitute an immense majority – desire liberty so as to be able to live in greater security. In all states, however organized, there are never more than forty or fifty citizens who attain a position that entitles them to command. A prince can either put them out of the way or give them a share in public honours and offices, according to their (social) condition or status. This will content them. The rest, who only care to live in security, are easily satisfied by institutions and laws that confirm at the same time the general security of the people and the power of the prince.

The kingdom of France has, in modern days, achieved precisely this. There the king is bound by laws that provide for the security of all his people. This is, clearly, a free government, because it is ruled by law backed by coercive sanction. The parallel with Aristotle's discussion in *Politics* V of how tyrants can secure their governments and achieve popular support by becoming constitutional monarchs is clear. It is also clear that Machiavelli has accepted the Ciceronian belief that the vast majority of the people want their liberty, meaning nothing more than security against the oppression of the wealthy and more powerful. What sustains liberty is rule by law and institutions. Corruption is the lack of both and where this is the case there is no constitution at all, only despotic whim. For Machiavelli it is clear that despotic whim can be expressed by a tyrant or by a people. He thinks Rome under Caesar had a people that was thoroughly corrupt, a faction, and hence, tyrannical.[179]

In the case of ancient Rome, Machiavelli thinks that kings had to be extinguished because they had become corrupt, while the people remained to some degree sound, their customs and institutions remaining alive. But a corrupt people living under the rule of a prince can never become free even should the prince be removed. A corrupt people is one without regulated customs and traditions. A corrupt people can only become settled if a new prince is created, whose own qualities can maintain their liberty. Where corruption has penetrated the people, the best laws are of no avail unless they are administered by a man of supreme power, that he may cause the laws to be observed until the mass has been restored to a healthy condition. Despite having provided advice for precisely this situation in *The Prince*, Machiavelli says in the *Discourses* that he does not know whether such a case has ever occurred or whether it possibly could ever occur!

Where there is corruption there is an incapacity to maintain free institutions, and such corruption results from there being a great inequality in a state. To reduce inhabitants to equality requires the application of extraordinary measures which few know how or are willing to employ.[180] It would require the complete destruction of gentlemen or *nobili*. It is beyond doubt that Machiavelli is no proto-democrat; he is speaking of creating an

179   *Disc.* I, 17.
180   *Disc.* I, 17 and 55.

equality before the law and not of a reduction of all citizens to the same social equality where there would be no differential rank and merit. His interest is in equality before the law while sustaining differentials in public honours and status. Indeed, he argues that free cities need to be rich in the sense that profits, say from military campaigns, are left to the public treasury, but their individual inhabitants ought to be kept poor. In this way the wealth and lack of virtue which riches induce may neither corrupt them nor enable them to corrupt others.[181] It is of the greatest advantage in a republic to have laws that keep the citizens poor. Poverty, if we take Rome as an example, never was allowed to stand in the way of the achievement of rank or honour.[182] Machiavelli's attitude to the populace is that they require relatively little to keep them content and that if properly guided, that is, controlled by laws, they are neither servile nor do they command with insolence.[183] Rank is maintained, as it was in Rome, supporting the laws and the magistrates. Men of merit are recognized. It is only an unbridled multitude that cannot be trusted. Contrary to the general (humanist) opinion which believes that the people, when they govern, are inconstant, unstable and ungrateful, Machiavelli concludes that these defects are not more natural to the people than they are to princes. The solution is to shape the character of a people by law backed by coercive sanction which habituates. Such a people is poor, healthy and can be trusted, but in what way?

Machiavelli makes the point that a people that governs and is well regulated by laws will be stable, prudent and grateful as much if not more than a prince who is esteemed wise. The wise prince is the Platonic philosopher–prince seen from a flattering perspective: he is above the laws. Seen from an unflattering perspective, he is a ruler, freed from the restraints of the law, and he will be more ungrateful, inconstant and imprudent than a people similarly situated. The difference in conduct is not, he says, due to any difference in their nature, for that is the same. The difference is that the people have a greater respect for laws under which they respectively live than does a prince. Their difference is in character. Machiavelli is not giving the people an opportunity to be involved in shaping legislation but rather in consenting to laws proposed by experts. Hence, he says that princes show themselves superior in making laws and in forming civil institutions and new statutes and ordinances, while the people are superior in maintaining those institutions, laws and ordinances.[184]

Machiavelli trusts law-bound princes and a law-bound people more than he trusts the nobles. He trusts constitutional monarchies and republics where the people play their role more than he trusts aristocracies and oligarchies, where the *nobili* are loose cannon. In *Discourses* II and III he provides an anthropology of the *nobili*, 'wealth without worth', self-indulgence and the pursuit of self-interested gain, as opposed to the devotion of energies to the common good, taking up the classical, medieval and humanist discourse on true nobility. But he always thought that the Florentine people, as amateurs in government, needed to have someone in charge. Orderly government is what Machiavelli calls *il vivere civile* or *il vivere politico*. Constitutional monarchs can provide this while despots cannot. And since most men want only security, to maintain their possessions and honour, then only a minority of a people will want to participate in political life.

---

181 *Disc.* III, 16 and 25.
182 *Disc.* III, 25.
183 *Disc.* I, 58.
184 *Disc.* I, 58.

Hence, the most satisfactory *vivere civile* is where that minority is offered roles in government. This is Machiavelli's 'republican' government, a mixed constitution with a role for a 'prince' and where the role of the vast majority of the people is constrained to selecting their leaders. This is his *governo largo*. Machiavelli is using the language of fifteenth-century humanism which assumes a vast proportion of the led and a tiny group of leaders.

What does it mean for Machiavelli to say that since every 'republic' is composed of nobles and people, the protection of liberty is best confided to those who have least desire in violating it? Remember that 'republic' is the by-now well-established humanist Latin word for any good constitution, Aristotle's *politeia*. Included in Machiavelli's examples of 'republics' are Sparta, Venice and Rome – all 'mixed regimes' – and both Sparta and Venice lasted longer than Rome. All 'states', whatever their constitutional form, are comprised of the rich and poor, the nobles and the people. Now the nobles have always and everywhere had a desire to dominate, while the people only have the wish not to be dominated. Hence, it is the people who have the greater desire to live in the enjoyment of liberty.[185] Machiavelli trusts the people because their only desire is to preserve that which they already possess. And if you have a 'state' that looks to found an empire, rather than merely preserving itself, then Machiavelli insists that the people as a whole, and well-armed, are better guardians of liberty. The nobles must have their aggression turned to conquering neighbours.[186]

Given that states naturally rise or decline and can never remain stable, Machiavelli takes ancient Rome's constitution as a model of success and despite all the difficulties he is prepared to tolerate the unavoidable conflicts between the nobles in the Senate and the people.[187] This is because the natural enmities between rich and poor can never be eliminated. Instead of trying to eliminate them they can be made to serve the public good, the *stato*. Hence, Rome's historical genius consisted in recognizing that the divided power of a mixed regime is naturally more effective than the concentrated power of a simple regime. And where principalities are usually not large, too few having a stake in their success, mixed regimes are those with an interest in glory gained from world conquest.[188] Furthermore, the older theoretical hope of achieving a concord between the people and nobles by eliminating civil discord – as this was expressed by thirteenth-century *dictatores* and modelled on an idealized interpretation of a Ciceronian 'concord of the ranks or orders' – is rejected. He thinks nothing can be gained by attempting to control cities by means of keeping alive one faction as opposed to another because it is

185   *Disc.* I, 5.
186   In his *Florentine Histories* 2.12 he speaks of the greatest and most prosperous moment in Florence's history, *c.* 1295–8, when Florence was strong, with thirty thousand citizen–soldiers and was obeyed by all of Tuscany: external tranquillity leads to internal unrest; hence, republics need to be engaged in external conquests to maintain their own internal peace and liberty; foreign wars are remedies for civil wars. See chapter 5 on Cicero, in *A History of Political Thought*, vol. 1, where in *De officiis* Cicero argues for conquering and taxing the empire.
187   *Disc.* I, 6.
188   'The affection for liberty arises in a people when they see that cities never increase in dominion or wealth unless they are free; it is not individual prosperity but the general good that makes cities great, and the general good is regarded nowhere but in republics because whatever they do is for the common benefit . . . the very reverse happening where the prince [is of such a kind that] his private interests are generally in opposition to those of the city, a state of affairs leading to tyranny.' *Disc.* II, 2.

the nature of man in all differences of opinion to prefer either the one side or the other.[189]

Where humanist contemporaries argued for institutions and laws that would give all citizens of whatever rank a sense of civic pride and patriotism so that each individual would seek to eliminate differences, equating his own good with that of the city, Machiavelli, reinterpreting Roman history, suggests something else: the maintenance of a fruitful, continuous conflict which cancels out sectional interests between rich and poor *in the end*. In a contest for public honours, the institutions of the state should be so regulated that the influence of citizens is founded only upon acts that benefit the state. The means to the acquisition of influence must be public rather than private: honours should be open to every citizen and suitable rewards established that will satisfy those who merit them. He believes that reputation and influence gained in this regulated, public manner will never prove dangerous to any state. A well-regulated republic, then, is one that opens the way to public honours to those who seek reputation by means that are conducive to the public good, and at the same time, closing it off to those whose aim is advancement of private ends. And distinguished, public-spirited men, engaged in conflicts by representing sectional interests of rich and poor, will ensure that the only laws that will be enacted will be those that benefit the community as a whole.

Successful 'self-government' and legislation that favours liberty always emerge out of the clash of the irreconcilable interests of nobles and people. History shows recurrent and natural enmities between rich and poor, between those who seek to command and those who seek not to obey or be oppressed. Enmities are not only natural but healthy if well managed. In well-ordered states they result in a balance of power in a mixed constitution, the balance itself resembling the common good. The common good is not, then, for Machiavelli, a concept that arises in each individual but, rather, is an interstitial emergence achieved in the right conditions, those of free government under law with *ordini* and institutions that provide for stability, success and policies of expansion.

Machiavelli believed that anyone who would foresee what has to be, should reflect on what has been, for everything that happens in the world has a genuine *resemblance* to what happened in ancient times. This is because agents who bring such things about are men, and he insisted that men have and always have had the same passions. To study how Romans achieved and maintained their liberty provides lessons about desires and their fulfilment that may be imitated in what are taken to be like circumstances. Machiavelli, in looking to old liberties, was not nostalgically escaping to the past but attempting to establish continuities in his present with that past. He was certainly not looking forward to what would become a new, arbitrary and conventionally established autonomy of subjects, a new individual liberty that would come into existence, and could be, and was, as easily destroyed by absolutist sovereigns' legal definitions that had no natural stability, based as they were on the sovereign's absolute will. Machiavelli's liberty, founded in a *populus liber*, was not Hobbes's liberty. Machiavelli's was perhaps one of the last great statements about the liberty that medieval theorists and practitioners, in successful monarchies and city-state republics, believed was natural to men and which the 'state', monarchy or republic was meant to acknowledge and secure.

189 *Disc.* III, 27.

Conclusion

Machiavelli's works were proscribed and placed on the Index of Prohibited Books in 1559. Times were changing and across Europe Machiavelli's *doctrina politica* was coming to be understood as political craft; he was taken to be an innovator in entirely secular civil prudence who was prepared not only to compromise on religious matters but to teach immorality. Shakespeare referred to him as 'murderous Machiavel'. In France and England he was regarded as godless. Sixteenth-century Italy saw the end of republican liberty, in 'state' theory and practice. The peninsula became a battleground for the great powers of Europe.[190] Arguments for mixed constitutions and a renewed conciliarism would, however, remain alive among scholastic theologians and lawyers a good deal longer, as would the late-medieval tradition of self-governing cities in, for instance, the Dutch republic.

But from the later sixteenth and early seventeenth centuries there would also emerge very different discourses of power, propaganda, which owed nothing to those supposed natural processes of conflictual enmities and their natural management in states with liberty, leading to the common good. Machiavelli had written at a time in which it was still possible to speak of a natural propagation of governing power whose aim, through education of a people's character, was to secure already-practised individual and collective liberties or to begin a process of establishing them. This was, for him, man's healthy condition.

This is the reason that the story of individual and collective liberties into the sixteenth century actually begins in the thirteenth, when strong monarchs or self-governing republics began their engagement in curtailing the territorial power of aristocratic magnates in the name of the various liberties of the members of their respective communities, be it called 'the community of the realm' or of ' the city-state republic'. The languages they used to defend such liberties were the languages with which we have already become familiar, that of the ancients, modified to suit innumerable *de facto* practices as these emerged during the Middle Ages and early Renaissance. The seventeenth-century of Hobbes was not, then, the teleological end of what some have taken to be a centuries-long ideological struggle between *respublica* and *regnum*, republic versus monarchy. In the period from the thirteenth century to the beginning of the sixteenth there was no groping towards the Hobbesian or our modern concept of the 'state', although we have seen that medieval and Renaissance theorists had *a* concept of the 'state' when they referred to sovereign government as constitutional or civic rule. Their problems with and experiences of republican and monarchical governments were not those of the seventeenth century. The opposition in the earlier period – and as it still would be presented in both of Machiavelli's works, *The Prince* and the *Discourses on Livy* – was not *between* monarchies and republics, but between *the liberty of the whole community* and the *licence of magnates*, be those magnates ecclesiastical, e.g. the papacy and the episcopacy, or secular lay lords, the *signori*, who still exercised or tried to recover old feudal liberties over and against the liberties of the community which the state was meant to serve.[191]

---

190   See Skinner, *Foundations* 1, pp. 186–9, 248–54; also Coleman, *The Individual in Political Theory and Practice*, chapters by I. Comparato and M. van Gelderen.

191   For Skinner's alternative view to the one I am proposing here, see Q. Skinner, 'The State', in T. Ball, J. Farr and R. Hanson, eds, *Political Innovation and Conceptual Change* (Cambridge, 1989), pp. 90–131; and Skinner, 'The Italian City-Republics', in J. Dunn, ed., *Democracy: The unfinished journey 508 BC to AD 1993* (Oxford, 1992), pp. 57–70. I have argued my case further in Coleman, 'Structural realities of power'.

The persistent political genres of propagandists well into the sixteenth century remained that of the *De regno* and the *Tractatus de potestate regia (vel) imperatoris ac papae* and not the *Tractatus de potestate regia/ monarchia* vel/contra *respublica*. When they wrote tracts *De regno* they were referring not to a prevailing constitutional regime but more generally to good government, by which was meant those immortal, coherent, public power structures which legitimately exercised the coercive control that served and preserved order within political communities. Only thereafter did they go on to show how different constitutions achieved this enduring, good government, be they monarchies or republics, given a people's traditions, history and circumstances. This is what Machiavelli meant when he opened his *Prince* with the statement: '*tutti li stati*, all the dominions that have had or now have power over men either have been or are republics or principalities'. It was the establishment of centralized good laws and arms, be they instituted in monarchical or republican constitutions, which were seen to enable the achievement of the common good as perceived by subjects or citizens. And it is for this reason that, despite his apparent preference for republics, Machiavelli argued that *un vivere politico* can be either a republic or a monarchy. Both a *regnum* and a republic can 'live politically' or civically; that is, both can have constitutional government.[192] What guarantees liberty is that regime which acts to promote the common good of its consenting and thereby sovereign-constituting body of citizens or subjects whose will is represented in collective assemblies. The coronation medal of England's fourteenth-century monarch Edward III was inscribed: *voluntas populi dat jura* (the people's will is law).

Now the modern notion of the state is said to distinguish state authority from that of the rulers entrusted with the temporary exercise of state powers. This view was already established during the Middle Ages and the Renaissance in the notion of 'office' and in the sense that customs and laws were meant to 'rule' in perpetuity for the common good. We need only recall Marsilius of Padua's view that all temperate regimes have something that distinguishes them, 'the people' or the human legislator by whose authority laws are enacted and executive governing offices are determined. But the modern state also distinguishes between state authority and that of the whole of the society/community over which its powers are exercised. This was neither a medieval nor a Renaissance view, because it drives a wedge between a society's perspective on its common good and the state's authoritative will to establish its own version of that 'good'. This modern state emerged out of a theory proposed by those who desired to legitimize the more absolute forms of government of the early seventeenth century, with their insistence that the powers of government must be something *other* than a mere expression of the powers and will of the governed.[193] Hobbes in particular saw it as essential that the individuals who construct the state must recognize that they are *renouncing and transferring* their original

---

192   See N. Rubinstein, 'The History of the Word *politicus* in Early-modern Europe', in A. Pagden, ed., *The Language of Political Theory in Early Modern Europe* (Cambridge, 1987), pp. 41–56: 'Like Fortescue's *dominium politicum, il vivere politico* or *civile* stands for constitutional government' (p. 53).

193   Here, I agree with Skinner, 'The State', pp. 116–19. P. Riesenberg, *Citizenship in the Western Tradition*, pp. xi and 185–6, observed 'that citizenship turned into subjectship, rejecting the older public citizenship which depended on birth or an act of will of the individual, replacing it with the prince's will alone which could create or destroy the relationship between citizen and community. In Bodin's understanding of sovereignty we see a kind of citizenship which is a form of subjectship that places the individual in direct subordinate relationship to the prince. This is what has prevailed, stripped of the institution of monarchy, as the basis of the relationship between the individual and the government in every modern country.'

sovereignty to a third party. Hobbes was discussing the nature of absolute sovereignty itself rather than a particular constitution, although he thought there were prudential grounds for favouring a monarchy. This state's authority and power, indeed will, remain distinct not only from the people who originally instituted it but also from that of office holders with rights to wield state power. Furthermore, the Hobbesian sovereign is not subject to the law, although he has obligations under the natural law for which he is answerable only to God. But technically there is no law that he may make that can be unjust, therefore no subject can claim against his injustice by right. From Hobbes's subjects has been removed the earlier liberty to exercise any judgement about political matters. The sovereign's commands do not require even consent. This is not Machiavelli's *vivere civile*. Rather, for Hobbes, political liberty has become what the sovereign defines it to be. Hobbes was to argue famously that to ascribe liberty to the human will is a mistake. Liberty consists in nothing more than the silence of the sovereign's law.

During the seventeenth century it would not be character but nature, including human nature, which came to be viewed as having to be conquered and transformed by absolute force and positive law. Whatever liberties were to be permitted would be artificially created by the sovereign state and its legal conventions. This would be as true of Hobbes's *Leviathan* as it would be of Rousseau's *Social Contract*.[194] An earlier understanding of the *natural* propagation of power, of a people's *virtù* responding to necessity, and seizing opportunities provided by fortune to establish a free state governed by laws about which they or those who represented their collective wills deliberated and to which they consented, with a common good in view, would be replaced by artificial conventions, the contractual state, sustained by the prudential prince's virtually unbridled will.

This volume ends with Machiavelli. To tell the subsequent story of European political theories and national states during the sixteenth and early seventeenth centuries would require a volume in itself, not least, one devoted to the Protestant Reformation and its various effects on notions and practices of governance. The confessional divide across Europe in fact helped to create somewhat different canonical traditions of political theorizing along national and confessional lines and it is for this reason, especially in the English-speaking world, that one tends to find a raft of English and Scottish political theorists, from Hobbes, Locke, Hume and Burke, who dominate courses in the history of political thought in Britain and America. Look to the European continent, however, and we find another set of 'great names', not least, Bodin. As was pointed out in the introduction to volume 1, Europeans reconstructed their histories and differentially forged their identities precisely by retrospective nominations of thinkers whom they believed important to their discrete national, political and religious 'traditions'. Before the Reformation, the canon was more stable than it would become after it.

From the seventeenth century, the undoubted flexibility of the new range of discourses on the artificial social contract would theoretically make available a range of choices, from creating society in the first place, or a sovereign, or even procedural rules of justice and morality itself. Hobbes in particular sought to ground the origin and legitimacy of political obligation and sovereignty, precisely by denying one of the central inspirations of much ancient, medieval and Renaissance political theorizing: he denied the very possibility of

---

194 On the variety of social contract theories, notably of Hobbes, Locke, Rousseau and from Kant to Rawls, Nozick and Gauthier, see D. Boucher and P. Kelly, 'The Social Contract and Its Critics: an overview', in D. Boucher and P. Kelly, eds, *The Social Contract from Hobbes to Rawls* (London, 1994), pp. 1–34.

morality by agreement. Thereafter, the story of original sin would come to be interpreted in a specific way: that we are now fallen and thereby incapable without something added to our nature ('grace' in Augustine's language, the contractual society with its coercive authority in ours) of loving and feeling obligations to anyone other than ourselves. This would help to open up a secular paradigm that all men are incorrigible knaves, passionate utility calculators with no capacity to live according to principle or act consistently in ways that they do not take to be in conformity with their present and shifting desires. The traditions of ethical and political discourse treated in these volumes, on the whole, resisted this vision, largely finding the man who answered to this description as the rare case of a non-cooperative isolate, the brute, incapable of character acculturation by norms that could make him a reliable citizen, by which was meant that his interests and duties were not simply to preserve himself but to live well with others of his kind.

For most of the earlier tradition we have examined, politics as a 'science' was not about knowledge but about action, not about knowing but about doing. Because politics as a practical 'science' concerned the type of life that was thought to be worthwhile, they thought it imperative to recognize that this must depend on the actions it contained. Hence, the frame of the debates about choosing well was always constrained by the ancient rhetorical, ethical and political realizations, adapted and modified by Christian discourse, that choosing well was caused by desiring the right end, which is doing well for the common good and then deliberating about the various means in human power to secure that rightly desired collective and human end. Underpinning this earlier discourse was the belief that social praise and blame were trained on the character dispositions men revealed towards the emotions, not on the observation *that* humans feel, say, anger, but rather, on what they get angry at, in which circumstances, to whom and for what purpose and this, for political leaders and citizens, was what mattered in human discourse and association. Hence, the heart of much of the earlier ethical and political discourse lay in discussions about the formation of moral character in the circumstances.

On the contrary, after Hobbes there would be produced a variety of discourses on the reasoned justifications of each individual's instrumental rationality in the 'state', itself construed as a site of self-preservative bargaining. From here there would eventually emerge a discourse with which we are all, today, terribly familiar: it is a discourse of the economists who explain that the reason we have laws, indeed the contractual society, is precisely because left to our own devices we are too rational and never play co-operatively whenever we calculate correctly, as we always try to do, that it is not in our self-interest to contribute to collective goods or to co-operate in general. Today, we often hear that naturally we are non-cooperators and even in social nexuses which we agree to construct, we will always be seeking an exit from co-operation when it proves rational, that is, in our self-interest, to do so. The term 'rationality' is now often applied strictly to the calculation of the means to a given end, but the rationality of the ends does not arise, except in so far as ends can be means to further ends. On this view we need to be conceived and conceive ourselves as primarily self-regarding choosers where the history of character formation is off the agenda, leaving us with a formal description of instrumental reasoning, a description of cognitive functioning in whatever milieu any individual may find him or herself. In having redefined the will as the last appetite in deliberation so that reason is to be understood as no more than a learned means to acquire what is simply desired, Hobbes dropped the classical, medieval and Renaissance tradition of speaking about what they took to be the major concern of humans to discuss and act upon: notably, what it is *reasonable* for men to will in concert. Instead, a new man with a new freedom was to emerge. This person's freedom in a society of equal but perpetual strangers would consist in the silence of the state's laws, that is, his or her free agency would appear especially clearly primarily and exclusively when the individual stood at a distance from his or her actual social roles and histories.

To Machiavelli, a people that stands at a distance from traditions of self-governance and is ignorant of its history is a corrupt people, in need of a prince. But Machiavelli's prince, in not being a tyrant, knows that men need an ethical identity, a character, and he will forge one for them through good arms and good law. Through his efforts sub-jects will come to identify with some set of principles, clarifying in the circumstances what, for the most part, it is rational for an agent to be and then do in accordance with what he is, so that being restored to health, subjects are turned into citizens who may then determine whether such ends, the common good, are being justified by the chosen means of achieving them. Co-operation for Machiavelli is an interstitial, rational emer-gence in societies which always harbour conflict between the rich and poor. It emerges from within an ethical, political and rhetorical tradition that believes it possible to per-suade men with characters formed from their experiences that it is rational to act in one way or another for the *salus populi*. Machiavelli was still writing within the tradition that insisted that action in the world is constrained and shaped less by deliberative and calculative reasoning of means to personally desired ends than by habits and by principles which establish the ends to be pursued, that is, in the tradition that insisted that moral virtue had to be acquired and a *vivere politico* in either a monarchy or a republic with good laws backed by coercive sanction ensured the acquisition. It is from the practice of moral virtue that humans learn to choose the right object and from which humans acquire a knowledge of the principles of good and bad in order to act towards a collective end. For Machiavelli, individuals may appear to be engaged in choices that seem 'simply' instrumental but they are actually engaged in choices about what or who to become and to be perceived as being in natural, social environments. Machiavelli was still within the tradition that was not simply interested in redescribing private interests and the calculative means to their achievement, but in forging men's social character, this being taken to be the aim of all legislators who seek the best means of acquiring the common good.

The prince who can do this for a corrupt people is a rare being in times where tradi-tions are forgotten. Indeed, he is a kind of god along the model of the lone non-coopera-tor, who shows himself through his choices to be a lover of war, resembling as Aristotle had said an isolated piece in a game of draughts, either a lower animal than man or a god. But his aim is to be loved, if also feared, and his success is the people's success in ulti-mately leaving them with a set of *ordini* and civic characters which no longer require his prudence or even presence to maintain their liberty. Neither his *Prince* nor his *Discourses* is sceptical of the moral domain in the way that many later political theories would insist upon. For Machiavelli, to save the life and preserve the freedom of one's country requires a momentary setting aside of considerations of justice, kindness, praiseworthiness. But a state that relies on such extraordinary measures, turning them into policy and dispensing with constitutional means, is nothing other than a tyranny and to be avoided at all costs. Machiavelli was writing within the tradition of absolute, legitimate, limited government, and not within a tradition that would later emerge, that of 'absolutism'.

Bibliography

In a work of this kind which, in two volumes, treats over two thousand years of political theorizing in different historical contexts, the bibliographies can only be selective. Below I have especially listed works in which a variety of approaches to our subject may be found and which refer to further extensive and more specialist bibliographies.

Abu-Lughod, J. L. *Before European Hegemony: the world system, AD 1250–1350* (Oxford, 1989).

Ackrill, J. L. 'Aristotle on *Eudaimonia*', in A. O. Rorty, ed., *Essays on Aristotle's Ethics* (Berkeley, 1980), pp. 15–33.

Adams, M. M. *William Ockham*, 2 vols (Notre Dame, IN, 1987).

Anderson, P. *Passages from Antiquity to Feudalism* (London, 1974).

Anscombe, G. E. M. and P. T. Geach, *Three Philosophers: Aristotle, Aquinas, Frege* (Oxford, 1973).

Bagge, S. 'Medieval and Renaissance Historiography: break or continuity?', *The European Legacy* 2 (1997), pp. 1336–71.

Ball, T., J. Farr and R. Hanson, eds, *Political Innovation and Conceptual Change* (Cambridge, 1989).

Baron, H. *Humanistic and Political Literature in Florence and Venice at the Beginning of the Quattrocento* (Cambridge, MA, 1955).

Baron, H. *The Crisis of the Early Italian Renaissance* (Princeton, NJ, 1966).

Baron, H., ed., *From Petrarch to Leonardo Bruni* (Chicago, 1968).

Becker, M. B. *Medieval Italy: constraints and creativity* (Bloomington, IN, 1981).

Bennett, R. F. and H. S. Offler, eds, *Guillelmi de Ockham, Opera Politica*, vol. 2 (Manchester, 1963).

Benson, R., G. Constable and C. Lanham, eds, *Renaissance and Renewal in the Twelfth Century* (Oxford, 1982).

Berlin, I. 'The Originality of Machiavelli', in *Against the Current*, ed. H. Hardy (London, 1979), pp. 25–79.

Bertelli, S. and G. Ramakus, eds, *Essays Presented to Myron P. Gilmore* (Florence, 1978).

Bertelli, S., N. Rubinstein and C. H. Smyth, eds, *Florence and Venice: comparisons and relations* (Florence, 1979).

Black, A. *Monarchy and Community: political ideas in the later conciliar controversy, 1430–50* (Cambridge, 1970).

Black, A. *Council and Commune: the conciliar movement* (London, 1979).

Black, A. *Guilds and Civil Society in European Political Thought from the Twelfth Century to the Present* (London, 1984).

Black, A. *Political Thought in Europe 1250–1450* (Cambridge, 1992).

Black, A. 'The Juristic Origins of Social Contract Theory', *History of Political Thought*, 14 (1993), pp. 57–76.

Black, A. 'The Commune in Political Theory in the Late Middle Ages', in P. Blickle, ed., *Theorie kommunaler Ordnung in Europa* (Munich, 1996), pp. 99–112.

Black, A. 'Individuals, Groups and States: a comparative overview', in J. Coleman, ed., *The Individual in Political Theory and Practice* (Oxford, 1996), pp. 329–40.

Black, R. 'Florence', in R. Porter and M. Teich, eds, *The Renaissance in National Context* (Cambridge, 1992).

Black, R. 'Higher Education in Florentine Tuscany: new documents from the second half of the fifteenth century' in Denley and Elam, eds, *Florence and Italy,* pp. 209–22.

Black, R, 'Machiavelli, Servant of the Florentine Republic' in Bock, Skinner and Viroli, eds, *Machiavelli and Republicanism* (Cambridge, 1990), pp. 71–99.

Bleienstein, F. *Johannes Quidort von Paris über königliche und papstliche Gewalt (De regia potestate et papali)* (Stuttgart, 1969).

Blickle, P., ed., *Theorien kommunaler Ordnung in Europa* (Munich, 1996).

Bloch, M. *La Societé féodale,* 2 vols (Paris, 1939/40).

Blockmans, W. 'Vers une societié urbanisée', in R. Doehaerd, ed., *Histoire de Flandre* (Brussels, 1983).

Blythe, J. M. *Ideal Government and the Mixed Constitution in the Middle Ages* (Princeton, NJ, 1992).

Blythe, J. M. trans., Introduction, *Ptolemy of Lucca, On the Government of Rulers (De regimine principum) with portions attributed to Thomas Aquinas* (Philadelphia, 1997).

Bock, G., Q. Skinner and M. Viroli, eds, *Machiavelli and Republicanism* (Cambridge, 1990).

Boehner, P. *Collected Articles on Ockham,* ed. E. M. Buytaert (St Bonaventure, NY, 1958).

Boggess, W. F. 'Hermannus Alemannus's Rhetorical Translations', *Viator* 2 (1971), pp. 227–50.

Bolgar, R. R., ed., *Classical Influences on European Culture AD 500–1500* (Cambridge, 1971).

Bolton, B. *The Medieval Reformation* (London, 1983).

Bosl, K. *Das Problem der Armut in der Hochmittelalterlichen Gesellschaft* (Vienna, 1974).

Boucher, D. and P. Kelly, 'The Social Contract and Its Critics: an overview', in D. Boucher and P. Kelly, eds, *The Social Contract from Hobbes to Rawls* (London, 1994), pp. 1–34.

Brams, J. and W. Vanhamel, eds, *Guillaume de Moerbeke* (Leuven, 1989).

Brett, A. S. *Liberty, Right and Nature: individual rights in later scholastic thought* (Cambridge, 1997).

Brown, A. *The Medici in Florence: the exercise and language of power* (Florence, 1992).

Brucker, G. *Renaissance Florence* (Berkeley, 1969).

Brucker, G. *The Civic World of Early Renaissance Florence* (Princeton, NJ, 1977).

Buckland, W. W. *A Text-book of Roman Law from Augustus to Justinian,* revd P. Stein, 3rd edn (Cambridge, 1975).

Bueno da Mesquita, D. M. 'The Place of Despotism in Italian Politics', in J. Hale, R. Highfield and B. Smalley, eds, *Europe in the Late Middle Ages* (London, 1965), pp. 301–31.

Burke, P. *The Renaissance Sense of the Past* (London, 1969).

Burke, P. *Tradition and Innovation in Renaissance Italy: a sociological approach* (London, 1974).

Burke, P. *The Renaissance,* 2nd edn (London, 1997).

Burns, J. H., ed., *The Cambridge History of Medieval Political Thought c. 350–c.1450* (Cambridge, 1988).

Burns, J. H. *Lordship, Kingship and Empire: the Idea of Monarchy 1400–1525* (Oxford, 1992).

Burns, J. H., 'Conciliarism, papalism and power, 1511–1518' in D. Wood, ed, *The Church and Sovereignty* (Oxford, 1991), pp. 409–28.

Burns, J. H. 'Absolutism: the history of an idea', *The Creighton Trust Lecture,* University of London, 1986, pp. 1–30.

Butters, H. C. *Governors and Government in Early Sixteenth-century Florence, 1502–1519* (Oxford, 1985).

Cabrini, A.-M. *Per una valutazione delle 'Istorie Fiorentine' del Machiavelli: note sulle fonti del Secondo Libro* (Florence, 1985).

Cadoni, G., ed., *Provvisioni Concernenti L'Ordinamento della Repubblica Fiorentina, 1494–1512,* vol. 1 (Rome, 1994).

Canning, J. *The Political Thought of Baldus de Ubaldis* (Cambridge, 1987).

Canning, J. *A History of Medieval Political Thought 300–1450* (London, 1996).

Canning, J. and O.-G. Oexle, eds, *Political Thought and the Realities of Power in the Middle Ages/Politisches Denken und die Wirklichkeit der Macht im Mittelalter* (Göttingen, 1998).

Cassirer, E., P. O. Kristeller and J. H. Randall Jr, eds, *The Renaissance Philosophy of Man* (Chicago, 1948).

Catto, J. I. 'Ideas and Experience in the Political Thought of Aquinas', *Past and Present* 71 (1976), pp. 3–21.

Catto, J. I. and R. Evans, eds, *The History of the University of Oxford*, vol. 1: *The Early Oxford Schools* (Oxford, 1984).

Celli, R. *Pour l'histoire des origines du pouvoir populaire: l'expérience des Villes–Etats Italiennes (xi–xii siècles)* (Louvain–La Neuve, 1980).

Chabod, F. *Machiavelli and the Renaissance* (London, 1958).

Chiappelli, F. *Nuovi studi sul linguaggio del Machiavelli* (Florence, 1969).

Chittolini, G. 'Organizzazione territoriale e distretti urbani nell' Italia del tardo Medioevo', in *L'organizzazione del territorio in Italia e Germania: secoli XII–XIV* (Annali del Istituto storico Italo-Germanico, 37) (Bologna, 1994).

Cipolla, C. *Before the Industrial Revolution: European society and economy, 1000–1700* (London, 1976).

Colas, D. *La Glaive et le fléau, généalogie du fanatisme et de la société civile* (Paris, 1992).

Coleman, J. *English Literature in History, 1350–1400: medieval readers and writers* (London, 1981).

Coleman, J. 'Medieval Discussions of Property: *ratio* and *dominium* according to John of Paris and Marsilius of Padua', *History of Political Thought* 4 (1983), pp. 209–28.

Coleman, J. '*Dominium* in Thirteenth- and Fourteenth-century Political Thought and its Seventeenth-century Heirs: John of Paris and Locke', *Political Studies* 33 (1985), pp. 73–100.

Coleman, J. 'The Interrelationship between Church and State During the Conciliar Period: theory and practice', in J. P. Genet and B. Vincent, eds, *Etat et église dans la genèse de l'état moderne* (Madrid, 1986), pp. 41–54.

Coleman, J. 'The Owl and the Nightingale and Papal Theories of Marriage', *Journal of Ecclesiastical History* 38 (1987), pp. 517–68.

Coleman, J. 'The Two Jurisdictions: theological and legal justifications of church property in the thirteenth century', *Studies in Church History* 23 (1987), pp. 75–110.

Coleman, J. 'Property and Poverty', in J. H. Burns, ed., *The Cambridge History of Medieval Political Thought c. 350–c.1450* (Cambridge, 1988), pp. 607–48.

Coleman, J. 'Guillaume d'Occam et la notion de sujet', in *Archives de philosophie du droit* 34 (1989), pp. 25–32.

Coleman, J. 'The Dominican Political Theory of John of Paris in its Context', in D. Wood, ed., *The Church and Sovereignty c. 590–1918: essays in honour of Michael Wilks* (Oxford, 1991), pp. 187–223.

Coleman, J. 'The Relation between Ockham's Intuitive Cognition and His Political Science', in (no ed.) *Théologie et droit dans la science politique de l'état moderne* (Rome, 1991), pp. 71–88.

Coleman, J. *Ancient and Medieval Memories: studies in the reconstruction of the past* (Cambridge, 1992).

Coleman, J. 'The Intellectual Milieu of John of Paris, OP', in J. Miethke, ed., *Das Publikum politischer Theorie im 14. Jahrhundert* (Munich, 1992), pp. 173–206.

Coleman, J. 'Medieval Discussions of Human Rights', in W. Schmale, ed., *Human Rights and Cultural Diversity* (Goldbach, 1993), pp. 103–20.

Coleman, J. 'The Uses of the Past (14th–16th Centuries): the invention of a collective history and its implications for cultural participation', in A. Rigney and D. Fokkema, eds, *Cultural Participation: trends since the Middle Ages* (Amsterdam, 1993), pp. 21–37.

Coleman, J. 'MacIntyre and Aquinas', in J. Horton and S. Mendus, eds, *After MacIntyre* (Cambridge, 1994), pp. 65–90.

Coleman, J. 'Machiavelli's *via moderna*: medieval and Renaissance attitudes to history', in M. Coyle, ed., *Niccolò Machiavelli's The Prince: new interdisciplinary essays* (Manchester, 1995), pp. 40–64.

Coleman, J., ed., *The Individual in Political Theory and Practice* (Oxford, 1996).

Coleman, J. 'The Science of Politics and Late Medieval Academic Debate', in R. Copeland, ed., *Criticism and Dissent in the Middle Ages* (Cambridge, 1996), pp. 181–214.

Coleman, J. 'Structural Realities of Power: the theory and practice of monarchies and republics in relation to personal and collective liberty', in M. Gosman, A. Vanderjagt and J. Veenstra, eds, *The Propagation of Power in the Medieval West* (Groningen, 1997), pp. 207–30.

Coleman, J. 'Some Relations Between the Study of Aristotle's *Rhetoric*, *Ethics* and *Politics* in Late Thirteenth- and Early Fourteenth-century University Arts Courses and the Justification of Contemporary Civic Activities (Italy and France)', in J. Canning and O.-G. Oexle, eds, *Political Thought and the Realities of Power in the Middle Ages* (Göttingen, 1998), pp. 127–58.

Coleman, J. 'The Practical Use of *Begriffsgeschichte* by an Historian of European Pre-modern Political Thought: some problems', *Huizinga Instituut: History of Concepts Newsletter*, 2 (1999), pp. 2–9.

Coleman, J. ed., *Scholastics, Enlightenments and Philosophic Radicals: essays in honour of J. H. Burns* (Exeter, 1999).

Colish, M. 'Cicero's *De officiis* and Machiavelli's *Prince*', *Sixteenth Century Journal* 9 (1978), pp. 81–94.

Condren, C. 'Democracy and the *Defensor Pacis*', *Il Pensiero Politico* 8 (1980), pp. 301–16.

Condren, C. and R. Pesman Cooper, eds, *Altro Polo: A Volume of Italian Renaissance Studies* (Sydney, 1982).

Copeland, R., ed., *Criticism and Dissent in the Middle Ages* (Cambridge, 1996).

Cortese, E. 'Cittadinanza (Diritto intermedio)', in *Enciclopedia del Diritto*, VII (Milan, 1960), pp.132–40.

Coulet, N. and J.-P. Genet, eds, *L'Etat moderne: le droit, l'espace et les formes de l'état* (Paris, 1990).

Courtenay, W. J. 'Covenant and Causality in Pierre d'Ailly', *Speculum* 46 (1971), pp. 94–119.

Courtenay, W. J. 'Nominalism and Late Medieval Religion', in C. Trinkaus, ed., *The Pursuit of Holiness in Late Medieval and Renaissance Religion* (Leiden, 1974), pp. 26–59.

Courtenay, W. J. 'The Reception of Ockham's Thought in Fourteenth-century England', in A. Hudson and M. Wilks, eds, *From Ockham to Wyclif* (Oxford, 1987), pp.89–108.

Courtenay, W. J. *Capacity and Volition: a history of the distinction of absolute and ordained power (Quodlibet 8)* (Bergamo, 1990).

Coyle, M., ed., *Niccolò Machiavelli's The Prince: new interdisciplinary essays* (Manchester, 1995).

Crowder, C. M. D. *Unity, Heresy and Reform 1378–1460: the conciliar response to the Great Schism* (London, 1977).

Dahan, G. 'Notes et textes sur la póetique au moyen âge', *Archives d'histoire doctrinale et littéraire du moyen âge* xlvii (1980), pp. 214–19.

Damiata, M. *Guglielmo d'Ockham: povertà e potere*, 2 vols (Florence, 1979).

Davies, B. *The Thought of Thomas Aquinas* (Oxford, 1992).

De Grazia, S. *Machiavell in Hell* (Princeton, NJ, 1989).

Dean, T. and C. Wickham, eds, *City and Countryside in Late Medieval and Renaissance Italy: essays presented to Philip Jones* (London, 1990).

Denley, P. and C. Elam, eds, *Florence and Italy: Renaissance Studies in Honour of Nicolai Rubinstein* (London, 1988).

Dilcher, G. 'The City Comunity as an Instance in the European Process of Individualization', in J. Coleman, ed., *The Individual in Political Theory and Practice* (Oxford, 1996), pp. 281–301.

Doehaerd, R., ed., *Histoire de Flandre* (Brussels, 1983).

Dolcini, C. *Crisi de poteri e politologia in crisi. Da Sinibaldo Fieschi a Guglielmo d'Ockham* (Bologna,

1988).

Dolcini, C. *Introduzione a Marsilio da Padova* (Bari, 1995).

Douie, D. *Archibishop Pecham* (Oxford, 1952).

Dronke, P., ed., *A History of Twelfth-century Western Philosophy* (Cambridge, 1988).

Dunbabin, J. 'The Reception and Interpretation of Aristotle's *Politics*', in N. Kretzmann, A. Kenny and J. Pinborg, eds, *The Cambridge History of Later Medieval Philosophy* (Cambridge, 1982), pp. 723–37.

Dunbabin, J. *A Hound of God: Pierre de la Palud and the fourteenth-century church* (Oxford, 1991).

Dunn, J., ed., *Democracy: The unfinished journey 508 BC to AD 1993* (Oxford, 1992).

Duvernoy, J.-F. *La Pensée de Machiavel* (Paris, 1974).

Dyson, R. W., ed., trans., Introduction, *James of Viterbo, On Christian Government* (*De regimine Christiano*) (Woodbridge, 1995).

Fasolt, C. *Council and Hierarchy: the political thought of William Durant the Younger* (Cambridge, 1991).

Finnis, J. *Aquinas: Moral, Political, and Legal Theory* (Oxford, 1998).

Flahiff, G. B. 'The Use of Prohibitions by Clerics against Ecclesiastical Courts in England', *Mediaeval Studies* 3 (1941), pp. 101–16.

Flahiff, G. B. 'The Writ of Prohibition to Court Christian in the Thirteenth Century', *Mediaeval Studies* 6 (1944), pp. 261–313 and 7 (1945), pp. 229–90.

Fleisher, M., ed., *Machiavelli and the Nature of Political Thought* (New York, 1972).

Flüeler, C. *Rezeption und Interpretation der Aristotelischen 'Politica' im späten Mittelalter*, 2 vols (Amsterdam/Philadelphia, 1992).

Fredborg, K. 'Buridan's *Quaestiones super Rhetoricam Aristotelis*', in J. Pinborg, ed., *The Logic of John Buridan* (Copenhagen, 1976), pp. 47–59.

Fredborg, K. 'The Scholastic Teaching of Rhetoric in the Middle Ages', *Cahiers de l'institut du moyen–âge grec et latin*, 55 (1987), pp. 85–105.

Fryde, E. 'The First Humanistic Life of Aristotle: the 'vita Aristotelis' of Leonardo Bruni', in P. Denley and C. Elam, eds, *Florence and Italy: Renaissance Studies in Honour of Nicolai Rubinstein* (London, 1988), pp. 285–96.

Fuhrmann, H. *Germany in the High Middle Ages c. 1050–1200* (Cambridge, 1986).

Garin, E., ed., *Prosatori latini del Quattrocento*, La letteratura italiana, Storia e testi, 13 (Milan–Naples, 1952).

Garin, E. 'La cultura fiorentina nella second meta del 300 e i "barbari britanni"', in *L'età nuova: Ricerche di Storia della Cultura dal XII al XVI secolo* (Naples, 1969), pp. 141–66.

Garin, E. *Moyen Âge et Renaissance*, trans. C. Carme (Paris, 1969).

Garin, E. *La Cultura del Rinascimento* (Bari, 1976).

Garver, E. 'After Virtù: rhetoric, prudence and moral pluralism in Machiavelli', *History of Political Thought* 17 (1996), pp. 195–223.

Geach, P. T. 'Aquinas', in G. E. M. Anscombe and P. T. Geach, *Three Philosophers: Aristotle, Aquinas, Frege* (Oxford, 1973), pp. 65–125.

Geary, P. J. *Phantoms of Remembrance: memory and oblivion at the end of the first millennium* (Princeton, NJ, 1994).

Genet, J.-P., ed., *L'Etat moderne: genèse. Bilans et perspectives* (Paris, 1990).

Genet, J.-P., ed., *L'Historiographie médiévale en Europe* (Paris, 1991).

Genet, J.-P. *Le Monde au moyen âge* (Paris, 1991).

Genet, J.-P., ed., *L'Histoire et les nouveaux publics dans l'Europe médiévale (xiiie–xve siècles)* (Paris, 1997).

Genet, J.-P. and G. Lottes, eds, *L'Etat moderne et les élites, xiie–xviiie siècles. Apports et limites de la méthode prosopographique* (Paris, 1996).

Genet, J.-P. and M. Le Mené, eds, *Genèse de l'état moderne: prélèvement et redistribution* (Paris, 1987).

Genet, J.-P. and B. Vincent, eds, *Etat et église dans la genèse de l'état moderne* (Madrid, 1986).

Gewirth, A. *Marsilius of Padua and Medieval Political Philosophy* (New York, 1951).

Gibson, M. 'The Early Scholastic *Glosule* to Priscian, Institutiones grammaticae: the text and its influence', in M. Gibson, *'Artes' and Bible in the Medieval West* (Aldershot [Variorum], 1993).

Gilbert, A. *Machiavelli's 'Prince' and its Forerunners: the Prince as a typical book de Regimine Principum* (Durham, NC, 1938).

Gilbert, F. *Machiavelli and Guicciardini* (Princeton, NJ, 1965).

Gilli, P. 'Dictature, monarchie et absolutisme en italie aux xiv–xv siècles', in: Colloque – Dictature, Absolutisme et Totalitarisme, *Revue française d'histoire des idées politiques* 6 (1997), pp. 275–89.

Gillingham, J. 'Crisis or continuity? The structure of royal authority in England 1369–1422', in R. Schneider, ed., *Das spätmittelalterliche Königtum in Europaischen Vergleich* (Sigmaringen, 1987), pp. 59–80.

Giordanengo, J. 'Etat et droit féodal en France, xii–xiv's', in N. Coulet and J.-P. Genet, eds, *L'Etat moderne: le droit, l'espace et les formes de l'état* (Paris, 1990), pp. 61–90.

Goldthwaite, R. *Private Wealth in Renaissance Florence* (Princeton, NJ, 1969).

Gosman, M., A. Vanderjagt and J. Veenstra, eds, *The Propagation of Power in the Medieval West* (Groningen, 1997).

Gouron, A. and A. Rigaudière, eds, *Renaissance du pouvoir législatif et genèse de l'état* (Montpellier, 1988).

Gregory, T. *Platonismo medievale* (Rome, 1958).

Gruen, E. 'The Exercise of Power in the Roman Republic', in A. Molho, K. Raaflaub and J. Emlen, eds, *City-states in Classical Antiquity and Medieval Italy* (Ann Arbor, MI, 1991), pp. 251–67.

Guenée, B. *L'Occident aux xive et xve siècles: les états* (Paris, 1971).

Guggisberg, H. R. 'The Secular State of the Reformation Period and the Beginnings of the Debate on Religious Toleration', in J. Coleman, ed., *The Individual in Political Theory and Practice* (Oxford, 1996), pp.79–98.

Gurevich, A.-J. *Categories of Medieval Culture*, trans. G. L. Campbell (London, 1985).

Hale, J. *The Civilization of Europe in the Renaissance* (New York, 1994).

Hankins, J. *Plato in the Italian Renaissance*, 2 vols (Leiden/New York, 1991).

Harding, A. 'Political Liberty in the Middle Ages', *Speculum* 55 (1980), pp. 423–43.

Harding, A. *England in the Thirteenth Century* (Cambridge, 1993).

Haren, M. *Medieval Thought: the western intellectual tradition from antiquity to the thirteenth century*, 2nd edn (London, 1992).

Haverkamp, A. *Medieval Germany 1056–1273* (Oxford, 1988).

Henley, J. A. 'Theology and the basis of human rights', *Scottish Journal of Theology* 39 (1986), pp. 361–78.

Herlihy, D., ed., *The History of Feudalism* (New York, 1970).

Herlihy, D. 'Family and Property in Renaissance Florence', in H. Miskimin, D. Herlihy and A. Udovitch, eds, *The Medieval City* (New Haven, CN, 1977), pp. 3–24.

Herlihy, D. and C. Klapisch-Züber, *Les Toscans et leurs familles* (Paris, 1978).

Hexter, J. H. *The Vision of Politics on the Eve of the Reformation* (London, 1973).

Highfield, J. R. L. and R. Jeffs, eds, *The Crown and Local Communities in England and France in the Fifteenth Century* (Gloucester, 1981).

Holt, J. C. *Magna Carta*, 2nd edn (Cambridge, 1992).

Holt, R. and G. Rosser, eds, *The Medieval Town, a Reader in English Urban History 1200–1540* (London, 1990).

Horrox, R. 'The Urban Gentry in the Fifteenth Century', in J. A. F. Thomson, ed., *Towns and Townspeople in the Fifteenth Century* (Gloucester, 1988).

Horrox, R., ed., *Fifteenth-century Attitudes: perceptions of society in late medieval England* (Cambridge, 1994).

Horton, J. and S. Mendus, eds, *After MacIntyre* (Cambridge, 1994).

Hudson, A. and M. Wilks, eds, *From Ockham to Wyclif* (Oxford, 1987).

Hulliung, M. *Citizen Machiavelli* (Princeton, NJ, 1983).

Hyde, J. K. *Society and Politics in Medieval Italy: the evolution of the civil life 1000–1350* (London, 1973).

Jones, P. 'La storia economica. Dalla caduta dell'impero romano al secolo XIV', in R. Romano and C. Vivanti, eds, *Storia d'Italia*, vol. 2 (Turin, 1974), pp. 1,469–1,810.

Jones, P. *The Italian City-state* (Oxford, 1997).

Kantorowicz, E. *The King's Two Bodies: a study in medieval political theology* (Princeton, NJ, 1957).

Kedar, B. *Merchants in Crisis: Genoese and Venetian men of affairs and the fourteenth-century depression* (New Haven, CN, 1976).

Kelley, D. R. *The Foundations of Modern Historical Scholarship: language, law and history in the French Renaissance* (New York, 1970).

Kelley, D. R. 'The Theory of History', in C. Schmitt, Q. Skinner, E. Kessler and J. Kraye, eds, *The Cambridge History of Renaissance Philosophy* (Cambridge, 1988), pp. 746–62.

Kenny, A. *Aquinas* (Oxford, 1980).

Kent, D. V. and F. W. Kent, *Neighbours and Neighbourhoods in Renaissance Florence: the district of the Red Lion in the fifteenth century* (New York, 1982).

Kirschner, J. 'Paolo di Castro on "cives ex privilegio": a controversy over the legal qualifications for public office in early fifteenth century Florence', in A. Molho and J. A. Tedeschi, eds, *Renaissance Studies in Honor of Hans Baron* (Florence, 1971), pp. 227–46.

Kirshner, J. '*Civitas sibi faciat civem*: Bartolus of Sassoferrato's doctrine of the making of a citizen', *Speculum* 48 (1973), pp. 694–713.

Kirshner, J. 'Between Nature and Culture: an opinion of Baldus of Perugia on Venetian citizenship as second nature', *Journal of Medieval and Renaissance Studies* 9 (1979), pp. 179–208.

Kraye, J., ed., *Cambridge Translations of Renaissance Philosophical Texts*, 2 vols (Cambridge, 1997).

Kretzmann, N. and E. Stump, eds, *The Cambridge Companion to Aquinas* (Cambridge, 1993).

Kretzmann, N., A. Kenny and J. Pinborg, eds, *The Cambridge History of Later Medieval Philosophy* (Cambridge, 1982).

Kristeller, P. O. *Studies in Renaissance Thought and Letters*, 2 vols (Rome, 1956–85).

Kristeller, P. O. *Medieval Aspects of Renaissance Learning: three essays*, ed. and trans. M. P. Mahoney (Durham, NC, 1974).

Kristeller, P. O. *Renaissance Thought and its Sources*, ed. M. Mooney (New York, 1979).

Krynen, J. *Idéal du prince et pouvoir royal en France à la fin du moyen âge* (Paris, 1981).

Kuttner, S. *Repertorium der Kanonistik* (Vatican, 1937).

Lagarde, G. de *La Naissance de l'esprit laïque au déclin du moyen âge,* 5 vols (Louvain and Paris, 1956–70).

Lambert, M. *Franciscan Poverty: the doctrine of absolute poverty of Christ and the apostles in the Franciscan Order, 1210–1323* (London, 1961).

Lane, F. C. *Venice, a Maritime Republic* (Baltimore, 1973).

Lane, F. C. and R. Mueller, *Money and Banking in Medieval and Renaissance Venice*, vol. 1 (Baltimore, 1985).

Leaman, O. *An Introduction to Medieval Islamic Philosophy* (Cambridge, 1985).

Leff, G. *William of Ockham: the metamorphosis of scholastic discourse* (Manchester, 1975).

Le Goff, J. *Pour un autre moyen âge: temps, travail et culture en occident* (Paris, 1977).

Lerner, R. and M. Mahdi, eds, *Medieval Political Philosophy: a sourcebook* (Ithaca, NY, 1963).

Lewry, O. 'Four Graduation Speeches from Oxford Mss (*c.* 1270–1310)', *Mediaeval Studies*, xliv (1982).

Lewry, O. 'Grammar, Logic and Rhetoric, 1220–1320', in J. I. Catto and R. Evans, eds, *The History of the University of Oxford*, vol. 1: *The Early Oxford Schools* (Oxford, 1984).

Leyser, K. 'The Polemics of the Papal Revolution', in B. Smalley, ed., *Trends in Medieval Political*

Thought (Oxford, 1965).

Lis, C. and H. Soly, *Poverty and Capitalism in Pre–industrial Europe* (Brighton, 1979).

Lopez, R. *The Commercial Revolution of the Middle Ages, 950–1350* (Cambridge, 1976).

Lottin, O. *Psychologie et morale aux xii⁽ et xiii⁽ siecles* (Gembloux, 1959).

Maccarone, M. *Vicarius Christi. Storia del titolo papale* (Rome, 1952).

McGrade, A. S. *The Political Thought of William of Ockham: personal and institutional principles* (Cambridge, 1974).

McGrade, A. S. 'Ockham and the Birth of Individual Rights', in B. Tierney and P. Linehan, eds, *Authority and Power: studies . . . presented to Walter Ullmann* (Cambridge, 1980), pp. 149–66.

McGrade, A. S., ed., *William of Ockham, A Short Discourse on Tyrannical Government* trans. J. Kilcullen (Cambridge, 1992).

McGrade, A. S. *William of Ockham, A Letter to the Friars Minor and Other Writings* (Cambridge, 1995).

McKitterick, R. *The Carolingians and the Written Word* (Cambridge, 1989).

Maclean, I. *Interpretation and Meaning in the Renaissance: the case of law* (Cambridge, 1992).

Maierù, A., ed., *English Logic in Italy in the Fourteenth and Fifteenth Centuries* (Naples, 1982).

Mallett, M. and N. Mann, eds, *Lorenzo the Magnificent, culture and politics* (London, 1996).

Mann, M. *The Sources of Social Power: a history of power from the beginning to AD 1760*, vol. 1 (Cambridge,1986).

Mansfield, H. C. *Machiavelli's New Modes and Orders: a study of the Discouses on Livy* (Ithaca, NY, 1979).

Mansfield, H. C. *Machiavelli's Virtue* (Chicago, 1996).

Marenbon, J. *Later Medieval Philosophy* (London, 1987).

Marsh, D. *The Quattrocento Dialogue: classical tradition and humanist innovation* (Cambridge, MA, 1980).

Martin, C., ed., *The Philosophy of Thomas Aquinas: introductory readings* (London, 1988).

Martines, L. *Power and Imagination: city-states in Renaissance Italy* (Harmondsworth, 1983).

Meier, U. *Die Stadt im Denken spätmittelalterlicher Theologen, Philosophen und Juristen* (Munich, 1994).

Meinecke, F. *Die Idee der Staatsräson* (Munich, [1924] 1957).

Michael, B. 'Buridans moralphilosophische Schriften, ihre Leser und Benutzer im späten Mittelalter', in J. Miethke, ed., *Das Publikum politischer Theorie im 14. Jahrhundert* (Munich, 1992), pp. 139–51.

Michaud-Quantin, P. *Universitas. Expressions du mouvement communautaire dans le moyen âge latin* (Paris, 1970).

Miethke, J. *Ockhams Weg zur Sozialphilosophie* (Berlin, 1969).

Miethke, J. 'Zur Bedeutung der Ekklesiologie für die politische Theorie im späteren Mittelalter', in A. Zimmermann, ed., *Soziale Ordnung im Selbstverstandnis des Mittelalter* (Miscellania Medievalia 12) (Berlin, 1980), pp. 369–88.

Miethke, J. 'Marsilius und Ockham: Publikum und Leser ihrer politischen Schriften im späteren Mittelalter' *Medioevo* 6 ([1980] 1983), pp. 543–67.

Miethke, J. 'The Concept of Liberty in William of Ockham', in (no ed.) *Théologie et droit dans la science politique de l'état moderne* (Collection de L'Ecole Française de Rome, 147) (Rome, 1991), pp. 89–100.

Miethke, J. 'Politische Theorien im Mittelalter', in H.-J. Lieber, ed., *Politischen Theorien von der Antike bis zur Gegenwart* (Bonn, 1991), pp. 47–156.

Miethke, J., ed., *Das Publikum politischer Theorie im 14. Jahrhundert* (Munich, 1992).

Miethke, J., ed., German trans. and commentary, *Wilhelm von Ockham, Dialogus, Auszuge zur politischen Theorie* (Darmstadt, 1992).

Miethke, J. 'Literatur über Marsilius von Padua (1958–92)', *Bulletin de philosophie médiévale* 35 (1993), pp. 150–65.

Miethke, J., ed. and trans., *Wilhelm von Ockham, Texte zur politischen Theorie* (Stuttgart, 1995).

Miethke, J. 'Wirkungen politischer Theorie auf die Praxis der Politik im Römischen Reich des 14. Jahrhunderts. Gelehrte Politikberatung am Hofe Ludwigs des Bayern', in J. Canning and O.-G. Oexle, eds, *Political Thought and the Realities of Power in the Middle Ages/Politisches Denken und die Wirklichkeit der Macht im Mittelalter* (Göttingen, 1998), pp. 173–210.

Miethke, J. and A. Bühler, *Kaiser und Papst im Konflikt: Zum Verhältnis von Staat und Kirche im späten Mittelalter* (Düsseldorf, 1988).

Milsom, S. F. C. *Historical Foundations of the Common Law*, 2nd edn (London, 1981).

Minnis, A. J. and A. B Scott, eds, *Medieval Literary Theory and Criticism, c. 1100–c. 1375, the Commentary Tradition* (Oxford, revd edn, 1991).

Miskimin, H., D. Herlihy and A. Udovitch, eds, *The Medieval City* (New Haven, CN, 1977).

Mock, E. and G. Wieland, eds, *Rechts und Sozialphilosophie des Mittelalters* (Frankfurt, 1991).

Molho, A. *Florentine Public Finances in the Early Renaissance, 1400–1433* (Cambridge, MA, 1971).

Molho, A. and J. A. Tedeschi, eds, *Renaissance Studies in Honor of Hans Baron* (Florence, 1971).

Molho, A., K. Raaflaub and J. Emlen, eds, *City-states in Classical Antiquity and Medieval Italy* (Ann Arbor, MI, 1991).

Monahan, A. P. *John of Paris on Royal and Papal Power* (New York, 1974).

Monfasani, J. *Language and Learning in Renaissance Italy: selected articles* (Aldershot, 1994).

Moore, R. I. *The Origins of European Dissent* (Oxford, 1985).

Moulakis, A., ed., 'Leonardo Bruni's Constitution of Florence', *Rinascimento*, 2nd ser., 26 (1986), pp. 141–90.

Muldoon, J. *Popes, Lawyers and Infidels: the church and the non-Christian World, 1250–1500* (Liverpool, 1979).

Murphy, J. J. ed., *Medieval Eloquence* (Berkeley, 1978).

Murray, A. *Reason and Society in the Middle Ages* (Oxford, 1978).

Nader, H. 'The More Communes, the Greater the King: hidden communes in absolutist theory', in P. Blickle, ed., *Theorien kommunaler Ordnung in Europa* (Munich, 1996), pp.215–23.

Najemy, J. '*Arti* and *ordini* in Machiavelli's *Istorie Fiorentine*', in S. Bertelli and G. Ramakus, eds, *Essays Presented to Myron P. Gilmore* (Florence, 1978), pp. 161–87.

Najemy, J. *Corporatism and Consensus in Florentine Electoral Politics, 1280–1400* (Chapel Hill, NC, 1982).

Nederman, C. J. 'A Duty to Kill: John of Salisbury's theory of tyrannicide', *Review of Politics* 50 (1988), pp. 365–89.

Nederman, C. J. 'Nature, Sin and the Origins of Society: the Ciceronian tradition in medieval political thought', *Journal of the History of Ideas* 49 (1988), pp. 14–24.

Nederman, C. J. 'Nature, Ethics and the Doctrine of 'Habitus': Aristotelian moral psychology in the twelfth century', *Traditio* 45 (1989/90), pp.87–110.

Nederman, C. J. 'Nature, Justice and Duty in the *Defensor Pacis*: Marsiglio of Padua's Ciceronian impulse', *Political Theory* 18 (1990), pp. 615–37.

Nederman, C. J. 'Toleration and Community: a medieval communal functionalist argument for religious toleration', *The Journal of Politics* 56 (1994), pp. 901–18.

Nederman, C. J. *Community and Consent: the secular political theory of Marsiglio of Padua's Defensor Pacis* (London, 1995).

Nederman, C. J. 'Constitutionalism – Medieval and Modern: against neo-Figgisite orthodoxy (again)', *History of Political Thought* 17 (1996), pp. 179–94.

Nederman, C. J. 'The Mirror Crack'd: The *Speculum Principum* as political and social criticism in the late Middle Ages', *The European Legacy* 3 (1998), pp. 18–38.

Nicholas, D. *Town and Countryside: Social, Economic and Political Tensions in Fourteenth-Century Flanders* (Bruges, 1971).

Nicholas, D. *The Van Arteveldes of Ghent* (Ithaca, NY, 1988).

Oakley, F. 'Medieval Theories of Natural Law: William of Ockham and the significance of the voluntarist tradition', *Natural Law Forum* 6 (1961).

Oakley, F. *The Political Thought of Pierre d'Ailly: the voluntarist tradition* (New Haven, CN, 1964).

Oakley, F. 'Almain and Major: conciliar theory on the eve of the Reformation', *American Historical Review* 70 (1965), pp. 673–90.

Oakley, F. 'Natural Law, the *corpus mysticum* and Consent in Conciliar Thought from John of Paris to Matthias Ugonis', *Speculum* 56, 4 (1981), pp. 786–810.

Oakley, F. *Natural Law, Conciliarism and Consent in the Later Middle Ages* (London, 1984).

Oakley, F. *Omnipotence, Covenant and Order: an excursion in the history of ideas from Abelard to Leibniz* (Ithaca, NY, 1984).

Oakley, F. 'Nederman, Gerson, Conciliar Theory and Constitutionalism: *sed contra*', *History of Political Thought* 16 (1995), pp. 1–19.

Oberman, H. *The Harvest of Medieval Theology: Gabriel Biel and late medieval nominalism* (Cambridge, MA, 1963).

Oberman, H., ed., *Forerunners of the Reformation: the shape of late medieval thought* (New York, 1966).

Oberman, H. A. *Masters of the Reformation: the emergence of a new intellectual climate in Europe*, trans. D. Martin (Cambridge, 1981).

Oberman, H. A. *The Dawn of the Reformation: essays in late medieval and early Reformation thought* (Edinburgh, 1986).

Offler, H. S., ed., *Guillelmi de Ockham, Opera Politica*, vol. 1 (Manchester, 1940; repr. 1974).

Offler, H. S. 'The Three Modes of Natural Law in Ockham: a revision of the text', *Franciscan Studies* 37 (1977).

Ozment, S. *The Age of Reform, 1250–1550: an intellectual and religious history of late medieval and Reformation Europe* (New Haven, CN, 1980).

Padoa–Schioppa, A., ed., *Legislation and Justice* (Oxford, 1996).

Pagden, A., ed., *The Language of Political Theory in Early Modern Europe* (Cambridge, 1987).

Palliser, D. M. 'Urban Society', in R. Horrox, ed., *Fifteenth Century Attitudes* (Cambridge, 1994), pp. 132–49.

Paradisi, B. 'Il pensiero politico dei giuristi medievali', in L. Firpo, ed., *Storia delle idee politiche, economiche e sociale*, vol. 2 (Turin, 1973).

Parel, A. *The Machiavellian Cosmos* (New Haven, CN, 1992).

Pennington, K. *Pope and Bishops: the papal monarchy in the twelfth and thirteenth centuries* (Philadelphia, 1984).

Pennington, K. *Popes, Canonists and Texts 1150–1550* (Aldershot [Variorum], 1993).

Pesman Cooper, R. 'Pier Soderini: aspiring prince or civic leader?' *Studies in Medieval and Renaissance History*, n.s. 1 (1978).

Peters, E. *The Shadow King: rex inutilis in medieval law and literature, 751–1327* (New Haven, CN, 1970).

Phillips, M. 'Representation and Argument in Florentine Historiography', *Storia della storiografia* 10 (1986), pp. 48–63.

Pinborg, J., ed., *The Logic of John Buridan* (Copenhagen, 1976).

Pitkin, H. *The Concept of Representation* (Berkeley, 1967).

Pitkin, H. *Fortune is a Woman* (Berkeley, 1984).

Porter, R. and M. Teich, eds, *The Renaissance in National Context* (Cambridge, 1992).

Post, G. *Studies in Medieval Legal Thought: public law and the state, 1100–1322* (Princeton, NJ, 1964).

Posthumus Meyjes, G. H. M. 'Exponents of Sovereignty: canonists as seen by theologians in the late Middle Ages', in D. Wood, *The Church and Sovereignty, c. 590–1918: essays in honour of Michael Wilks* (Oxford, 1991).

Price, R. 'The Senses of Virtù in Machiavelli', *European Studies Review* 3 (1973), pp. 315–45.

Price, R. 'Self-love, "Egoism" and *ambizione* in Machiavelli's Thought', *History of Political Thought* 9 (1988), pp. 237–61.

Prodi, P. *The Papal Prince, One Body and Two Souls: the papal monarchy in early modern Europe*, trans. S. Haskins (Cambridge, 1987).

Quaglioni, D. 'Il modello del principe cristiano. Gli specula principum fra Medio Evo e prima età moderna', in V. I. Comporato, ed., *Modelli nella storia del pensiero politico*, vol. 1 (Florence, 1987).

Quaglioni, D. 'The Legal Definition of Citizenship in the Late Middle Ages', in A. Molho, K. Raaflaub and J. Emlen, eds, *City-states in Classical Antiquity and Medieval Italy* (Ann Arbor, 1991), pp. 155–67.

Quillet, J. *La Philosophie politique de Marsile de Padou* (Paris, 1970).

Quillet, J. 'Universitas populi et représentation au xive siècle', in *Der Begriff des Repraesentatio im Mittelalter, Miscellanea Mediaevalia* 8 (1971), pp. 186–201.

Rahe, P. *Republics, Ancient and Modern: classical republicanism and the American Revolution* (Chapel Hill, NC, 1992).

Randi, E. *Il sovrano e l'orologiaio, due immagini di Dio nel dibattito sulla 'potentia absoluta' fra XIII e XIV secolo* (Florence, 1986).

Remer, G. *Humanism and the Rhetoric of Toleration* (University Park, PA, 1996).

Reynolds, S. *Introduction to the History of English Medieval Towns* (Oxford, 1977).

Reynolds, S. 'Medieval Urban History and the History of Political Thought', *Urban History Yearbook, Leicester* (1982), pp. 14–23.

Reynolds, S. *Kingdoms and Communities in Western Europe 900–1300* (Oxford, 1984).

Reynolds, S. *Fiefs and Vassals: the medieval evidence reinterpreted* (Oxford, 1994).

Reynolds, S. 'The History of the Idea of Incorporation or Legal Personality: a case of fallacious teleology', in *Ideas and Solidarities of the Medieval Laity: England and Western Europe* (Aldershot, 1995).

Reynolds, S. *Ideas and Solidarities of the Medieval Laity, England and Western Europe* (London, 1995).

Ridolfi, R. *The Life of Niccolò Machiavelli*, trans. C. Grayson (London, 1963).

Riesenberg, P. 'Citizenship at Law in Late Medieval Italy', *Viator* 5 (1974), pp. 333–46.

Riesenberg, P. *Citizenship in the Western Tradition* (Chapel Hill, NC, 1992).

Rigney, A. and D. Fokkema, eds, *Cultural Participation: trends since the Middle Ages* (Amsterdam, 1993).

Robinson, I. S. *The Papacy 1073–1198: continuity and innovation* (Cambridge, 1990).

Romano, R. and C. Vivanti, eds, *Storia d'Italia*, vol. 2 (Turin, 1974).

Roover, R. de *Money, Banking and Credit in Medieval Bruges: Italian merchant bankers, Lombards and money changers, a study in the origins of banking* (Cambridge, MA, 1948).

Roover, R. de *The Rise and Decline of the Medici Bank* (Cambridge, MA, 1963).

Rorty, A. O., ed., *Essays on Aristotle's Ethics* (Berkeley, 1980).

Rouse, R. H. and M. A. Rouse, 'John of Salisbury and the Doctrine of Tyrannicide', *Speculum* 42 (1967), pp. 693–709.

Rubinstein, N. *The Government of Florence under the Medici (1434–94)* (Oxford, 1966).

Rubinstein, N. 'Florentine Constitutionalism and Medici Ascendancy in the Fifteenth Century', in N. Rubinstein, ed., *Florentine Studies: Politics and Society in Renaissance Florence* (London, 1968), pp. 442–62.

Rubinstein, N. 'Oligarchy and Democracy in Fifteenth-century Florence', in S. Bertelli, N. Rubinstein and C. H. Smyth, eds, *Florence and Venice: comparisons and relations* (Florence, 1979), pp. 99–112.

Rubinstein, N. 'Florentina Libertas', *Rinascimento*, 2nd ser. 26 (1986), pp. 3–26.

Rubinstein, N. 'The History of the Word *politicus* in Early-modern Europe', in A. Pagden, ed., *The Language of Political Theory in Early Modern Europe* (Cambridge, 1987), pp. 41–56.

Rubinstein, N. 'Machiavelli and the Florentine Republican Experience', in G. Bock, Q. Skinner and M. Viroli, eds, *Machiavelli and Republicanism* (Cambridge, 1990), pp. 3–16.

Rubinstein, N. 'Italian Political Thought 1450–1530', in J. H. Burns and M. Goldie, eds, *The Cambridge History of Political Thought, 1450–1700* (Cambridge, 1991).

Rubinstein, N. *The Palazzo Vecchio 1298–1532: government, architecture and imagery in the civic palace of the Florentine republic* (Oxford, 1995).

Rubinstein, N. 'Lorenzo's Image in Europe', in M. Mallett and N. Mann, eds, *Lorenzo the Magnificent, culture and politics* (London, 1996), pp. 297–312.

Sabbadini, R. *Le Scoperte dei codici latini e greci ne' secoli XIV e XV*, 2 vols (Florence, 1905–14; reprinted Florence, 1967).

Sasso, G. *Machiavelli e gli antichi e altri saggi*, 3 vols (Milan, 1987).

Schmale, W. ed., *Human Rights and Cultural Diversity* (Goldbach, 1993).

Schmitt, C. *Aristotle in the Renaissance* (Cambridge, MA, 1983).

Schmitt, C., Q. Skinner, E. Kessler and J. Kraye, eds, *The Cambridge History of Renaissance Philosophy* (Cambridge, 1988).

Schneider, R., ed., *Das spätmittelalterliche Königtum in europaischen Vergleich* (Sigmaringen, 1987).

Scholz, R. *Wilhelm von Ockham als politischer Denker und sein Breviloquium de Principatu Tryannico* (Leipzig, 1944).

Senellart, M. *Les Arts de gouverner. Du regimen médiéval au concept de gouvernement* (Paris, 1995).

Shogimen, T. 'Ockham's Vision of the Primitive Church', in R. N. Swanson, ed., *Studies in Church History 33: the church retrospective* (Woodbridge, 1997), pp. 163–75.

Sigmund, P., ed., *St Thomas Aquinas on Politics and Ethics* (London, 1988).

Sirat, C. *La Philosophie juive médiévale en pays de chrétienté* (Paris, 1988).

Skinner, Q. *Foundations of Modern Political Thought*, 2 vols (Cambridge, 1978).

Skinner, Q. *Machiavelli*, revd edn (Oxford, 1985).

Skinner, Q. 'Ambrogio Lorenzetti: the artist as political philosopher', *Proceedings of the British Academy* LXXII (1986), pp. 1–56.

Skinner, Q. 'The State', in T. Ball, J. Farr and R. Hanson, eds, *Political Innovation and Conceptual Change* (Cambridge, 1989), pp. 90–131.

Skinner, Q. 'The Italian City-Republics', in J. Dunn, ed., *Democracy: The unfinished journey 508 BC to AD 1993* (Oxford, 1992), pp. 57–70.

Skinner, Q. *Reason and Rhetoric in the Philosophy of Hobbes* (Cambridge, 1996).

Smalley, B., ed., *Trends in Medieval Political Thought* (Oxford, 1965).

Smalley, B. 'Sallust in the Middle Ages', in R. R. Bolgar, ed., *Classical Influences on European Culture AD 500–1500* (Cambridge, 1971), pp. 165–75.

Southern, R. *Robert Grosseteste: the growth of an English mind in medieval Europe* (Oxford, 1986).

Southern, R. W. *Western Society and the Church in the Middle Ages* (Harmondsworth, 1970).

Staico, U. 'Retorica et politica in Egidio Romano', *Aegidiana 3. Documenti e studi sulla tradizione filosofica medievale*, III, 1 (1992), pp. 1–75.

Stephenson, C. and F. Marcham, *Sources of English Constitutional History* (London, 1972).

Sternberger, D. *Machiavellis 'Principe' und der Begriff des Politischen* (Wiesbaden, 1974).

Stieber, J. W. *Pope Eugenius IV, the Council of Basel and the Secular and Ecclesiastical Authorities in the Empire* (Leiden, 1978).

Strauss, L. *What is Political Philosophy? and other studies* (Glencoe, IL, 1959).

Strayer, J. R. *Feudalism* (New York, 1965).

Strayer, J. R. *On the Medieval Origins of the Modern State* (Princeton, NJ, 1970).

Strayer, J. R. *Medieval Statecraft and the Perspectives of History* (Princeton, NJ, 1971).

Struever, N. S. *Theory as Practice: ethical inquiry in the Renaissance* (Chicago, 1992).

Sullivan, V. B. *Machiavelli's Three Romes: religion, human liberty and politics reformed* (De Kalb, IL, 1996).

Tierney, B. *Foundations of the Conciliar Theory: the contribution of the medieval canonists from Gratian to the Great Schism* (Cambridge, 1955).

Tierney, B. *The Crisis of Church and State 1050–1300 with selected documents* (Englewood Cliffs,

NJ, 1964 and reprints).

Tierney, B. *Religion, Law and the Growth of Constitutional Thought 1150–1650* (Cambridge, 1982).

Tierney, B. *The Origins of Papal Infallibility, 1150–1350*, 2nd edn (Leiden, 1988).

Tierney, B. 'Origins of Natural Rights Language: texts and contexts 1150–1625', *History of Political Thought* 10 (1989), p. 638.

Tierney, B. *The Idea of Natural Rights: studies on natural rights, natural law and church law 1150–1625* (Atlanta, GA, 1997).

Tierney, B. and P. Linehan, eds, *Authority and Power: studies on medieval law and government presented to Walter Ullmann on his seventieth birthday* (Cambridge, 1980).

Toscano, A. *Marsilio da Padova e Niccolò Machiavelli* (Ravenna, 1981).

Trinkaus, C., ed., *The Pursuit of Holiness in Late Medieval and Renaissance Religion* (Leiden, 1974).

Ullmann, W. *The Carolingian Renaissance and the Idea of Kingship* (London, 1969).

Ullmann, W. *Law and Politics in the Middle Ages: an introduction to the sources of medieval political ideas* (Cambridge, 1975).

Vanderjagt, A. *'Qui sa vertu anoblist': the concepts of 'noblesse' and 'chose publicque' in Burgundian political thought* (Groningen, 1981).

Van Laarhoven, J. 'Thou Shalt *Not* Slay a Tyrant! The So-called Theory of John of Salisbury', in M. Wilks, ed., *The World of John of Salisbury* (Oxford, 1984), pp. 319–42.

Van Steenberghen, F. *Thomas Aquinas and Radical Aristotelianism* (Washington, DC, 1980).

Verger, J. 'The Contribution of Medieval Universities to the Birth of Individualism and Individual Thought', in J. Coleman, ed., *The Individual in Political Theory and Practice* (Oxford, 1996), pp. 59–77.

Vignaux, P. *Philosophy in the Middle Ages: an introduction*, trans. E. C. Hall (New York, 1959).

Villari, P. *The Life and Times of Niccolò Machiavelli*, 2 vols, 4th edn, trans. L. Villari (New York, 1969).

Villey, M. 'La Genèse du droit subjectif chez Guillaume d'Occam', *Archives de philosophie du droit* 9 (1964), pp. 97–127.

Villey, M. *La Formation de la pensée juridique moderne*, 4th edn (Paris, 1975).

Villey, M. *Le Droit et les droits de l'homme* (Paris, 1983).

Viroli, M. *From Politics to Reason of State: the acquisition and transformation of politics 1250–1600* (Cambridge, 1992).

Viroli, M. *Machiavelli* (Oxford, 1998).

Viroli, M. 'Machiavelli and the Republican Idea of Politics', in G. Bock, Q. Skinner and M. Viroli, eds, *Machiavelli and Republicanism* (Cambridge, 1990), pp. 143–72.

Waley, D. *The Italian City-Republics*, 2nd edn (London, 1978).

Walker, D. P. *The Ancient Theology: studies in Christian Platonism from the fifteenth to the eighteenth century* (London, 1972).

Walther, H. G. *Imperiales Königtum, Konziliarismus und Volkssouveränität. Studien zu den Grenzen des mittelalterischen Souveränitätsgedanken* (Frankfurt, 1976).

Walther, H. G. 'Die Gegner Ockhams: Zur Korporationslehre der mittelalterlichen Legisten', in G. Göhler and H. Münkler, eds, *Politischen Institutionen im Gesellschaftlichen Umbruch* (Opladen, 1988).

Walther, H. G. 'Die Legitimität der Herrschaftsordnung bei Bartolus von Sassoferrato und Baldus de Ubaldis', in E. Mock and G. Wieland, eds, *Rechts und Sozialphilosophie des Mittelalters* (Frankfurt, 1991), pp. 115–39.

Watt, J. A. *The Theory of Papal Monarchy in the Thirteenth Century: the contribution of the canonists* (London, 1965).

Watt, J. A. *John of Paris, on Royal and Papal Power* (Toronto, 1971).

Weigand, R. *Die Naturrechtslehre der Legisten und Dekretisten* (Munich, 1967).

Weinstein, D. *Savonarola and Florence: prophecy and patriotism in the Renaissance* (Princeton, NJ, 1970).

Weisheipl, J. A. *Friar Thomas d'Aquino* (Oxford, 1974; revd edn Washington DC, 1983).

Westburg, D. *Right Practical Reason: Aristotle, action and prudence in Aquinas* (Oxford, 1994).

Wieland, G. *Ethica–scientia practica. Die Anfange der philosophischen Ethik im 13. Jahrhundert* (Münster, 1981).

Wieland, G. 'The Reception and Interpretation of Aristotle's *Ethics*', in N. Kretzmann, A. Kenny and J. Pinborg, eds, *The Cambridge History of Later Medieval Philosophy* (Cambridge, 1982).

Wilcox, D. *The Development of Florentine Humanist Historiography in the Fifteenth Century* (Cambridge, MA, 1969).

Wilks, M. *The Problem of Sovereignty in the Later Middle Ages* (Cambridge, 1963).

Wilks, M. 'Corporation and Representation in the *Defensor Pacis*', *Studia Gratiana* 15 (1972), pp. 251–92.

Wilks, M., ed., *The World of John of Salisbury* (Oxford, 1984).

Wolin, S. *Politics and Vision* (Boston, 1960).

Wolin, S. *The Presence of the Past* (Baltimore, 1989).

Wood, D., ed., *The Church and Sovereignty, c. 590–1918: essays in honour of Michael Wilks* (Oxford, 1991).

Wood, N. 'Machiavelli's Concept of Virtù Reconsidered', *Political Studies* 15 (1967), pp. 159–72.

Index